mylabschool™
Where the classroom comes to life!

From watching actual classroom video footage of teachers and students interacting to building standards-based lessons and web-based portfolios . . . from a robust resource library of the "What Every Teacher Should Know About" series to complete instruction on writing an effective research paper . . . **MyLabSchool** brings together an amazing collection of resources for future teachers. This website gives you a wealth of videos, print and simulated cases, career advice, and much more.

Use **MyLabSchool** with this Allyn and Bacon Education text, and you will have everything you need to succeed in your course. Assignment IDs have also been incorporated into many Allyn and Bacon Education texts to link to the online material in **MyLabSchool** . . . connecting the teachers of tomorrow to the information they need today.

PEARSON

VISIT www.mylabschool.com **to learn more about this invaluable resource and Take a Tour!**

Here's what you'll find in mylabschool™
Where the classroom comes to life!

O9-ABH-747

VideoLab ▶

Access hundreds of video clips of actual classroom situations from a variety of grade levels and school settings. These 3- to 5-minute closed-captioned video clips illustrate real teacher–student interaction, and are organized both topically *and* by discipline. Students can test their knowledge of classroom concepts with integrated observation questions.

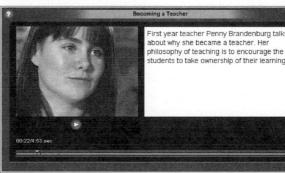

Becoming a Teacher

First year teacher Penny Brandenburg talks about why she became a teacher. Her philosophy of teaching is to encourage the students to take ownership of their learning.

00:22/4:53 sec

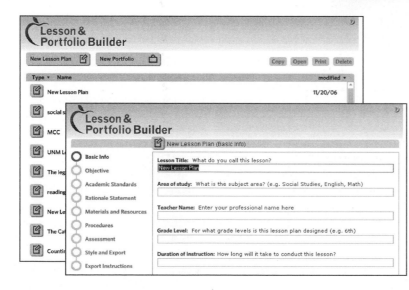

◀ Lesson & Portfolio Builder

This feature enables students to create, maintain, update, and share online portfolios and standards-based lesson plans. The Lesson Planner walks students, step-by-step, through the process of creating a complete lesson plan, including verifiable objectives, assessments, and related state standards. Upon completion, the lesson plan can be printed, saved, e-mailed, or uploaded to a website.

Here's what you'll find in mylabschool™

Where the classroom comes to life!

Simulations ▶

This area of MyLabSchool contains interactive tools designed to better prepare future teachers to provide an appropriate education to students with special needs. To achieve this goal, the IRIS (IDEA and Research for Inclusive Settings) Center at Vanderbilt University has created course enhancement materials. These resources include online interactive modules, case study units, information briefs, student activities, an online dictionary, and a searchable directory of disability-related web sites.

◀ Resource Library

MyLabSchool includes a collection of PDF files on crucial and timely topics within education. Each topic is applicable to any education class, and these documents are ideal resources to prepare students for the challenges they will face in the classroom. This resource can be used to reinforce a central topic of the course, or to enhance coverage of a topic you need to explore in more depth.

Research Navigator ▶

This comprehensive research tool gives users access to four exclusive databases of authoritative and reliable source material. It offers a comprehensive, step-by-step walk-through of the research process. In addition, students can view sample research papers and consult guidelines on how to prepare endnotes and bibliographies. The latest release also features a new bibliography-maker program—AutoCite.

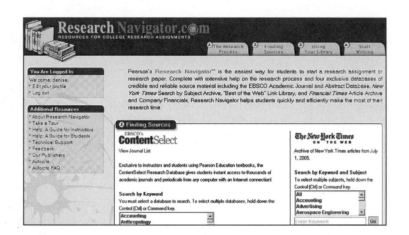

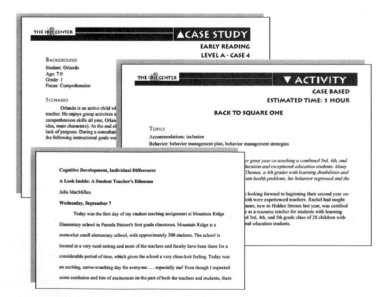

◀ Case Archive

This collection of print and simulated cases can be easily accessed by topic and subject area, and can be integrated into your course. The cases are drawn from Allyn & Bacon's best-selling books, and represent the complete range of disciplines and student ages. It's an ideal way to consider and react to real classroom scenarios. The possibilities for using these high-quality cases within the course are endless.

HANDBOOK OF
Reading Assessment

HANDBOOK OF
Reading
Assessment

Sherry Mee Bell
University of Tennessee

R. Steve McCallum
University of Tennessee

Boston   New York   San Francisco   Mexico City   Montreal   Toronto

London   Madrid   Paris   Hong Kong   Singapore   Tokyo   Cape Town   Sydney

Executive Editor: *Aurora Martínez Ramos*
Editorial Assistant: *Lynda Giles*
Executive Marketing Manager: *Krista Clark*
Production Director: *Elaine Ober*
Production Administrator: *Janet Domingo*
Manufacturing Manager: *Megan Cochran*
Composition Buyer: *Linda Cox*
Manufacturing Buyer: *Linda Morris*
Composition & Full Service Project Management: *NK Graphics/Black Dot Group*
Cover Coordinator: *Linda Knowles*
Printer Binder: *Edwards Brothers*

Between the time website information is gathered and then published, it is not unusual for some sites to have closed. Also, the transcription of URLs can result in typographical errors. The publisher would appreciate notification where these errors occur so that they may be corrected in subsequent editions.

ISBN: 10: 0-205-53177-6
ISBN: 13: 978-0-205-53177-6

Library of Congress Cataloging-in-Publication Data

Bell, Sherry Mee.
   Handbook of reading assessment / Sherry Mee Bell, R. Steve McCallum.—1st ed.
      p.   cm.
   Includes bibliographical references and index.
   ISBN 0-205-53177-6 (alk. paper)
   1. Reading—Ability testing. 2. Reading. I. McCallum, R. Steve. II. Title.
   LB1050.46.B45 2008
   428.4076—dc22   2007026362

Printed in the United States of America
10 9 8 7 6 5 4 3 2 1   11 10 09 08 07

Credits appear on pages 319–322, which constitutes an extension of the copyright page.

About the Authors

■ SHERRY MEE BELL

Dr. Sherry Mee Bell is an Associate Professor in the Department of Theory & Practice in Teacher Education at the University of Tennessee with over 25 years of accumulated experience in elementary education, special education, library information science, and school psychology. As a researcher and teacher educator, she has authored numerous journal articles and conference presentations with a particular focus on assessment of reading.

■ R. STEVE McCALLUM

Dr. R. Steve McCallum is professor and head of Educational Psychology & Counseling at the University of Tennessee. Co-founder and consulting editor of the *Journal of Psychoeducational Assessment,* Dr. McCallum is an internationally recognized expert in assessment. He is author of two books on assessment, a test of nonverbal cognitive ability published by Riverside Publishing Company, and over 200 journal articles and conference presentations focusing on assessment.

*To my partner, Steve; to my father, William L. (Bill) Mee,
who taught me persistence; to my mother, Marian J.
(Mickey) Mee, who always made sure I had books to read;
and to the family.*

—SMB

To my partner, Sherry, and to the family.

—RSM

Brief Contents

Chapter 1   ASSESSMENT OF READING: THE CONTEXT   1

Chapter 2   NATURE OF READING   39

Chapter 3   INFORMAL ASSESSMENT: INFORMING
             INSTRUCTION   69

Chapter 4   INFORMAL ASSESSMENT: PROGRESS
             MONITORING   131

Chapter 5   FORMAL ASSESSMENT OF READING:
             INDIVIDUALIZED ASSESSMENT   165

Chapter 6   FORMAL GROUP ASSESSMENT: FOCUS ON
             ACCOUNTABILITY   199

Chapter 7   USING INFORMAL AND FORMAL ASSESSMENT
             TO INFORM TEACHING   237

Contents

Preface   **xix**

    Rationale: Why We Wrote This Handbook   xix
    Enabling Educators to Speak the Same Language   xx
    Providing Inclusive Coverage of Reading Assessment   xxi

Chapter 1
ASSESSMENT OF READING: THE CONTEXT   **1**

Teachers in Action   **1**
    Meet Lesa Crockett   2
    Meet Greg Haywood   2
    Meet Harley Charles   3
    Meet Maria Sanchez   3

What Is the Role of Assessment in Instruction?   **4**

What Do Teachers Need to Know About Reading Assessment?   **6**

Purposes of Assessment   **8**
    Instructional Planning   8
    Progress Monitoring   9
    Ensuring Accountability   10
    Eligibility for Special Education Services   11

What Is Reading?   **12**
    What Are the Critical Areas of Reading?   14

What Is the Multitiered Model of Instruction?   **23**

What Is Scientifically-Based Research in Reading?   **25**
    Appreciating Effective Research   25
    Considering Peer-Reviewed Journals   25
    Reviewing and Using Evidence-based Research Findings   26
    What Is a "True Experimental" Design?   27
    What Is a "Quasi-Experimental" Design?   28
    What Is a Correlational Design?   29
    What Is a Single Subject Design?   30
    Quantitative versus Qualitative Research   31
    What Is a Qualitative Case Study?   31
    What Is Action Research?   32

How Does Scientifically-Based Research Help Teachers in the Classroom?   **32**

What Are the Reading Wars and How Are They Related to Assessment?   **33**

What Are the Major Types of Assessment?   **35**

Summary   **36**

Chapter 2

NATURE OF READING   39

Historical Context for Models of Reading   39

Developmental Models of Reading   41
Chall's Stage Model of Reading   41
Spear-Swerling and Sternberg Model of Reading   41
Frith's Developmental Phases Model   44

Adams' Cognitive Model of Reading   44

Information Processing Model of Reading   47

What Is the Relationship Between Reading and IQ?   51
Is It Helpful to Administer IQ Tests to Struggling Readers?   52

Transactional View of Reading   53

Speaking, Reading, and Writing   54

An Inclusive View of Reading   55

How Do We Know Whether a Student Has a Reading Disability?   57
What Are the Areas of Learning Disability?   58

How Do We Distinguish English Language Learning Challenges from Disabilities?   61

Low Literacy Adults   63

The Literacy Instruction Pie   64

Using Knowledge of Reading to Understand Reading Assessment   65

Summary   66

Chapter 3

INFORMAL ASSESSMENT: INFORMING INSTRUCTION   69

Observation and Interview   71

Teacher-Made and Teacher-Selected Curriculum-Related Assessment   72

Specific Skills Assessments   78

Error Analysis   80

Informal Reading Inventories   81
Getting Started with the IRIs   82
Quantitative Analyses of IRIs   88
Qualitative Analyses of IRIs   96
Abbreviated Assessment with IRIs   100
Using IRIs to Assess Listening Comprehension   100
Teacher-Made IRIs   100
Limitations of IRIs   100

Running Records   102

Curriculum-Based Assessment   105
Using Teacher-Constructed CBM to Assess Reading   107

Portfolio Assessment   113

Readability   116

Leveled Texts   119

Special Considerations in the Informal Assessment of Young Children   120

Special Considerations in the Informal Assessment of Adult Learners   123

**Special Considerations in the Informal Assessment of English
Language Learners   124**

Summary   125

Chapter 4

INFORMAL ASSESSMENT: PROGRESS MONITORING   131

The Assessment Continuum   132

Reliability and Validity   132
   Reliability   132
   Validity   134

Criterion-Referenced Assessment   137
   The BRIGANCE® Inventories   138

Progress Monitoring   142
   AIMSweb   145
   The Dynamic Indicators of Basic Early Literacy Skills   148
   Adequacy of Progressing Monitoring Systems   152

Computer-Based Assessment of Reading   152
   Lexiles   157

Special Considerations for Adult and English Language Learners   160

Summary   161

Chapter 5

**FORMAL ASSESSMENT OF READING: INDIVIDUALIZED
ASSESSMENT   165**

Development of Formal Reading Measures   167

Types of Scores   168
   Grade and Age-Equivalent Scores   169
   Limitations of Age and Grade Equivalents   169
   Percentiles   170
   Limitations of Percentiles   170
   Standard Scores   171
   Use of Standard Scores in Special Education   174
   Use of Standard Scores to Identify a Learning Disability   174
   Limitations of Standard Scores   175
   Stanines   175
   Normal Curve Equivalents   175

Administration and Scoring of Formal Tests   176
   Standard Error of Measure   176
   Establishing Basals and Ceilings   178

Determining Chronological Age   178

Individualized versus Group Tests   180

How Do Individualized Norm-referenced Measures Assess Reading?   181
Phonemic Awareness   184
Phonics   184
Automatic Word Recognition   184
Fluency   185
Vocabulary   186
Comprehension   187

Test Bias   188

Selecting Formal, Individualized Instruments   189

Summary   191

Chapter 6

FORMAL GROUP ASSESSMENT: FOCUS ON ACCOUNTABILITY   199

Context for Formal Standardized Assessment   200

Characteristics of Group Formal Standardized Testing   201
Tips for Administering and Scoring Formal
Group Tests   202

Group Achievement Tests for Instructional Planning and Progress Monitoring   206

High-Stakes Testing   209
Guidelines for High-Stakes Testing   210
Problems and Solutions Associated with High-Stakes Testing   212
High Stakes Testing of Students with Disabilities and English Language
Learners (ELL)   214

Formal Group Achievement Testing for Accountability: Two Well-Known Examples   216
NAEP   216
General Trends   218
Racial and Ethnic Trends   219
Gender Trends   219
NAAL   219

How Do Group Norm-referenced Measures Assess Reading?   221
Measures of Phonemic Awareness, Phonics, and Automatic Word
Recognition/Orthography   223
Measures of Fluency   224
Measures of Vocabulary   225
Measures of Comprehension   226

Special Considerations for Adult and ELL Learners   228

Summary   229

Chapter 7
USING INFORMAL AND FORMAL ASSESSMENT TO INFORM TEACHING   237

Selecting and Evaluating Assessments   238

Assessment of Writing: A Related Skill   240

Motivating Students to Read   245

    Relative Influence of Motivation   246

    Classroom Observations   248

    Reading Journals   249

    Sentence Completion Forms   249

    Thought-Bubble Technique   252

    Interest Inventories   254

    Attitude Inventories   255

    Elementary Reading Attitude Surveys (ERAS)   255

    The Reader Self-Perception Scale (RSPS)   256

    Interviews   256

    Using Affective Information   256

    Other Within-the-Individual Variables: Cognitive Correlates of Reading   257

    Teacher Self-Asssessment   259

Gathering and Evaluating Data   259

Putting It All Together!   261

    Assessment-to-Instruction for an Entire Class   261

    Assessment-to-Instruction for Individual Students   264

    Assessment-to-Instruction for a Typically Performing Student   264

    Assessment-to-Instruction for Students Who Struggle   265

Data-Based Problem-Solving   266

    Case Study: Todd   266

    Case Study: Emilio   268

    Case Study: Sammy   270

    Data-Based Problem-Solving and Multitiered Instruction   273

    Remediation versus Compensation   273

    Individual Education Program (IEP)   274

Assessment to Instruction   276

Summary   278

APPENDICES

Appendix A   **International Reading Association Professional Standards for Reading Assessment: Standard 3 Assessment   283**

Appendix B   **Inclusive Model of Reading   287**

Appendix C   **Literacy Instruction Pie with Overlay of Motivation   289**

Appendix D   **Resources for Assessment and Instruction of Reading**   291

Appendix E   **Instructional Tips**   295

Glossary   299

References   309

Credits   319

Index   323

Preface

■ RATIONALE: WHY WE WROTE THIS HANDBOOK

We believe the most important job teachers have is to teach their students to read and write, in essence, to acquire literacy. Unfortunately, many students have difficulty learning to read. According to Sweet (2004), about one-third of fourth-grade students in the United States cannot read simple books. Further, a 2005 report on adult literacy indicated that as a nation we made no substantial gains in improving adult literacy over the years 1992 to 2003; in fact, as of 2003, eleven million adults in the United States were categorized as illiterate in English (National Assessment of Adult Literacy 2005).

Not all experts believe the sky is falling, however. According to Allington (2001), students in U.S. schools perform about the same as other students across the world on tests of reading achievement. But, as Allington points out, students routinely perform better on tests measuring basic literacy—word analysis, phonics, and vocabulary in isolation—than on measures of higher-order comprehension skills. Also, some groups of students simply perform better than others. Students from families with low incomes and low parental educational levels and those who come from minority groups tend to lag behind peers who come from higher-income families and those with higher education levels (Allington, 2001). If schools in the United States are to fulfill their role of providing equal educational opportunities for all students, educators must address these inequities in achievement.

Not only do children from different socioeconomic groups perform differently, the percentage of students identified with learning disabilities has grown. The percentage of students enrolled in U.S. schools that are identified as having learning disabilities rose from 1.8 percent in 1977–1978 to 5.8 percent in 2001–2002 (Lerner 2006). Students identified as having learning disabilities currently comprise one-half of the total group of students receiving special education services (Turnbull, Turnbull, Shank, and Smith, 2004). Furthermore, an additional 80 percent of the students identified as having a learning disability have difficulty reading (Lyon 1996).

In addition to children from socioeconomically and ethnically diverse backgrounds and those with learning disabilities, students who enter school with English as a second language are at increased risk for reading difficulties. Many of the children who enter our classrooms with other challenges—such as mental retardation, speech-language disorders, and emotional disturbance—also struggle with reading. Consequently, classroom teachers, reading specialists, literacy coaches, special educators, educational diagnosticians, and school psychologists spend a significant portion of time engaged in identifying, diagnosing, and addressing reading problems. School administrators are also involved; the decisions they make about curriculum, professional development, resources, and programs must be informed by knowledge about how their students are performing, particularly in reading. In order to

help struggling readers, specialists from these diverse backgrounds must be familiar with basic assessment strategies; in addition, they need a common language and knowledge base in order to communicate effectively.

Recent federal legislation, including the No Child Left Behind Act (NCLB 2001), focuses on accountability for the education of students in diverse groups. Passage of the Individuals with Disabilities Education Improvement Act of 2004 (IDEA 2004), the federal special education law, provides an additional impetus for collaboration of educators across disciplines to assess and gauge progress of *all* students, particularly in the area of reading. The 2004 IDEA calls for early intervention in the general education classroom for those at risk for academic failure, and it requires educators to track students' instructional responsiveness; that is, teachers must continuously assess the progress of students in their classrooms, particularly in reading. This early intervention approach is more likely to be successful when classroom teachers, special educators, and other professionals work closely together.

ENABLING EDUCATORS TO SPEAK THE SAME LANGUAGE

We wrote the *Handbook of Reading Assessment* to share with educators from various disciplines the knowledge needed to make use of a variety of assessments and to communicate effectively about student progress and needs. We describe individually administered and group-administered tests, as well as formal, informal, curriculum-based, criterion-referenced, and norm-referenced measures. Also, this handbook provides an introduction to reading assessment for educators at the preservice level and serves as a resource for in-service educators and administrators who are responsible for instructional planning and for determining student progress. The content is relevant for general, special, and adult educators and serves as a valuable resource for reading specialists, literacy coaches, educational diagnosticians, reading tutors, school psychologists, and administrators.

One of our goals is to promote effective communication across these educational subdisciplines. Our backgrounds include formal education and work experiences in elementary education, special education, library science, school psychology, and reading disabilities; we have witnessed firsthand the harm that can occur when professionals from different areas and orientations use different terminology to reference the same or very similar educational practices. In a sense, educators have created a Tower of Babel effect, and all too often, fail to communicate effectively with colleagues, especially with those in other areas (even though in many cases, these colleagues work just down the hall). This communication failure often results in uncoordinated, fragmented, and ineffective instruction for the struggling readers most in need of consistency, particularly students in special education, which Allington and Cunningham (2002) refer to as the "second system" of education.

■ PROVIDING INCLUSIVE COVERAGE OF READING ASSESSMENT

This handbook describes, in one volume, the various approaches to reading assessment. It is designed to be inclusive, in contrast to most other current texts that tend to focus exclusively or too heavily on one type of assessment (such as informal classroom assessment or formal standardized assessment). In Chapter 1, we describe several purposes and types of assessment; common definitions of reading; areas of reading identified by the National Reading Panel (NRP; National Institute of Child Health and Human Development [NICHD] 2000) (phonemic awareness, phonics, fluency, vocabulary, and comprehension) and other important areas including orthography and automatic word recognition; and guidelines to help educators understand and appreciate scientifically-based reading literature. Chapter 2 presents some of the developmental and cognitive underpinnings of reading, various models of reading, how the models can help educators implement and interpret assessment strategies, and how the models can help educators understand the nature of common reading problems (including cultural/environmental and within-the-learner based difficulties).

Chapters 3, 4, 5, and 6 each address a different type of assessment— informal progress monitoring, and individual and group standardized assessments—and relate these assessment types to the areas of reading identified by the NRP. Purposes of assessment, administration and scoring procedures, types of information and scores yielded, interpretation, and psychometric properties of both informal and standardized assessments are presented. Also, these chapters feature authentic scenarios to give readers applied examples of assessment types. Tables, figures, and worksheets show particular assessment strategies and provide easy reference to a large amount of information. Informal classroom assessment techniques, including informal reading inventories, running records, miscue analyses, portfolio assessment, teacher-made and teacher-selected tests, and checklists are the focus of Chapter 3. These techniques are most likely to be used by classroom teachers, but they are quite useful as well for reading specialists, literacy coaches, special educators, educational diagnosticians, tutors, adult educators, and others.

Chapter 4 focuses on techniques that are frequently used in special education but, increasingly, are being used in general education classes. These include published criterion-referenced measures and curriculum-based measures, including some recently available instruments designed especially for progress monitoring. These measures are most likely to be administered by special educators, educational diagnosticians, and school psychologists. However, they have direct relevance for classroom instruction—classroom teachers need to understand, interpret, and effectively use their results.

Norm-referenced individual achievement tests are the focus of Chapter 5. These tests are typically administered by special educators, educational diagnosticians, or school psychologists and, sometimes, by reading specialists. Their most common purpose is to determine levels of achievement in specific areas such as reading comprehension. Also, these tests are used to determine eligibility for special education, especially for those who have learning disabilities, but also mental retardation, giftedness, and so on.

Chapter 6 addresses group norm-referenced tests, the so-called "high-stakes" tests that typically are administered toward the end of the school year to determine whether students are making adequate progress as compared to other students at the same grade level across the country. These tests usually are administered in the classroom by classroom teachers in accordance with strict protocols established by the test publisher. The tests are considered high stakes because school districts, schools, individual teachers, and students may experience negative consequences (such as the loss of federal dollars, closing of the school, reassignment or firing of teachers, and retention of students or failure to graduate) for failing to perform at some predetermined standard of acceptability. Adult educators also use group norm-referenced tests to monitor academic progress in adult education programs.

Chapter 7 is perhaps the most important chapter in the book. In this chapter, we present practical criteria educators can use to evaluate assessment tools. We also describe how to incorporate a variety of assessment data into a case study, with recommendations for instructional planning. To help the reader "pull it all together," we address affective factors in literacy, particularly motivation.

Finally, we include a glossary and several appendixes. Throughout the text, when an important term is first introduced, it appears in **bold** type. These terms are defined in the glossary and are referenced, along with other critical information, in the index. Appendix D includes a list of resources of assessment and instructional texts, materials, and online resources. Finally, we provide a set of instructional tips (Appendix E). All of these sources are useful for extending knowledge, applying various types of assessment, and linking assessment to instruction.

Hundreds, perhaps thousands, of reading assessments, tools, and strategies are available; this book cannot provide an exhaustive list. Instead, we introduce readers to the most commonly used and respected types of assessments. We clearly define the relevant terms and present the background knowledge necessary to administer and interpret many of these assessment strategies.

For some readers of this text, assessment may seem like a necessary evil and that teaching is the "good stuff" and not all that related to assessment. As you read this handbook, you will see how assessment and instruction are integrally related. In addition, you will learn vocabulary and concepts that will make you more effective in your role in the educational system.

Acknowledgments

Completion of this text would not have been possible without the contributions of committed colleagues, friends, and family. Obviously this book would not have come to fruition without the expert support and guidance of Aurora Martínez Ramos at Allyn and Bacon. Thank you to our reviewers who provided invaluable feedback for early drafts of the text: Bill Clarke, Blackstone Academy Charter School; Cheryl L. Cooke; Margaret A. Deitrich, Austin Peay State University; Cathleen Doheny, University of West Virginia; Sallie Averitt Miller, Columbus State University; and Susan Wegmann, Sam Houston State University.

Mary Catherine Hammon, our graduate assistant, was tireless in her efforts to acquire permissions for the numerous figures and tables that contribute significantly to the usefulness of the text. She also proofed various versions of the text and managed numerous details including acquiring authentic photographs. Other graduate assistants who contributed their time and talents include Lindsay Anne Thompson, Laura Whitford Flores, Olivia Halic, and Emily R. Kirk. We also acknowledge the numerous students, teachers, and parents whose literacy goals and challenges are the reason for this book. And we acknowledge Karen Walker for her continual unflagging support and optimism.

We are indebted to Tinah Utsman for her expertise in capturing our colleagues and students on film. We acknowledge the following people for their willingness to contribute to the photographs: Cynthia (Cindy) Mee Rule and Ralph Eugene (Sonny) Rule III, Hope Brooks, Gregory Hayworth, LeAnne McCracken Colquitt, Merna Schott, Hardy DeYoung, and Ferlin McGaskey.

Finally, we acknowledge the patience and support of our young adult children, whose evolving literacy lives have informed us as much as our professional experiences: Ross, Ryan, Daniel, and Lauren.

HANDBOOK OF
Reading Assessment

CHAPTER 1

Assessment of Reading: The Context

■ TEACHERS IN ACTION

We begin this book by introducing four teachers. If you are an educator or an educator-to-be, you will identify with one or more of these teachers because they work in real settings and experience real challenges, perhaps like those you have faced. Throughout the book, you will learn about the students of these four teachers and how the teachers use information from assessment to improve their instruction.

Meet Lesa Crockett

Lesa Crockett is a first-grade teacher with seventeen years of experience in a city school with a diverse population of students, primarily Caucasian, but also African American, Hispanic, and Asian, with **socioeconomic status (SES)** ranging from below poverty level to affluent. Increasingly, she has at least one student per year in her class for whom English is a second language. To teach reading, Ms. Crockett uses the **basal series** required by her school district. She supplements with **leveled readers** to ensure that students get plenty of practice with books they can read and with specific **phonics** activities that teach students to recognize patterns of letters and the sounds they typically make. Ms. Crockett thinks that teaching her students to read is the most important part of her job. And she is usually pretty successful. That is, most of her students leave her classroom reading short books or stories of connected text and can read orally between 25 and 75 words per minute. Importantly, most also seem to like reading. However, she also considers teaching reading to be her biggest challenge. As do most other teachers, she feels pressure to be accountable for the performance of all her students, even the ones who enter first grade not knowing the alphabet and who come from homes in which English is not spoken or read. Ms. Crockett routinely administers unit tests associated with the district-adopted basal series that measure progress on a variety of reading skills. However, she is concerned that she does not have the time to plan instruction based on these assessments. And, recently, her district has begun routine assessment of all students, a process called **progress monitoring.** She is concerned that she will have neither the time nor the skills to implement another assessment process in her class.

Meet Greg Haywood

Greg Haywood is a special education teacher in a rural K–8 school. Like Ms. Crockett, he believes his biggest challenge is teaching literacy skills. His school participates in a literacy project with a university in the area. The classroom teachers have implemented a **core program** that relies heavily on **guided reading,** use of leveled readers, and time to work on word skills and writing. Also,

his school participates in a federal initiative to boost reading skills at the lower grades; recently the school has begun implementing the **response to intervention (RTI)** model associated with federal special education laws. Mr. Haywood is concerned that the classroom teachers in his building are overwhelmed by seemingly contradictory approaches associated with the different initiatives and that reading and special education staff need to have better communication. Also, he is concerned that teachers and students have to spend so much time on assessment activities that teachers may not understand and, consequently, that may not be used to plan instruction.

Meet Harley Charles

Dr. Harley Charles is a tenth-grade biology teacher. He has twenty-four students in his class, but he finds it very difficult to hold the attention of all of them. In fact, almost a third of the students sit near the back of the class and requires intermittent prodding to keep them attentive. They whisper among themselves, yawn, stare off into space, and generally remain off task. Four or five of the very best students sit over near the window, doodle, stare outside, or read paperbacks they hide inside their huge biology textbooks. They do well on tests and are quiet during class lectures, but they obviously are bored much of the time. These students are typically able to answer questions when called on, and, on those occasions when Dr. Charles feels he can afford to take the time to engage the class in a discussion, these students become motivated and energized. The rest of the class is pretty well behaved and generally attentive, but Dr. Charles is frustrated because of the variable behavior of the students and the wide range of grades. He wonders whether it is possible to engage the whole class and how he could obtain the information to help him plan instruction better. He suspects that the most poorly behaved students cannot comprehend the content in the textbook, even though in order to graduate, they are required by state law to pass his course as well as an end-of-course test.

Meet Maria Sanchez

Maria Sanchez is an adult educator; she teaches older adolescents and young adults who have dropped out of school. Like Ms. Crockett and Mr. Haywood,

Ms. Sanchez believes her most important task is to teach literacy. Her students exhibit a wide range of reading levels; a few are beginning readers, many are reading between third- and fifth-grade level, and a few are reading at higher levels. Ms. Sanchez typically has very limited information about her students when they enter her class, often just a single measure of reading comprehension from a group-administered achievement test for adults. She wants to learn more about assessment so that she can group the students for instruction, plan appropriate experiences for the diverse learners in her class, and, more specifically, document their progress over time.

Throughout this book we revisit the classrooms of Ms. Sanchez and the other teachers—Ms. Crockett, Mr. Haywood, and Dr. Charles—as we discuss assessment strategies they can use to help their students.

WHAT IS THE ROLE OF ASSESSMENT IN INSTRUCTION?

It is difficult for some teachers to see the connection between their teaching and assessment, particularly between daily classroom instruction and large-scale, end-of-year assessment. But effective teachers appreciate the importance of assessment. They use assessment information to plan and implement instruction based on knowledge of what their students know and do not know and what they can and cannot do. Assessment can be as informal as listening to students express themselves in class or in the hallway or as formal as administering a standardized achievement test such as the National Assessment of Educational Progress, or NAEP (http://nces.ed.gov/nationsreportcard/).

Unfortunately, the relationship between assessment and instruction is only one of hundreds of things new teachers have to learn. Consequently, both new and in-service teachers sometimes have a vague understanding or even misconceptions about the role of assessment in planning instruction. For example, many educators tend to think of **assessment** and **testing** as interchangeable terms, though experts distinguish between the two. According to Overton (2006, 4), for example, assessment is "the process of gathering information to monitor progress and make educational decisions," while testing is "a method to determine a student's ability to complete certain tasks or demonstrate mastery of a skill or knowledge of content" (2006, 4). Thus, assessment defines a broader range of activities and includes testing as one technique to gather information. Overton's definition implies that assessment includes decision making regarding students' strengths and weaknesses and the match between those strengths/weaknesses and instruction, though some refer to the decision making itself as a separate process and refer to this component as "evaluation."

Teachers such as Ms. Crockett, Mr. Haywood, Dr. Charles, and Ms. Sanchez can be most effective when they routinely use assessment information. For example, the kindergarten teachers in Ms. Crockett's school use checklists throughout the year to assess their students' knowledge of the alphabet. Primary-level teachers may administer unit tests that accompany basal readers to ensure students' mastery of word analysis and comprehension skills. Intermediate and high school teachers, such as Dr. Charles, may use teacher-made worksheets and quizzes that are tied to units of study to gauge student mastery of instructional objectives; in addition, they can use **curriculum-based measurement** (**CBM**) and standardized test results to help them understand how their students vary on fundamental skills such as reading **fluency.**

Consider the dilemma Dr. Charles faces in his class, as described in the opening scenario. Obviously, several of his students are not motivated. This situation is not unusual. In fact, Hargis (2006) describes a very similar situation in an article in the *Phi Delta Kappan*. Of twenty-four students in a tenth-grade biology class he observed, nine students were reading at or below the eighth-grade level, seven were reading in the ninth- to tenth-grade range, and eight were at the eleventh-grade level or higher, but all were expected to read a textbook written at the 10.2 readability level! According to national data that Hargis presents, this level of variability is common, even expected, in schools, but this variability leads to many of the behavior problems teachers face. Consequently, he makes a case for using instructional materials of appropriate difficulty level, rather than expecting all students to work at a pace that is appropriate for middle-ability students.

Teachers such as Ms. Crockett, Mr. Haywood, and other school-based reading specialists sometimes use **informal reading inventories** to identify appropriate levels of instruction for their students and to target specific skill gaps for individuals. Effective educators use information from these assessments to plan further instruction, reteaching when necessary, to ensure mastery. These informal measures can be used in conjunction with information from many other types of assessment, including norm-referenced group achievement tests (typically given near the end of the school year to ensure progress of individual students, classes, schools, or systems) and individualized norm-referenced achievement tests, usually administered to determine eligibility for special education. At the most basic level, **norm-referenced tests** produce scores that identify how well the performance of a particular student compares to the performance of all others at the same age or grade. You are probably familiar with at least one type of norm-referenced test. You likely took either the ACT (American College Test) or the SAT (Scholastic Aptitude Test) prior to your admission into college. Your performance on either test was compared to the performance of others who took the test at about the same time. Norm-referenced testing is discussed at length in Chapter 5; for now, simply keep in mind that norm-referenced scores are obtained by comparing a particular student's performance with others like her or him.

In addition to helping teachers such as Mr. Haywood and Ms. Sanchez learn about the reading level of their students, how can norm-referenced assessments relate to instruction? Typically, there is no direct connection between scores on standardized tests and daily instruction. The primary purpose of norm-referenced measures is to compare a student or groups of students to a peer or **norm group;** this way, scores can be used to determine, essentially, "how are we doing" compared to a national, or even international, group. Recently, many of the norm-referenced tests have been refined and lengthened and can provide information to identify specific areas of academic strength and weakness for particular students, for groups of students, and for teachers trying to determine which areas of the curriculum may need more emphasis.

In contrast to yearly norm-referenced tests, authors and publishers have developed individualized probes to screen and monitor progress much more frequently in discrete skills such as oral word reading fluency. These measures represent a hybrid of traditional classroom assessment and norm-referenced assessment. They provide teachers with valuable information about whether a student is making adequate progress but may not provide enough specificity to guide instruction. The goal of this text is to provide teachers and other educators with the knowledge needed to understand, compare, and contrast all these types of assessment in order to design and deliver effective reading instruction for students with diverse abilities and needs.

WHAT DO TEACHERS NEED TO KNOW ABOUT READING ASSESSMENT?

The answer to this basic question is simple on the one hand, but extremely complex on the other. The simple answer is this—teachers need to know reading assessment content that experts have identified as the most important. Based on considerable thought and discussion, educators have developed standards to reflect this content. Presumably, these standards describe critical content, minimal information that teachers should possess. The complex answer is certainly more difficult to pin down, but perhaps it should be something like this: Teachers need to know enough about reading assessment to make them effective teachers of reading. This book addresses both answers, and we start by discussing how standards relate to reading assessment content.

Simply put, "an educational standard is a statement that depicts what students should know or be able to do as a result of teaching and learning" (Conley 2005). All teachers become familiar with reading, math, or other curriculum standards set by local or state policy for their students. Specific to reading assessment, professional standards describe what teachers should be able to know or do as a result of education and professional development in reading assessment. Although we believe standards represent a good starting point for defining essential content, not all would agree. One of our teacher education colleagues frequently says, with some negative affect, "We are awash in standards!" It is true—the field of education is inundated with standards; sometimes, total mastery seems too difficult, given all the other job expectations. However, familiarity with the standards provides guidelines for practice, so considering them is probably worth the time and energy required.

As teacher education candidates know (and as in-service teachers and other educators will remember), they must demonstrate proficiency on a variety of professional standards, such as those promulgated by the Interstate New Teacher Assessment and Support Consortium (INTASC), the National Board for Professional Teaching Standards (NBPTS), and the National Council for Accreditation of Teacher Education (NCATE). The International Reading Association (IRA) has developed a set of standards for reading professionals that takes into consideration the standards related to reading from INTASC, NBPTS, and NCATE. The 2003 version, *Standards for Reading Profes-*

TABLE 1.1   Standards for Reading Professionals (Revised 2003)

Standards	Standard 3 Assessment Subcategories
1.0 Candidates have knowledge of the foundations of reading and writing processes and instruction.	3.1 Use a wide range of assessment tools and practices that range from individual and group standardized tests to individual and group informal classroom assessment strategies, including technology-based assessment tools.
2.0 Candidates use a wide range of instructional practices, approaches, methods, and curriculum materials to support reading and writing instruction.	
3.0 Candidates use a variety of assessment tools and practices to plan and evaluate effective reading instruction.	3.2 Place students along a developmental continuum and identify students' proficiencies and difficulties.
4.0 Candidates create a literate environment that fosters reading and writing by integrating foundational knowledge, use of instructional practices, approaches and methods, curriculum materials, and the appropriate use of assessment.	3.3 Use assessment information to plan, evaluate, and revise effective instruction that meets the needs of all students including those at different developmental stages and those from different cultural and linguistic backgrounds.
5.0 Candidates view professional development as a career-long effort and responsibility.	3.4 Communicate results of assessment to specific individuals (students, parents, caregivers, colleagues, administrators, policy makers, policy officials, community, etc.).

Source: Standards for Reading Professionals–Revised 2003. Professional Standards and Ethics Committee of the International Reading Association. Copyright 2004 by IRA. Reprinted with permission.

sionals Revised, includes standards for paraprofessionals, classroom teachers, reading specialists/literacy coaches, teacher educators, and administrators. The five standards are presented in Table 1.1. As you will note, Standard 3 focuses on assessment. Also presented in Table 1.1 are the subcategories for Standard 3; these identify specific assessment knowledge and skills.

In addition to the five general standards and their subcategories, the IRA developed a matrix delineating expectations for each of the five types of reading professionals as defined by the IRA. The IRA standards stipulate that the classroom teacher must possess all the knowledge and skills of the paraprofessional plus have additional knowledge and skills. The reading specialist/literacy coach is expected to master all the standards for both paraprofessional and classroom teacher plus have additional knowledge and skills. In turn, the teacher educator must demonstrate mastery of standards for the paraprofessional, classroom teacher, and reading specialist/literacy coach plus have additional knowledge and skills. There is a separate set of standards for administrators. (The entire matrix for Standard 3, describing knowledge and skills in each subcategory for each of the five types of professionals is presented in Appendix A.) In addition, readers are encouraged to peruse the entire set of standards and the complete standards matrix, which are accessible on the IRA Web site: www/reading.org/resources/issues/reports/professional_standards.html

All the types of assessment described in Standard 3.1 are presented in Chapters 3–6 of this book. In order to help educators meet Standard 3.2, we present several models of reading in Chapter 2. Building on these models, we present an inclusive model of reading in graphic and chart forms. Educators can use one or more of the models as both a basis for understanding reading, identifying students' skill levels in different areas of reading, and applying assessment data. To ensure mastery of Standard 3.3, Chapter 7 describes how educators can combine various types of assessment information and use the information to inform instruction. Throughout the text, information presented will allow educators to communicate effectively with each other, with administrators, parents, and policy makers, consistent with Standard 3.4.

PURPOSES OF ASSESSMENT

The ultimate goal of all assessment information should be to create the most effective learning environment for each student. We can think of four related assessment purposes that help meet that goal. Assessment data should be obtained to: (1) guide instructional planning; (2) monitor progress of students on an ongoing basis; (3) determine accountability; and (4) aid in determining eligibility for special education services. These purposes can be thought of on a continuum from most directly related to instruction to least related to instruction. But, all are related, as will be seen. A summary of the four purposes of assessment is presented in Table 1.2.

Instructional Planning

Teachers are expected to do two sometimes contradictory things related to planning instruction. They are expected to teach students knowledge and

TABLE 1.2   Key Characteristics of the Four Purposes of Assessment

Instructional Planning	Progress Monitoring	Accountability	Special Education Eligibility
Determining specific skills mastered and not mastered	Screening students into categories (e.g., proficient, at risk, and below level)	Determining relative ranking among peers to inform parents, teachers, administrators, state and federal departments of education, and the public of progress	Determining whether there is a disability. For example, are criteria met for a particular disability category, such as Learning Disability or Mental Retardation?
Determining level of materials to be assigned by pinpointing instructional level	Frequent monitoring of at-risk and below-level students		
		Determining progress of disaggregated groups (e.g., low SES students)	Determining whether an educational need exists as a result of the disability
Determining assignment to instructional group	Measuring discrete skills such as oral reading fluency		
	Determining the need for more intensive instruction	Determining performance of intact classes/schools to track improvement over time	Determining the best curriculum goals through writing of an Individual Educational Program (IEP)
Determining most appropriate instructional activities			
Determining specific areas on which to focus instruction		Determining teacher effectiveness over time by monitoring classroom performance	

skills for a particular grade level or curricular area. At the same time, they are expected to individualize instruction to fit each student's entering skills. Specifically, grade-level teachers are expected to teach students to master literacy, mathematics, and content area skills to conform to standards or benchmarks defined by state departments of education and as assessed by end-of-year standardized achievement tests. But students enter school with incredible diversity in language skills, innate abilities and talents, background knowledge, motivation, and social-emotional characteristics. In fact, the reading levels of students in a typical first-grade class range from prekindergarten to fourth grade (Hargis 2006). Remember Dr. Charles, the high school biology teacher? How can teachers focus on meeting predetermined grade-level standards and also meet the academic needs of each student in their charge, regardless of the students' entering academic skills and backgrounds? This may be an impossible task. In our opinion, the best response teachers can make to these sometimes competing goals is to make effective use of assessment data. When the teacher knows where the student is performing academically, it is possible to use that information to solve what some experts call the **problem of the match** (Hunt 1972) by determining how best to match the curriculum to the student's entering skills.

The notion of matching the curriculum tasks to the learner's level of readiness is a common theme of developmental psychologists (e.g., Vygotsky 1978). If the match is optimal, students are more likely to be motivated to read and get involved with their assignments. As you will learn later in the book, various assessment techniques are available to help teachers get the information they need, such as informal reading inventories (IRIs), to pinpoint instructional reading levels, classroom worksheets, quizzes, projects, presentations to assess content mastery, curriculum-based measures, and norm-referenced tests for peer comparisons if needed. All can illuminate areas of strength and weakness for a given child or for a whole class. Finally, when information needs to be presented to parents, administrators, and others, educators may be asked to write a case study report, integrating information gleaned from assessment with relevant background educational, medical, and developmental history. Based on all these sources of information, a teacher or specialist can develop recommendations to maximize the student's literacy development. Excerpts from case studies for several students are presented in Chapter 7.

Progress Monitoring

Group achievement tests, typically given once per year, are costly and time consuming. Importantly, they are not designed to measure small gains in student progress. They compare student progress on a wide range of skills; that is, the content in group achievement tests is not designed specifically to match a particular classroom, school, or district curriculum. Consequently, it is important for teachers to monitor more often the progress of their students relative to specific curriculum goals. In addition, laws such as No Child Left Behind of 2001 (NCLB) and the Individuals with Disabilities Education Improvement Act of 2004 (IDEA, 2004) stipulate that progress of students should be screened routinely. Implementation of these laws, and their earlier versions such as the Elementary and Secondary Education Act of 1965 (ESEA), requires delivery of additional or specialized services to students deemed at risk for academic failure. These laws have funded the creation of what Allington (1994) calls a "second system" of education, which includes components outside general education (such as special education, Title 1 reading programs, accelerated tracks for highly capable students). In addition, both laws require extensive assessment of student outcomes for accountability purposes. To be consistent with the accountability requirements imposed on schools, teachers and support personnel (including special educators, reading specialists/literacy coaches, or school psychologists) may administer brief, frequent assessments to determine whether students are making progress consistent with expectations for their grade level.

Remember Mr. Haywood? He and another special educator in his school recently participated in professional development to gain the expertise needed to administer brief, routine assessments that can be used to track student progress over time. In order to monitor progress, some educators have advocated using a **multitier model of instruction,** the most common of which is a **three-tier model of instruction.** Specifically, the three-tier model is required for schools participating in Reading First, a multiyear, federally funded program to improve reading skills of children in the primary grades. The three-tier model also plays a crucial role in the response to intervention or **RTI** approach to identifying learning disabilities, a key change in the 2004 amendments to the federal special education law, IDEA 2004. A critical element of the three-tier model is the idea that students at all tiers receive **scientifically-based reading instruction.** We discuss both the three-tier model and scientifically-based instruction in later sections of this chapter.

Ensuring Accountability

Assessment is needed to ensure that children are acquiring reading and other academic skills according to expectations. For example, NCLB requires states to perform yearly assessments and guarantee that all students make **adequate yearly progress (AYP).** The law also requires systems to **disaggregate,** or separate, data for various groups. Specifically, the progress of students in minority groups, students in special education, students who have English as a second language, and students of low socioeconomic status must be tracked separately. Traditionally, schools have had difficulty educating students from these groups. NCLB requires that all but approximately 2 percent of students (i.e., those with the most severe disabilities) participate in the same accountability testing. States are free to choose their own tests, but they must meet certain criteria. These tests are the norm-referenced achievement tests that allow educators to compare progress of students to their same-grade peers. Some people refer to this type of testing as **high-stakes** because in some states, students are retained or not allowed to graduate if they do not attain certain cutoff scores on these tests. And if schools fail to demonstrate adequate yearly progress, they are in danger of losing funds and/or being taken over by the state education agency.

As you might guess, students in Dr. Charles' biology class must pass an end-of-course test in order to graduate. In some states (such as Tennessee), these group achievement test scores are also used as one measure of teacher effectiveness; using a sophisticated statistical formula, all the gain scores of the students taught by a particular teacher over a specific year are calculated. According to this strategy, there is an attempt to separate the impact of the teacher from the impact of other variables, such as socioeconomic status or school. These gains are used by administrators as an indication of a given teacher's effectiveness, which can be compared to gains by other teachers, school or system averages, and so on. This type of assessment is sometimes referred to as **value-added** (Sanders 1998) and also may have high-stakes consequences for the teachers involved.

Eligibility for Special Education Services

More than 10 percent of United States school children receive special education services. For example, 11.4 percent of the total school population was eligible for special education in 1999–2001 (Turnbull, Turnbull, Shank, and Smith 2004). This means that slightly more than one out of every ten school-age students is eligible for special education. These students are the concern of all educators—special educators, general educators, and administrators. Students who are referred for special education services are required by law to undergo a comprehensive, nondiscriminatory educational evaluation. Assessment data are collected from a variety of sources; that is, more than one test must be used to determine eligibility for special education services. In addition, the assessments must not be racially or culturally discriminatory and they must be administered in the student's native language or preferred mode of communication whenever feasible. The number of **English language learners (ELL),** students whose first language is not English, is increasing rapidly; assessments must be conducted fairly so that students with academic differences due to bilingualism are not misidentified as having a disability (Brown 2004), as we discuss in subsequent chapters.

Classroom and special education teachers usually provide some of the data for making a special education eligibility decision, but other specialists get involved, including speech-language pathologists and school psychologists. In many states, the assessment expert that gathers much of the data is the school psychologist, who may coordinate the assessment process and obtain data from teachers, parents, and medical and social services providers when necessary, and, of course, from assessments given to the student directly. Obviously, information showing academic progress is very important, and much of that comes from the classroom teacher. Other academic progress data may come from direct, individualized assessment and end-of-the-year group test scores. If information related to social and/or emotional functioning is needed, the school psychologist typically obtains it, again, either from the teacher, parents, or the student directly. For some decisions, cognitive testing (i.e., intelligence testing) is required. And speech-language pathologists sometimes assess language and auditory skills. All this information is written into a case report, typically by the school psychologist, and shared with all interested parties at a meeting held at the school.

Based on all the information gathered in the assessment process, including significant input from parents, a team of parents and professionals decides whether the student meets eligibility criteria for special education. Specifically, the team determines whether the assessment data are consistent with state and federal guidelines defining disabilities. IDEA 2004 recognizes thirteen different disability categories. The most commonly identified are learning disabilities (about 47 percent of all special education students), speech-language disorder (about 19 percent), and mental retardation (about 10 percent) (Turnbull, Turnbull, and Wehmeyer 2007). General education teachers will certainly encounter students with these disabilities, as well as students with attention problems. Though **attention deficit hyperactivity disorder (ADHD)** is not technically a disability category under IDEA 2004, some students with ADHD receive special education services under the Other Health Impaired category while some receive classroom accommodations under a separate law, **Section 504 of the Rehabilitation Act of 1975,** which also guarantees a free and appropriate public education to all students.

If a student is identified with a disability, the IEP team decides what services, if any, in addition to regular class instruction, are needed to meet the student's needs. These services then are documented in an **individual education program (IEP).** *A critical decision must be made at this point.* If the student has difficulty in reading, the team must decide whether the student is benefiting from participation in the core reading program used in the general classroom. If so, probably the most beneficial arrangement is for the special education teacher to provide supplemental, intensive instruction in identified areas of need, such as building a sight **vocabulary** and teaching comprehension strategies. However, if the core program does not meet the student's needs (usually because the materials and activities are too difficult), the special education teacher should provide alternative, appropriate instruction. In Mr. Haywood's school, the core program provides opportunities for students to spend considerable time reading from leveled readers, at an appropriate instructional level. Consequently, he typically provides instruction supplemental to the core program, rather than replacing it.

Suppose the IEP team evaluates the assessment data and decides the child is not eligible for special education. It is still necessary to provide appropriate instruction. In cases when students do not qualify for special education, the team considers other options, which may include tutoring, counseling, and accommodations under Section 504.

■ WHAT IS READING?

In order to assess effectively, educators must understand the phenomena they are assessing, in this case *reading*. Unlike language development, reading is not a natural process, according to Shaywitz (2003). While this assertion may be true, reading seems to come more naturally to some than others. Simply defined, reading is getting meaning from print. According to Snow, Burns, and Griffin, editors of the influential publication *Preventing Reading Difficulties in Young Children* (1998, vi), "reading should be defined as a process of getting meaning from print, using knowledge about the written alphabet and about the sound structure of oral language for the purpose of achieving understanding." Even though not everyone defines reading exactly the same—Calkins (2001, 359) defines it as "nothing more or less than thinking, guided by print"—and despite ongoing controversy about how to teach reading, everyone seems to agree that the purpose of reading is comprehension. However, as anyone who has ever tried to read text in an unfamiliar language can attest, even the most capable students cannot extract meaning from print when they cannot decipher or **decode** what the print says.

Reading is an undeniably complex interplay of visual, auditory, language, memory, and reasoning skills. And to make the process even more daunting, learning to read exists in a particular social context. Reading is guided by cultural and social rules. At the most fundamental level, these include assigning print left to right versus right to left versus top to bottom. But social and cultural mores also influence reading in more subtle ways. For example, in some cultures, reading for pleasure is not a valued or respected activity for males (Brozo 2002). Prior experiences in the world and past experiences with reading (i.e., reading with success versus difficulty) also shape what a reader experiences each time he or she engages in reading.

In this book we use as a focal point the five areas of reading as identified by the National Reading Panel (NRP, National Institute of Child Health and Human Development or NICHD, 2000) and we add a couple of important areas not specifically addressed by the panel. The NRP was commissioned by the U.S. Congress in 1997 to review the scientific literature on reading instruction. Their work culminated in a report published in 2000. The NRP began by **screening** more than 10,000 studies and reviewing those that met predetermined criteria for scientific rigor. Ultimately, the panel presented findings primarily in five areas of reading. Though criticized by some for excluding certain types of studies, including **correlational** and **qualitative studies,** and for overemphasizing the importance of phonics instruction, the NRP report provides a good starting point for beginners and those who need a refresher. (See Allington [2002] and Shanahan [2003, 2004] for discussion of the criticisms of the NRP report). The five areas provide a **scaffold** upon which educators can build.

Figure 1.1 depicts the five NRP areas, with the addition of **orthography,** and represents the interrelationships among them. Readers should not assume that the model is hierarchical. That is, even very young and beginning readers check for understanding. Phonics skills are influenced by fluency, vocabulary, and comprehension (and vice versa). **Phonemic awareness,** which is discussed in more detail as follows, has its influence on other reading skills primarily through its relationship to phonics.

Effective teachers must understand reading well in order to **task analyze** the process (i.e., break it down into teachable parts). We think of the five areas of reading from the NRP as a template upon which to build knowledge and skills in assessment and instruction, understanding that strengths or weaknesses in any one area are likely to affect and be affected by skill level in the other areas. We depict the NRP model in a figure at the risk of oversimplifying reading. There are other important **intra-individual** attributes that impact reading such as motivation, background knowledge and culture, and teacher/classroom and parent variables (Allington 2005). But educators who develop an understanding of these five areas and recognize how they are measured by the various assessment tools will be well equipped to begin effective assessment and instruction of their students. Literacy experts with differing philosophies seem to agree on the need for ongoing professional development in both assessment and instruction, and we endorse this

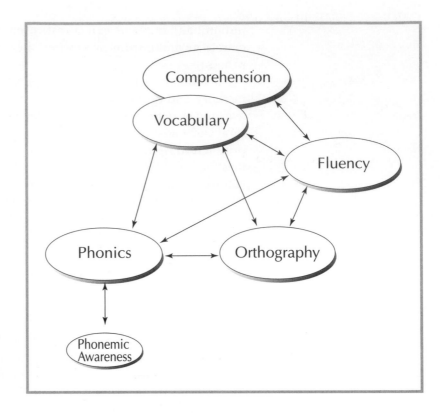

FIGURE **1.1 Areas of Reading Identified by the National Reading Panel Plus Orthography and their Interrelationships**

practice. Finally, IRA includes ongoing professional development as one of its standards.

What Are the Critical Areas of Reading?

In addition to labels applied by the NRP to five identified critical areas of reading—phonemic awareness, phonics, fluency, vocabulary, and comprehension—the panel uses additional terms that will be of interest to teachers. For example, the panel introduces the broad term **alphabetics** to include both phonemic awareness and phonics. Armbrister and Osborn authored *Put Reading First: The Research Building Blocks for Teaching Children to Read* (2001), a summary of the NRP findings for educators. They emphasize the importance of the **alphabetic principle.** In order to master phonemic awareness and phonics skills, students must "learn and use the alphabetic principle— the understanding that there are systematic and predictable relationships between written letters and spoken words" (Armbruster and Osborn 2001, 12).

What is phonemic awareness?

According to Adams, phonemic awareness is the "insight that every spoken word can be conceived as a sequence of phonemes" (cited in Adams and Treadway 2000, 17). Further,

> . . . phonemic awareness is the ability to notice, think about, and work with the individual sounds in spoken words. Before children learn to read print, they need to become aware of how the sounds in words work. They must understand that words are made up of speech sounds, or phonemes. Phonemes are the smallest parts of sound in a spoken word that makes a

TABLE 1.3   Six Subtypes of Phonemic Awareness

Phonemic isolation	Requires recognizing individual sounds in words (e.g., "Tell me the first sound in *paste*." **(/p/)**
Phonemic identity	Requires recognizing the common sound in different words (e.g., "Tell me the sound that is the same in *bike, boy,* and *bell*." **(/b/)**
Phonemic categorization	Requires recognizing the word with the odd sound in a sequence of three or four words (e.g., "Which word does not belong? *Bus, bun, rug*.") **(/rug/)**
Phoneme blending	Requires listening to a sequence of separately spoken sounds and combining them to form a recognizable word (e.g., "What word is /s/ /k/ /u/ /l/?") **(school)**
Phoneme segmentation	Requires breaking a word into sounds by tapping out or counting the sounds, or by pronouncing and positioning a marker for each sound (e.g., "How many phonemes in *ship?*" **(3: /sh/i/p)**
Phoneme deletion	Requires recognizing what word remains when a specified phoneme is removed (e.g., "What is *smile* without the /s/?" **(mile)**

Source: National Institute of Child Health and Human Development. (2000). Report of the National Reading Panel. *Teaching children to read: An evidence-based assessment of the scientific research literature on reading and its implications for reading instruction* (NIH Publication No. 00-4769). Washington, DC: U.S. Government Printing Office.

difference in the word's meaning. For example, changing the first phoneme in the word *hat* from /h/ to /p/ changes the word from hat to pat and so changes the meaning (Armbrister and Osborn 2001, 2).

What are the recommended strategies for teaching phonemic awareness? Six subtypes of phonemic awareness were identified by the NRP:

1. Phonemic isolation
2. Phonemic identity
3. Phonemic categorization
4. Phoneme blending
5. Phoneme segmentation
6. Phoneme deletion

A seventh, not identified by the NRP, is called **onset-rime** (Ehri 2004). The six types identified by the NRP are presented in Table 1.3.

In addition to the six subtypes, onset-rime manipulation requires isolation, identification, segmentation, blending, or deletion of onsets (the single consonant or blend that precedes the vowel in a syllable) or rimes (the vowel and following consonants), for example, *j-ump, st-op, str-ong, bl-ock* (Ehri 2004, 157).

Strategies are designed to teach the various subtypes. For example, teachers may use **Elkonin blocks** or boxes to teach students to isolate and manipulate phonemes. One such strategy involves giving the students blocks of different colors and asking one to say a word such as */bat/* and represent each different sound with a different-colored block. Then, the student can be led to manipulate phonemes by changing the block that corresponds with the changing sound when the word is changed to */hat/*. There are numerous commercial programs available to teach phonemic awareness; many involve a manipulative or kinesthetic component.

How is phonemic awareness different from phonological awareness? According to Adams (1990, 17), **phonological awareness** is a broad term; that is, it is a "more inclusive term than phonemic awareness and refers to the general ability to attend to the sounds of language as distinct from its meaning." Phonological awareness includes the types of phonemic awareness described above but also includes the ability to separate words into syllables, the ability to notice how sounds in words are alike or different and the ability to appreciate and create rhymes (Adams and Treadway 2000; Leu, Kinzer, Wilson, and Hall 2006).

What is phonics?   According to Leu et al. (2006), phonics consists of two elements: (1) knowledge of sounds and letters and their relationships and (2) the ability to synthesize or blend the sounds that are represented by letters. In English, this task is challenging because English is a phonologically complex language (Miles 2000). One sound in English, for example, may be represented by more than one letter (such as the sound made by the letter /f/, which may also be made by the combination of two letters (/ph/). Further, English contains many irregular spellings (such as /reed/ and /read/, which may be pronounced the same way). In contrast, /read/ may be pronounced two different ways depending on context.

What are recommended types of phonics instruction?   Armbruster and Osborn (2001) described six types of phonic instruction:

1. Synthetic—Readers are taught to recognize letters, convert them into sounds, and blend them into words;
2. Analytic—Readers are taught to recognize letter-sound relationships from words they have already learned; emphasis is not on sounds in isolation;
3. Analogic—Readers are taught to use parts of words they have already learned (**word families** or **rimes**) to figure out new words with the same patterns;
4. Through spelling—Readers are taught to segment words into letters or letter combinations that represent phonemes and make words by writing the letters for the phonemes in the words;
5. Embedded phonics—Readers learn letter-sound relationships as they read connected text (this approach is not considered systematic or explicit but can be used effectively to reinforce **systematic instruction** and promote generalization);and
6. Onset-rime—Readers are taught to identify the sounds of the first letter or letters (the onset) and the rime (common vowel-consonant patterns such as /an/ /ot/).

How important are phonemic awareness and phonics?   The NRP (2–41) concluded that "teaching phonemic awareness helps many different students learn to read, including preschoolers, kindergartners, and first-graders who are just starting to learn to read." According to several researchers, knowledge of the alphabet and phonemic awareness are the two best predictors of how well children will learn to read during their first two years of reading instruction (e.g., Adams 1990; Christiansen 2000; Liberman 1989).

Research on phonemic awareness virtually exploded in the 1990s, following the publication of Adams' *Beginning to Read: Thinking and Learning about Print* in 1990. Results of several studies identified phonemic awareness skills in kindergarten or first grade as an important predictor of later reading skills, including reading comprehension (Adams 1990; Christiansen 2000). According to Adams (1990), the important variable in phonemic awareness is the reader's ability to attend to sounds separate from meaning and to understand that the sounds can be manipulated. The NRP asserted that phonemic awareness instruction is effective for young beginning readers, older beginning readers, those at risk for developing reading problems, and older disabled readers (Ehri 2004; NICHD 2000).

The NRP concluded that systematic instruction in phonics is effective for younger readers and for those with reading difficulties. "Findings yielded solid support for the conclusion that systematic phonics instruction makes a more significant contribution to children's growth in reading than do non-systematic instruction or no phonics instruction" (Armbrister and Osborn 2001, 14). These findings corroborate the earlier results from Chall (1967; 1983) and Bond and Dykstra (1967). The important point for educators to remember is that the purpose of reading is comprehension—but for most readers, phonemic awareness and phonics skills instruction are critical aspects of reading instruction, especially in the early grades or for beginning readers of any age (Stanovich, 1986). In fact, even readers with deafness and hearing impairments apparently develop an appreciation of the alphabetic principle. Though they may not hear the sounds or phonemes in a language, they develop a sense that letters represent phonemes (McAnally, Rose, and Quigley 1999; Kathleen Warden, personal communication, January 26, 2006). According to Adams (1990, 65), it is not the working knowledge of phonemes that is so important but rather:

> . . . conscious, analytic knowledge. It is neither the ability to hear the difference between two phonemes nor the ability to distinctly produce that is significant. What is important is the awareness that they exist as abstractable and manipulable components of the language.

Despite the strong endorsements for their importance, there is disagreement about the relative importance of phonemic awareness and phonics in the overall reading process. Some argue that the NRP overstated the case for the importance of phonemic awareness and phonics instruction (Allington 2002; Hammill and Swanson 2006; Shanahan 2003, 2004). In fact, Allington and Cunningham (2002) describe phonics instruction as only one of four strategies to teach children to read—and all have unique and specific strengths. These authors acknowledge the value of phonics instruction, particularly for young children and those who have had limited exposure to reading and writing and fewer opportunities to master the alphabetic system. But they also discuss the relative strengths of the other three strategies, such as the value of learning to read "inside out" by writing and the value of the systematic variations in difficulty level and literature styles found in basal readers. Nonetheless, there seems to be at least a general consensus that these skills are important and crucial to assess for identifying **dyslexia** (International Dyslexia Association or IDA 2003; Shaywitz 2003). Dyslexia is a specific type of reading difficulty characterized by significant difficulty with phonological, and sometimes, orthographic, skills. It is discussed in more detail in subsequent chapters.

What is orthography?   Orthography is the system of printed symbols or marks, such as letters, that represents a spoken language. Though not specifically addressed by the NRP, along with phonemic awareness, letter-name knowledge is a strong predictor of later reading proficiency (Snow, Burns, and Griffin 1998). Orthographic processing is the "process of identifying letters in isolation, in individual words, and in running text" (Schumm 2006, 528). According to Rego (2006, 122), "fluent identification of letters facilitates word recognition, which in turn facilitates reading comprehension." Adams (1990) asserts the importance of automatic letter recognition in the early reading process, noting that both meaning and spelling are compromised when beginning readers struggle with letter recognition.

Most children in the United States learn to identify letters before or during kindergarten. These children are ready to learn letter-sound relationships. However, because the English alphabet contains several letters that differ only in spatial orientation (/b/, /d/, /p/), some early readers experience confusion and struggle with automatic recognition of letters. In addition to individual letter recognition, orthography includes common spelling patterns in a language, which gives readers clues to syllabication rules. According to Moats (2004, 276), "users of English orthography spell by both sound and meaning. To read the alphabetic orthography proficiently, learners must first appreciate that letters and letter groups, such as /oa/. . . and/igh/" combine in specific ways to represent sounds or phonemes. Further, "to read multisyllabic words fluently, learners must recognize the syllable spelling conventions and junctures of printed syllables that permit visual "chunking" of long letter sequences and assignment of a vowel sound to specific letter patterns" (2004, 276). Orthographic skills are related to spelling skills; to spell well, students must learn orthographic "patterns, principles, and rules" (2004, 276).

Building upon letter recognition and repeated exposure to print, proficient young readers learn to recognize whole words automatically. Automatic recognition of words has commonly been referred to as **sight word recognition;** the words a reader knows automatically are sometimes referred to as **sight vocabulary.** However, according to Leslie and Caldwell (2001, 37), "automatic word identification may involve a strong sound component"; consequently they prefer the term **automatic word recognition.** In any case, quick and effortless recognition of words is necessary for readers to read fluently.

What strategies are recommended to build automatic word recognition and orthography?   Bos and Vaughn (2006, 135) indicate that teachers need to teach students to recognize with automaticity high-frequency words and words that are phonetically irregular. They note it is "not practical to teach students to analyze all words in the English language because the patterns they follow may not occur frequently enough to teach." Like other experts, they recommend teaching words from a high frequency word list such as Gunning's (2000) list of 200 *high-frequency* words. They summarize recommendations by Cunningham (2000) and Gunning (2000) as follows:

- Teach the most frequently occurring words.
- Check to make sure that students understand the meaning, particularly if they have limited language, a specific language disability, or are English-language learners.

- Introduce these new words before students encounter them in text.
- Limit the number of words that are introduced in a single lesson.
- Reinforce the association by adding a kinesthetic component such as tracing, copying, and writing from memory.
- Introduce visually similar words, (e.g., *where* and *were*, *was* and *saw*) in separate lessons to avoid confusion.
- Ask students to compare visually words, (e.g., *what* for *when*) and highlight the differences between the two words.
- Provide multiple opportunities for the students to read the words in text and as single words until they automatically recognize the words.
- Review words that have been taught previously, particularly if the students incorrectly call them when reading text.
- Provide opportunities for the students to get automatic at recognizing the words such as games that require quick word recognition or power writing (i.e., writing the words multiple times in a short length of time). (Bos and Vaughn 2006, 136–137)

Because spelling and orthography are highly related, writing activities naturally lend themselves to building proficiency with recognizing and using familiar word patterns. Activities that provide practice with rime and onset and word patterns such as those found in Cunningham and Hall's *Making Words* (1994) and Cunningham's *Phonics They Use* (2005) are recommended to help students automatize familiar word patterns.

What is fluency?   "Fluency is the ability to read with efficiency and ease. Fluent readers can read quickly and accurately and with appropriate rhythm, intonation and expression" (Curtis and Kruidenier 2005, 6). According to McKenna and Stahl (2003), fluency involves accuracy, **automaticity,** and appropriate inflection or **prosody.** Finally, Rasinski and Padak (2004) describe fluency as the bridge between word recognition and comprehension, an important point because it reinforces the critical and reciprocal relationship between the two and emphasizes the value of developing fluency as a necessary ability in the acquisition of the ultimate reading skill—creating meaning from text. As implied in the definitions above, fluency is multidimensional; according to Zutell and Rasinski (1991) fluency includes phrasing and intonation, smoothness, and pacing.

Betts (1946) recommended that students read with 95 percent or better accuracy in order to achieve adequate comprehension. Reading with automaticity means that students read words automatically, without conscious effort (i.e., without relying on the mechanics and strategies required to break the phonetic code). And prosody means reading with inflection; in oral reading, the reader's voice goes up and down depending on whether one is reading a sentence or question, and readers pause at punctuation and between sentences.

What strategies are recommended to increase fluency?   According to Armbrister and Osborn (2001), when teachers provide opportunities for students to read and reread orally while monitoring and providing feedback, students get better at reading. Specifically, they improve in accuracy, speed, word recognition skills, and fluency. Students, especially weak readers, need lots of time to practice reading books they can read without much difficulty. Special techniques to improve fluency include reading with a tutor or with a peer, reading along with an audiotape, and small-group reading strategies such as **choral reading,** which is reading together with the teacher or another model, or **echo reading,** which is reading by following just after the teacher or a model (Allington 2001; Armbruster and Osborn 2001). Importantly, students will not gain much from being asked to read on their own when the material is too hard or when they are not monitored.

What is vocabulary? "A person's vocabulary consists of the individual words whose [sic] meaning he or she knows and understands. **Reading vocabulary** comprises those words that we know and understand as we read" (Curtis and Kruidenier 2005, 7). **Oral vocabulary** refers to "words we use in speaking or recognize in listening" (Armbruster and Osborn 2001, 34). Two types of oral vocabulary are **listening vocabulary,** which are the words we understand when we hear them and **speaking vocabulary,** the words we know how to use when speaking. Some students who are weak readers have much better developed listening and speaking vocabularies when compared to their reading vocabularies. Other students who are weak readers may be able to recognize words but not know their meanings. As might be expected, adult nonreaders and those with low level reading skills tend to have better developed oral vocabulary than reading vocabulary (Kruidenier 2002).

What strategies are recommended to enhance vocabulary? According to the NRP, vocabulary is the reading skill most likely to be improved through incidental reading as opposed to direct instruction. That is, students learn new words when engaging in class discussion, in conversation, when they are read to, and when they read on their own (assuming they can read the material with some level of understanding). But the NRP also found that some vocabulary needs to be taught directly through planned, teacher-guided instructional experiences. According to Beck, McKeown, and Kucan (2002), vocabulary is learned through context but it should also be taught explicitly if poor readers are to acquire vocabularies similar to stronger readers. Teaching specific word meanings before encountering them in text, promoting active engagement with words by having students create their own sentences using the words, and repeated exposure of the same words in text, in similar and different contexts, are all helpful in enriching vocabulary (Armbrister and Osborn 2001).

Bos and Vaughn (2006) recommend that teachers provide suggestions to parents to help build vocabulary. A few of these include: (a) play with words by choosing rhyming words, synonyms, and antonyms and by categorizing words (such as hot versus cold); (b) choose a "family" word of the day to use in different situations all day long; (c) use words encountered in everyday activities (such as on signs, in stores) as a basis for discussing meanings and how words may be used in certain contexts. Bos and Vaughn also recommend that teachers build on oral language by drawing on students' background knowledge; preteaching before reading and using specific word-learning strategies, including **contextual analysis** (using the context to derive meaning), and **morphemic analysis** (deriving meaning by breaking words down into their smallest meaningful parts **or morphemes**). Students who know the meanings of prefixes and suffixes can generally make good inferences about words that contain them. In addition, students may benefit from learning some of the most common Greek and Latin roots, such as *bio* and *phon*.

What is the relationship between vocabulary and comprehension?   Overall reading ability and vocabulary size are related, and vocabulary proficiency is related strongly to reading comprehension. According to Kamil (2004, 215), both vocabulary and comprehension "involve the meaning of the text, albeit at different levels. Vocabulary is generally tied closely to individual words, whereas comprehension is more often thought of in much larger units." Further, Kamil notes that "precisely separating" vocabulary and comprehension "is difficult, if not impossible, making it difficult to tell where one ends and the other begins" (2004, 215). Nonetheless, we know that vocabulary is influenced heavily by one's background experiences and that "limited vocabulary has been viewed as both a cause and an effect of poor reading achievement" (Bos and Vaughn 2006, 281). "Good readers know about twice as many words as do poor readers in the first grade, and as these students go through the grades, the gap grows" so that by the end of high school, good readers know about four times as many words as poor readers (Bos and Vaughn 2006, 281). Effective instructional strategies, both incidental and explicit, are necessary to help close the vocabulary gap between strong and weak readers. According to Beck et al. (2002), results of several research studies on teaching vocabulary showed positive effects for both vocabulary and comprehension.

What is comprehension?   "Reading comprehension is the process of constructing meaning from what is read" (Curtis and Kruidenier 2005, 9). Anderson, Hiebert, Scott, and Wilkinson (1985) describe it as a holistic act that relies on several factors, including the background of the reader, the purpose for reading, and the context within which reading occurs. Because comprehension is a complex act, it can occur with varying degrees of sophistication or complexity and may be literal, inferential, or applied. For example, a reader may interpret text at a literal level. If so, the phrase, "raining cats and dogs" might inspire a novice reader, one who interprets meaning in a literal fashion, to run for a substantial shelter, as opposed to reaching for an umbrella. Similarly, readers may make inferences from text and create meaning that goes beyond the printed word. For example, if a text conveys information that mammals are warm-blooded creatures, and the reader knows that rabbits are mammals, the reader might infer also that rabbits are warm-blooded. Finally, readers may elaborate on text so that meaning acquired in one context can be applied in other similar situations.

What strategies are recommended for comprehension instruction?   Comprehension is influenced by all other areas of reading. For obvious reasons, the readers' vocabulary heavily influences comprehension. According to Betts (1946), comprehension suffers when readers recognize fewer than 95 of 100 words and suffers significantly when readers recognize fewer than 90 of 100 words. McKenna and Stahl (2003) indicate that students may be able to comprehend adequately at lower recognition levels (85 percent accuracy) provided that teachers are available to provide support. From its examination of numerous studies on reading comprehension, the NRP identified eight strategies as especially effective.

Comprehension monitoring.   Teachers can help students learn to monitor their comprehension by teaching them to check for understanding. One strategy for checking is to ask themselves "Does that make sense?" after reading from text. Students with good comprehension skills know what they do and do not understand and they know how to use "fix" strategies as needed. If reading is thinking as Allington (2001) and Calkins (2001) assert, the importance of **metacognition,** or the ability to think about one's own thinking, is paramount. Students who read with comprehension can identify where in the text they are having difficulty and specifically what they do not understand. They can paraphrase the text to make it make sense and look back and forward to confirm or clarify meaning. According to the NRP, students tend to benefit from **explicit instruction** in comprehension monitoring strategies (NICHD 2000).

Application of graphic and semantic organizers.   **Graphic organizers** or pictorial depictions of relationships between concepts, such as the one in Figure 1.1, help illustrate ideas or concepts and their interrelationships. In fiction or **narrative text,** graphic organizers may be presented as story maps. In the content areas, such as science and social studies, graphic organizers may contain factual information and show how concepts or ideas are related. They may also depict processes. The NRP found that teachers can enhance student memory and comprehension of content in science and social studies by teaching them to use a visual graphic to organize reading content.

Question answering.   Effective teachers ask questions that help guide and monitor student comprehension. Asking questions gives students a specific purpose for reading, helps focus their attention and thinking as they read, and encourages comprehension monitoring (Armbrister and Osborn 2001). The NRP found a small but positive effect on comprehension for students whose teachers asked questions to aid in comprehension.

Question generation.   Not surprisingly, the NRP found that when students are taught to generate their own questions, their reading comprehension improves. Teaching students to generate and ask themselves questions promotes active engagement with the reading. This active involvement results in improved memory and may help students identify main ideas, and integrate and summarize material.

Building story structure.   "**Story structure** is a method by which the teacher teaches the reader knowledge and procedures for identifying the content of the story and the way it is organized into a plot structure" (NICHD 2000, 4–88). When teachers teach students to recognize story structures, the students remember better the stories and show deeper understanding and appreciation for them. The sequence of events in stories can be shown in **story maps,** a type of graphic organizer. The NRP found that instruction in story structure is particularly helpful for less capable readers.

Summarization.   Good readers can summarize and condense what they read by deciding what is most important, identifying the main ideas, making generalizations, and putting the information into their own words. When summarizing, readers also must leave out irrelevant or trivial information. According to the NRP, instruction in summarization improves comprehension.

Ensure cooperative learning.   With careful planning and management by teachers, students can be taught to work in groups to improve reading comprehension, particularly in the content areas. The NRP found that peer discussion and instruction can lead to increased student learning of comprehension strategies, heightened intellectual discussion, and improved reading comprehension.

Apply multiple strategies.   Good readers use more than one strategy to ensure comprehension as they read. Readers need to be able to use various strategies to understand content. For example, teachers can use a series of instructional strategies known collectively as **reciprocal teaching,** which was first introduced by Palinscar and Brown (1984). In reciprocal teaching, the teacher models and teaches students to ask questions, summarize, clarify what they do not understand, and predict what will come next in the text. Reciprocal teaching may be used with both narrative and **expository** (nonfiction) text. The NRP found strong evidence to support the use of more than one strategy in a natural context as students read routinely and as they complete content-area assignments.

Implement explicit instruction.   Explicit instruction is overt and planned by the teacher. The teacher models how to apply a strategy, explains the procedure directly, provides guided practice, and helps students practice until they can apply the strategy themselves. Explicit instruction is sometimes referred to as **direct instruction.** Indeed, explicit instruction requires action and planned activities on the part of the teacher. However, direct instruction sometimes is used to denote a specific type of explicit instruction in which teachers deliver lessons according to a curriculum script. While noted for their effectiveness in teaching mastery of basic skills, particularly phonics, these scripted direct instruction approaches sometimes are criticized for their heavy emphasis on phonics. Explicit strategies can be contrasted to less direct (more **implicit**) strategies, characterized by providing less salient cues to novice readers, cues that might help them "discover" the importance of structure embedded in text types (such as expository and narrative text, newspaper articles, and work-related manuals), incidental mastery of vocabulary, and word patterns.

◼ WHAT IS THE MULTITIERED MODEL OF INSTRUCTION?

Now that you know more about important elements of reading and about some of the more effective specific instructional strategies, we turn our attention to a general instructional model with direct relevance for reading, the so-called *multitiered model of instruction.* As you will remember, we described multitiered reading instruction briefly in the context of the Reading First initiative. In this generic model, teachers use sound instructional practices (i.e., scientifically-based instruction) in the regular class setting (referred to as Tier 1); student progress is monitored; and those who do not progress as expected receive increasingly intensive additional instruction. Teachers or

TABLE 1.4 Multitiered Model of Instruction

Level of Instruction	Person Delivering Instruction	Assessment	Educational Status of Students
Tier 1	General education teacher delivers a sound core program	Student progress is monitored several times per year	General education
Tier 2	General education teacher, reading specialist, tutor, or special educator delivers additional sound instruction in addition to Tier 1 instruction	Student progress is monitored frequently (such as once per week)	General education
Tier 3	Special education teacher delivers sound instruction in addition to or in lieu of Tier 1 and Tier 2 instruction	Student progress is monitored frequently (such as once per week)	Special education

other educators monitor student progress several times per year with screening tests. These tests measure specific skills, such as oral reading fluency, based on how many words a student can read per minute from a grade level list or passage. Students' performance is compared to **benchmarks,** which have been developed by gathering data on students in the various grades, at various times of year. If students perform below established expectations and if their rate of progress is significantly slower than expected, they will be targeted for extra instruction, several times per week. This extra instruction is referred to as Tier 2 instruction; it is not considered a special education service. Once students are targeted for Tier 2 instruction, teachers or other educators monitor their progress much more frequently (such as once per week) with assessments that tap specific skills, including oral reading fluency. Those students who continue to perform below expectation and at a slower rate than peers will be referred for special education, referred to as Tier 3 instruction. Table 1.4 presents the essential characteristics of the basic three-tier model.

In practice, implementation of this model varies from district to district and state to state. Some variations of the model include four tiers; in the four-tier model, Tier 3 represents additional intensive services but students are not identified as special education eligible unless they do not perform well in Tier 3 and are referred on to Tier 4, which includes special education services.

How is progress monitoring related to the multitiered model? Essentially, progress monitoring is the measure that tells whether the student is achieving at a rate and level similar to peers of the same age and grade. Consequently, it tells educators when a student should be moved into a different tier. Progress monitoring hinges on the use of benchmarks and documenting a student's performance over time, continually comparing performance to the benchmarks. The educator who assesses the student's performance charts the scores on a graph or uses a computer program to create the graph. Scores are compared to the typically expected performance for the child's age or grade. Progress monitoring is discussed in detail in Chapter 4.

Progress monitoring and other assessment information can give educators knowledge about which specific reading skills are weak and which are stronger. The next step is to select and implement the instructional strategies that are best for the student in the situation. How do educators know what strategies are effective? One avenue is through ongoing professional development; good professional development is essential to good teaching. But it is important that the strategies addressed in professional development are based on sound research supporting their effectiveness. There are volumes of research on various instructional strategies and their effectiveness with a variety of students. The NRP summarized some of this research in its 2000 report. But educators will want to expand their knowledge beyond what was addressed in the NRP report. To read and appreciate the research literature, educators need to know about scientifically-based methods and how those can be applied in research. In the following sections, we examine exactly what is meant by scientifically-based instruction and why it is important to teachers and other educators.

WHAT IS SCIENTIFICALLY-BASED RESEARCH IN READING?

Because teachers are expected to make decisions that ensure quality instruction, they are motivated to separate myth from reality, misinformation from information, and research-supported guidelines from conventional but unsupported wisdom. In practice, there are two important implications from this expectation. First, educators should rely on quality research that establishes the effectiveness of their instructional decisions. Second, educators should rely on the collection of data and solid theory to guide their decision making in the classroom and in schools.

Appreciating Effective Research

How can educators learn to distinguish between well-controlled, high-quality research, as opposed to poorly conducted research? As Gersten (2001, 45) noted, teachers are "deluged with misinformation." The following guidelines have been provided to help teachers evaluate the quality and credibility of information presented in the literature (Stanovich and Stanovich 2003):

1. Value conclusions found in **peer-reviewed journals** over those found in non–peer-reviewed journals;
2. Look for evidence that a finding has been corroborated by evidence from more than one study;
3. Look for a consensus among experts from a body of research;
4. If direct evidence about a particular practice is not available, look for support from related and "connected" studies.

Considering Peer-Reviewed Journals

Peer-reviewed journals are professional journals such as *The Reading Teacher* and *Reading Research Quarterly*, published by the International Reading Association, and *Teaching Exceptional Children*, published by the Council for Exceptional Children. Peer-reviewed means that the articles published in these journals have been screened through a blind review process. Experts, typically professors and practitioners, read anonymously manuscripts submitted for publication and provide critical feedback to the journal editor who makes a decision about the quality of the manuscript and its potential contribution to the field.

According to Stanovich and Stanovich (2003), some educators have not always valued knowledge obtained scientifically. In our view, educators work in a context that makes it difficult for them to exercise informed professional judgment. Stanovich and Stanovich (2003) argue that the dominant model for resolving disputes and guiding practice in education has been political rather than scientific. Political problem solving relies on expert opinion, and has led to what Stanovich and Stanovich (2003) have called the "authority syndrome," a model conducive to fads and gimmicks. In addition, teachers often rely on practical experience and on craft knowledge to guide their decision making, as opposed to the type of knowledge that emerges from the scientific enterprise (Fletcher and Francis 2004). Further, teachers often are told what materials and techniques to use in their classrooms by administrators who may not be aware of current best practices. Administrators typically are under pressure from various groups, such as school boards and legislatures, and may react to perceived problems by suggesting sweeping changes in curriculum. They may fall prey to vendors touting the effectiveness of certain programs when money would be better spent in ongoing professional development of teachers and other staff. One of the outcomes has been the loss of respect for education as a profession and colleges of education in particular.

George Will (2006), a noted political columnist, recently called for the close of colleges of education, in part because of what he perceives as lack of scientific rigor. Unfortunately, he is not alone in his opinion. The criticism of the field of education is not restricted to columnists or politicians. For example, see criticisms by professionals in the field (e.g., Sweet 2004) and most notably by Reid Lyon (Lyon et al. 2001) who headed the NICHD in the late 1990s and early 2000s.

We certainly do not endorse the call for closing colleges of education, nor do we agree with much of the harsh criticism leveled against them. But we do endorse the need for educators to have the knowledge and skills necessary to make sound educational decisions, based on knowledge of solid research coupled with expert clinical judgment. When educators are well informed, they are less vulnerable to fads and gimmicks and can resist the so-called authority syndrome.

Reviewing and Using Evidence-based Research Findings

Scientific inquiry is guided by several basic principles. First, decisions are based on information or data obtained **empirically;** that is, by direct observation. Second, data are organized systematically and based on reason and logic so that questions or hypotheses can be generated and investigated or tested. Third, data-gathering strategies must be clearly stated publicly so that others can copy or replicate the process and self-righting can occur. When data and related conclusions are made public, in professional journals and at professional meetings, others can conduct similar investigations and either corroborate or disconfirm findings.

There are a variety of types of studies that educators read about or use, including the **true experimental study, quasi-experimental study,** correlational study, **single-subject studies,** and qualitative studies, particularly the **case study.**

These types of studies examine the relationship between two (or more) variables or factors. Some are designed to determine cause and effect, while others are designed to yield descriptive information. The true experiment is generally considered the most powerful for determining cause and effect, but quasi-experimental and single-subject studies can also demonstrate causality. Not all types of studies have as a goal to establish cause and effect. Correlational studies demonstrate relationships between two or more variables, such as poverty and low reading achievement, but they do not establish that one variable causes the other. Also, qualitative research may be undertaken to clarify the perspectives or perceptions of students and their teachers under certain (or changing) classroom conditions such as curricula, physical (re)arrangements, grading schemes, and so on. For example, case studies often are written simply to provide descriptions of events, which may be a very useful endeavor, particularly when the goal is to determine the ease or acceptability of some intervention or to describe the characteristics of a student or classroom.

What Is a "True Experimental" Design?

When scientists seek answers to questions they typically begin by asking, "What is the relationship between or among variables?" In the simplest case, researchers are interested in investigating the relationship between only two variables, which we can call "X" and "Y." In reading, for example, a teacher might want to know the nature of the relationship between a beginning reader's vocabulary development and reading comprehension or use of a new reading instructional approach and reading fluency skills of the children participating in the approach. Both are legitimate questions for a teacher to ask. By using a true experimental design, the teacher might vary systematically one of the variables and assess the effect the variation has on the second. In doing so, students would be assigned randomly to one of the two (or more) groups. Random assignment occurs when students are assigned to groups completely on the basis of chance, such as when names are pulled blindly out of a hat so that the first name goes in Group 1, the second in Group 2, the third in Group 3 (if there is a need for three groups), and so on. Then, the members of the groups are treated differently based simply on which group they are assigned to, and measures are taken on the variable of interest so performance can be compared across the groups. So, a true experiment is characterized by random assignment to groups, followed by some manipulation of events that causes members of one group to be treated differently than members of another group. Let's consider a real-world example of how this design might work.

Ms. Sanchez, who teaches adults as you will remember, may be interested in the efficacy of implementing a new reading approach with one group while continuing to use the "old" approach with another, basically because there is no evidence that one is better than the other in increasing students' reading fluency. Suppose she read in an article in the *Journal of Adolescent and Adult Literacy,* a peer-reviewed journal published by the International Reading Association, about some strategies for increasing vocabulary of low-literate adults and she wants to try one out with her students. This is a classic kind of question that teachers face every day. Ms. Sanchez may ask, "Will my students perform better if I teach using Method A or Method B?" Ms. Sanchez divides her class into two groups, teaches one using the new approach and one using the old, then measures carefully the reading fluency of students in both groups. If the students in the class have been randomly assigned to the two approaches, the design is referred to as a true experiment because there is no reason to believe that the two groups differ on the reading fluency variable at the outset. Remember, they were assigned randomly; that is, without regard to their reading fluency. Therefore, if they differ after implementation of the two approaches, say Method A produces better performance in reading than Method B, the assumption is that the approaches were differentially effective.

Optimally, other teachers could replicate this study many times to verify the initial results. Typically, this is too costly, so scientists use statistics to determine whether or not the difference between the two groups is large enough to be "nonchance." Most often, the average scores of the two groups are compared to make this decision. The logic of this type of experimental design is strong, and results have strong cause and effect implications. So, when results from this type of study are available, teachers can have confidence in the findings and should look for results of true experimental studies in the literature.

What Is a "Quasi-Experimental" Design?

Realistically, in many (if not most) cases, teachers do not have the latitude to randomly assign students to two or more instructional approaches. Random assignment of students is not feasible for a variety of reasons, so less powerful designs are often used (for example, quasi-experimental or correlational). These less powerful designs sometimes are used because the use of the true experimental study in education is controversial. Some argue that it is very difficult to randomly assign students to different teaching approaches as a scientist would assign laboratory rats. And some argue that it is unethical to assign humans to different approaches because one might be superior to the other. See Fletcher and Francis (2004) and Shanahan (2004) for a discussion of the use of experiments in education. In our experience, teachers, schools, and school districts are much more likely to engage in quasi-experimental and correlational research than in true experiments with random assignment, particularly of children and adolescents, to groups.

As you know by now, the true experimental design is considered the strongest type of scientific study because of its relatively greater power to determine cause and effect relationships between variables. The quasi-experimental design is also powerful. Like the true experimental design, it relies on evaluating the result of varying some intervention or treatment, in the simple case, between two groups. However, unlike the true experimental design, the quasi-experimental design uses intact groups (rather than randomly assigned students) as a beginning point; consequently, the design does not assure equality of the groups at the outset.

To illustrate use of a quasi-experimental design, we can revisit the question Ms. Sanchez posed earlier about the efficacy of two reading approaches. If a quasi-experimental design is used, rather than a true experimental study, she might use the new reading approach in her class and ask Mr. Robinson, also an adult education teacher, to continue to use the old approach. After some period of instruction, held the same for both classes, a test of reading fluency is given and the results compared. Suppose the adult students in Ms. Sanchez's class score well above those in Mr. Robinson's class on reading fluency, usually called the **dependent variable** by the way, because it is subject to change when the other variable is manipulated. In this case, Ms. Sanchez may want to attribute the difference to the new approach. But she will have to rule out other causes, so-called alternative explanations. In this case, one difference between the two groups is the instructional approach, which we can call the **independent variable** because we are manipulating it to see if the manipulation causes a difference. But, because the groups were not assigned randomly at the beginning, it may be that one group was more capable than the other at the beginning. Also, in this case, the two groups were exposed to two different teachers, and Ms. Sanchez might be a more motivating teacher than Mr. Robinson. So, these alternative hypotheses must be examined and if possible, eliminated.

Take another example. Let's assume Ms. Crockett, our first-grade teacher, is interested in determining whether vocabulary instruction can lead to increased reading comprehension. In this case, she must vary the amount and type of vocabulary instruction across at least two groups. After two months, if the group with the most intensive vocabulary instruction also shows the highest score on comprehension, Ms. Crockett is inclined to attribute that gain to the type and increase in vocabulary instruction. But, the higher mean score of the group with the more intensive vocabulary instruction may have been the result of higher scores at the outset, or perhaps the students in this group were more motivated, had parents who read to them more, and so on. As is obvious, there are many possible reasons for the difference in mean scores that are unrelated to vocabulary instruction, and these alternative explanations must be eliminated before any cause and effect explanations can be made. There are a number of variations in the way quasi-experimental studies are structured to help eliminate these alternative hypotheses, but these more complicated designs are beyond the scope of our discussion (see Cook and Campbell, 1979, for a classic discussion of how quasi-experimental research designs can be rigorously designed and implemented).

What Is a Correlational Design?
A less powerful but perhaps more common type of design is typically referred to as correlational and allows conclusions regarding the strength of the relationship between two or more variables, but it does not allow cause and effect statements. This type of study is less powerful because it does not require the teacher to manipulate any variable, but simply to assess variables closely in time. The same variables already mentioned can be used again to illustrate this type of design. For example, Ms. Crockett may believe that there is a relationship between vocabulary instruction and comprehension, but she may have neither evidence nor a directional hypothesis. That is, she may not have a hunch about which one "causes" the other. So, she could assess the two variables and apply a particular statistical technique, typically yielding a value called a **correlation coefficient.** This statistical index, which ranges from −1.0 to 1.0, tells Ms. Crockett the magnitude or strength of the relationship, but not that one variable produces or causes an increase in the other.

TABLE 1.5 Magnitude of Correlation Coefficients

Range	Magnitude
.70 to 1.0	Very Large
.50 to .69	Large
.30 to .49	Moderate
.10 to .29	Small
.0 to .09	No relationship

Note: These descriptions are applicable whether the correlation coefficient is negative or positive. The magnitude is not determined by the sign.

What is a correlation coefficient? A correlation coefficient is a numerical representation of the relationship between two variables, such as vocabulary and comprehension. A positive correlation means that as the score on one variable goes up, so does the other. A negative correlation means that as one scores goes up, the other goes down. The closer the correlation is to 1.0, the stronger the positive relationship. The closer the correlation is to −1.0, the stronger the negative correlation. We know that vocabulary goes up with increased reading; this is an example of a positive relationship and if we assessed these variables and calculated a correlation coefficient it would be positive and robust—approaching 1.0. Does reading cause an increase in vocabulary development or do students who build their vocabularies choose to read more? The coefficient does not tell us which variable causes the other or whether a third variable may have caused both to increase. For example, students who are highly motivated to achieve may read more and engage in other vocabulary-building activities (such as word games). Correlations close to 0 mean that the two variables are not related. An example of this type of relationship is the number of hairs on the head of a student and the level of comprehension.

General accepted guidelines for interpreting correlations are presented in Table 1.5. Note that the magnitude or strength of the relationship is the same, whether the correlation coefficient is positive or negative. Remember, however, the direction or nature of the relationship differs; when a positive correlation occurs both variables move in the same direction. When a negative correlation occurs, one variable increases but the second decreases. We discuss correlations again in subsequent chapters when we consider the **reliability** or consistency of various types of reading assessments.

What Is a Single-Subject Design?

Another type of study that educators value is referred to as single-subject design studies. These studies usually focus on only one student, but they can be powerful in helping to understand the nature of that student's performance and under what conditions the performance may vary. That is, if the teacher is willing to vary instruction in systematic ways it is possible to determine what strategies or factors can lead to positive changes in student performance.

To ensure that the single-subject design lends itself to making cause and effect statements about the performance of one student, a teacher must be willing to systematically vary the approach in question (for example, assess the student's performance both when using the approach and when not using it). Typically, this means evaluating how change occurs (or fails to) when instruction is varied for some period of time, often for six to eight weeks. This technique requires the teacher to be very careful to define the two (or more) different types of strategies (such as fluency building by reading aloud with a partner versus silent reading simultaneously with a tape), or perhaps levels of a single strategy (such as varying time spent with a tutor), and the measure assumed to change (such as reading rate, which may be determined by words read accurately per minute). But, results from single-subject studies cannot be used to generalize about the effectiveness of a particular approach for other students. Because only one student is the focus of the experiment, the teacher does not know how the interventions would affect others. Single-subject studies are particularly common in the field of special education.

Quantitative versus Qualitative Research

The research designs described thus far can be considered quantitative in nature because they rely on statistics to determine significance of relationships under study. Only studies with quantitative designs (specifically experimental and quasi-experimental) were included in the review by the NRP. But other types of study also have value. As in many other areas of education, educators do not agree about the merits of quantitative versus qualitative research. The topic is particularly controversial in light of recent emphasis at the federal level on quantitative, experimental studies. Nonetheless, many argue that both types of studies have merit and, in fact, that they are designed to answer different questions. For example, Shanahan (2004) asserts that qualitative studies can provide valuable information about how or why a particular teaching approach might work, but they are less valuable in demonstrating cause and effect and determining whether the approach actually made a difference. Teachers and other educators benefit from reading qualitative research; they can gain deep and rich perspective into the experiences of other teachers and of students. Many peer-reviewed journals include a mix of quantitative and qualitative studies, while some feature generally only one type.

What Is a Qualitative Case Study?

The most common type of qualitative research is the case study. In case study research, the emphasis is placed on capturing the experiences of the participants from their point of view; that is, to give a voice to the participants. Case study research is primarily descriptive and focuses on only one student, a small group of students, or a particular classroom or school. According to Gall, Gall, and Borg (1999, 289), "researchers conduct case studies in order to describe, explain, or evaluate particular social phenomena." Data gathering for this type of study often requires researchers to interview participants to obtain their perspectives about some event or process. For example, case study research might be used to probe the attitudes and experiences of a school staff as they transition to using a new instructional approach, such as from using basal readers to a leveled reading approach. Frequently in case study research, the researcher interviews multiple participants and extracts themes and patterns from the interviews. Open-ended interviews, observation, analyses of documents, and questionnaires are popular data-gathering techniques in qualitative research.

What Is Action Research?

We conclude this discussion of **scientifically-based research** with a brief consideration of **action research,** research conducted by educators specifically to inform their practice. Increasingly, teacher education programs are requiring preservice and in-service educators to conduct action research.

> Action research (AR) is a way for classroom practitioners to study their own practices through the identification of problems or concerns, implementation of strategies to address these problems, and, ultimately, analysis and dissemination of their results. Methods can either be quantitative or qualitative, descriptive or experimental. With increasing attention to preparing teachers to be reflective practitioners, action research has become a prominent topic in the literature concerning instructional practices, particularly in the K–12 classroom arena (University of Tennessee 2006, 16).

> According to Abrams and Mohn (2007, 33), action research is a vehicle for teachers or groups of teachers to "systematically investigate issues or topics to inform practice or decision-making within a particular setting such as a classroom or school." At our university, teacher interns in all areas of teacher education complete an action research project, typically collaborating with their mentor teachers to investigate challenging issues such as weak achievement, poor motivation, and behavior problems. Some sample projects from recent years include: (a) teaching middle school students how to self-select books at an appropriate reading and interest level and documenting changes in reading habits and (b) implementing a timeline strategy to improve reading and writing skills (based on Wooten 2000).

HOW DOES SCIENTIFICALLY-BASED RESEARCH HELP TEACHERS IN THE CLASSROOM?

> Keep in mind that the primary job of most teachers is not to conduct research. Rather, it is to teach students to read, write, solve math problems, master content, and develop problem-solving and social skills that prepare them for life outside the school environment. Nonetheless, teachers should possess the skills to read the relevant research in the professional literature and to use basic research strategies to answer questions in their classrooms. As is apparent, several research strategies are available and each has unique strengths and weaknesses. No one research method can be used to answer all the questions raised by educators. The method chosen depends on the question under scrutiny, and one method is not necessarily better than another. Which one is "best" depends on the purpose of the research, the latitude of the researcher to control factors (such as setting) to assign

students/participants to a variety of instructional strategies, resources available to implement strategies according to best practices, and so on.

Educators can benefit from knowing about scientifically-based instruction and assessment practices. Specifically, teachers, support staff (such as school psychologists and reading specialists), and administrators should be aware of the strategies and approaches that are supported by research and should use materials and techniques consistent with these strategies. Understanding scientific research can empower educators to make informed decisions about which strategies and procedures to use. Currently, numerous instructional and assessment materials claim to be scientifically based but in fact, the efficacy of most commercial instructional programs has not been demonstrated through research (Allington and Cunningham 2002). Educators can obtain knowledge of effective practices by participating in professional organizations, attending conferences and workshops, reading professional journals such as those published by IRA, by participating in book clubs with other educators, and through professional development activities. For example, in one of our university's partnership schools, teachers recently participated in a book study of Lucy Calkins' *The Art of Teaching Reading* (2001). These teachers met twice a month for four months to talk about their experiences as they read and implemented strategies from the book. In our experience, solutions for many of the classroom problems experienced by our teacher education students can be found in the professional education literature. But teachers need support via well-planned professional development opportunities to read, practice, observe what happens when they apply new practices, assess, reflect, and so on.

When implementing new instructional and assessment practices, teachers can benefit by applying **reason-based practices** (Stanovich and Stanovich 2003), which is the application of scientific methodology directly by using systematic hypothesis testing to solve problems that arise in their classrooms. All teachers are problem solvers, and as such, can be scientifically-based problem solvers when they apply the scientific method to solving problems in their classrooms. In spite of the converging agreement in the field that teachers should rely on scientifically-based research, controversies still plague the reading literature. Some are addressed in the following section.

WHAT ARE THE READING WARS AND HOW ARE THEY RELATED TO ASSESSMENT?

All educators seem to agree that reading is a critical skill and that the purpose of reading is comprehension, which relies on lower-level decoding and word recognition skills. Further, there seems to be consensus that some students need more of certain types of reading instruction than others (e.g., some need more work on word skills, some on fluency, and some on comprehension). Beyond these basic points, professional agreement is less certain.

In the field of reading, there is an ongoing debate among educators about how to teach reading, the so-called **reading wars.** Jeanne Chall's *Learning to Read: The Great Debate,* published in 1967 and reissued in

1983, provides a synthesis of numerous and extensive studies, interviews, and analyses of mainstream and alternative reading programs and approaches. According to Adams (1990, 39), "the observations and data she amassed seemed inescapably to suggest that—as a complement to connected and meaningful reading—systematic phonic instruction is a valuable component of beginning reading instruction. Its positive effects appeared both strong and extensive." But Chall did not discount the importance of early authentic reading experiences. She concluded that "an early opportunity to do meaningful connected reading in addition to learning how to decode is needed to integrate both abilities" (1983, 11). Seemingly then, Chall's conclusions called for both **meaning-based** and systematic **code-based** instruction for beginning readers but the debate continues.

At the core of the debate is a philosophical difference with practical implications for both instruction and assessment. Some (for example, Goodman 1986) assert that learning to read happens naturally as children are exposed to language and reading. This view, called **whole language,** is a meaning-based philosophy that regards reading as an integral part of overall language development and focuses on meaning making and experience to teach reading. It follows from this philosophy that assessments would focus heavily on comprehension and vocabulary. Others (including Shaywitz 2003 and Sweet 2004) assert that reading does not happen naturally and that phonological processing skills are very important at the beginning stages of reading. According to this philosophy, reading comprehension cannot occur without well-developed phonics, word recognition, and fluency skills. Those ascribing to this philosophy emphasize teaching phonics and word skills to beginning readers. This approach sometimes is characterized as primarily code-based. From this perspective, assessments focus on skills such as sounding out words, recognizing words, and speed and accuracy.

Unfortunately, the debate between those in the whole language camp and those in the code-based camp has been rancorous at times, leaving teachers, administrators, and those who set reading policy at state and federal levels unsure about which approaches to instruction and assessment are best. Although the debate continues, there is some consensus that a **balanced literacy** approach—with many opportunities for students to read at their instructional level, practice in phonics and other word work, write, and use explicit fluency and comprehension strategies—is more effective than approaches that focus heavily on either phonics or whole language (NICHD 2000). It is our view that both philosophies have validity; both, for example, agree that the goal of reading is comprehension, but they differ on how to get there. Unfortunately, the debate becomes increasingly intense when focused on struggling readers. These readers need to read as much as possible so as not to become hopelessly behind their peers (Allington 2001). So, how and where should we focus instruction, particularly for those struggling readers?

Assessment tools can help determine the strengths and weaknesses of struggling readers so that teachers can focus on teaching needed skills—not those already mastered and not those that are too advanced. In some situations and for some students, word instruction may be emphasized over comprehension and meaning-making skills; for others, just the reverse may be true. For assessment purposes, the question is not which camp is correct, but which skill areas from which camp are appropriate to target. To help you think about the specific assessment strategy that might be most relevant for particular situations, we discuss the four major types of assessment next.

■ WHAT ARE THE MAJOR TYPES OF ASSESSMENT?

Four broad types of assessment are presented in this book: (1) informal; (2) **criterion-referenced** and curriculum-based; (3) formal, individual; and (4) formal, group. Information from all of these types of assessment may influence instruction. Information obtained from formal **standardized assessment** has the potential to influence instruction profoundly, though that effect is not likely to be immediate, nor specific. Data from informal assessment strategies are less likely to result in drastic shifts in a student's academic life, but they have the potential to effect instruction in a very effective and immediate manner.

Teachers are probably most comfortable using informal classroom assessments. These assessments provide information that tells a teacher what to teach next. The important point to remember is that teachers can use direct informal assessment to specifically and quickly adjust instruction. Examples of informal classroom assessments include **running records** (Clay 2000) in which a teacher listens to a student read orally and codes rate and types of errors. Similarly, informal reading inventories (IRIs) include assessment of reading rate, types of errors or miscues, as well as measures of word recognition. However, IRIs are typically not tied directly to a given classroom reading program.

Although teachers can create their own assessments to test mastery of knowledge and skills presented, more frequently they select and adapt published materials that accompany instructional materials. Increasingly, published criterion-referenced and curriculum-based measurement tools are available and frequently are used in special education. Criterion-referenced assessment tells how well a student has mastered a specific skill—for example, adding inflectional endings such as /ing/ to words. Initially designed to measure student progress in a given curriculum, current versions of curriculum-based measurement often are not based in the actual curriculum (Fuchs and Deno 1994). However, they are still considered more authentic, or similar to the actual curriculum, than standardized norm-referenced assessments. Informal classroom measures are presented in Chapter 3; criterion-referenced and curriculum-based measures are presented in Chapter 4.

Educators may use data gained from standardized assessment instruments to determine (a) which students should be promoted to the next grade; (b) which groups of students make adequate progress; (c) which schools and even individual teachers are effective; and (d) which students meet eligibility criteria for special programs, particularly special education. Some standardized tests are designed to be administered to groups of students (such as a whole third-grade class), while others are designed to be administered individually, in particular those used to determine eligibility for special education services. Both group and individual standardized assessments have common features. They are administered in a standard way, with scripted directions, time limits, and response formats, often on a bubble-in form that can be scanned and scored electronically. Both allow comparison of the performance of an individual or group of students to a norm group, a peer group on which the test was initially standardized. Individual standardized achievement tests are addressed in Chapter 5 and group measures in Chapter 6. Finally, Chapter 7 presents information on how to relate the various types of assessment information presented in previous chapters and to use that information to plan instruction. But before we address the various types of assessment, we consider the nature of reading in some detail in Chapter 2.

Summary

Chapter 1 provides an introduction to reading assessment and a context for it. You met four teachers—Ms. Crockett, a first-grade teacher; Mr. Haywood, a special education teacher; Dr. Charles, a high school biology teacher; and Ms. Sanchez, an adult basic educator. You will meet them again and some of their students in subsequent chapters. As is apparent, reading is a cognitively complex phenomenon that occurs in a social and cultural context. Because of the complexity, experts do not agree about how to teach reading nor about how best to assess reading. But, after reading this chapter, you should have a better understanding of the key elements, or pillars, of reading and the general types of assessment techniques available.

After introducing our teachers, we addressed what educators should know about assessment of reading by presenting standards, developed by the International Reading Association, for paraprofessionals, teachers, and reading specialists. Next, we described four purposes of assessment, including instructional planning, progress monitoring, accountability, and determining eligibility for special education. A key part of the chapter provided information about the five areas of reading identified by the National Reading Panel: phonemic awareness, phonics, fluency, vocabulary, and comprehension. In addition, we discussed the importance of orthography and automatic word recognition. We also discussed the multitiered model of reading instruction that requires teachers to use scientifically-based reading instructional procedures. The multitiered approach also requires frequent assessment or progress monitoring to determine whether students are benefiting from instruction as would be expected compared to typical progress. We described scientifically-based research and explained the most prominent types of quantitative designs, including experimental, quasi-experimental, correlational, and single-subject designs, and the qualitative case study design that may include open-ended interview and observation data-gathering techniques.

We close Chapter 1 with a discussion of the so-called reading wars; philosophical preferences for meaning-based versus code-based approaches have significant influence on policies and choices about instruction and assessment of reading. We hope the content of Chapter 1 piqued your interest in the assessment of reading and provided you with some fundamental knowledge of how assessment can contribute to the information teachers use to increase the reading skills of their students.

mylabschool
Where the classroom comes to life!

MyLabSchool is a collection of online tools for your success in this course, your licensure exams, and your teaching career. Visit www.mylabschool.com to access the following:

- *Online Study Guide*
- *Video cases from real classrooms*
- *Help with your research papers using Research Navigator*
- *Career Center with resources for:*
    Praxis exams and licensure preparation
    Professional portfolio development
    Job search and interview techniques
    Lesson planning

CHAPTER 2

Nature of Reading

Reading is very complicated. One strategy for understanding reading is to use a model to depict the relationships among components or processes. Also, models provide perspective and context to enhance understanding. In this chapter, we present several models. Before we share the details of these models, we describe some historical and current influences in the field of reading that shaped development of these models.

■ HISTORICAL CONTEXT FOR MODELS OF READING

Early models of reading were rooted in medicine. In fact, early accounts of reading problems were described by physicians. In 1676, a German physician named Dr. Johann Schmidt characterized one of his patients, Nicholas

Cambier, as being unable to read after suffering a stroke. This condition came to be known as **acquired alexia**. In 1896, Dr. W. Pringle Morgan described one of his patients, Percy F., as, ". . . a bright and intelligent boy, quick at games and in no way inferior to others his age. His great difficulty has been—and is now— his inability to read" (cited in Shaywitz 2003, 13). According to Dr. Morgan, Percy could not read in spite of having a good education, good visual acuity, and being good at arithmetic. Dr. Morgan described Percy as "word blind," a term used earlier by a German neurologist, Dr. Kussmaul. In 1887, another physician, Dr. Rudolf Berlin, described six cases of "word blindness" found in adults and traced the cause to brain lesions, noting that the symptoms might be extreme if the lesion site was large, but might be less severe if the damage was more localized, although there might still be ". . . very great difficulty in interpreting written or printed symbols . . . ," a condition he termed *dyslexia* (cited in Shaywitz 2003, 15).

Although educators are indebted to these early medical pioneers, the work of these men led to the belief that all problems could be fixed by addressing "within-the-individual" organic **etiology**(ies) or cause(s) for reading problems. Consequently, educators began to put too little emphasis on external factors. Only much later did the focus change to an emphasis on external causes (e.g., lack of exposure to print materials in the home, mismatch between a given instructional strategy and a particular student). In fact, some behaviorally-oriented educators in the middle part of the twentieth century may have gone too far. They emphasized environmental factors almost to the exclusion of individual differences within readers (Kazdin 1981; Skinner 1953).

As implied earlier, the medical model is a deficit model, and as such, it focuses attention almost exclusively on limitations within the individual. Consequently, the medical model does not provide much help to teachers as they think about what should be done in the classroom. There are not many medical interventions that can aid struggling readers, at least not until medical science advances significantly. There are no drugs available to "cure" limited sight word recognition for example. Consequently, the medical model of reading has fallen out of favor and some consider it irrelevant for educators (see McKenna and Stahl 2003 for a discussion of this issue).

But should we abandon the medical model altogether? Is it completely without value for educators? We don't think so. After all, it is conceivable that medical problems like poor eyesight or attention problems could be addressed with medical aids such as prescription glasses and medication. So when a student has difficulties in reading, the teacher should rule out medical causes early on, such as vision or hearing problems, fatigue caused by illness, and so on. For example, students with a history of chronic ear infections and students with hearing impairment are at risk for difficulty acquiring phonemic awareness. If medical problems are suspected, a referral to a physician is recommended. We can share a personal example. One of the authors of this text needed glasses early on in life, but the need was not recognized and remedied until the fifth grade, after significant learning opportunities were missed.

A criticism of the medical model is that it presumes there is a problem and, consequently, focuses on deficits. However, some models, derived from the medical tradition, focus on within-the-child characteristics, but unlike the medical model, do not presume a deficit. We address these later in this chapter, but for now, we describe some salient developmental models of reading; these focus almost exclusively on the acquisition of reading skills in a developmental progression.

DEVELOPMENTAL MODELS OF READING

The developmental models were among the first to recognize systematically the increasingly complex nature of the reading process. As children mature they develop more sophisticated central nervous system characteristics, which allow them to master the subtle and complex aspects of decoding and comprehension.

Chall's Stage Model of Reading

Some of the models that focus on the developmental nature of reading skills acquisition were developed by Chall (1996), Ehri (1998), Spear-Swerling and Sternberg (1996), and Frith (1985 as cited in Sawyer, Kim, and Lipa-Wade 2000). In general, these models show reading development beginning with early skills such as awareness of print, and they progress toward reading for higher-order comprehension. The first developmental model that we describe in some detail was developed by Jeanne Chall, a pioneer in the field of reading. McKenna and Stahl (2003) present an overview of Chall's model, which is reproduced in Figure 2.1.

Chall's model (1996) contains six stages, focusing initially on emerging literacy characterized by a rudimentary awareness that print can communicate and moving on to more advanced literacy abilities required to extract sophisticated meaning from academic material. The model provides information about the typical progression of reading and identifies reading milestones. For example, preschoolers at the stage of **emergent literacy** are learning to recognize and say the alphabet, learning how to rhyme and manipulate sounds in words, and learning the purpose and function of writing. At the stage of emergent literacy, young readers look at books and pretend to read them, and they sing the alphabet, repeat nursery rhymes, and engage in alphabet and rhyming activities. They read **predictable text** (stories in which certain phrases are repeated) in picture books, and they learn with manipulative letters. Chall's model outlines what the reader is learning, typical learning activities, and typical instructional materials used for readers from what she terms Stage 0 (emergent literacy) to Stage 5 (late college and graduate school). Although this model helps educators because it defines expectations about typical performance, it is mostly descriptive and may not be helpful in the analysis of reading difficulties (McKenna and Stahl 2003).

Spear-Swerling and Sternberg Model of Reading

Another stage model of reading that may be helpful in understanding reading and especially in troubleshooting reading problems was described by Spear-Swerling and Sternberg (1996). Their model, influenced by the work of Ehri (1998), is reproduced in Figure 2.2.

According to this model, readers progress through several qualitatively different stages/phases from the visual cue recognition stage to the strategic

FIGURE 2.1 Jeanne Chall's Model of Reading Development

Stage	Name	What Child Is Learning	Typical Activities	Materials
Stage 0 Birth to grade 1	Emergent literacy	Functions of written language, alphabet, phonemic awareness	Story reading, "pseudoreading," alphabet activities, rhyming, nursery rhymes, invented spelling	Books (including predictable stories), letters, writing materials, *Sesame Street*
Stage 1 Beginning grade 1	Decoding	Letter-sound correspondences	Teacher-directed reading instruction, phonics instruction	Preprimers and primers, phonics materials, writing materials, trade books
Stage 2 End of grade 1 to end of grade 3	Confirmation and fluency	Automatic word recognition, use of context	Reading narratives, generally about known topics	Basal readers, trade books, workbooks
Stage 3 Grades 4 to 5	Learning the new (single viewpoint)	How to learn from text, vocabulary knowledge, strategies	Reading and studying content area materials, use of encyclopedias, strategy instruction	Basal readers, novels, encyclopedias, textbooks in content areas
Stage 4 High school and early college	Multiple viewpoints	Reconciling different views	Critical reading, discourse synthesis, report writing	Texts containing multiple views, encyclopedias and other reference materials, magazines and journals, nonfiction books, etc.
Stage 5 Late college and graduate school	A world view	Developing a well-rounded view of the world	Learning what not to read as well as what to read	Professional materials

Taken from McKenna, M.C. & Stahl, S.A. (2003). *Assessment for reading instruction.* New York, NY: Guilford Press, p. 4.

reading stage. Readers in the first stage have very limited comprehension and word recognition skills while readers at the strategic stage can employ higher-order comprehension and have advanced phonological and orthographic skills. By examining Figure 2.2, it is easy to see that **comprehension**, the process of constructing meaning from what is read, improves as a function of developing orthographic and phonological skills.

Readers in early stages of reading proficiency apply visualization skills to identifying words, using distinctive visual cues such as two "eyes" (the letter "o" occurring together in the middle of the word) as in the word *look*. As beginning readers become exposed to an increasingly large number of words, the purely visual system becomes inefficient. When readers develop phonemic awareness and the alphabetic principle, including the idea that individual sounds are represented by letters, they begin to use individual letters. Early in this stage, they often rely only on the beginning or ending letters of words in decoding. They develop an appreciation of the sound-symbol relationship in the alphabet—an awareness that letters elicit certain sounds—and that a sequence of these sounds forms words.

Next, developing readers begin to focus their attention on more of the elements of words, for example **medial letters** and **blends**, as they try to

FIGURE 2.2 Stage Model of Reading by Spear-Swerling and Sternberg

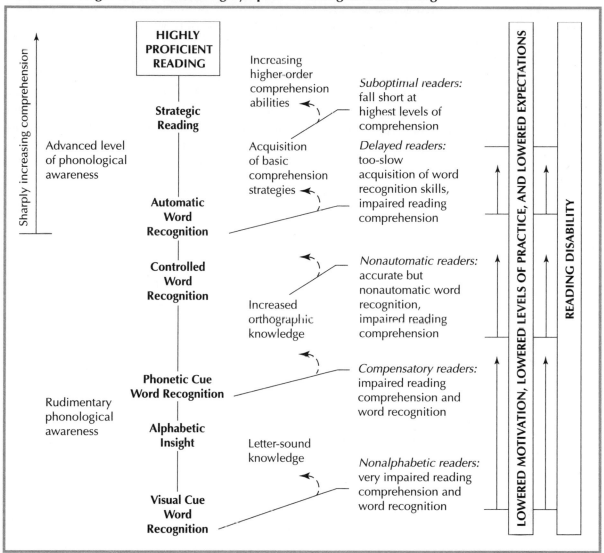

Source: Spear-Swerling, L. & Sternberg, R.J. (1996). *Off track: When poor readers become "learning disabled."* Copyright 1996. Boulder, CO: Westview Press.

analyze the sounds characterizing unfamiliar words. As readers move from alphabetic insight to phonetic cue recognition, they become proficient at **full alphabetic coding**, characterized by examination of each letter within a word. Ultimately, phonological awareness develops, as readers attend to and appreciate syllables, onsets and rimes, initial and final phonemes, and finally, vowels. Readers at this stage (controlled word recognition) are accurate at decoding, but the skill is not yet automatic. With instruction and practice, readers become efficient and are able to benefit from **consolidated word recognition**, such that chunks or groups of letters are recognized automatically; that is, they experience automatic word recognition. As readers are able to recognize words automatically, using orthographic and phonological skills, there is the opportunity for increased comprehension; that is, they can become strategic readers. This model, as with Chall's, helps teachers understand the developmental nature of reading and is somewhat more useful when considering when and why readers develop problems as they progress through the early grades. Another prominent developmental model, developed by Frith (1985), contains significant developmental detail.

Frith's Developmental Phases Model

As you have learned already, a model of reading can be used for a variety of purposes. Models can show important elements of reading, the developmental progression of reading skills, and the relationship between reading skills and cognitive abilities, and the use of the elements of the model may lead to prediction of later reading success. Frith's model is one of several that has been used to satisfy multiple purposes. In particular, it can be used to show developmental acquisition of reading skills, and as discussed next, it has been used to make predictions of future reading success.

Building on Frith's phase model of reading acquisition (1985) and Ehri's (1994) elaboration of that model, Sawyer, Kim, and Lipa-Wade (2000) and others from the Tennessee Center for the Study and Treatment of Dyslexia developed a checklist of competencies that readers exhibit within each phase. This checklist shows the hierarchy of reading skills (such as identifying initial sounds in spoken words, identifying final sounds in spoken words, and producing rhyming words) and is organized within developmentally appropriate phases, including **logographic**, early alphabetic, late alphabetic, early orthographic, and late orthographic. In typical development, children acquire skills within a particular phase, then they consolidate the skills to form the basis for news skills within the next phase. This checklist was used successfully by Sawyer and colleagues to identify a set of variables that predict later reading achievement. Seven of the ten predictor variables significantly helped explain or account for later reading achievement, with the letter-sound association variable being the most consistent and powerful predictor. Apparently, Frith's model provides a solid foundation for building an assessment tool capable of effectively identifying kindergarten students who are at risk of failure in reading and spelling. Excerpts from the Developmental Phases checklist are presented in Figure 2.3.

Adams' Cognitive Model of Reading

Cognitive models, so called because they trace the origins of reading to underlying mental processes, describe linkages between reading skills and intellectual or cognitive activity. One of the most influential of the cognitive models was developed by Marilyn Adams (1990). As shown in Figure 2.4, the model includes four major components, two of which are primarily responsible for receiving information from the environment, either from an **orthographic processor** (print) or a **phonological processor** (speech/sounds). A third processor, a **meaning processor**, is responsible for determining what the information means and a fourth, **context processor**, for determining how the information relates to context. Stated another way, the context processor helps create meaningfulness based on the specific situation in which the word is used. In this manner, the reader builds a vocabulary by determining the meaning of a new word from context cues (contextually-evoked meaning) and relates that meaning to the structural image of the word and to the sounds as well. Of course, this happens only when the reader engages in meaningful reading *and* attends to the spelling (and shape) of the newly encountered word.

FIGURE 2.3 Selected Skills from the Development Phases Checklist Based on Frith's Developmental Phases Model by Sawyer, Kim, and Lipa-Wade (2000)

Logographic Phase: Can the student...
segment spoken words, sentences?
write the alphabet letter?
recognize familiar words?
recognize words that rhyme?

Early Alphabetic Phase: Can the student...
identify sounds in words?
produce words that rhyme?
produce the sound of consonants?
segment two or three phonemic words?

Late Alphabetic Phase: Can the student...
segment four or more phonemic words?
read and spell (pre)consonant blends and nasals?
read and spell short vowels in one-syllable words?

Early Orthographic Phase: Can the student...
differentiate within a spoken word short from long vowels sounds?
evidence improvement in word recognition automaticity?
correctly spell most homophones?
read simple words with at least two syllables?
read and spell various vowel patterns?

Late Orthographic Phase: Can the student...
evidence improvement in reading content with automaticity?
demonstrate understanding of syllable patterns?
spell plurals and inflectional endings correctly?
demonstrate learning with additional types of syllables (e.g., stressed and unstressed)?
demonstrate improvement in reading/writing fluency?

Source: Adapted excerpts from Sawyer, D.J., Kim, J.K., & Lipa-Wade, S. (2000). Frith's Developmental Phases Model Checklist, pp. 87–103. *Prediction and prevention of reading failure.* Baltimore, MD: York Press.

Reciprocal nature of the processors. It is apparent from looking at the arrows in Figure 2.4 that reciprocal communication exists between and among the various processors. The activity of each processor influences and is

FIGURE 2.4 Adams' Cognitive Model of Reading *Source:* Adams, M.J. (1990). *Beginning to read: Thinking about learning and print.* Figure 8.1, p. 158. Copyright 1990. MIT Press. Reprinted by permission.

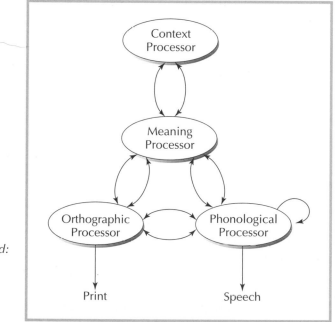

influenced by the others. Although readers acquire new vocabulary words by attending to how the words look (orthography), it is also the case that readers acquire new orthographic patterns by attending to meaning. Specifically, when the orthographic processor sends a meaningful spelling pattern to the meaning processor, the meaning processor returns excitatory feedback, thereby reinforcing and consolidating the activated spelling pattern. More simply, the systems work together and reinforce one another. So the productivity of the system can be understood by attending to elements working in isolation, but the system can best be understood as it engages a number of processors both simultaneously and sequentially during the act of reading. And the most efficient readers are those who read quickly and with accuracy. That is one reason why slow, nonfluent readers tend to have weaker comprehension than those who read more fluently. The associative linkages within and among processors work inefficiently when words are processed too slowly or with poor understanding. When an individual reads slowly, the connections among the processors are not activated efficiently or thoroughly. This results in limited meaning-making, or comprehension. When readers must use a significant portion of their working memory to process the sounds or shapes of relatively unfamiliar words in a sentence, they have little memory left to support comprehension.

Adams' model describes hypothetical constructs (processors) that ultimately have some substance and reality within the reader's central nervous system. The four components she describes operate independently and cooperatively to influence the way the language system's **graphemes,** which are letters or combinations of letters, symbolize its phonemes (via the connections between the orthographic and phonological processors), and ultimately to make meaning out of print (via the connections between the meaning processor and the context processor). Print comes into the system through the orthographic processor and is relayed to the phonological processor for a phonological translation so that a reader can look at a word and almost instantaneously process its sounds.

Of interest, skilled readers can neither remember nor comprehend a complex sentence unless they are allowed to **subvocalize**—to read the sentence quietly to themselves (Baddeley, 1979). Even though subvocalization occurs, the process is fast. Even before a word has been read completely, its representation is relayed to the meaning processor. For skilled readers, the letters of familiar words are combined to form words by the orthographic processor almost instantaneously, and the meaning processor is stimulated by the orthographic processor to receive a whole word; then almost as fast, the meaning processor is able to communicate the meaning of the word. Almost simultaneously, the meaning processor receives stimulation from the phonological processor of the integrated phonological translation of the complete word. So the meaning processor gets information based on both how the word looks and sounds.

Meaning-making is less effective whenever the orthographic processor cannot handle a word effectively or must send the elements of the word slowly in phonological patterns or letters. In these cases, meaning-making depends on a host of variables, such as the familiarity of the word and the context cues provided. Of course, teachers can help readers be more efficient by teaching strategies to build the skills of each of the four processors. Also, good assessment can inform teachers about the particular limitations of each, such as poor phonological awareness or phonics skills, slow response to word shapes, limited oral vocabulary, or poor ability to extract meaning from context.

We find the Adams model appealing and believe that the developmental models also have good information to offer. Next, we consider the extent to which basic information processing theory and study of the cognitive correlates of reading can contribute to the understanding of reading.

■ INFORMATION PROCESSING MODEL OF READING

Information processing models often trace information coming in from the environment through the meaning-making system of the individual. This tradition has focused on identifying individual difference variables, specifically cognitive processing abilities or skills. Presumably, these processing strengths and weaknesses are related to and probably underpin academic progress, and knowledge of these strengths and weaknesses can be used to help tailor instructional interventions. For example, students with good visual-spatial and **fluid reasoning** abilities should profit optimally from graphic organizers, semantic maps, and so on. To show how cognitive and academic components might work together, experts have constructed graphic displays of information processing models. A generic model is displayed in Figure 2.5 and shows specifically how stimuli (sensory information) come in from the environment initially through receptors (such as the ears and eyes), how the information interacts with information in memory, and how new knowledge can be produced in working memory through the interaction of incoming information and information stored in memory. As a result of attention to and operation on the stimuli coming into the system, an output is produced (including thinking, speech, and movement). The quality of this output is influenced by the sophistication of the cognitive underpinnings, including

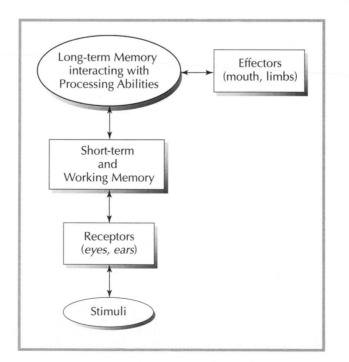

FIGURE 2.5 General Information Processing Model

processing speed, memory, and auditory processing, and the support offered by the environment (such as teachers, peers, and parents).

The heart of any information processing model is the interaction between stimuli coming in, new or novel information, and old information already in long-term memory. This interaction takes place in **working memory**. Basically, working memory contains the ideas that are in **awareness**. Gagne, Yekovich, and Yekovich (1993) define working memory as the crucible on which new knowledge is added to old knowledge. New knowledge develops in working memory when students relate and integrate new information to old to create unique content. Teachers understand the importance of helping students build on and relate new ideas and experiences to their prior knowledge. Some students learn much more efficiently than others. The most efficient learners tend to have the best internal environment, including strong cognitive abilities such as long-term memory, and external support system, including curriculum matched to ability and good teacher and parent support.

One of the most helpful information processing models for teachers of reading was developed by Gagne et al. (1993), which shows how the reading process begins by attending to relevant stimulation coming from the eyes (or through the fingers for blind students using Braille) and concludes with comprehension, which may lead to external responses such as speech or internal responses such as thinking. The activities that occur between the input (a printed page, for example) and output are enormously complex, beginning with the memory system that consists of three components: (1) short-term memory (rote recall without transformation of content); (2) working memory, the ability to hold several elements in mind and transform or use them; and (3) long-term memory, the ability to retrieve information stored from one's experience. Good readers develop and hold an enormous amount of information in long-term memory stores and can access that information efficiently.

In the Gagne et al. (1993) model, long-term memory consists of two fundamental memory stores: **declarative knowledge** and **procedural knowledge**. Declarative knowledge is knowing about something or knowing that something is the case; it is relevant for reading. Readers need to know how to break the code in the text, and they need to know background information related to particular text. Specifically, to make meaning of text, readers need to know *about* letters, phonemes, morphemes, words, word meanings, grammatical and semantic structure, content knowledge, typical text structure, and so on. In contrast to knowing about the elements of reading, which include letters, sounds, and the like, procedural knowledge is knowing *how* to do something; and, in the case of reading, knowing how to engage the processes necessary to extract meaning from printed text. This occurs when the reader actually makes meaning from the symbols.

How does the reading process contribute to creation of knowledge in long-term memory *and* rely on this stored information to develop even better reading skills? Guidance for this process occurs as stimuli from the environment interact with the memory systems, controlled by a metacognitive or executive function, presumably **mediated** or processed primarily in the frontal lobes of the brain (Das, Kirby, and Jarman 1979; Flavell 1985). This metacognitive function allows the student to set reading goals, plan and implement strategies for decoding and comprehending, and monitor the extent to which comprehension actually occurs.

According to the Gagne et al. model, the declarative knowledge base, which contains sounds, letters, words, and the like, is activated when the reader begins to decode, either by using a template, a whole word matching process, or a **recoding** phonological process. These decoded words or phrases stimulate a literal and/or **inferential comprehension** process. Full comprehension of a passage requires integration (putting logically related ideas together), **summarization** (attaching themes to more isolated ideas), and elaboration (extrapolating to form logically consistent but new ideas).

Obviously, comprehension requires complex processing of information; consequently, some experts refer to reading as a thinking process. All these processes are guided by the metacognitive or strategy-building component. This executive portion of the information processing model produces reading-related questions about goal setting (e.g., Is the purpose to read for pleasure, or to gain technical information?), strategy setting (e.g., Will the reader use the chapter title and headings to get an overall idea before reading?), goal checking (e.g., Will the reader generate questions to check understanding?), and finally, remediation (e.g., Will the reader ask for help or will he or she reread if necessary?). This information processing model, as do most, assumes an interaction of existing knowledge with new information coming through the senses and requires engagement of several internal cognitive processes. Many information processing models do not describe these internal processes with any degree of specificity, except for the memory components. Some of these processes, and the exciting opportunity medical research offers in identifying their central nervous system (CNS) sites, are discussed next.

Information processing models supported by brain research.   Recent advances in medical technology allow us to examine cognitive correlates of reading at a whole new level—within the CNS and the brain. New medical scanning techniques provide an actual window into the working brain of readers. Consequently, research findings continue to grow showing CNS differences between good and weak readers and between weak readers with different types of difficulties, such as problems with phonics versus problems with fluency. Also, apparently brain functioning and physiology actually are changed by certain types of instruction. As technology advances, a recycled medical or clinical model may offer sophisticated insight into the relationship between CNS functioning and reading (Papanicolaou, Pugh, Simos, and Mencl 2004; Shaywitz and Shaywitz 2004).

Cognitive correlates of reading.   As the brain research advances, so does the sophistication of our educational assessment techniques. As mentioned earlier, some researchers (including McGrew and Woodcock 2001) have shown how cognitive abilities influence the reading process. The cognitive processes most important for reading development appear to be:

- **Auditory processing**—includes phonemic awareness and impacts ability to master phonics

- **Processing speed**—ability to attend and quickly respond to simple task demands; may be assessed by rapidly naming letters, words, or objects, sometimes called **rapid automatic naming**
- **Short-term memory** and **long-term memory**, particularly **auditory memory**

Table 2.1, based on the cumulative research of Woodcock and colleagues (Mather and Jaffe 2002; McGrew and Woodcock 2001), presents some of the relationships between cognitive ability and reading performance, as well as the closely related academic area of writing. Note that in the table, **basic reading skills** refers to phonetic decoding and sight word recognition; written expression refers to writing composition skills, and **basic writing skills** refers to punctuation, grammar, editing, and proofreading skills.

TABLE 2.1   Cognitive Abilities and Related Reading/Writing Skills

Cognitive Ability	Associated Literacy Skill
Long-Term Memory/Retrieval	
Storage and retention of information	Basic reading skills
Ability to retrieve and use previously stored information	Reading comprehension
	Written expression
Auditory Processing	
Discrimination, analysis, and synthesis of auditory stimuli	Basic reading skills
Auditory attention, perception, and discrimination despite background noise	Written expression
Phonemic Awareness	
Manipulation, analysis, and synthesis of discrete sounds	Basic reading skills
	Spelling
	Written expression
	Basic writing skills
Visual Processing	
Perception, analysis, and synthesis of visual stimuli	Not strongly related to achievement
Storage and memory of visual stimuli	
Short-Term Memory (Auditory)	
Processing and holding auditory stimuli in awareness and manipulating/using it within a few seconds	Basic reading skills
	Reading comprehension
Processing Speed	
Rapid cognitive processing without higher-order thinking	Basic reading skills
Attentiveness and fluency in processing	Written expression
Verbal Reasoning	
Reasoning and comprehension using language	Basic reading skills
Verbal expression	Reading comprehension
Vocabulary	Written expression
General Information and Knowledge	
Acquired knowledge	Basic reading skills
Long-term memory	Reading comprehension
	Written expression
Fluid Reasoning	
Inductive and deductive reasoning	Reading comprehension
Problem-solving of novel tasks	Written expression

The cognitive abilities described in Table 2.1 tend to be related moderately to reading level. For example, the stronger a person scores on a test of auditory processing, the higher his or her reading scores are likely to be. In fact, correlation coefficients, numerical values expressing the strength of the relationship between variables, typically range from .30 to .60 between certain cognitive abilities and measures of reading (McGrew and Woodcock 2001). These magnitudes are considered to be in the fair to moderately strong range. (Use of correlation coefficients to express relationships was discussed in Chapter 1.) Do the coefficients mean that basic cognitive processing cause reading? We cannot draw that conclusion. But it is obvious that students cannot perform complex activities such as reading, without some processing activity within the brain; and the accumulating evidence is that some cognitive processing abilities, such as auditory processing and processing speed, are likely involved in learning to read and that some of the processes are more important to reading than are other processes (e.g., auditory processing is probably more important to reading than is quantitative processing).

In our experience, assessment of these underlying cognitive variables for readers who struggle excessively can provide some valuable information for explaining the source of the difficulty and for planning instruction. For one thing, this type of assessment tells us where a student's strengths lie; we can make educational suggestions to build upon these strengths. And, we need to address weaknesses with explicit instruction, starting with what students know. For example, for those few readers with very poor auditory processing skills, supplemental instruction in structured approaches that focus heavily on word decoding and sight word acquisition skills tends to be beneficial. Knowledge of cognitive strengths and weaknesses can provide insight for the bright struggling readers who have come to think of themselves as stupid. Taken together, the cognitive abilities described in Table 2.1 comprise a portion of what experts consider to be **intelligence**.

■ WHAT IS THE RELATIONSHIP BETWEEN READING AND IQ?

There is an ongoing controversy about the definition and nature of intelligence, about the cognitive elements that comprise it, and about whether or not **intelligence quotient (IQ)** tests can help predict and explain reading failure. Our view is that the research establishes a relationship between IQ and reading achievement, more or less, depending on the age of the child and how IQ is measured. We purposely titled this section "The Relationship between Reading and IQ" and not "The Relationship between Reading and Intelligence." Probably all would agree that intelligence and reading are related. But because test developers have not always done a good job of measuring intelligence, one *might* argue that reading and IQ are unrelated. It is not only intuitively appealing and consistent with the experience of most teachers to believe that **intellectually gifted** students master reading more easily than those with less intelligence, but there are hundreds of studies that show a significant relationship between student performance on measures of reading achievement and IQ, despite some claims to the contrary (Gersten and Dimino 2006). Experts in the field have described the specifics of the reading/IQ relationship for years (for example, see the manuals of recently developed intelligence tests for validity studies showing these relationships, including Wechsler 2003; Roid 2003; McGrew and Woodcock 2001). Not only is the relationship strong between verbal measures of intelligence, which is to be expected because most verbally-laden intelligence tests assess reading like skills such as vocabulary, but the relationship is also robust between nonverbal measures of intelligence and reading (Bracken and McCallum 1998; Brown 2003; Naglieri 2003). Obviously, the more a student reads, the larger and more enriched his or her vocabulary becomes (Stanovich 1986) and the higher the student's score should be on verbal IQ measures; but the strong relationship between nonverbal measures of IQ and achievement suggests that intelligence contributes significantly to reading and that the strength of the relationship cannot be explained totally by the reciprocal positive influence of reading and IQ gain.

The prediction between IQ and reading is low at the primer and first-grade level, in part because of difficulty associated with assessing reading for that age student. In fact, at this age, reading usually is defined as letter and word identification primarily. In addition, the IQ measures used by virtually all researchers reporting low beginning reading/IQ relationships used IQ tests that fail to include perhaps the strongest cognitive ability associated with beginning reading—auditory processing (phonological awareness and precursor phonics skills). So reports by Fletcher et al. (1994) and Lyon (1995) showing that IQ fails to differentiate between good and poor readers when reading achievement is defined as word identification and phonological decoding are not surprising. IQ measures used in these analyses do not include the most relevant intellectual or cognitive elements that underpin these reading abilities. The relationship between beginning reading and cognitive tests that are related more naturally to reading are relatively strong (McGrew and Woodcock 2001). So the findings of "no relationship" between IQ and reading are limited significantly by the definitions of intelligence used by the researchers. Further, the difficulty associated with measuring reading at young ages complicates matters. In contrast, the picture changes considerably when reading achievement is defined as comprehension; IQ predicts reading comprehension significantly (Fuchs and Young 2006; Rathvon 2004).

Is It Helpful to Administer IQ Tests to Struggling Readers?
We do not believe most teachers would benefit from routinely knowing the IQ scores of their students, though some reading experts advocate this as a way of determining expectations (including Mariotti and Homan 2005). But we do believe that students vary in the cognitive processes or abilities they bring to the reading process and that these processes matter. Although we agree with Rathvon—that routine administration of IQ tests are not needed—we do believe that practitioners (typically school psychologists and educational diagnosticians) who assess specific reading skills should, in some cases, assess reading-related cognitive abilities (including auditory processing, short-term auditory memory, and authentic speed-of-processing tasks such as rapid automatic naming tasks) in order to obtain information about the roots of reading problems and ideas for instruction. Other assessment

strategies may be important to include as well. Just as at-risk readers vary on important cognitive precursors of reading, they also vary on other important characteristics that have an impact on reading acquisition, including persistence, motivation, energy level, alertness, and so on. We talk more about assessment of these characteristics in Chapter 7.

■ TRANSACTIONAL VIEW OF READING

So far, we have discussed models that primarily address factors operating within the reader. In the next section, we discuss the **transactional view** of reading, which focuses attention on situations in which literacy experiences occur and emphasizes the importance of context interacting with the reader to construct new knowledge. Figure 2.6 shows the variety of influences, both within the child (and situational), that can have an impact on the reading abilities and experiences of a particular student.

Louise Rosenblatt is widely credited with developing a transactional view of reading. She argues that "reading is transaction, a two-way process, involving a reader and a text at a particular time under particular circumstances" (2001, 269). Rosenblatt addresses the importance of the reader's selective attention during the reading process; that is, the reader attends more to certain aspects of the text, such as rhyming words in a poem, and less to others. Further, Rosenblatt distinguishes between reading primarily for

FIGURE 2.6 Inclusive View of Reading

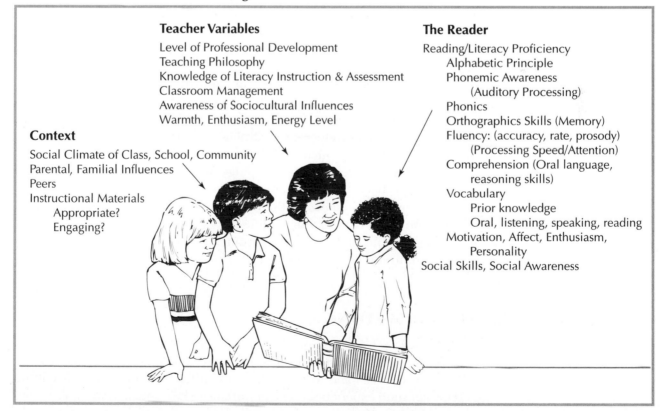

Teacher Variables
Level of Professional Development
Teaching Philosophy
Knowledge of Literacy Instruction & Assessment
Classroom Management
Awareness of Sociocultural Influences
Warmth, Enthusiasm, Energy Level

The Reader
Reading/Literacy Proficiency
    Alphabetic Principle
    Phonemic Awareness
        (Auditory Processing)
    Phonics
    Orthographics Skills (Memory)
    Fluency: (accuracy, rate, prosody)
        (Processing Speed/Attention)
    Comprehension (Oral language,
        reasoning skills)
    Vocabulary
        Prior knowledge
        Oral, listening, speaking, reading
    Motivation, Affect, Enthusiasm,
        Personality
Social Skills, Social Awareness

Context
Social Climate of Class, School, Community
Parental, Familial Influences
Peers
Instructional Materials
    Appropriate?
    Engaging?

appreciation and aesthetic purposes versus reading primarily for information-gathering reasons. She notes that what a reader experiences and takes away from a given reading experience is shaped generally by his or her cultural and social experiences and specifically his or her stance or approach to the particular text. For example, does the reader approach a text to learn specific facts or to experience emotion? Importantly, Rosenblatt argues that it is rarely the case, perhaps impossible, for one to read for only one purpose (1996).

McEneaney, Lose, and Schwartz (2006) also describe a transactional view of reading; their view emphasizes the importance of the context in which reading occurs and deemphasizes within-the-reader variables. "In this view, reading ability is not a property of the reader and may vary widely depending on contextual circumstances" (2006, 120). According to McEneaney and colleagues, individual differences in reading skills are viewed as normal variability. The emphasis is on normal variability as opposed to disability. McEneaney and colleagues argue that reading ability can and should be expected to vary within a given classroom setting as well as across different settings.

Certainly, research supports the notion that readers in any classroom will vary in reading ability (Hargis 2006; Shaywitz 2003). Further, we acknowledge that learning takes place in context and that the social context of the classroom influences how students will make meaning of what they are reading and of their other experiences (Gee 2001). We agree that the context in which literacy instruction occurs is very important. To disagree would be to discount the importance of teacher; of classroom climate; of instructional materials; and of a host of social, cultural, and affective factors. It is critical that teachers remain attentive to these factors and that they appreciate the need to focus on what they can do to create the most conducive climate for literacy development. We address some of these factors in Chapter 7, including the need to assess and focus instruction based on the needs and preferences of students.

We acknowledge the importance of context, and as do others (such as McGill-Franzen 2006), we believe that effective educators must focus attention on individual readers' competencies in order to instruct effectively. For example, when using **cooperative learning** or **partner reading**, teachers must know about student's proficiencies and their social relationships with specific peers in order to make effective groupings. McEneaney and colleagues argue that there has been too much emphasis on identifying reading disabilities and not enough acceptance of the natural variability of readers in different settings. We agree that reading abilities vary widely and that effective educators recognize this and instruct accordingly, in spite of state standards that reflect and promote expectations of grade-level achievement for all students (Hargis 2006).

■ SPEAKING, READING, AND WRITING

In addition to considering social and contextual factors, teachers must appreciate that reading does not occur in isolation of other literacy skills, particularly oral vocabulary and writing, which are influenced, of course, by culture and background experiences. The importance of vocabulary was noted by the

National Reading Panel (NRP, National Institute of Child Health and Human Development [NICHD] 2000), and we reemphasize it here. Some researchers have argued that vocabulary is more important than phonological awareness in predicting early reading skills (Gee 2001). And, writing sometimes is thought of as the inverse of reading. If reading requires extracting meaning from existing print, writing requires the generation of print to convey meaning. Both require knowledge of the meaning of symbols and are learned more easily by those with good visual and auditory memory, the ability to process information quickly, and a strong capacity to understand relationships among ideas and information (including categorically, hierarchically, and semantically). According to Rosenblatt, "both writer and readers are drawing on personal linguistic/experiential reservoirs in a to-and-fro transaction with a text. . . . Their composing and reading activities are both complementary and different" (2001, 384). Similarly, Rasinski and Padak point out that "children learn a great deal through writing that applies to their reading" (2004, 205). Through writing, children have the opportunity to practice and apply phonics, and they develop facility with forming words and sentences. In short, writing gives developing readers inside/out experience with the reading process. In summary, the reciprocal relationships among reading and writing, as well as listening, speaking, and spelling, are critical to the use of instructional approaches advocated by Clay (1983, 1986); Cunningham, Hall, and Sigmon (1999); and Goodman (1986).

■ AN INCLUSIVE VIEW OF READING

All the models just described provide information to help teachers appreciate the complexity of reading. For a student to read successfully, many internal processes must be engaged, as is obvious from tracing the reading through the steps in an information processing model. In addition, many (external) environmental influences are at work. Reading success and interest may be influenced by the teacher, peers, parents, extended family members, school administrators, community opportunities, and so on. For example, teachers determine the difficulty and content of the material students read but they are also influenced by school administrators from a distance. Administrators often determine the core program and which content texts are chosen. Hopefully, reading and content-area specialists have input into these decisions. Principals and the community have strong influences on the overall school climate and expectations within the school.

Teachers have most control over their immediate classroom environment; ideally, they set the occasion for success. Peers may be helpful by offering direct support, such as partner reading, or indirect support, such as behaving themselves, thereby producing a conducive climate. Similarly, parents can provide direct support by reading to or with a child or indirect help by creating a facilitative study schedule and climate. Community decision makers typically offer more indirect help. For example, community leaders may create a reading enrichment program through the local public library in the summer. These outside-the-child variables may help or hinder literacy acquisition and are important. All these influences, internal and external, should be the focus of an inclusive assessment.

We believe it is important to try to describe the influences of reading, internal and external, all in one place and within one graphic. In addition, we want the graphic to have utility for teachers and other educators. Ideally, the graphic would provide some space for teachers to make notes about the progress for a student, a sort of worksheet. The goal of providing such a graphic is ambitious, but we have made an attempt. An Inclusive Model of Reading is shown in Figure 2.7, in which we depict the complicated array of elements that influence the reading process, building on the work of theorists discussed previously in the chapter. Of course, an inclusive model of reading would not be complete without mention of specific reading skills themselves. Also shown in the model and taken from the NRP are alphabetics, fluency, vocabulary, and comprehension as well as orthography and sight word recognition, not specifically mentioned by the NRP. Understanding reading—how it develops and the process of reading—requires knowledge of these areas of reading, the relevant cognitive processing elements, and the social context within which these skills develop.

We hope the graphic depiction of the model provides a visual aid that will

FIGURE 2.7 Inclusive Model of Reading

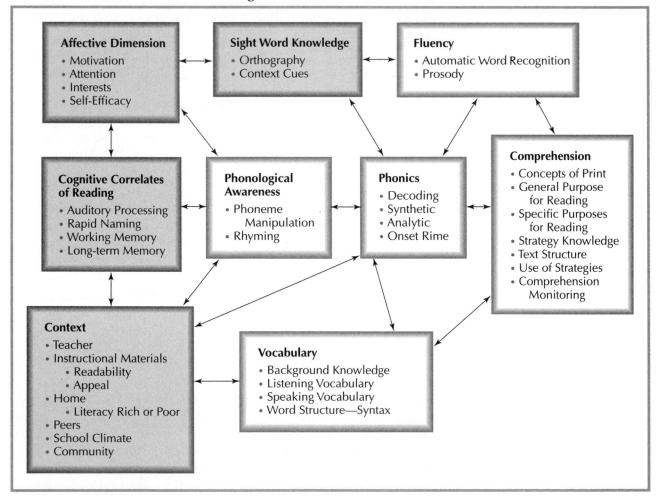

Note: Non-shaded boxes represent areas of reading identified by the National Reading Panel.

help you begin to appreciate the complex interaction of all these activities (and others) that are required during the act of reading. Because we believe it will be a useful reference for you throughout the book, it is also reproduced in Appendix B. Remember, the elements listed in Appendix B are not exhaustive nor are they written in stone. Rather, they are pulled from the current literature on reading, information processing, and cognitive development, and as you know by now, rarely is there consensus on the importance of any particular component of any model or theory. We offer the figure only as a device to stimulate your thinking and to motivate you to learn more about the awesome phenomenon of reading! We conclude this chapter with a discussion of students who find reading difficult, even when they are instructed by highly motivated and competent teachers.

HOW DO WE KNOW WHETHER A STUDENT HAS A READING DISABILITY?

How do we know whether a student who struggles with reading has one or more **learning disabilities**, such as dyslexia? When a student is not making progress in reading despite exposure to sound instruction, a motivating classroom environment, good school attendance, and a stable home environment, classroom teachers may consider some within-the-child characteristics. Teachers who are concerned about student performance should first check the student's cumulative records to be sure he or she has not already been assessed for special education eligibility. The federal law, Individuals with Disabilities Education Improvement Act of 2004 (IDEA 2004), stipulates that K–12 students suspected of having a disability must undergo a **nondiscriminatory comprehensive educational evaluation**. This process can seem daunting, so teachers should keep in mind that a comprehensive assessment is the responsibility of a team of professionals, which often includes reading specialists, special educators, school psychologists, and speech/language specialists. Classroom teachers' awareness of and involvement in the process is crucial, but the responsibility for conducting the assessments is a team responsibility.

IDEA 2004 identifies thirteen disability categories; the most common include learning disabilities, **mental retardation**, and **speech-language impairment**. The disability categories are defined in the law (see the complete list on the Internet at: www.ed.gov/about/offices/list/osers/osep/index.html). Also, the Council for Exceptional Children provides information about the various disability categories at: www.cec.sped.org Students in most exceptionality categories will experience difficulty with reading. Unfortunately, students with disabilities are far more likely than nondisabled peers to drop out of school and to be unemployed or underemployed following high school (Turnbull et al. 2007). We know that of the many adults who cannot read proficiently in the United States, a disproportionate number have disabilities (NCES 2006). Because low-literate adults represent a unique and underserved population, subsequent chapters will feature special tips for assessment of adults in boxed text.

As discussed in Chapter 1, the learning disability category is the most common type of exceptionality. Since the initial passage of the federal special education law in 1975, now called IDEA 2004, learning disabilities have been defined in many states by comparing individual measures of IQ and academic achievement to determine whether students underachieve. There is also the presumption that some type of underlying psychological processing problem exists, such as weak short-term memory, that is related to or that causes the achievement problem. And, it is necessary to rule out other causes for the academic problem, including excessive absences, insufficient or inappropriate instruction, and significant **emotional disturbance**.

What Are the Areas of Learning Disability?

IDEA indicates that a learning disability may exist in one or more of seven areas of academic achievement. These include basic reading skills, reading comprehension, written expression, listening comprehension, oral expression, math calculation, and math reasoning. How do the areas identified under IDEA relate to the areas identified by the NRP? Typically, basic reading skills include both automatic word recognition skills (sometimes referred to as sight word recognition) and phonetic decoding skills, while reading comprehension includes vocabulary and comprehension skills. It is unclear where reading fluency falls in this dichotomy, but we suggest it may fit best with basic reading skills. Figure 2.8 contains a graphic displaying the relationships of the areas of reading as depicted by both the NRP and IDEA.

The IQ-achievement discrepancy method for determining learning disabilities has increasingly come under attack and we do not advocate using it in the manner it has typically been used. This method became the most common strategy to identify learning disabilities following passage of the original federal special education law in 1975. The method requires that a significant difference, usually defined as about 15 **standard score** points, exist between IQ and a particular measure of achievement, with achieve-

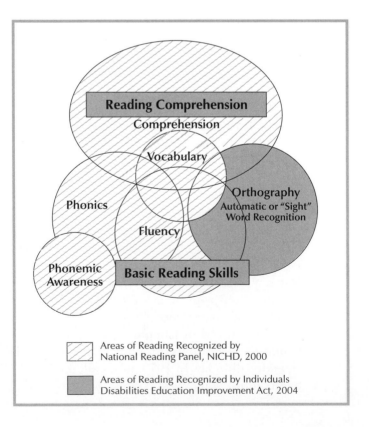

FIGURE 2.8 Areas of Reading Identified by the Individuals with Disabilities Education Act/National Reading Panel

ment being lower. This has been called a **wait to fail** method because it is very difficult to obtain a discrepancy for young children simply because of their lack of experience with academics and the limited nature of the tests for children this young. Another major criticism of the discrepancy model is that the process is not implemented in the same way across the country; that is, different cutoff scores have been used in different states such that a student identified as having a learning disability in one state may not be so identified in another state. Another problem is that different professionals apply the same criteria differently, sometimes identifying a disability even though the scores do not support it. Perhaps a more serious criticism is that the discrepancy concept itself may be flawed. Some argue that students with learning disabilities are no different from other low achievers who do not exhibit a discrepancy (Reschly and Grimes 2002).

Learning disabilities is a valid construct. We recognize that the IQ-achievement discrepancy has not been used effectively to identify learning disabilities. However, there is research evidence to support that the concept of learning disabilities is valid (Learning Disabilities Roundtable 2004; Scruggs and Mastropieri 2002). And, in our collective experience as teachers and psychologists, we have assessed, taught, tutored, and advocated for many bright children, adolescents, and even adults for whom reading is more difficult than it should be given their overall ability. A learning disability is best defined as a pattern of intra-individual strengths and weaknesses, and dyslexia is the most common type of learning disability.

Dyslexia defined. Shaywitz characterizes dyslexia as a weakness in a "sea of strengths" (2003, 58). Individuals with dyslexia have difficulty automatizing the code of a language. Estimates of the prevalence of dyslexia vary between 5 percent and 10 percent of the population (British Dyslexia Association 2005; Shaywitz 2003). Dyslexia, as defined by the International Dyslexia Association, is characterized by:

> . . . difficulties with accurate and/or fluent word recognition and by poor spelling and decoding abilities. These difficulties typically result from a deficit in the phonological component of language that is often unexpected in relation to other cognitive abilities and the provision of effective classroom instruction. Secondary consequences may include problems in reading comprehension and reduced reading experience that can impede the growth of vocabulary and background knowledge.

Because of these difficulties, students with dyslexic tendencies typically require more in-depth assessment and more intensive instruction than other students in order to read successfully.

In Figure 2.9, we present a list of characteristics typically exhibited by students with dyslexia. Generally, individuals with dyslexia tend to have most difficulty with basic reading skills, particularly phonological skills but also orthography and fluency. Spelling, as well, is usually very difficult for individuals with dyslexia. Though the term *dyslexia* is mentioned in the definition of learning disabilities in the federal law (IDEA), it is not specifically included in the regulations. So in many states and school districts, students with characteristics of dyslexia may simply be identified as having a learning

FIGURE 2.9 Characteristics of Dyslexia

Characteristics of Dyslexia	
Individuals with Dyslexia tend to have **higher** scores on measures of	Dyslexia
• Cognitive Abilities	• Is *Not* a Visual Problem
• Listening Comprehension	• Is characterized by poor basic reading skills and relatively stronger comprehension
• Reading Comprehension	• Is exhibited by 5–10% of the population
• Visual Skills	
Individuals with Dyslexia tend to have **lower** scores on measures of	Individuals with Dyslexia may have:
• Basic Reading Skills, Especially Phonetic Decoding	• Difficulty rhyming
• Auditory Skills, Especially Phonemic Awareness	• Difficulty associating sounds and letters
• Spelling	• Confusions with names and sounds of letters that look alike
• Written expression	• Slow and dysfluent reading
• Rapid Naming	• Problems with phonology
	• Problems with orthography

disability in basic reading skills, though often reading comprehension and written expression disabilities may also be identified.

It may not come as a surprise that the construct of dyslexia is controversial, primarily because of lack of consensus about how it should be identified and because some fear use of the label may make teachers less likely to take responsibility for teaching reading (if they believe a student has an inherent disability that makes reading difficult). In our experience, students with the most significant characteristics of dyslexia are well aware of their relative difficulties and often find it a relief to realize they have an identifiable pattern of strengths and weaknesses and that the weaknesses can be addressed through good instruction and hard work.

Quantifying learning disabilities. Keep in mind that dyslexia and other learning disabilities are difficult to quantify with test scores. When cutoff scores are established, the decision making that follows is necessarily arbitrary. The important point of an individual, comprehensive assessment should be to help determine strengths and weaknesses, to engender self-awareness, and to inform instruction. However, the reality is that schools must have a reliable way of determining which students need more instructional help. And, the most obvious type of help has been special education services, in which a student is supposed to receive individual instruction to meet his or her unique educational needs.

Because of the steady increase in the percentage of students identified as having a learning disability, the associated rising financial costs of special education services, and the fact that many other students, not identified as having learning disabilities also need extra assistance to achieve adequate literacy and other achievement goals, the federal law deemphasized the IQ-achievement discrepancy approach to identifying learning disabilities. IDEA 2004 allows school districts to use the traditional IQ-achievement discrepancy model to identify learning disabilities *but* provides an important second option—the response to intervention model.

The response to intervention (RTI) method requires using a tiered approach and progress monitoring of all students. Using some criteria (such as students who perform within the lowest 10 percent on some measure, say oral reading, and who fail to make adequate progress compared to most peers), students are selected to participate in extra, more rigorous instruction. If these students continue to fail to make adequate progress, based on predetermined criteria, they are assigned more intensive interventions at another tier. (A multitiered model of reading instruction was described in Chapter 1.)

Ultimately when students fail to meet predetermined criteria for adequate progress, even with the most intensive general education interventions, they may be tested by a team of professionals. Assessment instruments may include individualized tests of achievement, language, intelligence, **adaptive behavior** (ability to function independently in the environment) and personality to rule out learning disabilities, mental retardation, emotional disturbance, and so on. In such instances, an IQ test may be used to help determine whether a student has mental retardation (for example, the student displays intellectual and adaptive behavior performance significantly below the average). Also, an IQ test that includes measures of the cognitive processes known to be most important in reading can be part of a useful assessment battery for the small percentage of students who appear to have significant learning disabilities in reading.

■ HOW DO WE DISTINGUISH ENGLISH LANGUAGE LEARNING CHALLENGES FROM DISABILITIES?

The population of the United States is increasingly diverse; according to U.S. Census data reported in 2000, almost two million had no English-speaking ability and 31,844,979 people did not speak English as their primary language. In addition, individuals with limited or no English represent the fastest growing population in the United States. As early as 1994, there were more than 200 languages spoken in the Greater Chicago area (Pasko 1994) and in 1997, in California more than 150 languages were spoken (Unz 1997). In fact, in the nation's two largest school districts, ELL students make up almost half of all students at the kindergarten level. (McCallum, Bracken, and Wasserman 2001). These changing demographics mean a significant increase in both school-age students and adults whose first language is not English (English language learners). Teaching and testing students who are learning English as a second (or third) language poses special challenges. NCLB demands that the progress of students in minority groups be documented. Schools are accountable for progress of ELL learners just as they are for students with disabilities.

Brown (2004, 225) reports that from 1987 to 2001, the "percentage change in the general population who did not speak English increased by

2.5 percent," while the "... percentage of students from these homes who were identified for special services increased 10.9 percent." Despite this trend, data apparently are mixed as to whether Hispanic students, the fastest growing group of ELL students, are actually overrepresented in special education (Figueroa and Newsome 2006). Nonetheless, experts express concern that ELL students are being overreferred (Brown 2004; Figueroa and Newsome 2006). That is, there is a fear that teachers will confuse typical challenges associated with bilingualism with signs of a disability. For example, bilingual students tend to read more slowly, particularly in the nonnative language. Students who are learning English as a second language may learn basic interpersonal communicative skills (BICS) within two to three years of school, but they may take much longer to develop cognitive academic language proficiency (CALP), essentially the ability to read, speak, write and learn, with ease in English (Cummins 1984). To guard against misidentification of bilingual students as disabled and against their overrepresentation in special education, IDEA has set clear guidelines calling for nondiscriminatory assessment. In addition, the standards set by the Teachers of English to Speakers of English and Other Languages (TESOL 1997; www.tesol.org/s_tesol/seccss.asp?CID=3&DID=4) dictate best practices in assessment of ELL students as well.

Second Language Acquisition-Associated Phenomena. Brown (2004) proposes a new definition she calls Second Language Acquisition-Associated Phenomena (SLAAP). According to Brown, the "major causes of SLAAP stem from myriad external factors involved in moving from one's homeland to a new country" (2004, 227). Further, the transition may cause "cultural shock, feelings of isolation, downgraded socioeconomic conditions, and linguistic challenges related to immersion in a totally different language" (2004, 227). Brown notes that SLAAP may include very low performance in reading, expressive language and writing but that this low performance is not because of dyslexia or other within-the-student disabilities.

Brown (2004) provides a list of practices to help educators avoid misidentifying students exhibiting SLAPP as having a disability. Some of these are summarized as follows: (a) Consider the student's performance in his or her native language. Is it at or near grade level? (b) Does the student perform similarly to other ELL students with similar background and experiences? (c) Does the student exhibit high BICS relative to CALP? (d) Does he or she respond favorably to sound instructional practices? (e) Does he or she perform higher on nonverbal versus verbal measures of ability? Brown recommends that teachers document ELL students' response to instructional interventions, as described in the multitiered model of instruction. When ELL students do not progress despite appropriate instruction, Brown recommends that assessment include materials taken directly from the curriculum and that examiners test the limits or go beyond typical assessment procedures to probe and understand student responses.

When ELL students are referred for special education, educators should adhere to best practices for nondiscriminatory assessment; one of the most important of these is to use measures of cognitive ability that are either in the student's native language or that are nonverbal in nature. McCallum, Bracken, and Wasserman (2001) provide a review of nonverbal assessment techniques as well as advice on avoiding common pitfalls in assessment of ELL learners. Because of the increasing need for educators to provide appropriate instruction and assessment for ELL learners, Chapters 3–6 will feature special boxed matter with tips designed specifically to address the needs of ELL learners.

■ LOW LITERACY ADULTS

Individuals with disabilities and individuals whose first language is not English are overrepresented in the **adult basic education** population, the population of adults who exhibit low literacy levels in English and do not hold a high school diploma. Not all adults with low literacy skills are alike. Information on adult literacy is available from the National Assessment of Adult Literacy, "a nationally representative and continuing assessment of English language literacy skills of American adults." An assessment occurred in 2003. According to these results, 11 million adults in the United States were nonliterate in English; of those, seven million could not answer the most simple test questions in English and another four million could not take the test because of language barriers. In addition, 21 percent of the adults scoring at the lowest level on the National Assessment of Adult Literacy (NAAL) were identified as having disabilities, as compared to 9 percent of the overall adult population in the United States. Results suggest adult literacy is an ongoing concern in the United States. Of the four general levels of proficiency, 14 percent scored below basic, 29 percent scored at basic, 44 percent scored at intermediate, and 13 percent scored at proficient level. Results of the 2003 NAAL are discussed further in Chapter 5 in the context of formal group testing (http://nces.ed.gov/NAAL/index.asp?file=KeyFindings/Demographics/Overall.asp&PageId=16).

To better determine the status of adult readers, Strucker and Davidson (2003) conducted the massive Adult Reading Components Study; they

assessed 995 adult learners in eight states in the areas of phonemic awareness, rapid naming, word recognition, oral reading, spelling, vocabulary, and
background knowledge. Of these adult learners, 676 were identified as Adult
Basic Education and 279 had English as a second language. Strucker and
Davidson used assessment results to clump the learners into clusters (based
on similarities in various test scores). Ten separate clusters were identified,
indicating wide variability in adult learner reading and language skills. It is
important for instructors to understand that adult readers may achieve similar scores on a silent reading comprehension test, the type typically administered upon enrollment in adult education classes but still vary greatly in
other reading skills such as fluency, word decoding, and vocabulary.

■ THE LITERACY INSTRUCTION PIE

By now you have an awareness of the complexity of the reading process and
the multitude of influences that have an impact on the development of literacy. Given this complexity, it is natural to feel a little humbled, perhaps even
overwhelmed. But teachers successfully teach millions of children to read
every year. The most successful know how to translate assessment data into
effective instruction. Effective teachers assess the progress of their students in
the various areas of reading discussed in Chapter 1 and provide instruction
accordingly. Figure 2.10 depicts a Literacy Instruction Pie with pieces cut to
reflect equal amounts of instruction in word analysis (including phonological
awareness, phonics and sight word acquisition), fluency, vocabulary, comprehension, and the reading-writing connection. We visualize this pie as a conceptual planning tool. Teachers in lower grades will spend considerable time
on building word analysis skills but will not ignore the other areas of reading.
Teachers in middle school will spend relatively less time than their lower
grade colleagues on word analysis; further, the type of word analysis skills will
be different (e.g., rime-onset activities for lower grades versus sophisticated
morphology for middle grades). Teachers of students with reading disabilities
and struggling secondary and adult readers will spend more time on word
analysis than teachers of typically performing secondary students.

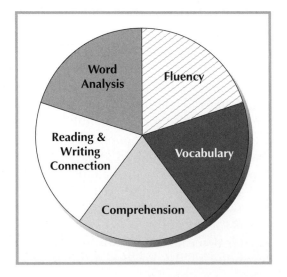

**FIGURE 2.10 Literacy
Instruction Pie**

We envision teachers using the Literacy Instruction Pie in two ways. They may: (a) construct a pie to represent the balance of instruction for a class as a whole, such as determining how much instructional time and energy are actually spent in each of the important areas of reading; and, (b) construct a pie to determine the balance of time and energy that should be devoted to each individual student. Because we hope you will refer to the pie throughout your reading of this book, we reproduced it in Appendix C. For typically performing students, the pieces of the pie will be the same size as the pieces in the pie constructed for the class as a whole. But for struggling and advanced readers, the size of the pieces of the pie should be of different sizes. The different sizes of the pie reflect the need for "personalizing instruction," as advocated by McGill-Franzen (2006, 12). For example, a student who is learning English will need relatively more time on vocabulary development than a high-achieving student with an advanced vocabulary. Similarly, a student with significant weaknesses in phonemic awareness will need relatively more instructional time on word analysis skills.

Keep in mind that the Literacy Instruction Pie can serve as a useful tool for evaluating the amount of instructional time spent in various types of activities. That is, a teacher might establish a goal of building reading fluency, and consequently, plan to provide time for students to practice reading at instructional level. As mentioned above the pie can also serve as a planning tool both for an entire class and for individual students; that is, teachers and other staff can collect assessment data (from various sources that are described in later chapters of this book) and use these data to build a pie indicating which areas of reading need the most instructional attention. Once the general areas of reading are identified, of course, teachers must identify specific instructional activities appropriate to students' level of performance.

USING KNOWLEDGE OF READING TO UNDERSTAND READING ASSESSMENT

Familiarity with various models and facets of reading provides you the background to appreciate various types of reading assessment. In Chapter 3, we address aspects of the context depicted in the Inclusive Model of Reading, specifically instructional materials, and techniques for matching readers to appropriately **leveled** materials. Assessments of skills less tied to classroom instruction (e.g., recurring probes of oral reading fluency) are important for monitoring progress and are addressed in Chapter 4. In Chapters 5 and 6, assessments that allow for both **intra-individual comparison** (essentially a profile of a student's strength and weaknesses) and comparisons of student progress with peers are addressed. These assessments are used primarily for accountability purposes and to determine eligibility into special education and other programs. Individually administered assessments are addressed in Chapter 5 and group administered ones in Chapter 6. These assessments provide measures of the NRP's five areas of reading as well as other aspects of the Inclusive Model (e.g., cognitive abilities such as rapid naming and auditory processing). Such assessment may help a teacher understand why one reader is so much more effective than another and provide information about how to structure the teaching environment to compensate for these differences among students. The techniques in Chapters 5 and 6 are considered formal because, in order to make intra- and inter-student comparisons, specific test construction guidelines must be adhered to (such as the use of scripted or standard administration directions, collection of normative data). Other aspects of the Model (such as motivation and interest) are addressed in Chapter 7.

Summary

In Chapter 2, we described the history of the development of reading models, which dates from early medical models designed to identify deficits such as "word blindness." We agree with critics that medical models are based on an assumption that the reader has an internal deficit that needs to be addressed and thus may not be particularly useful for most teachers. Even so, we urge teachers to rule out simple medical problems such as poor vision and hearing when students struggle with reading. As research methods become more sophisticated, we anticipate discovery of more brain-based explanations of individual variation in reading skills. These discoveries will likely increase understanding of reading acquisition, and perhaps lead to brain altering interventions that we can only dream of today.

Later in Chapter 2, we discussed several developmental models of reading including those espoused by Chall and Spear-Swerling, and the Sawyer et al. (2000) adaptation of Frith's model. Although particulars vary, these models depict stages of reading proficiency, moving from emergent or nonreader to proficient reader, and all recognize the importance of phonological, orthographic, and comprehension skills. These models may be particularly useful when considering where a student has gotten "off track" (McKenna and Stahl 2003, 3). We discuss in some detail Adams' model because it has been highly influential and depicts the reading act in process, involving phonological, orthographic, syntactical, and semantic systems. Somewhat similar to Adams', though more general, is the information-processing model. We also described cognitive correlates of reading, particularly auditory processing, processing speed, and memory and followed with a discussion of the controversy surrounding the relationship between reading and IQ. Despite some arguments to the contrary, there is a body of evidence concluding that reading and IQ are related, particularly when reading comprehension is correlated with IQ scores. Although this relationship does not confirm that higher IQ causes higher reading achievement, there is evidence to suggest a reciprocal relationship, particularly between reading and verbal measures of IQ. We close the review of models with a discussion of the transactional view of reading that takes into account the social context and the background experiences the reader brings to reading at any given time. Finally, we presented an inclusive model of reading, drawing upon the various models described in the chapter. The Inclusive Model accounts for within-the-reader *and* external influences.

Because struggling readers represent one of the most important challenges educators face, we included some details about how learning disabilities and in particular, dyslexia, may be identified. We presented a graphic that depicts the relationship between areas of reading identified by the National Reading Panel (and discussed in Chapter 1) and areas of reading disabilities as recognized by the Individuals with Disabilities Education Improvement Act. We also point out the importance of nondiscriminatory assessment to ensure that nondisabled English language learners are not misidentified as having a disability, and the relationship between disabilities and reading problems in adulthood among ELLs and non-ELLs. We closed this chapter with a discussion of the Literacy Instruction Pie, which is presented again in Appendix C. You may want to refer to it in subsequent chapters as a tool for thinking about student needs in the various areas of reading instruction and assessment.

mylabschool
Where the classroom comes to life!

MyLabSchool is a collection of online tools for your success in this course, your licensure exams, and your teaching career. Visit www.mylabschool.com to access the following:
- *Online Study Guide*
- *Video cases from real classrooms*
- *Help with your research papers using Research Navigator*
- *Career Center with resources for:*
    Praxis exams and licensure preparation
    Professional portfolio development
    Job search and interview techniques
    Lesson planning

Informal Assessment: Informing Instruction

In this chapter, we examine informal assessment procedures—those most commonly used in the classroom, particularly by teachers of students in primary grades and in special education, though many of the techniques can be used or adapted for use with adolescents and adults with low literacy skills. Informal assessment can be defined as "nonstandardized methods of evaluating progress, such as interviews, observation, and teacher-made tests" (Overton 2006, 15). Informal assessments are often criterion-referenced. That is, they assess mastery of a certain skill or objective. Criterion-referenced techniques tell teachers what students "got" and "didn't get" from their teaching. They can also be used as pretests to tell teachers where to focus instruction. Traditionally, informal assessments (such as quizzes, checklists, and worksheets) have been

teacher-made, although commercially published informal assessments increasingly are available.

To help put informal assessment in perspective, think back to the Inclusive Model of Reading discussed in Chapter 2 and shown in Appendix B. According to that model, successful reading results from the interaction of a number of influences, some typically considered to exist within the student (such as memory, visual and auditory processing, interests, and motivation) and some within the environment (such as instructional materials, parental support, and school and classroom climate). These influences are depicted in Appendix B; reading outcomes, the goals of reading assessment and instruction, are shown in the right side of the figure, i.e., phonemic awareness, phonics, orthography, vocabulary, fluency, and comprehension, and the supporting, underlying elements of reading are to the left. In fact, the ultimate goal of reading—comprehension—is the rightmost component. As you look at the model, which of the elements do you think could be assessed using informal assessment measures, and in particular, informal tests, strategies, and techniques that inform instruction? If you concluded that informal assessment measures that inform instruction might be most closely related to the actual act of reading you would be right—strategies that assess word attack skills, fluency, vocabulary, prosody, knowledge of print and text structure, ability to monitor and remediate comprehension strategies as needed, and so on. These informal techniques are described in Chapter 3 and are the most important assessment strategies of all, in part because they yield the most authentic information available—information about student reading progress and information a teacher can use to make instructional decisions right away.

In Chapter 3, we focus on the informal tests, techniques, strategies, and procedures that are most capable of informing instruction, and the focus of these assessments is tied closely to the reading curriculum. Early in the chapter, we describe assessments that are most familiar to classroom teachers—those that accompany published curriculum materials, such as a basal reading series. Next, we address informal checklists and skills assessments, **error analysis** techniques, informal reading inventories (IRIs), **miscue analysis,** running records, curriculum-based measurement (CBM), and **portfolio assessment** (authentic student work and documentation of progress). Because a primary purpose of assessment is to match readers to appropriate text, we include a section on determining readability of text and using leveled readers in instruction.

Near the end of this chapter, we focus on three somewhat unique populations: kindergarten students, adult beginning readers, and English language learners (ELLs). Because experiences in kindergarten can have a significant impact on later literacy development, we include a special section focusing on assessments most appropriate for these young students. Similarly, assessment of adult reading skills and those for ELLs is somewhat specialized, and we address that need. As we describe informal techniques in this chapter, we make an effort to address the areas of reading they assess based on the categories provided by the NRP (NICHD 2000). We conclude the chapter with a table (Table 3.9) that summarizes the types of assessments described. Because this table provides a concise visual summary of informal classroom assessment, we have placed it at the end of the chapter. You may want to refer to it as you read about the various informal techniques.

Very early in the life of young readers, teachers use observational strategies to obtain estimates of skill level, to discern attitudes toward reading, and to note students' problem-solving strategies. In some cases, teachers pair the information they obtain from these observations with brief interviews. We begin this chapter by describing simple observational and interview techniques.

◼ OBSERVATION AND INTERVIEW

The most fundamental assessment strategy involves simple observation of a student performing the task of interest; in this case, reading or a related literacy task. Observation allows teachers to determine whether readers understand and can apply what they read and whether they enjoy the activity. In fact, this is the most common type of assessment in the classroom, and when properly planned, can even inform the teacher about the students' speech, hearing, vision, affect, and general health. Teachers engage in observation-based assessment every day, and for the most part, they do so in a nonsystematic fashion, noting bits of behavior, making inferences about the behavior, or simply filing the information away mentally. Goodman (1985) calls this activity "kidwatching" and notes that teachers may use this information to make judgments about their students' success when communicating with peers, when involved in a social activity, and when working with instructional materials, such as texts, worksheets, and so on. Once collected, anecdotal information is available to teachers for analyses of specific errors or error patterns.

Some experts recommend employing a systematic structure in order to maximize the information gained from observation. For example, to inform teachers about emerging literacy skills of very young readers, Mariotti and Homan (2005) recommend using the Modified Concepts about Print Test, adapted from Clay's Concepts about Print Test by Klesius and Searls (1985 as cited in Mariotti and Homan 2005). This instrument, referred to as the Klesius-Searls Test by Mariotti and Homan, assesses emergent literacy skills and requires that the teacher provide a children's book, pencil, and eraser. The teacher asks a series of questions and records the answers on the Test of Print Concepts Answer Sheet (reproduced in Figure 3.1). The questions are reproduced in Box 3.1. Using the information gained from the administration of this brief informal test, teachers can determine some important instructional goals for the student regarding emergent literacy skills.

In addition to the concepts about print described earlier, the following five areas are assessed: (a) oral reading, (b) letter identification, (c) word naming, (d) writing, and (e) dictation. Mariotti and Homan (2005) and others (e.g., McGill-Franzen 2006; Ruddell 2002) recommend additional observational techniques to assess literacy stages, including the ability to identify rhyming words, lower and upper case letters, specific sound-symbol relationships, reading with inflection.

After observational information is obtained, teachers sometimes interview students to gain an understanding of their problem solving skills. For example, teachers may ask questions such as, "If you wanted to read a story about trains what is the first thing you would do? What do you do when you read a word you do not know? What do you do when you cannot understand what you have read?" These questions are directly related to the reading process and inform

FIGURE 3.1 Modified Test of Print Concept Answer Sheet

TEST OF PRINT CONCEPTS
Answer Sheet

Student _____ Age ____ Grade ____ Date _____
Examiner _____

	Correct	Incorrect
1. Directional Terms		
Front	_____	_____
Back	_____	_____
2. Function of Print		
Print function	_____	_____
Start at top left	_____	_____
3. Left-to-Right Direction		
Left to right	_____	_____
Return to lower line	_____	_____
4. Concepts		
First	_____	_____
Last	_____	_____
End of story	_____	_____
5. Directional Terms		
Top (page)	_____	_____
Bottom (page)	_____	_____
Top (picture)	_____	_____
Bottom (picture)	_____	_____

TEST OF PRINT CONCEPTS (CONTINUED)
Answer Sheet

	Correct	Incorrect
6. Word and Letter Boundaries		
1 Word	_____	_____
2 Words	_____	_____
1 Letter	_____	_____
2 Letters	_____	_____

Interpretation and Recommendations

_____
_____
_____
_____
_____
_____
_____
_____
_____
_____
_____

Adapted by Klesius & Searls (1985) in Mariotti, A.S. & Homan, S.P. (2005). *Linking Reading Assessment to Instruction: An Application Worktext for Elementary Classroom Teachers.* (4th ed.). Mahwah, NJ: Lawrence Erlbaum.

the teacher about the student's general reading attack strategies and independence. They do not focus on the student's affect and motivation. Interviews and tests related to assessing these reader characteristics are addressed in Chapter 7. The questions mentioned earlier can be used as a starting point, and teachers may add questions of interest to fit specific situations. We recommend that teachers be careful to limit the interview to only a few minutes, particularly for young readers.

TEACHER-MADE AND TEACHER-SELECTED CURRICULUM-RELATED ASSESSMENT

If you are or have been a teacher, you are probably most familiar with assessment that is designed to evaluate mastery of specific knowledge and skills within a given set of curriculum materials. In reading, these materials are often from a

BOX 3.1 Questions from the Concepts about Print Test

1. Directional Terms: Front and Back. Hand the student a simple illustrated book with the spine facing the child and say, "Show me the front of the book." "Show me the back of the book."

2. Function of Print. Open the book to a place where the print is on one page and a picture is on the other and say, "Show me which page tells the story." Observe whether the child points to picture or print. If the child points to the page of print, say, "Show me where I begin to read on this page."

3. Left-to-Right Orientation. On the same page say, "Show me where I go next when I read." Observe whether the student sweeps finger across the printed line from left to right, then ask, "Where do I go from there?" Note whether the child correctly makes the return sweep to the left and drops down one line.

4. Concepts: First and Last. Turn to a new page and say, "Point to the first word on this page." Then say, "Point to the last word on this page." Then ask, "Where is the end of the story."

5. Directional Terms: Top and Bottom. Turn to another pair of pages with print on one page and a picture on the other, then say, "Show me the bottom of the page. Show me the top of the page." Point to the picture and say, "Show me the top of the picture. Show me the bottom of the picture."

6. Word and Letter Boundaries. Hand the child the eraser end of a pencil and say, "Circle one word. Circle two words. Now, circle one letter. Circle two letters."

Source: Clay, M.M. (1993). *Observation Survey of Early Literacy Achievement.* (2nd ed.). Portsmouth, NH: Heinemann.

basal reading series. There is a growing trend toward teaching literacy using leveled readers, such as guided reading described by Fountas and Pinnell (1996) or the four blocks approach described by Cunningham, Hall, and Sigmon (1999), but the reality is that many systems continue to use basal reading series as the core reading program. According to Lerner (2006, 94), a basal reader is a "sequential and interrelated set of books and supportive material that is intended to provide the basic material for the development of fundamental reading skills" and "is the predominant instruction tool that is used to teach reading in 90–95 percent of the classrooms across the country."

Basal readers have been around for more than a century. Most fall into one of three types or frameworks (Allington and Cunningham 2002) and emphasize either: (a) stories with high frequency and severely restricted word selection, such as the old Dick and Jane readers; (b) text emphasizing decodable (phonetically regular) vocabulary words; and (c) a shared reading experience using texts that rely on topic familiarity and predictability based on storylines from language and artwork cues, and patterns of language repetition. Most current reading series reflect a balanced literacy philosophy and include explicit phonics instruction in the early levels. They also address other areas identified by the NRP—fluency, vocabulary, and comprehension. In fact, some teachers we know struggle to determine which instruction and assessment activities to include, mainly because the typical reading series offers so many options. Consequently, teachers often find themselves selecting what they hope will be the most appropriate and useful assessments from a whole host of materials available.

Most basal reading series include routine assessment of phonics, vocabulary, and comprehension. A unit test from first grade of the Scott Foresman Reading Series (2007), published by Pearson Education, is reproduced in Figure 3.2. You will see that word analysis skills, vocabulary, and comprehension are all assessed. This is the series used in the system of our first-grade

FIGURE 3.2 Unit Test

Name_____

Phonics Words

1 wish with wing
   ○ ○ ○

2 rack rake race
   ○ ○ ○

3 nose nick nice
   ○ ○ ○

4 those this tones
   ○ ○ ○

5 call cute cut
   ○ ○ ○

Name_____

6 waved walk walked
   ○ ○ ○

7 white when wipe
   ○ ○ ○

8 pig page wage
   ○ ○ ○

9 chime crime chin
   ○ ○ ○

10 tree these free
   ○ ○ ○

Name_____

High-Frequency Words

11 Jane could not find _____ hat.
   ○ her
   ○ she
   ○ look

12 Do you _____ this shell?
   ○ from
   ○ want
   ○ where

13 When you go out, put on _____ hat.
   ○ like
   ○ said
   ○ your

14 I like to _____ eggs.
   ○ eat
   ○ here
   ○ now

15 Three cats ran on the path. We _____ them.
   ○ go
   ○ saw
   ○ down

Name_____

A Place Called Lee Drive

At one time Lee Drive had trees. 7
It had lots of space for games. 14
Kids ran and played on Lee Drive. 21

Now Lee Drive is packed with homes. 28
It has lots of traffic. 33
There is less space for trees. 39
There is less space for games. 45

Can kids play on Lee Drive now? 52
Yes. Kids have a fun place on Lee Drive. 61
Kids go there to run and swing 68
and slide. 70

Scott Foresman Reading Series, Grade 1 (2007). *Intensive Reading—Assess Book.* Glenview, IL: Pearson Education, Inc.

teacher, Ms. Crockett, who was introduced in Chapter 1. She administers these unit assessments routinely and keeps careful records about student progress in each of the areas assessed.

Figure 3.3 is a reproduction of a summary sheet Ms. Crockett uses to note progress for each student during a unit of instruction as well as individual student performance on the unit test, such as the one shown in Figure 3.2. In addition to unit tests, most series also offer numerous worksheets for skill practice, reinforcement, and ongoing assessment. Examples from the Scott Foresman series are presented in Figures 3.4, 3.5, and 3.6 (pp. 76–78); measures of phonics, vocabulary, and comprehension are presented.

As you have learned, basal readers have distinct advantages such as preselected and developed skill strands, controlled text difficulty, suggestions for material use, and "built-in" assessment strategies. However, there are disadvantages. Use of basal readers limits the range and variability of the literature to

Child's Name _____ Level A

Record Chart for Unit Tests

		Score Individual/Group		Reteach ✔	Individual Retest Score	Comments
Unit 1	Letter Naming	/36	/18		/36	
	Letter-Sounds	/18	/9		/18	
	Word Reading: Phonics	/56	/28		/56	
	High-Frequency Words	/5	/5		/5	
Unit 2	Letter Naming	/16	/12		/16	
	Letter-Sounds	/9	/9		/9	
	Word Reading: Phonics	/30	/19		/30	
	High-Frequency Words	/5	/5		/5	
Unit 3	Word Reading: Phonics	/20	/15		/20	
	High-Frequency Words	/5	/5		/5	
	Fluency WCPM					
	Retelling Score					
Unit 4	Word Reading: Phonics	/20	/15		/20	
	High-Frequency Words	/5	/5		/5	
	Fluency WCPM					
	Retelling Score					
Unit 5	Word Reading: Phonics	/20	/15		/20	
	High-Frequency Words	/5	/5		/5	
	Fluency WCPM					
	Retelling Score					

Record Scores Use this chart to record scores for the Level A Unit Tests.

Reteach Reteach phonics skills or provide additional practice with high-frequency words if the child scores below 80% on either portion of the Unit Test.

Retest The Individual Unit Test may be used to retest skills that have been retaught.

© Pearson Education A

To move into the next unit of *Sidewalks*, children should	The child may be more appropriately placed in *Sidewalks Early Reading Intervention* if
• score 80% or better on their cumulative Unit scores for Word/Sentence Reading (See Teacher's Guide Vol. 1, pp. 189–190 and Vol. 2, pp. 281–283.) • score 80% or better on the preceding Unit Test	• the child makes little progress in Unit 1, scoring 60% or lower on the Unit 1 Test • and is struggling to keep up with the Level A group • and, based on teacher judgment, the Level A materials are not at the child's level

FIGURE 3.3 Unit Work Summary Form

Scott Foresman Reading Series, Grade 1 (2007). *Intensive Reading—Assess Book.* Glenview, IL: Pearson Education, Inc.

FIGURE 3.4 Phonics Review Worksheet

Scott Foresman Reading Series, Grade 1 (2007). *Intensive Reading—Practice Book.* Glenview, IL: Pearson Education, Inc.

which students are exposed. And, because basals are designed to correspond to a given reading level or grade level, a primary concern is that they do not allow teachers to differentiate instruction enough to meet the range of needs present in most classrooms. Finally, some experts (Ruddell 2002) argue that use of basal readers can encourage tracking, a controversial practice. Historically, many teachers placed students in reading groups associated with different levels of basal readers, leading potentially to secondary ill effects, such as poor reading self-concept among the students in the lower tracks.

Obviously, the decision to use a basal reading series is complex. If you are asked to help determine whether to adopt a basal reading series for your school (or which one to adopt), please consider carefully the particular

Name _____

Mister Bones

HIGH-FREQUENCY WORDS

Directions
Read each sentence. Mark the ○ for the word that fits.

1 Ray _____ his dog to the park.

○ go   ○ took   ○ will

2 That big man was _____ small.

○ fire   ○ see   ○ once

3 Rose _____ her cat under the bed.

○ found   ○ glass   ○ for

4 I eat with my _____.

○ right   ○ mouth   ○ here

5 There are _____ animals in the forest.

○ from   ○ very   ○ wild

© Pearson Education 1

GO ON

FIGURE 3.5
Vocabulary Test

Scott Foresman Reading Series, Grade 1 (2007). *Intensive Reading—Selection Tests—Teacher's Manual.* Glenview, IL: Pearson Education, Inc.

characteristics of the students and the claims by the publisher. Although most publishers of commercially prepared curriculum materials provide claims that their materials are supported by research, it is very difficult to verify these claims (Allington and Cunningham 2002). Consequently, teachers should read carefully all promotional materials and look for independent evidence that the materials and approaches will provide sound instruction.

Even though publishers of basal readers provide abundant assessment information, not all informal assessment needs are met in this way. For example, the techniques we describe in this chapter are particularly useful when determining needs of a reader new to the class, when a reader struggles with the core reading program, when the core program is not a basal reading series, and for low literate older readers. Reading specialists/literacy

COMPREHENSION

Directions

Read each question. Mark the ○ for the answer.

6 **What happens first in *Honey Bees?***
○ The bees make a hive.
○ The little bees eat pollen.
○ The bees wake up.

7 **How is the queen bee different from the drone bees?**
○ The queen bee rules the hive.
○ The queen bee makes honey.
○ The queen bee feeds the little bees.

8 **What will happen if you make a bee mad?**
○ The bee will fly away.
○ The bee will attack.
○ The bee will look for food.

9 **How are the worker bees and the drone bees alike?**
○ They both make new hives.
○ They both look for food.
○ They both work for the queen.

10 **Why did the author write *Honey Bees?***
○ to show how bees work together in the hive
○ to tell how bees make honey and nectar
○ to show where bees make new hives

© Pearson Education 1

**FIGURE 3.6
Comprehension Test**

Scott Foresman Reading Series, Grade 1 (2007). *Intensive Reading—Selection Tests—Teacher's Manual.* Glenview, IL: Pearson Education, Inc.

coaches are increasingly available in systems to help teachers with assessment and instructional planning, particularly for struggling readers. These support professionals sometimes perform the in-depth assessments that the classroom teacher does not have time to conduct. But teachers need to be familiar with the different types of assessment, even those they do not routinely administer, and to know how to use and explain the information they yield.

SPECIFIC SKILLS ASSESSMENTS

In addition to the informal techniques and assessments tied to basal reading series, there are hundreds of informal teacher checklists for specific skills in the various areas of reading. Over the years, teachers tend to gather these instruments and keep the ones they find most useful. McKenna and Stahl present some of these in their 2003 book *Assessment for Reading Instruction.* For example, the San Diego Quick Assessment provides an assessment of word recognition for students aged 5 to 16. Shearer and Homan (2005) provide several informal assessments, including measures of phonics, word recognition, and comprehension. Such assessments are typically quick to administer and help the teacher track skill development of individual students. One notable example is the Yopp-Singer Test of Phoneme Segmentation, which was published initially in *The Reading Teacher* (Yopp 1995); the author and publisher International Reading Association (IRA) granted permission to teachers to reproduce and use it at no cost. The twenty-two items in the test are useful for beginning readers, in kindergarten and first grade, as well as for older nonreaders, and the test can be administered in five to ten minutes (reproduced in Figure 3.7).

Yopp-Singer Test of Phoneme Segmentation

Student's name ______________________ Date __________

Score (number correct) __________

Directions: Today we're going to play a word game. I'm going to say a word and I want you to break the word apart. You are going to tell me each sound in the word in order. For example, if I say "old," you should say "/o/-/l/-/d/." (*Administrator: Be sure to say the sounds, not the letters, in the word.*) Let's try a few together.

Practice items: (*Assist the child in segmenting these items as necessary.*) ride, go, man

Test items: (*Circle those items that the student correctly segments; incorrect responses may be recorded on the blank line following the item.*)

1. dog	______	12. lay	______
2. keep	______	13. race	______
3. fine	______	14. zoo	______
4. no	______	15. three	______
5. she	______	16. job	______
6. wave	______	17. in	______
7. grew	______	18. ice	______
8. that	______	19. at	______
9. red	______	20. top	______
10. me	______	21. by	______
11. sat	______	22. do	______

The author, Hallie Kay Yopp, California State University, Fullerton, grants permission for this test to be reproduced. The author acknowledges the contribution of the late Harry Singer to the development of this test.

FIGURE 3.7 Yopp-Singer Test of Phoneme Segmentation

Yopp, H. K. (1995). A Test for Assessing Phonemic Awareness in Young Children. *The Reading Teacher, 49,* pages 20–29.

Similarly, *The Reading Teacher's Survival Kit* (Miller 2001) and *Alternative Assessment Techniques for Reading and Writing* (Miller 1995) contain numerous reproducible quick assessments for a wide range of reading skills. Finally, the short three-minute reading assessments provided by Rasinski and Padak (2005a; 2005b) provide user-friendly, teacher-based evaluation of word recognition, fluency, and comprehension. The efficiency provided by the Rasinski and Padak assessments is impressive, particularly given the wealth of information provided (e.g., indicators of word recognition accuracy, fluency, expression and volume, phrasing and intonation, smoothness, pacing, and comprehension). In addition, these authors provide record keeping forms and even instructional recommendation for the various areas of reading assessed. These and similar short instruments can contribute significantly to the knowledge teachers need to provide effective and unique instruction. For example, they can be administered at various times throughout the school year and maintained in the students' portfolios to document progress over time.

ERROR ANALYSIS

Whether using assessments taken directly from teachers' manuals or monitoring routine daily work, effective teachers know how to analyze and correct student errors. Error analysis is a technique all teachers use, whether or not they know the terminology. Error analysis is a technique for determining patterns or reasons for student errors or difficulties. For example, Ms. Crockett is concerned because one of her students, Misha, reads slowly and does not pause at the end of sentences or raise her voice at the end of a question. When Misha reads **connected text** orally, she reads slowly and laboriously, as though the text were a long list of unrelated words. Her oral reading is not fluent. Ms. Crockett wants to know more about why Misha reads this way so she asks Misha to read orally a selected passage of appropriate difficulty. When Misha reads, Ms. Crockett notices that she appears not to attend to punctuation. She reads slowly but does not pause or change her voice at the end of each sentence.

After listening to Misha read a few sentences orally, Ms. Crockett points to a period and asks Misha to identify it. Misha is able to tell her that a period comes at the end of a sentence. Then Ms. Crockett asks Misha why the period is there. Misha hesitates and essentially restates that the period means the end of the sentence. Ms. Crockett discusses the meaning of the period with Misha. The goal is to teach Misha that the period indicates the end of a thought or idea and that it conveys the need to pause before launching into a new idea or thought. Then Ms. Crockett models reading a short selection from the same text orally, pausing appropriately between sentences. Finally, she asks Misha to read again and gives her feedback on her performance. Ms. Crockett has used error analysis to identify and correct a problem in Misha's reading. Of course, Misha will need more opportunities to read orally to practice this new skill.

To effectively perform error analysis, teachers must also be proficient at task analysis. According to Overton (2006, 167), task analysis is "breaking down of the actual task or response expected to determine which prerequisite skills are lacking or have not been mastered." In other words, teachers must have working knowledge of various reading processes and the tasks and subtasks that are necessary for effective reading. In Ms. Crockett's case, she knows that fluent reading involves reading at an appropriate pace (relatively quickly) with accuracy and with appropriate intonation or prosody. Further, she knows that prosody requires the reader to attend to punctuation and to modulate the voice accordingly. And, even more specifically, she knows that the reader must be able to recognize the punctuation (in this case, a period) and to react appropriately by pausing and slightly changing voice inflection. So recognizing the punctuation and changing the voice are subtasks required for acquiring prosody when reading. When teachers are aware of the subskills of various areas of reading, such as phonemic awareness, phonics, orthography, fluency, vocabulary and comprehension, they can perform the appropriate error analyses.

■ INFORMAL READING INVENTORIES

Although checklists and specific skills assessments focus on narrow areas of reading, informal reading inventories, or IRIs, provide both specific and comprehensive information to the teacher. In fact, the IRI is the most comprehensive informal assessment technique available. A pervasive characteristic of informal assessment is its similarity to the act of reading, reflecting its "authentic" nature. Since the 1950s, educators have developed and used information gleaned from IRIs to determine their student's reading levels—independent, instructional, and frustration (Leslie and Caldwell 2006). At a minimum, IRIs typically include graded word lists and passages designed to assess oral and silent reading and listening skills. As the name implies, IRIs are administered individually. As the student reads orally to the teacher, the teacher can obtain a measure of reading rate and accuracy and can note the types of errors or miscues the student makes. Following reading, the teacher asks the student comprehension questions and may ask the student to retell what was read. The passages may or may not include pictures, and comprehension questions may be either explicit (i.e., directly stated), implicit (i.e., inferred from the text), or both.

IRIs provide information about students' reading level and rate, insight into the types of reading errors students make, and information regarding their proficiency with different types of reading comprehension tasks. In this way, IRIs provide a rather comprehensive picture of a student's reading skills. IRIs do not provide standardized or norm-referenced scores, so they are not used to compare one student's performance with another except in a gross way. Their primary use is to inform instruction, plan for grouping, and identify skills to target. IRIs can also be used to measure progress, though the skills measured may not be specific enough for them to be useful for monitoring weekly or monthly progress.

As should be obvious by now, an informal reading inventory provides considerable information to teachers about readers. In fact, some schools require teachers to administer an IRI to every student at the beginning of the year to determine reading levels and specific instructional goals. Ms. Crockett routinely administers an IRI to her entering first-graders each fall. In Mr. Haywood's school, the school's reading specialist administers an IRI to students who are formally referred for a special education evaluation because of reading difficulties. Teachers may create their own informal reading inventories, but increasingly they use published inventories rather than creating their own assessment materials. One of the most widely used is the *Qualitative Reading Inventory-4* or *QRI-4*, by Leslie and Caldwell (2006).

Getting Started with the IRIs

The first step in using most IRIs is to ask the student to read from a graded word list, typically twenty words. In commercially published IRIs, words that are commonly mastered at each grade level are included. Many IRIs have alternate lists; that is, two or more sets of twenty words at each level. Levels usually range from early first grade, sometimes called **primer,** through middle or high school level. For example, the QRI-4 has graded word lists and reading passages ranging from preprimer level to level 6, and even upper middle school and high school levels.

A teacher begins an IRI assessment by selecting the word list expected to most closely match the student's reading level. Ms. Crockett begins with the preprimer level for all her entering first-graders. Figure 3.8 shows three word recognition lists from the QRI-4 administered to a student named Jesse from Ms. Crockett's first-grade class. The purpose of the word recognition lists primarily is to determine a starting point for administering the oral reading passages. However, the QRI-4 also allows the teacher to distinguish between words the student recognizes automatically and those the student identifies using decoding strategies. According to Leslie and Caldwell (2006, 47), "if a student reads a word within one second, we can assume that the student has identified the word automatically." The words a student can read automatically sometimes are referred to as sight vocabulary words because students appear to recognize them on sight. However, Leslie and Caldwell recommend the use of the term *automatic word recognition,* because there is some evidence that students use auditory skills when retrieving "sight" words from memory.

Teachers hope to help students build large automatic or sight vocabularies so they can read fluently and focus on comprehension. By examining Figure 3.8,

FIGURE 3.8 Word Recognition Lists for Levels Preprimer through Grade 1

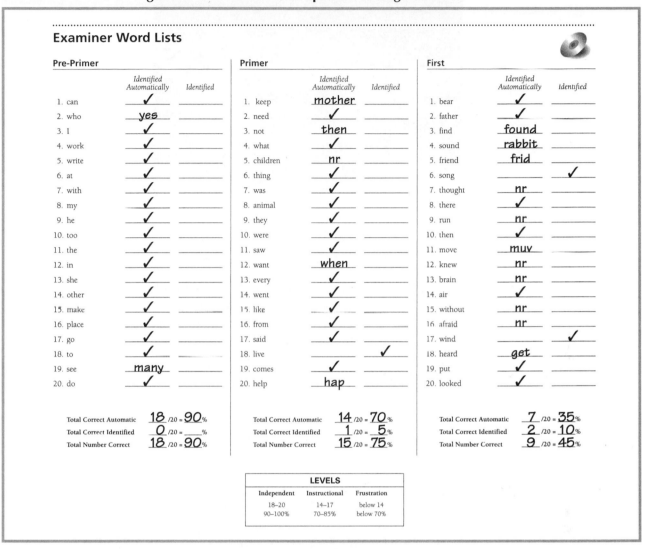

Examiner Word Lists

Pre-Primer

	Identified Automatically	Identified
1. can	✓	
2. who	yes	
3. I	✓	
4. work	✓	
5. write	✓	
6. at	✓	
7. with	✓	
8. my	✓	
9. he	✓	
10. too	✓	
11. the	✓	
12. in	✓	
13. she	✓	
14. other	✓	
15. make	✓	
16. place	✓	
17. go	✓	
18. to	✓	
19. see	many	
20. do	✓	

Total Correct Automatic **18** /20 = **90**%
Total Correct Identified **0** /20 = ___ %
Total Number Correct **18** /20 = **90**%

Primer

	Identified Automatically	Identified
1. keep	mother	
2. need	✓	
3. not	then	
4. what	✓	
5. children	nr	
6. thing	✓	
7. was	✓	
8. animal	✓	
9. they	✓	
10. were	✓	
11. saw	✓	
12. want	when	
13. every	✓	
14. went	✓	
15. like	✓	
16. from	✓	
17. said	✓	
18. live		✓
19. comes	✓	
20. help	hap	

Total Correct Automatic **14** /20 = **70**%
Total Correct Identified **1** /20 = **5**%
Total Number Correct **15** /20 = **75**%

First

	Identified Automatically	Identified
1. bear	✓	
2. father	✓	
3. find	found	
4. sound	rabbit	
5. friend	frid	
6. song		✓
7. thought	nr	
8. there	✓	
9. run	nr	
10. then	✓	
11. move	muv	
12. knew	nr	
13. brain	nr	
14. air	✓	
15. without	nr	
16. afraid	nr	
17. wind		✓
18. heard	get	
19. put	✓	
20. looked	✓	

Total Correct Automatic **7** /20 = **35**%
Total Correct Identified **2** /20 = **10**%
Total Number Correct **9** /20 = **45**%

LEVELS

Independent	Instructional	Frustration
18–20	14–17	below 14
90–100%	70–85%	below 70%

Leslie, Lauren & Caldwell, Joanne. (2006). *Qualitative Reading Inventory-4*. Boston, MA: Allyn and Bacon. Reprinted by permission of the publisher.

it is obvious that Jesse identified eighteen of twenty words automatically at the preprimer level; fourteen of twenty at the primer level and seven of twenty at the first-grade level. Note the criteria for independent, instructional, and frustration level used by Leslie and Caldwell at the bottom of Figure 3.8. Do not be surprised to find that these criteria vary somewhat depending on the source and depending on whether the criteria are applied to words read from lists versus words read in context. We discuss independent, instructional, and frustration levels at some length in the following sections.

Once Ms. Crockett determined the instructional, independent, and frustration levels for Jesse based on his performance on the word recognition lists, she administered the oral passages. Because Jesse was a beginning first-grader and because his word list performance indicated independent level at the preprimer level, Ms. Crockett began by administering to Jesse an oral passage at the preprimer level. Jesse read "Lost and Found," a narrative selection; Ms. Crockett's marking of the passage is shown in Figure 3.9. Jesse read 71 **words correct**

per minute (wcpm) and answered all comprehension questions correctly at the preprimer level, confirming that he does read independently at this level.

Ms. Crockett next administered another narrative selection, "The Pig Who Learned to Read"; her markings are shown in Figure 3.10 (p. 86). As you can see, Jesse had a little more difficulty with this passage. He read 36 wcpm and answered four of six comprehension questions correctly. Based on his performance on the passage and the word recognition list, Ms. Crockett determined that Jesse is reading primer material at the instructional level.

To confirm the upper limit of Jesse's reading level, Ms. Crockett asked Jesse to read orally a third narrative passage, "The Bear and the Rabbit." Jesse's reading slowed down considerably, and he self-corrected more frequently as he read this passage (Figure 3.11, p. 87). He read 28 wcpm and answered three of four comprehension questions. Ms. Crockett determined Jesse currently reads first-grade material at frustration level. It is important to note that the formulae in Figures 3.9, 3.10, and 3.11 for wcpm taken from the QRI-4 require that the number of errors from the entire passage be subtracted from words per minute (wpm). Calculation of wcpm in this fashion inflates the error rate significantly. It is common practice to calculate wcpm by subtracting **errors per minute** from wpm (rather than subtracting the total number of errors), and we recommend following this practice.

Importantly, to calculate wcpm most experts require the reader to read one minute and simply subtract the number of errors from the total number of words read. There is a simple formula available for passages longer than one

---

"Lost and Found"

I̲ lost m̲y̲ cat.

Where was s̲h̲e̲?

I̲ looked inside t̲h̲e̲ house.

I̲ looked under t̲h̲e̲ bed.

I̲ looked outside t̲o̲o̲.

I̲ lost m̲y̲ dog.

Where was h̲e̲?

I̲ looked inside t̲h̲e̲ house.

I̲ looked under t̲h̲e̲ bed.

I̲ looked outside t̲o̲o̲.

I found m̲y̲ cat.

I found m̲y̲ dog.

Where were they?

They were in the same place.
       in c
They were under t̲h̲e̲ table. (64 words)

Number of Miscues
(Total Accuracy): *64 -1 = 63 = 98%*

Number of Meaning-Change Miscues
(Total Acceptability): *64 - 0 = 64 = 100%*

Total Accuracy		Total Acceptability
(0–1 miscue)	✓ Independent	(0–1 miscue)
2–6 miscues	___ Instructional	___ 2–3 miscues
7+ miscues	___ Frustration	___ 4+ miscues

Rate: 64 × 60 = 3,840/ *53* seconds = *71* WPM

72 WPM – *1* errors = *73* CWPM

Questions for "Lost and Found"

1. What did the person in the story lose?
   Explicit: cat or dog

   her cat

2. What else did the person in the story lose?
   Explicit: cat or dog, depending on the answer above

   dog

3. Where did the person in the story look?
   Explicit: inside the house, under the bed, or outside

   under the bed

4. Where else did the person in the story look?
   Explicit: inside the house, under the bed, or outside, depending on the answer above

   outside and inside

5. Where did the person find the dog and cat?
   Explicit: in the same place or under the table

   under the table

Number Correct Explicit: _5_

Total: _5_

✓ Independent: 5 correct

___ Instructional: 4 correct

___ Frustration: 0–3 correct

FIGURE 3.9 Jesse's Reading of "Lost and Found"

Leslie, Lauren & Caldwell, Joanne. (2006). *Qualitative Reading Inventory-4.* Boston, MA: Allyn and Bacon. Reprinted by permission of the publisher.

minute; it requires that the quotient obtained by dividing the number of words read correctly by the number of seconds to read the passage be multiplied by 60 (Figure 3.12, p. 87). Suppose Shelby, a fifth-grader served by Mr. Haywood, the special education teacher, reads orally from a passage of 190 words. She makes fifteen errors and reads the passage in one minute, fifty-eight seconds (118 seconds). Her wcpm is calculated in Figure 3.13 (p. 88). We will discuss other applications of these simple formulas later in the chapter.

Because most IRIs do not require strict standardization procedures, such as the use of exactly the same administration directions each time, teachers may not obtain the same kind of information from the word lists each time it is administered. If time allows, it is safest to begin by administering a passage at the student's independent reading level, and administering passages until

"The Pig Who Learned to Read"

> *c*
> (Once) there was a pig. His name was Pete. He lived
> *the*
> *Pet*
> on a farm. He was not like other pigs. He was
> *is c*
> (special) He wanted to learn to read. His father said,
> *Pet*
> "But pigs can't read!" "I don't care," said Pete. "I
> want to read."
>
> *Pet*
> One day Pete went to a boy who lived on the farm.
> *c*
> (Teach) me to read," he said. The boy said,
> "But you're a pig. I don't know if I can. But I'll do
> what my mother and father did with me." Every
> night before bed, the boy read to the pig. The pig
> *lived*
> loved the (stories) He liked one called "Pat the
> *the c*   *Pat*
> Bunny" best. A week later Pete asked to take the
> *brarn*
> book to the barn. He looked at the words. He
> thought about what the boy had said. He did that
> every day. One day he read a story to the boy. He
> was so happy! After that he read to the other
> animals every night. The boy was happy too,(be-)
> (cause) he'd taught his first pig to read. (176 words)

Number of Total Miscues
(Total Accuracy): *176 -11 = 165 = 94%*

Number of Meaning-Change Miscues
(Total Acceptability): *176 - 5 = 171 = 97%*

Total Accuracy		Total Acceptability
0–4 miscues	___ Independent	0–4 miscues
(5–18 miscues)	✓ Instructional	(5–9 miscues)
19+ miscues	___ Frustration	10+ miscues

Rate: 176 × 60 = 10,560/*273* seconds = *39* WPM

___ WPM – ___ errors = ___ CWPM

Questions for "The Pig Who Learned to Read"

1. Who was this story about?
   Explicit: Pete the pig
   Pet
   pig

2. What did Pete want?
   Explicit: to learn to read
   to read

3. What did Pete do to get what he wanted?
   Explicit: he asked the boy who lived on the farm to teach him
   he asked the boy
   to teach him to read

4. Why was the boy not sure he could teach the pig to read?
   Implicit: because pigs didn't learn to read or because the boy had never taught anyone to read before
   because he was an animal

5. What did the boy do to teach Pete to read?
   Explicit: he read to him every night
   he read a little bit to him
   and let him read a little bit

6. What did the pig do in order to learn how to read?
   Implicit: he matched the words with what the boy had said. He did that every day.
   he - don't know

Number Correct Explicit: __3__

Number Correct Implicit: __1__

Total: __4__

___ Independent: 6 correct

✓ Instructional: 4–5 correct

___ Frustration: 0–3 correct

FIGURE 3.10 Jesse's Reading of "The Pig Who Learned to Read"

Leslie, Lauren & Caldwell, Joanne. (2006). *Qualitative Reading Inventory-4.* Boston, MA: Allyn and Bacon. Reprinted by permission of the publisher.

instructional and frustration levels are determined, as Ms. Crockett did with Jesse. The idea is to determine the highest level at which the student can read with success. Complicating matters is the fact that many students may perform at instructional level at two or more levels. And struggling readers sometimes perform at two or more instructional or frustration levels but fail to obtain an independent level. This inconsistency should not be considered a flaw in IRIs; rather, it reflects the nature of how readers learn, with variability and inconsistency. To maximize what they learn from administering an IRI, teachers perform both quantitative and qualitative analyses of IRI results.

"The Bear and the Rabbit"

Once there was a very big bear. He lived in the
side said
woods. He was sad (because) he didn't have anyone

to play with. He said to his father, "How can I find

a friend?" His father said, "By being you." "But all
for lot
the animals are afraid of me," said the bear. "I can't
ever
even get near them."

But one day the bear was sitting by a river. He
so
was singing softly to himself. A rabbit lived near the
hid
river. He looked out of his hole when he heard the

bear's song. He thought, "Anyone who sings like

that must be nice. Maybe I don't need to be afraid of

him. It would be nice to have a friend." The rabbit

went and got his horn. Very softly he began to play.
must wet
His music went well (with) the bear's song. The bear
The con   sowly
looked around. He couldn't see the rabbit. Slowly,

the rabbit walked up to the bear. He kept playing
the c
and the bear kept singing. They were both happy
and c   the janned
that they had (found) a friend. And a bird joined in
sing c
the song. (181 words)

Number of Total Miscues
(Total Accuracy): *181 - 20 = 161* = 89%

Number of Meaning-Change Miscues
(Total Acceptability): *181 - 17 = 164* = 91%

Total Accuracy		Total Acceptability
0–4 miscues	___ Independent ___	0–4 miscues
5–19 miscues	___ Instructional	5–9 miscues
(20+ miscues)	✓ Frustration ___	(10+ miscues)

Rate: 181 × 60 = 10,860/ *345* seconds = *31* WPM

31 WPM – *17* errors = *14* CWPM

Questions for "The Bear and the Rabbit"

1. Why was the bear sad at the beginning of the story?
   Explicit: because he didn't have anyone to play with

   √ *because he didn't have a friend*

2. Why did the father think that the bear could find a friend just by being himself?
   Implicit: the bear was nice and being nice makes friends

   ✗ *because - I don't know*

3. What was the bear doing as he sat by a river?
   Explicit: singing

   √ *singing*

4. What did the rabbit think when he heard the bear singing?
   Explicit: that the bear must be nice; he doesn't have to be afraid of him; it would be nice to have a friend

   √ *he was nice*

5. What did the rabbit do?
   Explicit: went and got his horn; played his horn

   ✗ *said hello*

6. Why did the bear and the rabbit become friends?
   Implicit: because of their love of music

   ✗ *they knew each other was nice*

Number Correct Explicit: _*3*_

Number Correct Implicit: _*0*_

Total: _*3*_

___ Independent: 6 correct

___ Instructional: 4–5 correct

✓ Frustration: 0–3 correct

FIGURE 3.11 Jesse's Reading of "The Bear and the Rabbit"

Leslie, Lauren & Caldwell, Joanne. (2006). *Qualitative Reading Inventory-4.* Boston, MA: Allyn and Bacon. Reprinted by permission of the publisher.

FIGURE 3.12 Formula to Determine Words Read Correctly per Minute (WCPM)

$$\text{WCPM} = \frac{\text{Number of words (correct)}}{\text{Number of seconds read}} \times 60 = \underline{\quad}$$

FIGURE 3.13 Shelby's Words Read Correctly per Minute

$$\text{WCPM} = \frac{175}{118} \times 60 = \underline{89}$$

Quantitative Analyses of IRIs

Independent, instructional, and frustration levels. Quantitative analyses help teachers understand how students are performing, their inter-reader variability (reading area strengths and weaknesses between students) and intra-reader variability (strengths and weaknesses within the same student). One index of performance is reading level. Level is important to determine early on to help match a student's skill level to the appropriate level of reading material. As previously mentioned, to aid in this process teachers quantitatively determine a student's independent, instructional, and frustration reading levels by counting the number of reading errors the student makes while reading the selected passage orally and comparing the counts to some standard.

Betts (1946) developed one of the first and most useful standards for determining independent, instructional, and frustration levels, and his criteria are reproduced in Table 3.1. In his system, pleasure reading occurs at the independent level, and homework can be assigned at this level. According to Betts,

TABLE 3.1   Betts Criteria for Determining Reading Level

Reading Level	Word Recognition		Comprehension	Symptoms of Difficulty
Independent	99%	1/100	90%	None
Instructional	95%	5/100	75%	Some
Frustration	90%	10/100	50%	Many

Note: Adapted from RISE Reading (1976). Edited by J. Estill Alexander, College of Education (University of Tennessee, Knoxville).

there are no overt signs of difficulty at this level, such as lip movements, pointing at individual words, slow word by word reading, fidgeting, and grimacing; the student reads fluently, achieves maximum comprehension, and needs very little if any help. On the other hand, the student who reads at the frustration level gains very little from the activity and has difficulty pronouncing words and comprehending passages. Neither pleasure reading nor instruction can occur at this level; reading at this level is often accompanied by signs of tension and anxiety. Instruction should occur at the intermediate or instructional level; word recognition and comprehension are challenging, but they do not preclude general understanding of the content. Students will gain significantly from content presented at the instructional level, particularly when teachers provide support such as preteaching and guided reading activities.

Interestingly, in using the Betts criteria, Powell (1969) and Powell and Dunkeld (1971) found that younger students could make more word recognition errors at their instructional level and maintain higher levels of comprehension than could older students. Specifically, ending first-grade students could make 16–17 errors of 100 words read and still maintain a 70 percent comprehension rate. But the comprehension of sixth-grade students suffered more when the students made the same number of errors. In fact, in order to maintain a 70 percent comprehension rate, they needed to exhibit no more than 5–6 errors. Consequently, Powell developed leveled criteria, by grade, as shown in Table 3.2. In addition to determining comprehension levels, teachers can analyze the errors students make when reading passages orally.

TABLE 3.2   Powell Criteria for Determining Reading Level

Reading Level	Grade Level of Passage	Word Recognition	Comprehension
Independent		94% and above	81% and above
Instructional	2nd and below	87%–93%	55%–80%
Frustration		below 87%	below 55%
Independent		96% and above	85% and above
Instructional	3rd to 5th	92%–95%	60%–85%
Frustration		below 92%	below 60%
Independent		97% and above	91% and above
Instructional	6th and above	94%–96%	65%–90%
Frustration		below 94%	below 65%

Note: Adapted from Mariotti and Homan (2005). *Linking Reading Assessment to Instruction.* Mahwah, NJ: Lawrence Erlbaum.

Miscue analysis and its role in the IRI.   Oral reading errors are often referred to as **miscues,** a term first used by Goodman in the 1960s, to refer to unexpected responses a reader makes to a text. Miscue analysis is a special type of error analysis, a technique we discussed earlier in this chapter. Although miscues represent departures from the printed text, they ". . . are not random, capricious, or evidence of carelessness but reveal the logical predictions readers make based on their background knowledge, experience, and what they know about language" (Cousin, Berghoff, and Martens 1999, 153). The use of the term *miscues* rather than error is based on the assumption that readers are using some "cues" about a word, such as phonics, structure, and context, and ignoring others (McKenna and Stahl 2003).

What are the most common miscues?   Major types of miscues include: (a) **omission** (a word skipped during oral reading); (b) **insertion** (a word or phrase read that is not in the text); (c) **substitution** (one word replaced by another); (d) **reversal** (a change in the printed word order); (e) **helper supplied word** (a word supplied by a helper when the reader pauses too long); (f) **repetition** (a word repeated unnecessarily); (g) **lack of prosody** (reading without attention to punctuation such as commas, periods, and question marks; (h) **hesitation** (a pause in oral reading, but one not long enough to force the helper to supply the word); (i) **mispronunciation** (incorrect sounding out of a word); and (j) **self-correction** (rereading a word or phrase a second time within three seconds to eliminate an error).

This list of miscues is not exhaustive, but it represents the most common ones. How can a teacher know which miscues should be scored? Are some more critical to understanding beginning reading than others? Unfortunately, experts do not agree universally about the meaningfulness and relevance of some of the miscues. For example, should substitutions that maintain meaning and repetitions be considered healthy beginning signs of comprehension monitoring and, like immediate self-corrections, be ignored in the miscue scoring process? Because of the lack of consensus regarding the importance of the miscues, there is a corresponding controversy surrounding the best proce-dure for determining which miscues should be scored, which may affect con-clusions about characterizing a student's reading performance as representing easy text (e.g., 95–100 percent correct), instructional text (90–94 percent cor-rect), or hard text (80–89 percent correct), according to Clay (2000).

According to McKenna and Stahl (2003) teachers should define miscues by adhering to the directions found in the assessment instrument being used if possible; if the instrument contains no directions regarding this point, or the analysis comes from informal assessment (such as running records) taken from the curriculum, score the following six miscues: (a) omissions, (b) insertions, (c) substitutions, (d) reversals, (e) helper supplied words, and (f) repetitions. Importantly, all miscues, even those not scored, should be marked, because they may provide useful information regarding reading skills. McKenna and Stahl also urge the teacher to address four important questions when evaluat-ing passages read and the related miscue analysis, namely:

a. For substitution miscues, did the reader substitute a word or phrase that preserves meaning?
b. Did the reading follow grammatical rules so that the reading sounded like a language?

c. When a word was miscalled, did it have sound or graphic similarity to the actual word in the passage?

d. When errors were made, did the reader make self-corrections? If so, how?

By answering these questions, teachers can evaluate qualitatively the level of reading sophistication, the extent to which readers use context cues, and ultimately, the need for specific interventions. Students who fail to preserve meaning, to follow grammatical rules, to demonstrate awareness of the graphic quality of words, or to attempt credible self-corrections may need more intensive remediation than those who exhibit one or more of these skills.

Student Name **Jesse**   Selections **The Pig Who Learned to Read**

1. Text Word	2. Miscue Substitution Mispronunciation	3. Is Similar: Beginning Letter Patterns	4. Is Similar: Ending Letter Patterns	5. Is Similar: Vowel Patterns	6. Retains Acceptable Grammar	7. Retains Meaning	8. Is Self-Corrected
once	omitted						yes
Pete	Pet	yes	yes	no	yes	yes	no
the	a	no	no	no	yes	yes	no
special	omitted						no
said	in	no	no	no	no	no	yes
teach	omitted						yes
loved	lived	yes	yes	no	no	no	no
stories	omitted						no
Pete	Pet	yes	yes	no	yes	yes	no
barn	brarn	yes	no	yes	no	no	no
because	omitted						no
Total Miscues: Mispronunciations/ Substitutions	11	Similar Beginning	Similar Ending	Similar Vowel	Acceptable Grammar	Retains Meaning	Self-Corrected
Analysis: Columns Total		4	3	1	3	3	3
Columns Total/Total Miscues = %		36	27	9	8	27	27

FIGURE 3.14 Jesse's Miscues from "The Pig Who Learned to Read"

Leslie, Lauren & Caldwell, Joanne. (2006). *Qualitative Reading Inventory-4.* Boston, MA: Allyn and Bacon. Reprinted by permission of the publisher.

Coding miscues.   How should miscues be coded on the teacher's printed page? Typically, a teacher uses a second copy of the printed material the student reads from to indicate miscues. Jesse's miscues from his reading of "The Pig Who Learned to Read" are presented in Figure 3.14 on page 91. Although some inconsistencies exist in how experts advise teachers to code miscues, some conventional strategies are generally acceptable. No matter which code is chosen to indicate which miscue, the most important point to keep in mind is this—be consistent. Use the same mark to indicate the same miscue each time it occurs, and when multiple teachers are comparing students' records, all teachers should use exactly the same code. Typically, an omission is indicated by a circle, a repetition by an underline, an insertion by adding the word above the print line, and the like. Table 3.3 provides specific directions about some of the most commonly used codes.

Calculating miscues in connected text.   Once scored, miscues can be included in a formula to determine words read correctly by simply subtracting the number of miscues from the total number of words in a passage, and dividing that number by the total number of words (in the passage). Figure 3.15 shows

TABLE 3.3   Types of Miscues and How to Code Them

Type of Miscue	Description	Scored	Coding
Omission	Reader skips one or more words	yes	over (the) hill *over hill*
Insertion	Reader adds one or more words	yes	**big**, over the hill *over the big hill*
Substitution	Reader replaces a word (or phrase) with another word (or phrase)	yes	**a** over the hill *over a hill*
Reversal	Reader switches order of words	yes	**~** over the hill *over hill the*
Helper-supplied word	Reader does not attempt the word; teacher gives help	yes	**H** over the hill *over the ___*
Repetition	Reader repeats one word or consecutive words	yes	**R** over the hill *over the the hill*
Self-correction	Reader re-reads within a few seconds to correct an error	no	**there SC** over the hill *over there the hill*
Hesitation	Reader pauses but reads the word correctly	no	**P** over the hill *over the (pause) hill*
Lack of prosody	Reader ignores punctuation	no	**I** . . . over the hill. He ran. . . *over the hill he ran.*

Note: Text is printed in nonitalics. What student reads is printed in *italics*. Coding is printed in **bold.**

FIGURE 3.15 Formula to Determine Percentage of Words Correct in Passage

$$\text{Percentage of WC} = \frac{\text{Total words in passage} - \text{miscues}}{\text{Total words in passage}} = \underline{\hspace{1cm}}$$

this formula. (Remember, if the intent is to calculate the number of words correct per minute [wcpm], use Figure 3.12.) Figure 3.16 shows an application of the formula in Figure 3.15 for Shelby, the fifth-grade student identified with a learning disability who receives reading instruction from Mr. Haywood, the special education teacher. The score in Figure 3.16 reflects Shelby's performance (percentage of words read correctly) on a third–grade-level reading passage.

By examining either Betts' (Table 3.1) or Powell's (Table 3.2) criteria, Mr. Haywood can characterize Shelby's reading level as independent versus instructional versus frustration. Using either criterion, her percentage correct score on the third–grade-level passage places her at instructional level. It is possible to use miscue data to calculate additional quantitative scores, if desirable. For example, if Mr. Haywood is interested in comparing Shelby's performance over time to determine whether her self-corrections increase, a self-correction score may be computed by dividing the number of self-corrections by the total number of miscues. Similarly, the number of helper words the teacher supplies might be compared from time 1 to time 2, either by using the raw score when the passage lengths are the same or by calculating a percentage (of helper miscues relative to total miscues). In fact, percentages may be calculated for any type of miscue, or for that matter, for other literacy measures (using the formula presented in Figure 3.15). Using this formula, a student's tendency to make certain types of errors, relative to other types, can be tracked.

Quantifying comprehension. Not only are teachers interested in calculating quantitative measures of oral reading, but they are also interested in quantifying comprehension, and for the same reasons (such as determining differences between students and differences within one student across type of comprehension questions or over time). The formula presented in Figure 3.15 can be changed slightly to accommodate results from assessment of comprehension. The starting point typically is a set of questions, posed to a student after a passage has been read. The basic formula is presented in Figure 3.17; scores for Shelby's responses to questions about the third-grade passage are presented in Figure 3.18.

The numbers generated from the comprehension percent correct formula represent Shelby's score (75 percent correct) on a third–grade-level

FIGURE 3.16 Shelby's Percentage of Words Correct in Passage

$$\text{Percentage of WC} = \frac{100 - 5}{100} = \frac{95}{100} = \underline{95\%}$$

FIGURE 3.17 **Formula to Determine Percentage of Comprehension Correct**

$$\text{Comprehension Percent Correct} = \frac{\text{Total number of questions} - \text{errors}}{\text{Total number of questions}} = \underline{\quad}\%$$

FIGURE 3.18 **Percentage of Comprehension Correct for Shelby**

$$\text{Comprehension Percent Correct} = \frac{20 - 5}{20} = \frac{15}{20} = \underline{75\%}$$

passage. According to Betts' and Powell's criteria, Shelby's word reading and comprehension levels are at the instructional level on the third-grade passages she read. The reading specialist administered an IRI to Shelby when she was first referred for special education because of reading problems at the beginning of her fifth-grade year. Her scores on the IRI are presented in Table 3.4. On a second-grade passage, Shelby obtained a word recognition percentage correct score of 99 and a comprehension percentage correct score of 90. On a fourth-grade passage, she obtained a word recognition percent correct score of 70 and a comprehension percent correct score of 45. She appears to be appropriately placed at the third-grade level using either Betts' or Powell's criteria.

Saimah is another fifth-grade student who has supplemental reading instruction with Mr. Haywood. Her IRI scores are presented in Table 3.5. Saimah earned a word recognition percent score of 99 and a comprehension percent correct score of 90 on level 2 material. She earned a word recognition percent correct score of 95 and a comprehension percent correct score of 40 from reading level 3 material. On a level 4 passage, she earned a word recognition score of 93, and a comprehension percent score of 25. This is a pattern of scores consistent with good word recognition skills, but poor ability to comprehend the content. To further check this assumption, Mr. Haywood reads orally a level 3 passage to Saimah. Her comprehension level is 50 percent, similar to how she scored when she read the passage herself. Consequently, Mr. Haywood knows that Saimah will need supplemental help

TABLE 3.4   **Word Recognition and Comprehension Scores for Shelby**

	Word Recognition	Reading Comprehension
Level 2	99	90
Level 3	90	75
Level 4	70	45

TABLE 3.5   Word Recognition, Reading Comprehension, and Listening Comprehension Scores for Saimah

	Word Recognition	Reading Comprehension	Listening Comprehension
Level 2	99	90	
Level 3	90	40	50
Level 4	93	25	

in building oral and listening vocabulary, relating what she reads to what she already knows, and preteaching vocabulary before reading. With this support, he will attempt to group her with Shelby at times and also to work with her individually to build vocabulary and comprehension.

Sammy, a beginning third-grade child in Mr. Haywood's school has been referred by his parents for a special education evaluation. They are concerned that he is frustrated with reading and calls himself "stupid." The school reading specialist administered an IRI to Sammy to gain information before pursuing a full evaluation to determine whether he has a learning disability. His IRI scores are presented in Table 3.6. On the level 3 passage, Sammy earned a word recognition percentage correct score of 74 (frustration level), but a comprehension percent correct score of 90 (independent level). Sammy scored at the independent level on both word recognition and comprehension on a beginning second-grade passage, but at the frustration level in both on a fourth-grade passage. Sammy has great difficulty decoding words, but he uses context cues very well. In addition, he has a good educational background in general and an enriched home life. He was tested recently by an independent psychologist who was not working within the school system, and the psychologist indicated that Sammy exhibits characteristics of dyslexia because, in part, he has difficulty mastering sound-symbol relationships. (Dyslexia is discussed in Chapter 2.)

TABLE 3.6   Word Recognition and Comprehension Scores for Sammy

	Word Recognition	Reading Comprehension
Level 2	95	100
Level 3	74	90
Level 4	50	70

School personnel decide that Sammy will benefit from instruction in the core program in his classroom, which provides blocks of time for students to read books independently and with peers and to receive explicit instruction and practice in working with words. In addition, he will participate in small group tutoring beyond the regular school day in a code-emphasis (i.e., phonics emphasis) program. The reading specialist will monitor his progress every few weeks. If he does not make progress, he will be referred for a full evaluation for special education. Specific techniques often used for progress monitoring are addressed in Chapter 4.

Qualitative Analyses of IRIs

In addition to providing scores and percentages, teachers can use IRIs to yield qualitative information by examining the specific nature of both miscues and comprehension errors. A qualitative analysis provides insight into the nature of the reader's strengths and weaknesses.

Qualitative analysis of miscues.   The teacher may ask several questions about miscues. For example, if the miscue is a substitution, the teacher should examine whether the substituted word is similar to the printed word, not only because of the way it looks (graphically), but also in terms of semantics

(meaning) and **syntax** (function). For example, consider substitution of the word "him" for "he." "He" is graphically similar to "him," at least initially; both reference some male previously mentioned in the passage so they share the same meaning. Also, both are pronouns. Finally, it is important to note self-corrections. Effective readers monitor themselves, and when miscues do not make sense, good readers will notice the lack of fit and at least make an effort to self correct. Table 3.3 presents common miscues and how to score them.

Consideration of these miscue patterns for a struggling reader can be important as the teacher plans instruction. Also, over time teachers develop a sense of developmental patterns that helps make the deviations characteristic of weak readers more apparent. To help beginning teachers understand the context of miscue analyses, McKenna and Stahl (2003) collected some statistics from the literature regarding the frequency of various types of miscues. From their analyses, they offer several conclusions:

a. Approximately one-half of first-graders' miscues are omissions.
b. Insertions comprise only about 10 percent (or less) of all miscues.
c. As students mature, substitutions become more common and omissions less common.
d. For beginning readers, substitutions are simply guesses based on the first letter of the word.
e. As readers gain sophistication, their substitutions begin more to resemble the phonetic structure of the printed word.
f. Letter reversals, such as *no* and *on,* are common in the first grade but typically disappear by second grade.

Qualitative analysis of comprehension.   Different informal reading inventories may provide different types of activities for assessing comprehension. For example, directions may require students to retell as much of a passage as possible after reading it, and without cues—at least initially, a simple **retelling** of content. Other directions may require students to respond to specific questions about the passages, with and/or without looking back at the passages. Again, the teacher can get valuable information by analyzing differential performance on these item types. For example, even though a student may have forgotten the answer to a specific question within a particular passage, the student may be able to look back quickly at the passage and find the answer, indicating some level of comprehension. And when teachers compare student responses after they read passages with pictures to responses after they read similar passages without pictures, teachers gain insight regarding the extent to which students rely on **context cues** for help.

According to Calkins (2001), teachers can use retelling to determine use of context cues. Typically, the teacher asks the reader to retell the passage as though the listener had never read or heard the content before. After the reader has finished retelling the content, the teacher may ask whether there is anything else. If the student gives no other information, the teacher may read the title of the passage to the reader and ask whether revisiting the title helps to prompt some ideas. The teacher gives no other help. Scoring is determined by comparing the ideas recalled by the reader to those listed by the authors of the IRI.

The QRI-4 uses retelling scoring sheets for each passage selection. The scoring sheet from Jesse's retelling of "The Pig Who Learned to Read" is shown in Figure 3.19. This sheet provides a systematic mechanism to determine how many of the ideas embedded in a story or passage can be recalled. Although the scores are not used typically to make comparisons across students, they may be helpful to a teacher who uses the same stories for

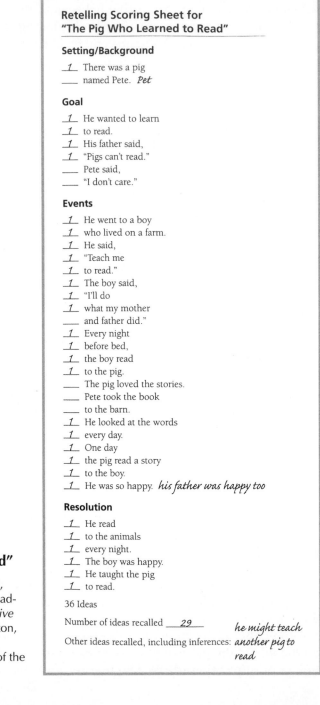

FIGURE 3.19 Jesse's Retelling of "The Pig Who Learned to Read"

Leslie, Lauren & Caldwell, Joanne. (2006). Primer Reading Passage from *Qualitative Reading Inventory-4.* Boston, MA: Allyn and Bacon. Reprinted by permission of the publisher.

Retelling Scoring Sheet for "The Pig Who Learned to Read"

Setting/Background

_1_ There was a pig
___ named Pete. *Pet*

Goal

_1_ He wanted to learn
_1_ to read.
_1_ His father said,
_1_ "Pigs can't read."
___ Pete said,
___ "I don't care."

Events

_1_ He went to a boy
_1_ who lived on a farm.
_1_ He said,
_1_ "Teach me
_1_ to read."
_1_ The boy said,
_1_ "I'll do
_1_ what my mother
___ and father did."
_1_ Every night
_1_ before bed,
_1_ the boy read
_1_ to the pig.
___ The pig loved the stories.
___ Pete took the book
___ to the barn.
_1_ He looked at the words
_1_ every day.
_1_ One day
_1_ the pig read a story
_1_ to the boy.
_1_ He was so happy. *his father was happy too*

Resolution

_1_ He read
_1_ to the animals
_1_ every night.
_1_ The boy was happy.
_1_ He taught the pig
_1_ to read.

36 Ideas

Number of ideas recalled ___29___

he might teach

Other ideas recalled, including inferences: *another pig to read* multiple students over time. That is, teachers may develop "informal norms," and can determine students' comparative performance based on those, i.e., compare the quality of many stories heard over the years. Also, the retelling scoring sheet can be used to answer fundamental questions, such as:

a. Do the retellings of narrative content maintain the basic structure of the narrative?
b. Is the most important information provided?
c. Do the retellings of expository material contain the main ideas and supporting detail?
d. Is the content told in sequential order?
e. How accurate is the retelling?

Leslie and Caldwell (2006) suggest use of these questions and note that long passages, appropriate for late middle school and high school, can also be qualitatively analyzed using similar questions:

a. Did the retelling include appropriate summary/gist statements or main ideas?
b. Did the retelling provide supportive details (to the main ideas)?
c. Did the retelling include specific ideas, as opposed to vague and general ones?
d. Did the retelling contain generally accurate content?

Leslie and Caldwell also recommend that explicit and implicit questions be developed and used to assess comprehension after passages have been retold. Answers must either come directly from the text or be able to be inferred from the text, and students who provide accurate answers to 90 percent (or more) of the questions are assumed to read at the independent level, from 67 percent to 89 percent correct at the instructional level, and below 67 percent at the frustration level on the passage read.

Think-alouds. Another kind of comprehension item type provided to examiners by the authors of some informal reading inventories requires metacognition and may be referred to as process-aloud or **think-aloud** items. These items require students to stop during reading and describe the thought processes they are engaging to comprehend passage content. For example, students might reveal their efforts to self-monitor by asking themselves questions about the content, by asking themselves to summarize key points, by asking themselves to remember section headings, and so on. The think-aloud process requires thinking about thinking; hence, the "metacognitive" descriptor, a term used to refer to the process of knowing about knowing, whatever the cognitive task, whether it be reading comprehension, reading decoding, or math problem-solving (Flavell 1985). Students who can comprehend well are much better at monitoring how much they know as they read, and applying needed metacognitive strategies as needed; these strategies have been described by the NRP as discussed in Chapter 1 and include tasks such as summarizing, question generation, and comprehension monitoring.

Student response to different types of text. Another feature of some IRIs is the provision of different types of text. In school, students are asked to read stories (narrative text) and to read for technical information in content courses such as biology, geology, and history (expository text), and the more complete informal inventories include both types of passages. Teachers can gain additional **diagnostic** information from differential comprehension of these passages, particularly when the inventory includes prereading items designed to assess prior knowledge of content of expository items. These prereading items can help educators determine the extent to which prior knowledge contributed to successful performance.

Abbreviated Assessment with IRIs

Finally, it is possible to use a brief IRI assessment whenever the teacher is interested only in determining the extent to which students are at or near grade level. In this case, the teacher would administer only the passages appropriate for that particular grade level and for that particular time of the year. For example, if a first-grade teacher wanted this information at year's end, only the passages appropriate for year-end administration would be used. This assessment takes only about 25 percent as long as a full IRI administration.

Using IRIs to Assess Listening Comprehension

Because some students read at a level significantly below the readability level of materials used in the class, particularly at the middle and upper grades, some IRIs include a mechanism for assessing listening comprehension. Assessment of listening comprehension tells teachers generally whether students can benefit from oral reading of content at a given level without significant preteaching of vocabulary and extensive support work. Essentially, the teacher reads a passage at a selected level to the student, then asks the student the corresponding comprehension questions or asks the student to retell the passage. Students who demonstrate better listening comprehension, relative to reading comprehension, will need instruction focused on word recognition, word decoding, and fluency.

Teacher-Made IRIs

Teachers typically do not construct their own IRIs. However, it is sometimes useful to be able to construct an IRI based on a particular set of curriculum materials. Why would a teacher want to construct an IRI? A teacher-made IRI will tell the teacher whether students can read with comprehension the material from a given basal series or other material. Adult educators may wish to construct IRIs with age-appropriate reading materials. Figure 3.20, taken from Ruddell (2002), describes the steps a teacher follows to create an IRI from a basal reader or other reading material.

Limitations of IRIs

Although informal reading inventories can provide extremely useful information, their use does not meet all assessment needs. For example, the data do not allow for peer comparisons, except in a crude way and only relative to those who read the same passages in the same classroom. In addition, technical problems plague this type of assessment, as is true to some extent of all assessment techniques. For example, comprehension levels can change as a function of any number of variables, including changing or rewording questions, using expository versus narrative text (expository text is typically more

FIGURE 3.20 How to do an Informal Reading Inventory

1. From your basal reader or from literature selections, select reading passages that are approximately one hundred to two hundred words long.
   - Try to find passages that represent a self-contained part of a story, such as an introductory episode or one complete story event.
   - Identify six to eight selections that represent different levels of difficulty from grades one through six (e.g., sample different grade-level stories from a basal reader).
   - Use your own judgment about difficulty level, because stories within a given grade level of a basal reader can vary by one or even two grade levels in difficulty.
   - Check your judgment on approximate grade level, using the Fry Readability Graph.
   - Make up a title for each of your selections.
2. Photocopy the selected pages, some of which will contain illustrations; type the title on each; mount them on tagboard; and place your sample passages in a three-ring binder for easy use.
3. Develop six to eight comprehension questions for each passage, including factual (two or three), interpretive (two), applicative (two), and transactive (one or two) questions.
4. Retype the passages in double-spaced format for your binder, to facilitate miscue coding during the student's oral reading.
   - Write the number of words at the end of the passage, to help you estimate the percent of miscues.
   - Make several photocopies of the passages and your accompanying comprehension questions for future use. (One complete set of passages and comprehension questions will be needed for each administration of the IRI, so you will want to save your originals, too.)
5. Before you administer the IRI, determine a reading level starting point (passage difficulty) for the student, based on your instructional observations.
6. As the first passage, use the passage at the level just below the starting level, to ensure reading ease. Use a tape recorder, especially at first, to assist you in checking and refining your coding.
7. Create a comfortable and informal setting for the administration of the IRI, and explain to the student that you are interested in learning more about his or her reading.
8. Begin by asking the child to read the title of the selection and tell what he or she thinks this selection might be about. As each passage is read, use the miscue notational system discussed earlier and ask the questions you have prepared. Or you may wish to use the running record procedure.
9. During the reading, carefully observe the child's interest and persistence in reading the passage.
   - Continue to administer the IRI passages until comprehension drops to approximately the 75 percent level and/or you note about 15 significant miscues per hundred words (15 percent). At this point, you have reached the child's frustration level.
   - Use the information in the table to determine the child's approximate instructional and independent reading placement levels.
10. Complete your analysis and interpretation of the IRI information, and incorporate your insights into your instructional planning and selection of reading experiences for the student.

Ruddell, R. B. (2002). *Teaching Children to Read and Write. Becoming an Effective Literacy Teacher.* (3rd ed.). Boston, MA: Allyn and Bacon.

difficult to comprehend), using different forms of an IRI, using pictures, varying level of prior knowledge of passage content, length of passages, the match between IRI content and classroom tasks, frequency of teacher prompts during reading, and so on (Mariotti and Homan 2005). Similarly, word calling errors may be influenced by the design elements of a particular IRI (e.g., whether the scoring criteria of the particular IRI scoring system counts a semantic miscue as an error, a repetition as an error, etc.). In general, the psychometric qualities (reliability and validity) of elements within the same IRI and among different IRIs vary considerably. It is the responsibility of the teacher to read the manual and the research literature to determine the best products available. In this chapter, we use excerpts from the QRI-4 to provide examples. Some of the most common commercially available IRIs and a description of some of their properties are presented at the end of this chapter in Table 3.9.

■ RUNNING RECORDS

Teachers of reading are sometimes interested in analyzing the oral reading strengths and weaknesses of a student but do not have access to (or prefer not to use) graded passages required to determine frustration, instructional, and independent levels. Perhaps the most widely used strategy is simply to listen to a student read orally *from any source,* code the errors and self-corrections, and determine the reading level of the student according to standard criteria. This procedure leads to creation of a running record and can be especially useful when the teacher is using leveled reading material (discussed later in this chapter). Clay first described this procedure in 1993, along with the following criteria for establishing three levels of proficiency: If the student reads with 95 to 100 percent accuracy the text is considered easy; if the student reads with 90 to 94 percent accuracy the content is considered to be at the student's instructional level; if the student reads with 80 to 89 percent accuracy the content is considered hard. Obviously, the categories represent only crude guidelines to help teachers make decisions about assigning students to reading groups, helping students decide what books may be appropriate for pleasure reading, and so on.

Clay offers several reasons for using running records, including: (a) evaluation of text difficulty; (b) instructional grouping; (c) progress monitoring; and (d) analyses of errors and self-corrections to guide individualized instruction. Clay (1993) and Johnston (2000) discuss the importance of evaluating and coding types of errors, pattern of responses, and self-corrections, in part to determine the extent to which the student obtains phonemic information for the printed letters. In addition, they emphasize the importance of addressing three questions:

1. Did the meaning (semantics) of the text influence errors?
2. Did the structure (syntax) of the text leading up to the error have an impact on the type of error made?
3. Did the visual elements (graphophonic/orthographic) influence the error?

Clay suggests using the symbols *M, S, and V* in the running record to indicate the influence of *m*eaning (semantics), *s*tructure (syntax), and *v*isual information (orthography), respectively, on error production. She presents guidelines for her somewhat unique error analyses coding system and a strategy for recording an Error Ratio, Accuracy Ratio, and Self-Correction Ratio. We prefer to use a modified system and to calculate Percentage Accuracy, rather than focusing on determination of error ratios. See Figures 3.21 and 3.22 for an example of how we calculate and use percentages of accurate reading to determine reading performance.

FIGURE 3.21 Scoring for Running Records

See some of the commonly used scoring conventions below, taken from Clay (2000) and others e.g., McKenna & Stahl, 2003; Temple, Ogle, Crawford, & Kreppon, 2005).

1. Assume an examinee read correctly the following text; it could be scored as below, with each correct response indicated by "+." These marks can be placed over the original text if there is room, or on a separate score sheet.

Sally is playing.	+	+	+			
"Sally is playing," said Jane.	+	+	+	+	+	
"I want to play," said Jane.	+	+	+	+	+	+
Sally and Jane are playing.	+	+	+	+	+	

2. Score an incorrect response by writing the incorrect response above the correct word taken from the text.

Examinee:	run
Text:	ran

one error

3. Record all attempts to read a word.

Examinee:	stay	st	stop
Text	step		

one error

Examinee:	st	st	+
Text:	step		

no error

4. When the examinee corrects a previous error, record a self correction (SC)

Examinee:	fat	farm	SC
Text:	father		

no error

5. No response is indicated by a dash; insertion is indicated by a word recorded over a dash.

Examinee:	— big
Test:	the family

one error, each case

6. When an examinee makes an error, then hesitates for more than 5 seconds the examiner reads the word, and marks the hesitation with a "T," for told.

Examinee:	Silly	
Text:	Sally	T

one error

7. When the examinee asks for help mark the spot with an "A."

Examinee:	----	A	saw
Text:	share		T

one error

8. When the examinee balks, and cannot seem to continue say "try that again," indicate by brackets around the passage, count as one error, and begin scoring again at the point where the balk began.

Examinee:	+	+	(−	−	−)	TTA
Text:	Jane	saw	Sam	and	Jim	one error

9. Indicate a repetition with an "R" and the number of repetitions with a numerical indicator. In some cases a repetition is made but the error is not corrected, or another error occurs. These should be marked as errors.

Examinee:	Show me the cat	R	R2	SC
Text:	Show me the cow			

no error

10. When the examinee reads from right to left, or bottom to top, mark the direction of the effort with an arrow.

FIGURE 3.22 Quantifying the Running Record

We use the following figures to illustrate how a running record can be quantified, based on guidelines established by Clay (2000) and others (Temple, Ogle, Crawford, & Kreppon, 2005).

Step 1. Count the words in the text of interest, minus the number of words in the title

Step 2. Count the errors, and calculate a Proportion (of Errors)

Step 4. Calculate Proportion of Accurate Responses by subtracting the Proportion of Errors from 1

Step 5. Calculate Percentage Accuracy by multiplying the Proportion of Accurate Responses by 100

Step 6. Calculate the Self-Correction Ratio, if needed.

Example: Suppose a text excerpt contains 110 words. To satisfy Step 1 above, simply count the words. To calculate the Proportion of Error, count the number of errors, for example, 20, and divide the total number of words in the passage into the number of errors.

$$\frac{\text{Errors}}{\text{Words}} = \frac{20}{110} = .18$$

To calculate the Proportion of Accurate Responses, subtract .18 from 1, which equals .82.

To calculate Percentage Accuracy, multiply .82 by 100, which equals .82%. This value is less than 90%, which is the minimum value Clay recommends for adequate processing of text. Readers who exhibit a Percentage Accuracy values of 89 or below often fail to comprehend context.

To calculate the Self-Correction Ratio assume that there were 4 self corrections (SC) in the passage of 110 words above. The 4 self corrections represent 4 additional potential errors (E). In total, there were 24 chances to make self corrections, and 4 self corrections. See the following equation:

$$\frac{\text{SC}}{\text{E} + \text{SC}} = \frac{4}{24} = 1:6, \text{ or 1 in 6}$$

Clay cautions against using a copy of the text the student reads as a scoring template because of the lack of room (to record scoring data). Of interest, she also cautions against using a tape recorder because it limits analysis and does not provide a visual record. A copy of a scoring sheet we developed is presented in Figure 3.23. However, not everyone agrees that using the printed text to aid scoring is problematic. In fact, Mariotti and Homan (2005) suggest use of the printed page as part of a traditional miscue analysis coding system to score running records if the teacher already possesses that knowledge. Their scoring scheme is a more traditional strategy; Figure 3.24 presents a contrast of the two (p. 106). Either system can provide helpful information to the teacher, and there is significant overlap. Whichever system is chosen, we recommend consistency, both within teachers who will use the data for progress monitoring, and among teachers who assess the same students for joint decision making.

In summary, a running record provides an authentic assessment. That is, the assessment is directly related to a task the student is asked to perform in the classroom or for homework. Consequently, the assessment data represent real world outcomes, not contrived tasks. Running records typically are used to

FIGURE 3.23 Worksheet and Example Worksheet for Summarizing Running Records

Summary of Running Records

Name: _____   Age: _____   Grade: _____

Examiner: _____   School: _____

Text Titles/Number of words:	Number of errors	%age accuracy*	Number of self corrections/ratio
1. Easy _____	_____	_____	_____
2. Instructional _____	_____	_____	_____
3. Hard _____	_____	_____	_____

Analysis of Errors (cues used, cues neglected, directionality, motivation)

Easy _____

Instructional _____

Hard _____

_____

Page Number	Actual Errors	Error Score	Self Correction

To score errors:
M refers to meaning, S to structure, and V to visual (graphic) characteristics
*Easy, 95% accuracy and above, Instructional, 90–94%, Hard, below 90%

assess automatic word recognition, word decoding skills, and reading fluency. Because errors are analyzed qualitatively to determine whether the reader is using meaning as a decoding strategy, running records also provide some insight into vocabulary and comprehension skills. Further, when comprehension or retelling techniques are used to follow up the oral reading, they can also provide assessment of reading comprehension and vocabulary.

CURRICULUM-BASED ASSESSMENT

Curriculum-based assessment (CBA), curriculum-based measurement (CBM), and curriculum-based evaluation (CBE) are terms sometimes used interchangeably, though some make a distinction among the three (refer to Shinn 1989 and Travers, Eliot, and Kratchowill 1993, for discussion of differences

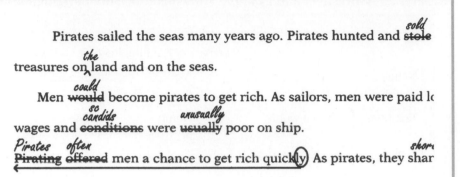

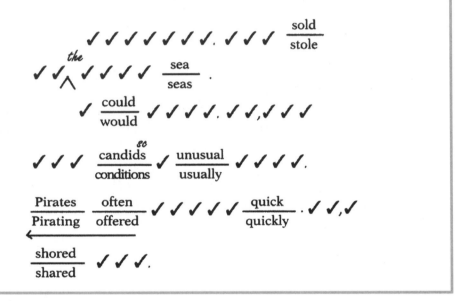

FIGURE 3.24 Comparison of Running Records and Traditional Miscue Analysis

Mariotti, A. S. & Homan, S. P. (2005). *Linking Reading Assessment to Instruction: An Application Worktext for Elementary Classroom Teachers.* (4th ed.). Mahwah, NJ: Lawrence Erlbaum.

among models). After a brief review of curriculum-based models, Travers et al. (1993) conclude that even though each model can be characterized by some uniqueness, the models are more alike than different. Of note, although CBA/CBM/CBE strategies can be used to assess any academic product, our goal for this chapter is to describe how these strategies can be employed to assess reading. Importantly, some of the strategies central to curriculum-based assessments are similar to strategies presented earlier in this chapter, including guidelines for scoring and recording miscues and determining wcpm.

Overton (2006) defines CBA broadly, to refer to teacher-made assessments, often given at the end of an instructional period (such as a unit test), measuring mastery of specific instructional objectives. Using this definition, the teacher-made and teacher-selected assessments that teachers use routinely to assess mastery of instructional objectives and to determine grades are considered CBA. Overton distinguishes between CBA and CBM by noting that CBM refers only to measures of the same skill (such as reading rate) that can be repeated frequently to monitor progress. These measures may be derived from content and materials actually used in the classroom, but Fuchs and Deno (1994) present an argument for using materials that are not curriculum-specific to reduce measurement error. Consider the following example. If Ms. Crockett wants to know whether students in her first-grade class are making adequate progress in reading, she could select reading passages from the basal reader she uses. However, as Fuchs and Deno point out, the readability level of basal readers tends to vary greatly. Consequently, these authors argue for the use of graded material, not specific to the classroom for progress monitoring. Later in the book (Chapter 4), we review some commercially available CBM measures. In this chapter, we address how teachers can construct their own CBM measures. The most appropriate use for teacher-made CBM measures is to gauge student progress in the particular curriculum materials used by the teacher in a given classroom.

CBM of achievement began in earnest during the 1970s with Stanley Deno's efforts to develop an efficient and accurate strategy for assessing the effects of his special education student teachers' interventions. Drawing on the developing field of applied behavior analysis, his goal was to provide a mechanism allowing **operationalization** or measurement of performance, frequent assessment, ease of recording and graphing, and evaluation of responsiveness to a student's curriculum. In principle, this type of assessment should provide a set of standard simple directions to measure short-duration behaviors taken as indicators of basic student achievement in important academic areas, the "vital signs" of student achievement (Shinn and Bamonto 1998).

Following that tradition, we suggest that teachers can conduct a curriculum-based measurement by choosing and then presenting to the student a reading passage from the curriculum. This procedure assesses level of mastery, typically defined as percentage correct (although other indicators may be used such as types of errors, speed of performance, or some combination).

Using Teacher-Constructed CBM to Assess Reading

What kind of specific information can a teacher obtain from using CBM to assess reading fluency? CBM yields measures of reading rate (speed), accuracy, or both. Typically, for young students, the teacher asks the student to read a passage of 100 words taken directly from reading material routinely used in the classroom, as shown in Figure 3.15. To reduce error associated with varying administration procedures, we recommend using proscribed directions. The directions provided by Shinn (1989) are recommended by numerous experts, including McKenna and Stahl (2003), and we see no reason to deviate from this common procedure. Shinn's directions provide very specific guidelines regarding the language used to convey the nature of the task, definitions of error types (such as mispronunciations, substitutions, omissions, hesitations), and scoring (such as using a vertical line through a word to denote an error, allowing a student up to three seconds to self-correct). We reproduce this procedure in Figure 3.25. Using this procedure, it is possible to determine how many words the student read correctly per minute (wcpm), using the formula we mentioned in Figure 3.12.

What does this information mean? Is 50 wcpm good? Is 100 wcpm? The answer is—it depends. Teachers can compare the oral reading scores their students get with norms, based on data taken from large groups of readers at

FIGURE 3.25 Curriculum-Based Measurement Procedures for Assessing and Scoring Oral Reading Fluency

Say to the student: "*When I say 'start,' begin reading aloud at the top of this page. Read across the page* [demonstrate by pointing]. *Try to read each word. If you come to a word you don't know, I'll tell it to you. Be sure to do your best reading. Are there any questions?*"

Say, "*Start.*"

Follow along on your copy of the story, marking the words that are read incorrectly. If a student stops or struggles with a word for 3 seconds, tell the student the word and mark it as incorrect.

Place a vertical line after the last word read and thank the student.

The following guidelines determine which words are counted as correct:

1. *Words read correctly.* Words read correctly are those words that are pronounced correctly, given the reading context.
   a. The word *read* must be pronounced *reed,* not as *red,* when presented in the context of "He will read the book."
   b. Repetitions are not counted as incorrect.
   c. Self-corrections within 3 seconds are counted as correctly read words.
2. *Words read incorrectly.* The following types of errors are counted: (a) mispronunciations, (b) substitutions, and (c) omissions. Further, words not read within 3 seconds are counted as errors.
   a. *Mispronunciations* are words that are misread: *dog* for *dig.*
   b. *Substitutions* are words that are substituted for the stimulus word; this is often inferred by a one-to-one correspondence between word orders; *dog* for *cat.*
   c. *Omissions* are words skipped or not read; if a student skips an entire line, each word is counted as an error.
3. *Three-second rule.* If a student is struggling to pronounce a word or hesitates for 3 seconds, the student is told the word, and it is counted as an error.

Note: Adapted from Shinn (1989, pp. 239–240). Copyright 1989 by The Guilford Press. Adapted by permission.

McKenna, M. C. & Stahl, S. A. (2003). *Assessment for Reading Instruction.* New York: Guilford.

various grade levels. Table 3.7 presents oral reading fluency norms collected by Hasbrouck and Tindal (1992), and more recently, by Edformation from 1999–2002. The table lists the average score for students at various grade levels for the fall, winter, and spring. This makes sense because we know that students increase their reading rate over the school year, particularly at the lower grades. The table includes scores for students in the "middle of the pack"—at the fiftieth percentile; for those scoring above average—seventy-fifth percentile; and for those scoring below—twenty-fifth percentile. As students get older, they tend to show less increase in rate per year. Consequently, most of the normative information available focuses on lower grades. In the right-hand column, we present norms collected by Harris and Sipay in 1990, as cited in Allington (2001). These norms are based on information from several standardized reading tests. Allington urges teachers to use these tests with caution, because they were developed based on both silent and oral rates. People tend to read more slowly when reading orally.

TABLE 3.7   Average Reading Fluency Rates for Students at Different Grade Levels

Grade Level	Per-centile	Edformation Fluency Standards (1999–2002) Oral Reading Fluency			Hasbrouck and Tindal (1992) Oral Reading Fluency			Harris-Sipay (1990) Based on Oral and Silent Reading Fluency
		Fall	Winter	Spring	Fall	Winter	Spring	
1	25		10	24				
	50		20	46				60–90
	75		38	73				
2	25	24	40	59	23	46	65	
	50	49	69	86	53	78	94	85–125
	75	73	97	114	82	106	124	
3	25	48	54	70	65	70	87	
	50	75	87	100	79	93	114	115–140
	75	101	115	130	107	123	142	
4	25	74	89	99	72	89	92	
	50	99	113	126	99	112	118	140–170
	75	124	140	154	125	133	143	
5	25	89	99	112	77	93	100	
	50	114	126	141	105	118	128	170–195
	75	143	157	171	126	143	151	
6	25	103	120	131				
	50	131	146	159				195–220
	75	158	169	182				
7	25	110	117	131				
	50	135	142	157				215–245
	75	162	172	182				
8	25	135	147	151				
	50	158	173	177				235–270
	75	185	194	200				
9	—							250–270
12	—							250–300

It is possible to use Table 3.7 to make some meaningful comparisons. For example, when a beginning second-grader reads orally fifty words correct per minute, the teacher is likely to breathe a sigh of relief. Using the oral reading fluency norms from Hasbrouck and Tindal, we can see that the beginning second-grader obtained an average score of 53 (fiftieth percentile rank). And the Edformation norms indicate that 49 is the average score for second-graders assessed in the fall. So the beginning second-grade student who obtained a score of 50 wcpm is pretty typical. Such a score would not be good for a beginning third-grader. As is apparent from Table 3.7, the average oral reading score for a beginning third-grader is 75 to 79 and for a beginning fourth-grader, it is 99. So the score of 50 wcpm is just fine for a beginning second-grader, and a score of 100 is just fine for a beginning fourth-grader. The Harris-Sipay norms tend to be higher; this difference reflects the fact that some of those numbers are based on silent reading.

In a 1972 study of adult literacy, reading rates for adults aged 26 to 35 reading tenth-grade level and college level passages were determined. The average silent reading rate for adults in the sample was 185 words per minute; for weaker readers (those scoring at the twenty-fifth percentile), the average score was 145 words per minute. For stronger readers (those scoring at the seventy-fifth percentile), the average score was approximately 245 words per minute (cited in Kruidenier 2002).

Recall the challenges faced by Dr. Charles from Chapter 1, the high school biology teacher whose class, like most high school classes, is composed of a diverse group of students. Because of his concern that many of his students could not read the text, he consulted with a reading specialist from his district. Together, they used the biology textbook to construct a curriculum-based measurement. They selected reading passages of 200 words in length from three different sections of the text; high school students typically read faster than 100 words per minute so 200 word passages were chosen. On the first few days of each new semester, Dr. Charles assigns cooperative group activities, then calls up students individually to read a passage. He times each student and marks errors on a copy of the passage. He calculates reading rate (wcpm) and percent accuracy.

How does Dr. Charles use the information from the CBM? First, he compares reading rate to the norms presented in Table 3.7 to determine a rough estimate of fluency. Though there is limited research available describing the reading rates of adolescents and adults, he knows his students will have difficulty when they read orally at less than approximately 150 to 175 words per minute. He knows that slower readers are less likely to remember what they read and that they will comprehend more and be more likely to complete reading assignments when the assignments are short. Importantly, Dr. Charles also determines his students' ability to recognize words in the text. Because one of the purposes of the text is to expose students to new vocabulary and concepts, he uses the lower end of the word recognition criteria by Powell (refer to Table 3.2). He also notes whether students have more difficulty with specialized terms (such as "photosynthesis") versus more generic terms (such as "eruption"). Because he is familiar with research on independent, instructional, and frustration levels, he knows that students with word recognition rates lower than 94 percent will have difficulty comprehending the text and will benefit from explicit work on vocabulary before reading, and during discussion of content.

Because each assessment takes only a couple of minutes, Dr. Charles is able to accomplish the assessments in two to three class days. He does not have latitude to abandon the text; the text is aligned with the content for which his students will be held accountable in the district's high-stakes tests, including the end-of-course tests that students must pass is a graduation requirement.

The rough knowledge Dr. Charles gathers regarding his students' proficiency with the biology text helps him plan instruction. He knows he cannot rely solely on a lecture and discussion format, assuming students have read the relevant material with understanding. His instructional plans include alternative strategies such as cooperative grouping, in which he purposely groups students of various reading levels together to find answers and solve problems. Dr. Charles also will preteach and reinforce both content-specific and more general vocabulary terms, use traditional lectures, and discuss salient concepts and issues.

It is possible for any teacher to use data from Table 3.7 for any assigned curriculum materials to determine appropriateness of the material. Reading level can be obtained by choosing a passage (of any length) and using the generic formula we presented in Figure 3.12 to find wcpm. Of course, experienced teachers build a set of internal or working norms, developed each year by working with multiple students, and over the years by working with multiple classes. This information can be formalized by taking local norms within the classroom, within a grade or school, or even within a system. We discuss this process in more detail in Chapter 4, in which we present some standardized CBM measures.

In addition to allowing teachers to compare student rate and accuracy to predetermined age/grade level expectations, a benefit of CBM is the potential for clearly showing progress over time. The results from CBM can be graphed to show a student's progress over the school year. To do this, teachers first determine a measure of progress, typically oral reading rate, by administering three passages from the text and averaging the reading rate; taking the median rate is also appropriate. Taking three measures over a relatively short time, say a week, is recommended to ensure the score is accurate. A student's scores can be plotted on a simple graph as indicated in Figure 3.26. Then, when a new measure is taken, it is plotted as before, with time on the horizontal axis (such as weekly or monthly average) and the wcpm on the vertical axis. To provide a more sophisticated trajectory of expectation, teachers can use information from research literature about typical skill acquisition to develop an **aimline,** which is simply a line showing the typical development. See Figure 3.27 for typical weekly growth rate of general and special education students for reading from Fuchs, Fuchs, Hamlett, Walz, and Germann (1993).

Remember Shelby from Mr. Haywood's special education reading group? Assume she achieves an oral reading rate gain score of about one word per week. Is this reasonable? Mr. Haywood constructed the graph in Figure 3.26

FIGURE 3.26 Aimline and Growth Rate in Oral Reading for Shelby, a Fifth-Grade Student in Special Education

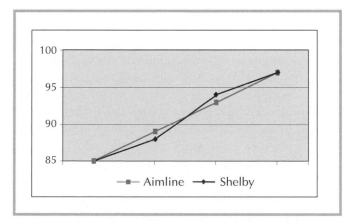

FIGURE 3.27 Expectancy Rates for Oral Reading

Grade	Realistic Growth Rate	Special Education Students	General Education Students	Ambitious Growth Rates
1	2 words	.83 word	1.8 words	3 words
2	1.5 words	.57 word	1.66 words	2 words
3	1 word	.58 word	1.18 words	1.5 words
4	.85 word	.58 word	1.01 words	1.1 words
5	.5 word	.58 word	.58 word	.8 word
6	.3 word	.62 word	.66 word	.65 word

Adapted from "Formulative evaluation of academic progress: How much growth can we expect?" by Fuchs, L. S., Fuchs, D., Hamlett, C. L., Walz, L., & Germann, G. (1993). *School Psychology Review, 22,* 27–48, and "Using curriculum-based measurement to establish growth standards for students with learning disabilities," by Deno, S. L., Fuchs, L., Marston, D., & Shin, J. (2001). *School Psychology Review, 30,* 507–524.

Overton, T. (2006). *Assessing Learners with Special Needs* (5th ed.). Upper Saddle River, NJ; Pearson Education.

with Shelby's scores and an aimline based on the information in Figure 3.27. The aimline is based on the "ambitious growth rate" shown in Figure 3.27 because he has confidence in the reading instruction he provides. And Shelby's oral reading rate does approximate the rate depicted in the aimline. Apparently, Shelby is making good progress, compared to special education and general education students. Any teacher can construct such a graph showing CBM performance over time, relative to expected progress. This graph can be a powerful part of a student **portfolio;** portfolio assessment is discussed later in this chapter.

It is possible to use CBM to assess mastery of comprehension as well, but it is used less extensively. One simple process requires that the teacher pose questions, some of which tap factual knowledge and others inferential knowledge of the content read. Percentage correct (i.e., questions answered correctly/total number of questions) can be taken to reduce problems associated with using varying passage lengths and numbers of questions. Overton (2006) describes a procedure for assessing reading comprehension using CBM. This procedure is called **maze** or **cloze.** The teacher selects passages from curriculum material as described earlier and types them into a word processing program. The first sentence is left intact, but the teacher deletes every *nth* word (e.g., every sixth word). The teacher then asks the student to read the passage and supply the missing word. In the cloze procedure, the student simply is asked to tell the missing word. In the maze procedure, the teacher develops three choices from which the student can choose. Teachers should follow guidelines such as those suggested by Fuchs and Fuchs (1992) when developing **distracters** (alternative word choices). The distracters should: (a) be of about the same length as the correct choice; (b) be a real word; (c) be of about the same difficulty level as the correct word and should *not* (a) make sense in the context; (b) resemble the correct word in sound or sight; (c) rhyme with the correct word. The correct word should be derived realistically from the content, and the student should not have to read ahead to figure it out.

One of the benefits of this type of CBM is that it allows direct assessment of progress in the curriculum. Although the procedures presented earlier are relatively straightforward, they are somewhat time consuming in terms of constructing and administering. These procedures have been used in special education settings and by school psychologists much more frequently than by classroom teachers. With mandates from No Child Left Behind (NCLB 2001) and the Individuals with Disabilities Education Improvement Act of 2004 (IDEA 2004), these techniques are likely to be used more frequently in classrooms, before students are referred for special education. Special educators and school psychologists can be of assistance to general education teachers and reading specialists as they comply with new accountability and progress monitoring expectations.

■ PORTFOLIO ASSESSMENT

Artists, photographers, and architects use portfolios, so why not elementary school students? Portfolios can contain samples of the various types of informal assessments addressed in this chapter. To create a portfolio, a student's work is collected over time and evaluated according to prescribed criteria. According to Arter and Spandel (1992, 36) a portfolio is a "purposeful collection of student work that tells the story of the student's efforts, progress, or achievement in (a) given area(s)." According to Valencia (1999), portfolio assessment relies on the assumption that assessment should be authentic, ongoing, multidimensional, and collaborative (between student and teacher). She notes that portfolio assessment can capture and capitalize on the best each student offers while encouraging teachers to vary their evaluation techniques. Portfolio assessment provides an integrity and validity that distinguishes it from most other types of assessment. That is, it is "real world."

In order to increase students' motivation to engage in portfolio assessment, students should help decide the content to be included and the criteria used to judge the content. In addition, students should be allowed to include in the portfolio a personal statement, a reflection about the contents. One purpose for using portfolios is to humanize and make more natural the evaluation process (Payne 2003). Portfolios should reflect real classroom work samples and may include journal entries, photographs, essays, drawings, videos, self-reflections, and so on. The goal of portfolio assessment is to preserve the richness and detail of student's work, unlike other more summative measures such as report cards. Report cards represent an efficient strategy for conveying information, and they serve that purpose well. But they do not provide much information about a student's day-to-day work.

How large should a reading portfolio be? The brief answer—it should be bigger than a report card but smaller than a suitcase. Teachers often choose an expandable file folder. It may consist of sections that contain not only permanent products generated by the student, but also observations about the work by the teacher, the student's self-evaluations, and any other progress notes or evaluative comments (such as from parents and peers). The portfolio should be available for the student to review at will and to make comparisons about the contents relative to current products. It should contain a well-conceived selection of the student's work not be simply a holding tank for all the permanent products the student completes over some prescribed period of time. The decision about what to include should be based on curricular and instructional priorities and be related to school and system goals, but also tied to specific student needs.

As is the case for every type of assessment, there are advantages and disadvantages associated with portfolio assessment. According to Payne (2003) and Ruddell (2002), portfolio assessment allows the student and teacher to: (a) track progress over time; (b) exhibit realistic examples of everyday academic and real-world products; (c) work together to design the evaluation process; (d) include artifacts (i.e., especially relevant samples of work) with high personal significance; (e) choose artifacts to include that motivate; and (f) involve others such as parents in the evaluation process. But the drawbacks are significant. For example, portfolio assessments are difficult to score reliably. Because it is difficult to get agreement among several raters about quality, or even within the same rater over time, scoring rules (or rubrics) should be predetermined and clear. Several indicators of any particular goal should be included; for example, varied work samples should reflect progress in vocabulary development. In addition, portfolio assessments may take considerable space in the classroom. Artifacts may be time consuming to develop and in some cases expensive. Finally, unless the work samples are representative, they may not convey well the typical work of the student.

As is obvious from the description of the pros and cons presented here, several questions must be addressed before portfolio assessment can be implemented (Payne 2003; Ruddell 2002). For example, to what extent will students be allowed to develop the ground rules? What is the purpose for the portfolio? What criteria will be used to grade the work samples? What is the time line for collecting the samples? Exactly what defines a sample of work for inclusion? How will the work samples be graded? How can the portfolio assessment be integrated into the classroom routine? Obviously, much thought and time are required before assessment can begin.

Portfolio assessment seems to lend itself naturally to some fields better than others. As mentioned earlier, art and architecture come to mind quickly. It is possible to visualize a struggling artist carrying work samples to prospective buyers. Strategies for using portfolio assessment to evaluate reading are less obvious. According to Overton (2006) a portfolio of reading might include several products showing mastery of decoding, such as completed teacher-made tests, curriculum-based work samples, homework papers, error analyses taken from IRIs or running records, as well as samples revealing comprehension level (such as retelling of a story, either written or on tape, and content mastery tests). We describe how to obtain many of these measures in this text. Importantly, reading is intimately related to other academic areas, particularly spelling and writing, and samples of these activities may be used to assess various elements of literacy.

One of the most difficult aspects of implementing a portfolio assessment of reading is establishing criteria for grading. In some cases, this may be rather straightforward, particularly for a reading assignment. Samples of products taken from an IRI might be scored according to the miscue analysis procedure recommended in the manual of the particular IRI in use. In this case, there is little latitude for scoring, and often the score for a measure of oral reading simply is a tally of errors or words read minus errors. However, other products may be more difficult to quantify and score, particularly creative reading products. For example, a student might retell a story but be asked to create a different ending. Alternately, the student might be asked to create a story map depicting the elements of a story in visual form. These products are more difficult to grade, leading to subjective decisions about scoring and potentially to disagreement and conflict. This problem cannot be eliminated, and subjectivity will always be part of the process. However, to reduce grading subjectivity for such products, we have developed a grading **rubric.** As is apparent from Table 3.8, it is not inclusive, but it may be helpful to teachers who are trying to establish a systematic method of assigning grades. You may use this rubric as a starting point to create your own. You may eliminate some of the items and replace them with items that are more appropriate for a particular product and situation.

Another strategy for grading is to make comparisons across students. In this case, grades are determined by making relative comparisons of the quality of work. As you might guess, this kind of system can produce competition whenever grades are determined strictly by the relative quality of products. Usually a better approach requires students and teacher to arrive at prescribed criteria in a collaborative spirit. For example, checklists can be prepared in advance, so that all have a clear understanding of the specific behaviors and products required for a given grade. Portfolios can be used to document progress in all areas of reading—from basic skills including phonics and automatic word recognition, to fluency, vocabulary, and comprehension. The task of the teacher is to collect materials that reflect the instructional goals for each student.

TABLE 3.8   Illustrative Reading Portfolio Rubric

Student	_____	Date	_____
Evaluator	_____	Teacher	_____
Work Sample	_____	Score	_____

On a scale of 1 to 5, rate the work characteristics from Low (poor quality) to High (excellent quality).

	Low				High
1. Shows mastery of assignment	1	2	3	4	5
2. Is well organized	1	2	3	4	5
3. Is neat	1	2	3	4	5
4. Was created on time	1	2	3	4	5
5. Reflects higher-order thinking and logic	1	2	3	4	5
6. Is representative of student's work	1	2	3	4	5
7. Is authentic	1	2	3	4	5
8. Is creative	1	2	3	4	5
9. Reflects adherence to directions	1	2	3	4	5
10. Reflects significant effort	1	2	3	4	5

■ READABILITY

The extent to which a passage is readable is always determined by two elements, the content and reader proficiency. So far, we have discussed ways to assess reader proficiency using various informal measures. Once reading level is determined, readers can be matched with reading material of appropriate difficulty. Readability of content is primarily a function of: (a) word difficulty; (b) sentence complexity; and (c) paragraph length. Reader proficiency is a function of innate ability and experience. The teachers' goal ultimately is to match the readability of the text with the reading proficiency of the student.

Often, teachers "guesstimate" readability of narrative and expository texts by simply thumbing through a book, reading a few passages here and there, and mentally comparing elements of readability such as word difficulty and sentence complexity with other passages they know. But there are more formal strategies, or formulae, for assigning readability. In fact, Hargis (1999) lists six: (1) Dale-Chall, (2) Fry, (3) Flesch, (4) Harris-Jacobson, (5) SMOG, and the (6) Spache; we add one more, the Flesch-Kincaid. These formulae typically report readability as a **grade-equivalent score,** based on systematic determination of word difficulty, sentence complexity, and so on. These grade equivalent scores should be taken as crude estimates only; the scores differ considerably depending on which formula is used, and there is not a consensus regarding which one is best.

As suggested above, readability is typically determined by various criteria, including word difficulty, word and sentence complexity, and the number of ideas in a sentence and paragraph. Most often, word difficulty is determined by comparing words in text to standard lists of common words at a given grade level, and words not on those common word lists are considered to be difficult. The more common method of determining difficulty is simply counting the number of syllables contained in a word; for years, experts have known that polysyllabic words are more difficult than monosyllabic words (Johnson 1930). Sentence complexity is determined by counting the number of words, ideas, and relationships in the sentence—the longer the sentence, the more difficult the text.

One of the most widely cited (and used) formula is provided by Edward Fry, which relies on a count of the average number of syllables in a word and the number of words in a sentence. The graph in Figure 3.28 can be used to determine approximate grade level.

One of the most conservative estimates of readability was developed by McLaughlin (1969) and is referred to as the SMOG grading formula. The steps for determining SMOG readability are:

   a. Count ten consecutive sentences near the beginning, middle, and end of the text, for a total of thirty sentences.

   b. Count every word of three or more syllables, including repetitions, and strings of letters or numbers beginning and ending with a space or punctuation mark, assuming they comprise three distinguishable syllables.

   c. Obtain the square root of the number of polysyllabic words counted.

   d. Add 3 to the square root.

FIGURE 3.28 Fry Readability Graph

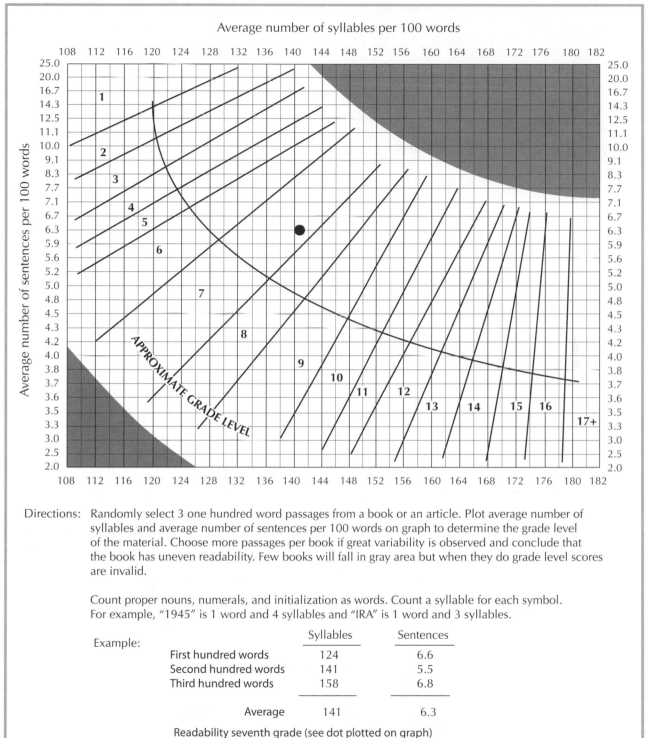

Directions: Randomly select 3 one hundred word passages from a book or an article. Plot average number of syllables and average number of sentences per 100 words on graph to determine the grade level of the material. Choose more passages per book if great variability is observed and conclude that the book has uneven readability. Few books will fall in gray area but when they do grade level scores are invalid.

Count proper nouns, numerals, and initialization as words. Count a syllable for each symbol. For example, "1945" is 1 word and 4 syllables and "IRA" is 1 word and 3 syllables.

Example:		Syllables	Sentences
	First hundred words	124	6.6
	Second hundred words	141	5.5
	Third hundred words	158	6.8
	Average	141	6.3

Readability seventh grade (see dot plotted on graph)

This value is the SMOG Grade, which is the reading grade a person must have attained to fully comprehend the text. There are two problems with this procedure, and both have been addressed satisfactorily by Hargis (1999). First, the SMOG Grade estimate is approximately two grade levels more difficult than most other procedures. For this reason, Hargis suggests modifying the last step in the SMOG procedure; rather than adding 3 to the square root of the value obtained in the previous step, add only 1. The second problem encountered when using the SMOG procedure is one of applicability. According to Hargis, the SMOG formula cannot be applied to primary material because a value cannot be calculated when there are fewer than four words of three syllables or more in a sample. In addition, in the original formula the number 3 is added to the value obtained from extracting the square root of the number of polysyllabic words counted, Step C earlier. Consequently, all obtained scores start with at least 3 grade levels of difficulty.

In order to address the problems with the original SMOG formula, Hargis (1999) developed a modified SMOG procedure he refers to as the Primary-SMOG Grading, which can be used to determine readability of primary materials. The steps include: (a) obtain a sample of thirty sentences, ideally ten from the beginning, middle, and end if the passage is long enough; (b) count every word of three or more syllables and if there are more than three words of three or more syllables use the SMOG procedure; (c) when there are three or fewer words of three or more syllables, count all the words of two or more syllables, but do not count repetitions; (d) obtain the square root of the number of words of two or more syllables; (e) subtract 1 from the square root—this is the Primary-SMOG grade equivalent score; (f) if the thirty-sentence sample has fewer than three two-syllable words, count the number of words in the sentences; (g) if the thirty-sentence sample has fewer than 100 words, it has a grade equivalent score at the preprimer or primer level; and if it has more than 100 words, it is at the first reader level.

These two SMOG-based formulae can be obtained with little effort. The most difficult part, obtaining the square root, is no longer difficult because all calculators perform this function. In addition, the **modification** by Hargis makes the SMOG grade equivalent scores more similar to the other formulas. Consequently, we can recommend use of the SMOG and Primary-SMOG formulae.

Other convenient options are available. It is possible to use readability formulae in common word processing programs. Most programs provide that function and it is easy to use. In fact, the Readability section of this chapter has a Flesch-Kincaid readability grade equivalent score of 11.6. It was obtained from the word processing program used to compose this text, Microsoft Word, and more specifically by following several easy steps:

a. Select the text to be checked.
b. Click on the Tools icon.
c. Click on the Spelling and Grammar option.
d. Click on Options.
e. Click on the Show Readability Statistics option.

It has been estimated that the SMOG procedures take about nine minutes to compute. It takes about thirty seconds to obtain the Flesch-Kincaid via the computer. Of course, the passage has to be typed or scanned into the computer first, which may take from thirty seconds to a few minutes, depending upon the length of the passages and whether they are scanned or typed.

Once readability has been determined, it is possible to categorize passages, stories, and texts for use by readers of varying ability. This process helps teachers develop resources. Teachers may also use professionally prepared materials that have been leveled. These materials have been analyzed and categorized according to levels of difficulty and related criteria to determine content readability and sophistication by publishers. Of course, determining the optimal match between the readability of particular material and a particular reader can be determined best by using IRIs and related assessment materials. The very best match can be attained only after spending time with the student, assessing levels of word recognition, fluency, and comprehension in the specific text assigned.

▪ LEVELED TEXTS

Once a teacher knows the reading level of individual students, it is possible to help a reader choose an appealing book at the appropriate level. Allowing a student to choose a book that focuses on a topic of interest should increase motivation to actually engage the text.

How can teachers determine the reading level of books in their classroom libraries or from other sources? Some teachers use readability formulas, as discussed earlier, to establish difficulty level. Fortunately, teachers have a number of available leveling systems. For example, Fountas and Pinnell (2006) have rated more than 18,000 children's book by difficulty level. The leveling systems available use criteria much like authors of the readability formulas use, except they seem more inclusive. Typical criteria include sentence complexity (length), vocabulary (number of high-frequency words), print features (frequency and size of pictures, length of book), language features (similarity to oral language versus technical language), and content (themes). Reading Recovery leveled books are rated from A to Z, with levels A–C for kindergarten, D to E for first grade, E to H for second grade, and so on. There are a number of leveling systems available, and all use similar criteria. Some systems have been used to level existing books (including Fountas and Pinnell 2006); other systems require that books be created and written within their established parameters (including *Reading a–z,* which is available at: www.readinga-z.com/guided/correlation.html. The *Reading a–z* Web site also equates existing leveling systems, for example, it shows how the *Reading a–z* level "K" is equal to the Fountas and Pinnell Guided Reading level "J," which is equal to Reading Recovery level 17, which, in term, is equal to Developmental Reading Assessment (DRA; www.pearsonlearning.com/index.cfm?a=37) level 18. Calkins describes a strategy she and colleagues have used to assign books to levels as follows:

> When working with books for emergent and early readers, there are so many resources the work is almost clerical at first. We grab a book, and then use references—the Reading Recovery leveling list, publishers' levels, the levels from *Guided Reading* and *Matching Books to Readers*—to slot the book into bins. After a bit, we pause to review these bins and decide which to combine to create a classroom lending library. By this time, we tend to have six or so books in a bin, and we find that this gives us a sense

of the books at that particular level so we can begin to make decisions about books that have not been previously leveled. We rarely feel absolutely certain, but our rule of thumb is that if we're not certain we put a book in the higher level (which means it's more likely to be too easy than too hard) (Calkins 2001, 129).

The advantage of being able to assign levels to reading material in the classroom library is crucial for helping match the ability of readers to the difficulty of the books. However, Calkins (2001) suggests that teachers not mark all their books. She suggests using a clearly marked system for leveling a portion of the books in the library, but leaving some significant portion unleveled to encourage children to independently explore and to choose books of appropriate difficulty.

When a book is not leveled but a child requests that you help choose an appropriate book, some general rules are available to help determine difficulty level (Clay 1987; 2000; Leslie and Caldwell 2006). Some teachers actually use a "rule of thumb" criterion to determine whether text is too difficult. In this case, the teacher asks the student to read a 100-word passage while marking errors by lifting the fingers on one hand. If the thumb is lifted before the passage is completed, indicating five errors, the passage is too difficult. Similarly, others use the "five finger" rule. They ask children to read a page in a book and to lift a finger each time a word cannot be identified; if more than five words cannot be called, it is too difficult; others use a two- or three-finger rule (Allington and Cunningham 2002). Others use the "90 percent" rule. If the child can read accurately 90 percent of the words, the book is probably reasonably assigned. Summarizing from several sources, it may be reasonable to consider an error rate of one in twenty words as "easy" and an error rate of between one in twenty and one in ten as "instructional." A rate of more than one error in ten words may be considered "hard."

In addition to the techniques just described, some districts use **Lexile** scores to match students to text and to keep track of a student's reading performance across the school years. Lexile levels are discussed in some detail in the context of computerized assessment in Chapter 4. In summary, it is important to have some strategies available to assess the difficulty level of the available books and to match the books to the reading level of the reader. Only then will students be motivated to read on their own.

■ SPECIAL CONSIDERATIONS IN THE INFORMAL ASSESSMENT OF YOUNG CHILDREN

Perhaps the most important single year in a student's life is the kindergarten year, particularly for developing literacy. Teachers who focus on the student's needs during that year, not the curriculum, will be most effective in moving the student forward (McGill-Franzen 2006). What does a student-centered approach require for young children? First and foremost, a teacher must know what skills a student brings to the classroom, then prescribe the just-next goals and steps for reaching those goals. Obviously, good assessment is necessary, and good assessment begins with good observation skills, as we suggested earlier in this chapter. Based on the information learned from the models of readings we presented in Chapter 1, it is apparent that teachers have to master both declarative knowledge (about early reading and child development) and procedural knowledge (how to engage and motivate the student). In addition, teachers must gain direct information from the students as they enter the classroom, beginning in September, and follow up by checking progress along the way. McGill-Franzen offers a Schedule for Kindergarten Literacy Assessment that we find appealing (reproduced in Figure 3.29).

As is apparent, there are eight essential literacy skills that are appropriate for kindergarten students to learn, including letter and sound associations, phonological awareness skills, print concepts, phonemic segmentation/ representation, word reading, word writing, text reading, and text writing. This schedule provides kindergarten teachers with an advanced organizer for

Suggested Schedule for Kindergarten Literacy Assessment

The 8 Skills		Beginning of Year To inform instruction	Midyear and as Appropriate To communicate to parents and inform instruction	End of Year To document progress and to communicate to parents and first-grade teachers
Letter and Sound Association Use card stock or letter tiles	Names and Sounds	Assess	Assess unknown letters and sounds	Assess unknown letters and sounds
	D'Nealian			*Your Purpose*
Phonological Awareness Use picture sorts	Rhyme	Assess	Assess unknown concepts	Assess unknown concepts
	Beginning Sounds	Assess	Assess unknown concepts	Assess unknown concepts
Print Concepts Use a Level A book		Assess all concepts, depending on book	Assess unknown concepts	Assess unknown concepts
Phonemic Segmentation and Representation Use paper and pencil or letter tiles	Spelling List 1	Assess	Assess	Assess
	Spelling List 2	*You select these lists (see sample, page 77)*		Assess if all words on List 1 are spelled correctly
Word Reading Use card stock or word cards	List 1	Assess	Assess unknown words	Assess unknown words
	List 2		Assess only those students who know most of List 1 words	
Word Writing "Write all the words you know"		Administer prompt and record number of words in writing vocabulary		
Text Reading Ask the child to read a text— • a "pretend reading" of a familiar book or story, such as *Have You Seen My Duckling?* or • the child's own writing, or • an appropriate guided reading leveled book, depending on what level of text is appropriate		Record observations as appropriate *See pages 103–113*		
Text Writing "Draw a picture and write all about yourself"		Administer prompt and analyze writing sample		

In general, assess only things child missed on previous assess.

FIGURE 3.29 Suggested Schedule for Kindergarten Literacy Assessment

McGill-Franzen, A. (2006). *Kindergarten Literacy. Matching Assessment and Instruction in Kindergarten.* New York: Scholastic.

thinking about structuring their time. Additional tips she offers include: (a) set aside thirty minutes each morning during the first few weeks of school to assess students' literacy skills, taking advantage of paraprofessionals and parents; (b) place materials on a strategically placed small table that allows monitoring of the whole class; (c) assess in the prescribed order from the Schedule, with deviations in order only after acquiring some familiarity with the process; (d) assess one-on-one for a full ten minutes or longer each day; and (f) keep track of students' progress. She suggests using a Student Profile Sheet for this purpose, and we reproduce it in Figure 3.30.

In order to keep track of student progress, teachers will probably want to use portfolios. We recommend using the guidelines suggested earlier in the chapter to guide portfolio development. What materials should teachers include? McGill-Franzen (2006) offers several suggestions, including student self-assessment forms, pages from core workbook, personal word banks or dictionaries, reading logs, and writing samples. In addition, she offers very

Student Profile Sheet

Student _____   Teacher _____

		Observation Dates		
		Beginning of Year	**Midyear**	**End of Year**
Letter and Sound Association	Names			
	Sounds			
	D'Nealian			
Phonological Awareness	Rhyme			
	Beginning Sounds			
Print Concepts	Book			
	Directionality			
	Voice-to-print Match			
	Word Concept			
	Letter Concept			
	First & Last Word			
	Punctuation Total Concepts* (period, question mark, exclamation point)			
Phonemic Segmentation and Representation	Spelling List 1			
	Spelling List 2			
Word Reading	List 1			
	List 2			
	List 3			
Word Writing "Write all the words you know"				
Reading				
Reads from Memory				
Reads Own Writing				
Reads Leveled Text	Book Title			
	Guided Reading Level			
	Accuracy			
	Rate/Word Correct per Minute			
Writing "Draw a picture and write about yourself"				
Drawing & Letterlike Forms				
Copied & Random Letters				
Name				
Words				

FIGURE 3.30 Student Profile Sheet

McGill-Franzen, A. (2006). *Kindergarten Literacy. Matching Assessment and Instruction in Kindergarten.* New York: Scholastic.

specific suggestions about how to informally assess each of the eight areas critical for kindergarten students.

SPECIAL CONSIDERATIONS IN THE INFORMAL ASSESSMENT OF ADULT LEARNERS

Informal assessment of adults proceeds pretty much like assessment of children and adolescents, with a few exceptions. First, adults learning to read are typically sensitive, and in some cases, ashamed of their reading limitations. Consequently, the teacher should work hard to put the adult learner at ease. It helps when the assessment material is based on adult themes (such as work and family life). Kruidenier (2002) provides other suggestions for assessing reading skills of adults based on research findings. His book may be considered a description of "best practices" for reading assessment (and instruction) for adults because of its reliance on empirical research. However, many of the findings are tentative and more research on adult reading instruction needs to be conducted. Importantly, Kruidenier categorizes research findings according to the NRP's areas of reading, as we described in Chapter 1 (phonemic awareness, phonics, fluency, vocabulary, and comprehension). In addition, other experts such as Venezky, Bristow, and Sabatini (1994) have focused their research on the particular needs of adult learners. Specifically, McShane (2005) has identified three specific purposes for adult assessment: (1) identifying individual goals, strengths, and needs for initial planning; (2) providing ongoing progress monitoring and trouble shooting; and (3) assessing learning over time for outcome measures, such as the General Education Diploma (GED). Some specific suggestions for assessing adults are presented in Box 3.2.

BOX 3.2 Tips for the Informal Assessment of Adult Learners

1. Take time to establish rapport with the learner, explain the nature and purpose of the assessments, and ensure that scores will be confidential.

2. Assess the various areas of reading for adult beginning readers, rather than assuming that adults possess basic word analysis skills.

3. Use multiple measures to provide a complete assessment of what the learner can do.

4. Assess oral reading rate. Adults who read at 125 wcpm or less will need further assessment.

5. Many of the informal assessment strategies and techniques described for children and adolescents will be acceptable for assessing adults, assuming the stimulus reading material is age-appropriate.

6. Assess adult learners' educational histories, background experiences, and interests as well as specific reading skills.

7. Use alternative or authentic measures as appropriate; for example, portfolio assessment, journals and work samples.

8. Use teacher-constructed CBM with authentic materials such as domestic or work-related reading materials.

9. Phonemic skills of adult nonreaders should be assessed much like young beginning readers because they possess virtually no phonemic awareness knowledge.

10. Adults have stronger vocabularies than young children because of their life experiences, and this knowledge should be assessed and used as a building block of reading.

SPECIAL CONSIDERATIONS IN THE INFORMAL ASSESSMENT OF ENGLISH LANGUAGE LEARNERS

Not all ELL students are alike. In fact, according to Freeman and Freeman (2004), ELLs fall into four categories: (1) newly arrived students with limited formal schooling; (2) newly arrived students with adequate formal schooling; (3) students exposed to two languages simultaneously; and (4) long-term, English-language learners. Knowledge of these categories can help teachers develop the most appropriate assessments; that is, assessments that match the literacy background of the particular student. In addition, Lenski, Ehlers-Zavala, Daniel, and Sun-Irminger (2006) recommend that teachers construct a predictability log (PL) to help them understand the types of literacies ELLs bring to the classroom. This log is completed by obtaining answers to questions about the student's functioning in several areas, including:

a. Language use (including the languages the student knows and uses and the language and literacy experiences of interest to the student).
b. Knowledge (including the student's cultural background and what the student enjoys doing after school).
c. Experiences/events that matter to the student (including whatever has been of great interest to the student recently).
d. Narrative (including the kinds of stories the student enjoys and the stories the student knows).
e. Relationships (including the students family situation, whether the student has left anyone behind in the home country, and the student's best friends).
f. Aesthetics and ethics (including the personal belongings the student brings to school or wears).

Once a teacher knows about the student's literacy background and knowledge base, the purpose of assessment should be considered. Next, particular assessment strategies should be determined. Remember, effective assessment leads to effective instruction. To help you think about appropriate informal assessment of ELLs, several tips were generated. These appear in Box 3.3.

BOX 3.3 Tips for the Informal Assessment of English Language Learners

Ensure that the assessment conforms to the general assessment standards set by the Teachers of English to Speakers of Other Languages (TESOL; www.tesol.org/s_tesol/seccss.asp?CID=3&DID=4

1. When language is the target of assessment, ensure the student understands nature of the tasks by ample use of sample and demonstration items, gestures, pantomime, as needed.
2. Assessment activities should represent authentic learning activities.
3. Assessment should be designed to assess progress over time, as possible.
4. Elements (items) of informal assessment should be linked to classroom instructional objectives.
5. When possible, use alternative assessment in naturally occurring situations (such as journals, observations, checklists, conferring, portfolios, and anecdotal records).

Summary

In writing this chapter, our goal was to familiarize you with informal assessment strategies most commonly used by classroom teachers and to provide you with real-world assessment skills and resources; consequently, it is the longest chapter in the book. First, we described some basic observational and interview strategies. Effective teachers learn much from simply "kidwatching," but they are also informed by interviewing students to find out what they know about print and by using checklists of various skills and reading behaviors as they go about daily instruction. Next, we discussed tests and assessments that accompany commercial reading programs. Though not considered best practice by some experts, most school districts in the United States use commercial basal reading series as the primary means of literacy instruction. These series contain built-in assessments of the wide range of reading skills, and we shared some of those.

We addressed the generic technique of error analysis and how it is applied specifically in miscue analysis (a systematic system of analyzing student reading errors to determine skill strengths and weaknesses) and running records (a method of listening to a student read from authentic text and recording and analyzing errors). We devoted a large section to informal reading inventories because of the rich amount of information they can provide; a major purpose of IRIs is to yield information about students' independent (read and comprehended with ease), instructional (read and comprehend with some support) and frustration (too difficult) reading levels. Another rich source of data comes directly from the curriculum, and teachers can develop direct measures by using excerpts from reading materials used in class. Teacher-constructed curriculum-based measurement can yield indices of reading rate and accuracy via use of simple formulae.

Knowing a student's reading level allows the teacher to recommend books at an appropriate (i.e., instructional) level. Book-leveling systems make this task easier by providing teachers with a predetermined reading level. In cases in which reading level is not already determined, there are several readability formulae available, including the Fry and the SMOG as well as the Flesch-Kincaid, which is included in some computer word processing programs, specifically Microsoft Word. Finally, we discussed some special considerations for assessment of kindergarteners, ELLs, and of adults with low literacy levels. Because literacy instruction in kindergarten tends to be less structured than in other grades, we recommend McGill-Franzen's schedule for assessment and instruction to ensure that students are making progress at this critical time. In order to maximize instruction teachers work to match the difficulty level of texts to the ability of readers. This goal is incredibly important and is the subject of considerable literature in educational psychology and education. We provide examples showing how to accomplish this goal in the area of reading.

Consideration of a real case may help you begin to think about how elements of the Instruction Pie relate to the classroom. Remember Mr. Haywood's fifth-grade special education students Shelby and Saimah and third-grader Sammy from his school? (Take a quick look back at their reading levels based on their IRIs in Tables 3.5 through 3.7). Mr. Haywood knows that Shelby is making pretty even progress in all the areas of reading, though she is performing below her same-age peers. In contrast, Saimah appears to need more work in vocabulary and background knowledge. And Sammy appears to need relatively more work on word analysis. Consequently, their personalized Pies have different sizes of slices to reflect different instructional emphases. Effective teachers and specialists use assessment data from various sources to construct appropriate Instruction Pies for their students. We revisit the Instructional Pie in subsequent chapters.

In closing, we present a table summarizing the types of assessment addressed in this chapter, the publisher (if appropriate), intended age ranges, and the areas of reading addressed by each assessment. Table 3.9 is not exhaustive because there are so many assessments available. The table provides a visual summary of the types of assessment described as well as information about specific techniques and tests. We think Table 3.9 will be a handy reference for practical use. In Chapter 4, we address informal assessments that are used in a somewhat more formal manner than those presented here, primarily for progress monitoring and for accountability.

mylabschool

Where the classroom comes to life!

MyLabSchool is a collection of online tools for your success in this course, your licensure exams, and your teaching career. Visit www.mylabschool.com to access the following:

- *Online Study Guide*
- *Video cases from real classrooms*
- *Help with your research papers using Research Navigator*
- *Career Center with resources for:*
    Praxis exams and licensure preparation
    Professional portfolio development
    Job search and interview techniques
    Lesson planning

TABLE 3.9 Measures of Informal Assessments That Inform Instruction

Name of Technique or Measure	Publisher/Source/Date	Grades/Ages	Administration Time	Administration Format	Facet of Reading				
					Basic Reading Skills			Vocabulary	Reading Comprehension
					Word Recognition	Phonics/PA	Fluency		Comprehension
Teacher-Made Curriculum Generated Assessment									
Curriculum-Based Measurement (CBM) of Oral Reading	Shinn, 1989	K–Adult	Usually read 3 passages for 1 minute each	Individual	X		X		X
Miscue Analysis	Goodman, 1985	K–Adult	Varies		X	X	X	X	X
Portfolio Assessment	N/A	K–Adult	Varies		X	X	X	X	X
Running Records	Clay, 1993	K–Adult	Varies		X	X	X	X	X
Specific Skills Checklists and Assessments									
Auditory Analysis Test (AAT)	Rosner & Simon, 1971	K–6	3–8 minutes	Individual	X				
Basic Early Assessment of Reading (BEAR)	Riverside, 2002	K–3	30–40 min. per subtest; 90 minutes for screener	Classwide and Individual	X	X	X	X	
Berninger Modification of the Auditory Analysis Test (B-AAT)	Berninger, Thalberg, DeBruyn, & Smith, 1987	K	3–8 minutes	Individual	X				
Book Buddies Early Literacy Screening (BBELS)	Johnston, Invernezzi & Juel, 1998	1–2	30–40 minutes	Individual	X	X			
Catts Deletion Test (CDT)	Catts, Fey, Zhang, & Tomblin, 2001	K	3–8 minutes	Individual	X				
Consortium on Reading Excellence (CORE) Phonics Survey	Honig, Diamond, & Nathan, 1999	K–8	10–25 minutes	Individual	X	X			
Criterion Test of Basic Skills, 2nd Ed.	Academic Therapy, 2002	Age 6–11	15–20 minutes	Individual	X	X		X	
Developmental Reading Assessment 2nd Ed.	Celebration Press/ Pearson Learning Group	K–8	Varies	Individual	X	X	X	X	X

(Continued)

TABLE 3.9 (Continued)

Specific Skills Checklists and Assessments

Name of Technique or Measure	Publisher/Source/Date	Grades/Ages	Administration Time	Administration Format	Word Recognition	Phonics/PA	Fluency	Vocabulary	Comprehension
					Basic Reading Skills			Facet of Reading	Reading Comprehension
Diagnostic Assessments of Reading 2nd Ed.	Riverside, 2005	Age 5–Adult	40 minutes	Individual	X	X	X	X	X
Early Reading Diagnostic Assessment, 2nd Ed.	Harcourt, 2003	K–3	40–60 minutes	Individual	X	X	X	X	X
Exception Word Reading Test (EWRT)	Adams & Huggins, 1985	2–5	5–7 minutes (list); 10–15 minutes (sentence)	Individual	X				
Fox in a Box: An Adventure in Literacy	CTB/McGraw-Hill, 2000	K–2	1¾ hours–2 hours	Individual, small-group, and classwide	X	X	X		X
An Observation Survey of Early Literacy Achievement, Rev. 2nd Ed.	Heinemann, 2006	K–3	Varies	Individual	X	X	X	X	X
Phonological Awareness Literacy Screening (PALS)	University of Virginia Press, 2002	PreK–3	20 minutes for group; 30 minutes for individual	Individual, small-group, and classwide	X	X	X		
Phonological Awareness Screening Test (PAST)	Brookes, 1998	K–1	20–30 minutes	Small-group		X			
San Diego Quick Assessment	See McKenna & Stahl, 2003	Age 5–16	Few minutes	Individual	X				
Spadafore Diagnostic Reading Test	Academic Therapy, 1983	Age 6–Adult	30 or 60 minutes	Individual	X				X

Name of Technique or Measure	Publisher/Source/Date	Grades/Ages	Administration Time	Administration Format	Basic Reading Skills			Reading Comprehension	
					Word Recognition	Phonics/PA	Fluency	Vocabulary	Comprehension
Specific Skills Checklists and Assessments									
Test of Auditory Analysis Skills (TAAS)	Academic Therapy, 1979	K–3	3–8 minutes	Individual	X				
Texas Primary Reading Inventory (TPRI)	University of Houston, 2002	K–2	5–7 minutes (screening); 20 minutes (inventory)	Individual and Group	X	X	X		X
3-Minute Reading Assessments Grades 1–4	Scholastic, 2005	1–4	3 minutes	Individual	X		X		X
3-Minute Reading Assessments Grades 5–8	Scholastic, 2005	5–8	3 minutes	Individual	X		X		X
Yopp-Singer Test of Phonemic Segmentation (YST)	Yopp, 1995	PreK–1	5–10 minutes	Individual		X			
Informal Reading Inventories									
Analytical Reading Inventory, 8th Ed.	Prentice Hall, 2007	K–3 and higher	Varies		X	X	X		X
Basic Reading Inventory: Pre-Primer Through Grade Twelve and Early Literacy Assessments, 9th Ed.	Kendall/Hunt, 2005	Pre-primer– 12	20 minutes	Individual	X	X	X		X
Burns/Roe Informal Reading Inventory: Preprimer to Twelfth Grade, 6th Ed.	Houghton Mifflin, 2002	Pre-primer– 12	40–50 minutes	Individual	X	X	X		X

(Continued)

TABLE 3.9 (Continued)

Name of Technique or Measure	Publisher/Source/Date	Grades/Ages	Administration Time	Administration Format	Basic Reading Skills — Word Recognition	Basic Reading Skills — Phonics/PA	Basic Reading Skills — Fluency	Vocabulary	Reading Comprehension
Informal Reading Inventories									
Cooter/Flynt/Cooter Comprehensive Reading Inventory	Pearson-Prentice Hall, 2006	PreK–12	Varies		X	X	X	X	X
Ekwall/Shanker Reading Inventory, 4th Ed.	Allyn & Bacon, 2000	K–9	20–30 minutes or more	Individual	X	X	X		X
Qualitative Reading Inventory, 4th Ed.	Allyn & Bacon, 2006	Pre-primer– high school	Varies	Individual	X	X	X	X	X
Reading Inventory for the Classroom & Tutorial Audiotape Package, 5th Ed.	Prentice Hall, 2004	PreK–12	Varies	Individual	X	X	X		X
Stieglitz Reading Inventory, 3rd Ed.	Allyn & Bacon, 2002	Emergent— Advanced	Varies	Individual	X	X	X		X

Note: PA = Phonemic Awareness.

Information is based on a combination of published and online materials (including independent test reviews, content from tests and test manuals, and publisher/author promotional materials). Strenuous efforts were made by authors to ensure accuracy but information may contain errors and omissions due to updates in the tests reviewed, errors in published materials, and conflicts in reported information. Lists are not exhaustive.

CHAPTER 4

Informal Assessment: Progress Monitoring

In Chapter 3, we considered assessments used most often in the classroom, by general and special education teachers to guide instruction. In this chapter, we consider informal tests that have some characteristics of "formal" instruments. These instruments are not teacher constructed; they may have time limits, they follow standard administration procedures, and they typically provide a score that is evaluated against a criterion, benchmark, or cutoff.

For context, think back to the Inclusive Model of Reading presented in Chapter 2 and shown in Appendix B. Recall that reading outcomes, the goals

of reading assessment and instruction, are shown on the right side of the figure while the processes and factors contributing to reading are to the left. Informal assessment measures that directly inform instruction and are most closely related to the actual act of reading, the outcome, arguably yield the most authentic information. However, as discussed in Chapter 3, they tend to be subjective and appropriate interpretation is based heavily on the teacher's experiences, training, and dedication.

Assessments of skills less tied to specific classroom instruction, such as recurring probes of oral reading fluency, offer more objectivity and increasingly are used for monitoring student progress. Such tests, as described in this chapter, often are administered in classroom settings by teachers, special educators, reading specialists, and sometimes, by educational diagnosticians or school psychologists. Unlike the high-stakes and norm-referenced tests considered in Chapters 5 and 6, these tests are used primarily to determine whether students have mastered certain skills or are performing at specified levels on various types of reading tasks. The information gleaned from these assessments is used to determine whether instruction is effective and whether it should be continued, intensified, or changed.

THE ASSESSMENT CONTINUUM

As implied previously, some informal assessment measures are standardized (administered according to prescribed directions and time limits), yet they yield primarily criterion-referenced data, information about whether students have mastered a particular skill or set of skills. Unlike norm-referenced tests, however, the focus is on individual students' mastery of specific skills relative to some criterion. As tests become more sophisticated, the distinction between formal and informal and criterion and norm-referenced assessments become blurred. It is increasingly difficult to compare and contrast types of assessment, because current technology allows test publishers to combine elements of several types in one package. Figure 4.1, a graphic organizer, depicts a range of reading assessments. However, keep in mind that some assessments may yield more than one type of information, which we refer to as "hybrid" measures.

RELIABILITY AND VALIDITY

Before considering various types of hybrid assessments, we discuss briefly two essential aspects of tests—reliability and validity—two important concepts that provide background knowledge. Remember the importance of building vocabulary and background knowledge to reading comprehension? Similarly, knowledge of these terms will give you background needed for understanding, evaluating, and using published assessments.

Reliability

Reliability is typically defined as the extent to which a test yields consistent scores and is directly related to test error. In fact, reliability is technically defined as:

1 — error

FIGURE 4.1 Reading Assessments Ranging Generally from Less Formal to More Formal

	Informal	**Formal**
Informing Instruction	*Monitoring Progress*	*Eligibility* and *Accountability*
Quizzes	Commercial Criterion-Referenced	Individual Norm-Referenced
Checklists	Progress Monitoring (Hybrids)	Group Norm-Referenced
Interviews	Computer Assessments	
Observations		
Informal Reading Inventories		
Miscue Analysis		
Teacher Constructed Curriculum-Based Measurement		
Portfolios		
Readability		
Leveled Texts		

Conversely, error is defined as:

1 — reliability

Reliability is defined technically from one of several possible formulas and may range from 0 to 1, although in reality, no test will exhibit perfect reliability. For illustrative purposes, assume that the manual of a particular reading test reports a reliability of .91. In this case, 91 percent of the variability (relative placement of scores within a distribution) earned on the test can be attributed to a systematic or "real" cause, say ability to decode if that is the purpose of the test. Conversely, 9 percent of the variability is unsystematic (1 − .91 = 9), cannot be predicted, and consequently represents error.

Traditionally, test authors use reliability estimates, calculated from specific formulas, as numerical indicators of the quality of a test. Certain types of reliability are based on the correlation coefficient as a starting point, which we discussed in Chapter 1. The higher the reliability, the better the test. According to Salvia and Yesseldyke (1998), tests that yield a reliability index of .90 and higher can be used for important decisions such as special education placement; those that yield scores from .80 to .90 can be used for screening; those that yield scores of .60 or better can be used for research purposes.

Types of reliability.   As indicated earlier, various statistical estimates of reliability can be calculated and each is related to a slightly different type of reliability, although all estimates reference the extent to which the test produces consistent or systematic measurement.

Table 4.1 provides a description of the main types of reliability, including inter-rater reliability, intra-rater reliability, alternate forms reliability,

TABLE 4.1   Types of Reliability

Type of Reliability	What Is Measured?	How Is It Calculated?
Inter-Rater	Consistency between two or more raters or observers	Percentage agreement
Intra-Rater	One rater's consistency in scoring across different assessments	Percentage agreement
Alternate Form	Consistency of scores over two alternate or equivalent forms of same test	Pearson r coefficient
Internal Consistency	Consistency of scores on items within same test	Spearman Brown; Cronbach's alpha
Test-Retest	Consistency of scores from one testing time to another, usually within a few weeks	Pearson r coefficient

internal consistency reliability, and test-retest reliability. All these variations are tied to somewhat unique specific data analyses and statistical procedures, but all the analyses are based on determining the extent to which there is consistency within or between raters or between items. Consistency between different examiners or raters is called **inter-rater reliability,** and consistency over time by the same rater(s) is called **intra-rater reliability.** Consistency among items, which can be determined by comparing scores across two halves of the same test, is called **internal consistency reliability.**

Consistency among items can also be estimated by **test-retest reliability,** which is determined by administration of the same test twice to the same individuals within a relatively short period of time, and **alternate forms reliability,** which is obtained by administration of parallel or equivalent forms of a test at the same time to the same individuals. Intra-rater reliability and inter-rater reliability estimates typically are determined by calculating the percentage of agreement by the raters on the total number of items rated. Consistency or reliability of items typically is determined by the results of calculation of a Pearson Product Moment correlation coefficient, or r, or some reliability estimate using the Pearson r as a starting point, such as the Spearman-Brown formula. The specific procedures associated with calculating the Pearson r and related reliability formulae are beyond the scope of this book, but they can be found in many introductory measurement texts (for example, Payne 2003).

Validity

Just as reliability indexes represent the extent to which a test yields consistent measurement across examiners and items, validity indexes represent the extent to which the test assesses what it was designed to assess. Validity is the "most fundamental consideration in developing and evaluating tests" according to the Standards for Educational and Psychological Testing (American Educational Research Association [AERA], American Psychological Association [APA], & National Council on Measurement in Education [NCME], 1999, 9). There are various strategies for determining validity, including content validity, construct validity, predictive validity, and treatment validity. For informal tests, content and treatment validity are perhaps the most critical types. **Content validity** refers to the extent to

TABLE **4.2** **Types of Validity**

Type of Validity	What Is Measured?	How Is It Determined?
Content	How well do items assess the desired content	Expert review Test blueprint
Construct	How well do the items assess a particular construct, domain, or skill area	Correlation coefficients with other measures of the same construct or other measures of intent
Concurrent	How well do two or more measures of same construct agree (administered at same time)	
Predictive	How well do two or more measures of same construct agree (one administered several months or years before the other)	
Treatment	How well do the items predict students' learning gains	Analysis of gain scores following instruction

which a test reflects the content that the teacher or school district considers important. **Treatment validity** refers to the extent to which a test yields information that relates directly to instruction. See Table 4.2 for a summary of validity types and some techniques used to determine them.

Content validity. Content validity evidence typically is determined by examining the items contained within a test and the extent to which they reflect knowledge of interest. Usually this is determined by creating a test blueprint. Figure 4.2 shows a blueprint for a test we designed with a colleague to assess teachers' knowledge of reading instruction and assessment practices. You will see that items were developed to assess mastery of knowledge at a basic recall or recognition level and at a more advanced application level in the areas of alphabetics, fluency, vocabulary, and comprehension. A quick glance at the test blueprint provides a visual summary of the number of items assessing each category. By using a blueprint, test authors can ensure a balanced coverage of the content they wish to assess.

Construct validity. Another type of validity, **construct validity,** can be determined by evaluating the relationship between the test of interest and other established measures of the construct of interest. One type of construct validity is **concurrent validity;** in this case, the measures are administered to the same examinees at approximately the same time. In our case, if an author wants to determine the validity of a newly developed informal reading test, the author may administer the new test and an older well-constructed test measuring the same or similar content to a group of students on the same day. The scores then are subjected to a statistical formula, in this case, the Pearson Product Moment correlational procedure. A high positive score, approaching 1, is an indication that the newly constructed test has construct validity because it measures the same construct as the older, established measure. For example, correlations between measures of oral reading fluency, such as those used in AIMSweb (Edformation 2001; Harcourt, 2007) and DIBELS (Good and Kaminski 2002) with the Woodcock Reading

FIGURE 4.2 Sample Test Blueprint

	Alpha-betics	Fluency	Vocabulary	Comprehension	General	Total
Assessment						
# of Items	2	2	2	2	2	10
Knowledge	21, 70	53, 63	19, 69	48, 79	3, 45	
# of Items	3	3	3	3	3	15
Application	10, 42, 44	1, 12, 23	18, 9, 43	28, 30, 81	20, 61, 67	
Total per Scale/ Assessment	5	5	5	5	5	25
Instruction						
# of Items	5	5	5	5		20
Knowledge	8, 25, 31, 35, 38	14, 29, 41, 50, 66	17, 22, 39, 52, 80	6, 36, 55, 58, 76		
# of Items	9	9	9	9		36
Application	7, 11, 13, 46, 56, 59, 62, 65, 77	4, 16, 32, 37, 40, 47, 68, 71, 74	24, 26, 27, 49, 54, 57, 73, 75, 78	2, 5, 15, 33, 34, 51, 60, 64, 72		
Total per Scale/ Instruction	14	14	14	14		56
Total per Scale	19	19	19	19	5	
Total						81

Ziegler, M., Bell, S. M., & McCallum, R. S. (in press). Test Blueprint for *Assessment of Reading Instructional Knowledge-Adults*. National Institute for Literacy.

Mastery Test (Woodcock 1987/1998) were .91 and higher, according to information from the AIMSweb Training Workbook, published on the AIMSweb Web site (www.aimsweb.com). Another type of construct validity is predictive validity. **Predictive validity** is the extent to which a test predicts success on some variable of interest. For example, the goal for developing an informal test of reading might be to predict reading success in class, as represented by a language arts grade. In this case, a Pearson *r* might be calculated to determine the relationship between the test score and grades; and if the Pearson *r* yields a score approaching positive 1, the author would conclude that the test has solid predictive validity.

Treatment validity. Treatment validity is the extent to which a test yields information that is useful in treatment, or, in the context of this book, reading instruction. Although treatment validity is more difficult to establish than other types, there are two strategies to achieve the goal. First, treatment validity may be determined by examining the specific content assessed by test items and relating that content to a teacher's instructional goals. For example, remember Misha in Ms. Crockett's first grade class? She reads slowly and haltingly. The most appropriate type of assessment is one that allows Ms. Crockett to hear her read and assess her rate and accuracy. A procedure that allows Ms. Crockett to gain information about the specific skills in question is more appropriate than a generic test, such as one that requires the student to read words from an oral word list and allows her to target specific instruction.

A second way to determine the treatment validity of a test is to evaluate how well the test predicts progress or gains made by students, based on the information taken from the test. That is, the extent to which a test predicts instruction gain may be evaluated by assessing students' achievement gain scores over a prescribed period of time during which the test results were used to guide instruction. For example, assume that Misha is targeted for extra instruction (Tier 2 in a multi-tiered instructional approach) based on her oral reading fluency scores from the DIBELS. According to this *rate* measure, Misha needs instruction designed to increase reading rate. In Tier 2 instruction, she gets lots of practice reading books at her instructional reading level, a strategy designed to increase rate. If, after eight weeks of Tier 2 instruction, her oral reading fluency score on the DIBELS improves, we can assume that the DIBELS oral reading score has treatment validity in this limited context (as a measure for determining the need for fluency instruction). Statistically, the relationship between Misha's DIBELS score on measures of oral reading fluency and her grades after instruction could be established by calculating a Pearson *r* between the test scores and grades after instruction.

In the remaining sections of this chapter, we address three types of commercially available assessments that are used primarily to gauge student progress: (a) criterion-referenced, (b) progress monitoring, and (c) computerized.

CRITERION-REFERENCED ASSESSMENT

Special educators, educational diagnosticians, and others who work in remedial programs often use commercially published criterion-referenced assessments that measure a wide variety of academic skills across many grade levels. These instruments have been particularly useful for (a) assessing mastery of objectives as determined in the Individual Education Program (IEP) of students in special education; (b) determining present levels of performance, as required in federal special education law, and (c) establishing specific curricular objectives.

Criterion-referenced assessments have been extremely useful in establishing IEP objectives for students below grade level or with inconsistent performance across different types of academic skills. For example, Mr. Haywood, our special education teacher, has used the BRIGANCE® Diagnostic Comprehensive Inventory of Basic Skills–Revised (CURRICULUM ASSOCIATES®, Inc.© 1999, 1983) for the past five years with his special education students. The BRIGANCE® Inventories have been used primarily in special education to determine student mastery on a wide variety of academic skills dating back to the 1970s. These assessments have been used by thousands of special educators to determine student progress toward specific curriculum goals. An example of a specific reading goal might be: *the student demonstrates ability to substitute initial consonant sounds in words*. This specificity allows teachers to set particular educational goals and gauge progress.

All teachers conduct some type of criterion-referenced assessment. The unit tests and worksheets used by our first-grade teacher, Ms. Crockett, and featured in Chapter 3 are criterion-referenced in that they provide information about how well a student can perform a specific skill or task, such as matching words that rhyme or choosing the correct definition for a word read in context. Criterion-referenced tests, as the name implies, tell the teacher the extent to which a student has mastered specific criteria, including curriculum objectives. These tests are used to assess student mastery of the curriculum rather than to compare a student's performance to that of other students. Most reading instructional programs include criterion-referenced assessments to measure skill mastery as students progress through the instruction. Classroom teachers typically use these assessments routinely as described in the beginning of Chapter 3.

In contrast to classroom teachers, special education students historically have used a variety of instructional materials, often different from or in addition to the core program used in the regular classroom. And formal instruction in reading often ends at about sixth grade. Consequently, adolescents and adults with low reading levels may not receive instruction from a basal reader or a core reading program. To gauge progress of primary students in special education and older students reading below grade level, there are numerous commercially available criterion-referenced measures that are not tied directly to a given set of instructional materials. The BRIGANCE® Inventories are the most comprehensive and are widely used in special education programs across the United States (Overton 2006). Next, we specifically describe some of the BRIGANCE® Inventories.

The BRIGANCE® Inventories

Several BRIGANCE® instruments are available, but not all are directly relevant for reading assessment. Some are designed as screening instruments (including BRIGANCE® K & 1 Screen II [2005]; BRIGANCE® Preschool Screen II [2005]) and are often administered when children first enter a school setting. Preschool, kindergarten, and first-grade classroom teachers often administer these instruments at the beginning of a school year, when a child enters a program, and sometimes to assess progress in a program. Other BRIGANCE® instruments are designed for secondary-level special education and vocational education students (such as the BRIGANCE® Life Skills Inventory 1994). Most relevant for our purpose are the BRIGANCE® Diagnostic Inventory of Early Development—Second Edition (IED-II; CURRICULUM ASSOCIATES®, Inc.© 2004, 1991, 1978) and the BRIGANCE® Diagnostic Comprehensive Inventory of Basic Skills—Revised (CIBS-R; CURRICULUM ASSOCIATES,® Inc.© 1999, 1983). These provide in-depth assessment of reading, reading readiness, and reading-related skills as well as many other academic skills. Rather than provide an exhaustive review of these instruments, our goal is to inform teachers and other assessment specialists about the basic structure and utility of the instruments, particularly about administration guidelines, depth and breadth of reading-related content, and usefulness of the information the instruments provide.

Structure. Typically, the BRIGANCE® Inventories contain multiple subtests; each inventory is contained within a large, ringed binder that resembles a traditional notebook. These binders contain examiner and examinee pages that can be removed from the notebooks for ease of administration. For any particular student, only selected subtests should be administered. In addition, there is a student record book in which the teacher/examiner records specific information about the student's performance. On the first page of the student record book, the teacher circles the skills the student masters and underlines the skills to be targeted as objectives. In addition, the system allows the same student booklet to be used up to six times, with the teacher using a pen of a different color each time the student is assessed. This system works well for students in special education, whose progress needs to be assessed frequently throughout a given school year. See Figures 4.3 and 4.4 for examples of the student profile and examiner record book pages.

FIGURE 4.3 Page from Student Record Book, BRIGANCE® Diagnostic Comprehensive Inventory of Basic Skills–Revised

G. WORD ANALYSIS (CONTINUED)

Assessment	Page	
G-12	217–219	**READS SUFFIXES:**

(page 217)
[1]1. s
2. ed with *t* sound
3. 's
4. ed with *d* sound
5. ing
6. es
7. double final consonant and add *ing*
8. double final consonant and add *ed*
9. drop final *e* and add *ing*
[2]10. er
11. y
12. ly

(page 218)
13. est
14. y to i and add *es*
15. y to i and add *est*
16. remove y and add *ily*
17. n
18. en
[3]19. ful
20. f to v and add *es*
21. or
22. th
23. ness
24. ion

(page 219)
25. ous (drop final *e*)
26. ment
27. al
28. drop final *e* and add *ation*
[4]29. ward
30. ist (drop final *e*)
31. less
32. ian (remove y)
33. able (drop final *e*)
34. ship
35. ance (drop final *e*)
[5]36. ish[6]

| G-13 | 220 | **READS PREFIXES:** |

[2]1. un 3. re 5. in [4]7. en 9. inter [5]11. mis 13. pre
[3]2. dis 4. im 6. non 8. super 10. de 12. fore 14. ir[6]

| G-14 | 221 | **DIVIDES WORDS INTO SYLLABLES:** |

[2]1. one vowel sound
2. like consonants between vowels
3. unlike consonants between vowels
4. consonant blends and digraphs between two vowels
5. one consonant between two vowels
6. suffixes
[3]7. three vowel sounds
8. ending *le*
9. prefixes[4]

Brigance, A. H. Page from Student Record Book of the *BRIGANCE® Diagnostic Comprehensive Inventory of Basic Skills–Revised.* © 1999, 1983. N. Billerica, MA: CURRICULUM ASSOCIATES®, Inc. Reprinted/Adapted by permission.

FIGURE **4.4** Page from Examiner Book, BRIGANCE® Diagnostic Comprehensive Inventory of Basic Skills–Revised

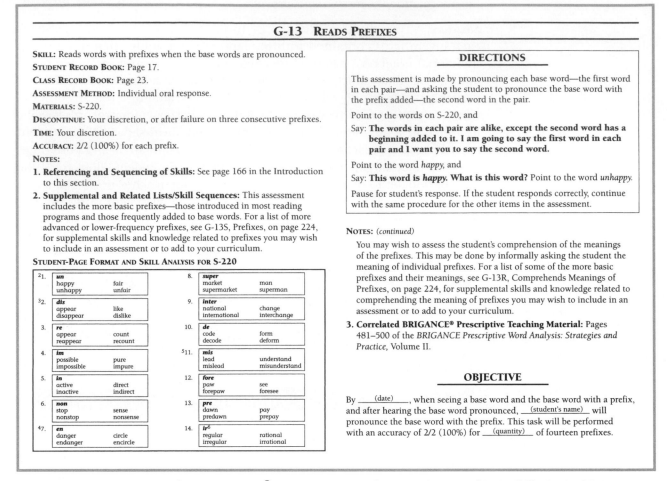

Brigance, A. H. Examiner Page from *BRIGANCE® Diagnostic Comprehensive Inventory of Basic Skills–Revised* © 1999, 1983. N. Billerica, MA: CURRICULUM ASSOCIATES®, Inc. Reprinted/Adapted by permission.

As is apparent from Figures 4.3 and 4.4, the tasks are clear and straightforward and each skill area to be assessed is described. Each skill is tied to an objective, and the objective is provided with blanks embedded and to be completed by the examiner, showing the projected date of completion and the criterion required for mastery. Some of the subtests yield norm-referenced information, such as standard scores (with a mean of 100 and a standard deviation of 15), grade/age equivalents, and percentiles, (these scores are described in Chapter 5). The primary purpose of the administration, however, is to obtain information about students' present levels of performance and to aid in developing instructional goals and monitoring progress.

Perhaps the most widely used inventory, the CIBS-R, contains three global components that can be used to screen, determine readiness for kindergarten or first grade, and assess specific skills for students performing at instructional levels typical of students in grades 1 through 6. Because special education students are generally performing below typical grade-level expectations in one or more areas, the CIBS-R may be used with older students or even adults, depending on instructional level.

Administration.   As mentioned earlier, not all sections should be administered to particular students. The examiner selects the skills areas to be assessed, presumably relative to teacher and curricular goals. Specific administration directions are provided, as are suggestions about scoring criteria, administration time, discontinue rules, and so on (see Figure 4.4).

Content.   BRIGANCE® Inventories are designed to provide in-depth information sufficient to inform instruction. In fact, teachers are encouraged to use the information to set instructional objectives, particularly for IEPs required for special education students. The reading and reading-related skill areas assessed by the CIBS-R include: readiness, speech, listening, word recognition, oral reading, reading comprehension, word analysis, functional word recognition, spelling, writing, reference skills, graphs, and maps. Within the functional word recognition skill area, the following specific content can be assessed: basic sight vocabulary, direction words, number words, warning and safety words, information sign words, warning label words, and food label words. Within the direction word area are specific word lists related to writing, speaking, physical activities, and studying. Additional supplemental sections include content assessing contractions, abbreviations, and so on. So assessment data can be very specific and may be tied directly to specific classroom goals.

Usefulness.   BRIGANCE® data can inform specific reading goals, based on direct assessment of what the student can and cannot do. Use of the system allows examiners to create very specific learning objectives. Multiple assessments can be generated to chart progress and determine ultimate mastery of the objectives. So **intra-individual comparisons** are readily available. **Inter-individual comparisons** are also available for some subtests and some ages, based on norm-referenced scores.

Psychometric integrity.   **Psychometric** data are available in standardization and validation manuals. Data show moderate to good test-retest, internal consistency, inter-rater, and alternative forms reliabilities, as well as evidence for various types of validity. For example, robust correlations are shown

between examinee raw scores and age. (Because achievement should progress steadily with development, this relationship between age and raw scores is expected). Several correlation coefficients show evidence for concurrent validity between the BRIGANCE® scores and related instruments, such as the Peabody Individual Achievement Test-Revised (Markwardt 1989) and the Wide Range Achievement Test-3 (Wilkinson 1993). Although appreciable psychometric data are available in the CIBS-R Standardization and Validation Manual, not all agree on its merits. For example, according to a review of the CIBS-R by Cizek (n.d.) "Overall, the level of content validity evidence provided falls short of 'abundant' as claimed in the technical manual" (Validity section ¶ 1). Cizek calls for the collection of additional information to support content validity claims and the mastery/nonmastery cutoffs provided, as well as the development of new items that more clearly differentiate between the constructs assessed. Finally, Cizek (n.d.) recommends cautious use of the standardization data for making eligibility decisions; rather, the BRIGANCE® is best used as an information gathering tool. In that role, it appears to be strong indeed, and it can help teachers determine instructional goals and monitor progress of those goals.

Let us look at an example of a BRIGANCE® assessment for a student from Mr. Haywood's special education class. In Chapter 3, you learned that Shelby, a fifth-grade student who receives reading instruction from Mr. Haywood, was administered an informal reading inventory by the reading specialist at the beginning of fifth grade (refer to Table 3.4 to see her scores on comprehension and word recognition). According to results from the IRI, Shelby's instructional reading level is 3, even though she is in fifth grade. Mr. Haywood is responsible for much of Shelby's reading instruction and, consequently, wants more in-depth information about her reading. From the CIBS-R, he chooses several sections to obtain a more in-depth picture of Shelby's skills in reading; based on this assessment, he will set goals that are reflected in Shelby's IEP. He will assess her progress every six weeks, in accordance with state and federal special education guidelines, and will set new goals as she masters current ones. Figure 4.5 depicts a section from the CIBS-R and shows Shelby's performance the first time she was assessed by Mr. Haywood.

■ PROGRESS MONITORING

The passage of the Individuals with Disabilities Education Improvement Act (IDEA 2004) in late 2004 provides a strong impetus for collaboration of educators across disciplines to assess and gauge progress of all students, particularly in the area of reading. IDEA 2004 calls for early intervention for those at risk for academic failure and demands that educators track students' instructional responsiveness. The intent is to prevent academic failure, especially in reading, and consequently reduce the percentage of students ultimately identified as eligible for special education.

Recall the multitiered model of reading instruction and the Response to Intervention (RTI) model described in Chapters 1 and 2. The success of these models relies on two important components: (a) effective instruction and (b) accurate assessment. Our first-grade teacher, Ms. Crockett, uses a core reading program that is generally effective with most of her students.

FIGURE 4.5 Shelby's Scores on Selected Sections of the BRIGANCE® Diagnostic Comprehensive Inventory of Basic Skills–Revised

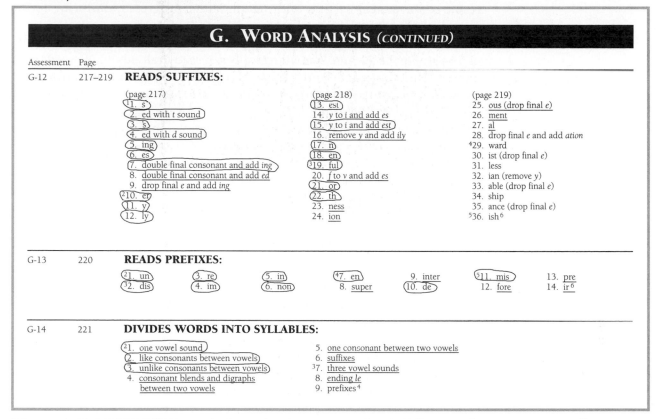

G. WORD ANALYSIS (CONTINUED)

Assessment	Page	
G-12	217–219	**READS SUFFIXES:**

(page 217)
1. s
2. ed with *t* sound
3. s
4. ed with *d* sound
5. ing
6. es
7. double final consonant and add *ing*
8. double final consonant and add *ed*
9. drop final *e* and add *ing*
²10. er
11. y
12. ly

(page 218)
13. est
14. y to i and add *es*
15. y to i and add *est*
16. remove y and add *ily*
17. n
18. en
³19. ful
20. *f* to v and add *es*
21. or
22. th
23. ness
24. ion

(page 219)
25. ous (drop final *e*)
26. ment
27. al
28. drop final *e* and add *ation*
⁴29. ward
30. ist (drop final *e*)
31. less
32. ian (remove y)
33. able (drop final *e*)
34. ship
35. ance (drop final *e*)
⁵36. ish⁶

G-13	220	**READS PREFIXES:**

²1. un
²2. dis
3. re
4. im
5. in
6. non
⁴7. en
8. super
9. inter
10. de
⁵11. mis
12. fore
13. pre
14. ir⁶

G-14	221	**DIVIDES WORDS INTO SYLLABLES:**

²1. one vowel sound
2. like consonants between vowels
3. unlike consonants between vowels
4. consonant blends and digraphs between two vowels

5. one consonant between two vowels
6. suffixes
³7. three vowel sounds
8. ending *le*
9. prefixes⁴

Brigance, A. H. *BRIGANCE® Diagnostic Comprehensive Inventory of Basic Skills–Revised* © 1999, 1983. N. Billerica, MA: CURRICULUM ASSOCIATES,® Inc. Reprinted/Adapted by permission.

However, some fail to progress with their peers. Some enter first grade knowing only a few letters and sounds, and others enter with limited English proficiency. Occasionally, she has a student with enriched oral vocabulary who has extreme difficulty mastering phonics and remembering words automatically. For these students, early intervention is essential. Most students who do not read well by the end of third grade will never read well (Badian 1988). Consequently, there is a strong need for accurate monitoring of student progress, particularly in the early grades.

Ideally, teachers are well-informed about assessment and instruction. In many cases, effective use of the assessment techniques described in Chapter 3 will provide teachers with the knowledge needed to determine when students need additional or different types of instruction. However, teacher knowledge and expertise in the use of informal classroom techniques is extremely variable. Because too many students reach middle and upper grades with inadequate reading skills, large-scale progress monitoring is included in the multitiered model RTI models. The rationale is to assess students several times per year. Their progress on certain key indicators of reading (including quick oral reading of words at grade level) is compared to the typical progress of students in the same grade. Students whose progress is below the typical performance of students in the same grades are targeted for more intensive instruction, and their progress is gauged more frequently. The National Center on Student Progress Monitoring has been established as a resource for educators, and information about progress monitoring tools is available at: www.studentprogress.org/chart/chart.asp#.

Benchmarks are expected levels of performance; for example, at the end of first grade, the average student typically can read orally about 50 words per minute (Hasbrouck and Tindal 1992). **Slope** is actually a term taken from the element of a graph that shows the relationship between performance (say oral reading fluency—defined as number of words read correctly per minute) and instructional time. Using this example, the steepness of the line showing rate of oral reading progress relative to time spent in instruction is called the slope. Consequently, we can graph the performance of Jesse in Ms. Crockett's class to see whether he is making progress consistent with expectations for his age and grade. We know that the average first-grader acquires 1.75 new sight words per week (Fuchs and Fuchs 2005). Figure 4.6 shows progress monitoring for Jesse. We can see that he appears to be making adequate progress. He generally increases his oral reading speed by about two words per week.

Because progress monitoring provides information about the student's level of performance—such as how many words the student can read in a minute and rate of acquisition (slope)—implications for instructional placement are pretty straightforward. If the child is below benchmark (i.e., expected performance at some given time) but rate is adequate, current instruction is probably effective. However, if the child performs below benchmark and rate is also slower than typical, instruction needs to be intensified. In this case, the child would begin receiving supplemental instruction (Tier 2 in the context of multi-tiered instruction). For effective progress monitoring, tools should be reliable (consistent) and valid (accurate). These measures should also provide measures of discrete skills so that teachers can target instruction.

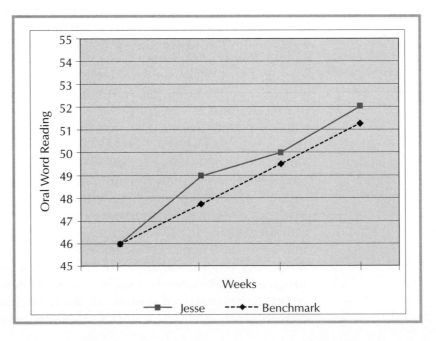

FIGURE 4.6 Oral Reading Fluency (Words Correct Per Minute) for Jesse, a First Grader

In order to meet the multiple needs of informal assessment, hybrid measures have emerged that combine some characteristics of informal and formal assessment. Curriculum-based measures (CBM), like those in Chapter 3, historically have been developed by teachers using actual school curriculum. However, according to Fuchs and Deno (1994), curriculum-based measurement may actually be more effective when not derived from the actual curriculum in use. There is an increasing trend toward use of standardized skills assessments in which a student's performance is compared to the typical performance for his or her grade. In this scenario, students are screened three to four times per year on one or more key measures of reading. If progress is within expected range, great! If not, students are targeted for more frequent instruction and assessed much more frequently (e.g., once per week). Two assessments that are widely used are the AIMSweb progress monitoring system (Edformation 2001) and the Dynamic Indicators of Basic Early Literacy Skills, or DIBELS (Good and Kaminski 2002).

AIMSweb

AIMSweb (www.aimsweb.com) is published by Edformation, Inc., which was acquired in 2007 by Harcourt Assessment, and is updated regularly. AIMSweb is the name of a software assessment system that can be used by school systems and individual teachers to assess, monitor, and track student progress. Also, it can be used to track students in systems that already use DIBELS (addressed in the following section of this chapter); alternatively, system personnel have the option of using unique but somewhat similar measures built into the AIMSweb system. In fact, AIMSweb includes unique measures of reading fluency, comprehension, early literacy skills, Spanish early literacy skills, early numeracy skills, mathematical computation, spelling, and written expression. These measures are curriculum-based in the sense that they are designed to assess real-world skills that teachers consider essential in the classroom and are appropriate for assessing benchmarks for students in grades K–8 and for progress monitoring for students of any age. According to the authors, AIMSweb provides a proactive, evidence-based solution for universal screening, strategic assessment, progress monitoring, and special services eligibility.

Structure.   AIMSweb provides not only testing materials, but also a tracking service. Typically, system administrators or other personnel make a decision to "subscribe" to AIMSweb services, which are differentially priced depending on system needs. For example, according to the AIMSweb Internet site, a system site license can be purchased for a small fee per student, which varies depending on the type of service needed. Additional site or individual licenses can be purchased and, as with the others, prices depend on the services, academic areas assessed, and data needed (such as preservice instructor package, benchmark data package, progress monitoring data package, and RTI data package). The prices include computer scoring and monitoring, downloadable test materials, manual, online support, and training. Directions for administering the materials and tracking the scores are provided.

Administration and scoring.   Teachers or other personnel individually administer assessments to students; each assessment takes from one to five minutes, administration is fairly straightforward. The tests can be administered by a teacher or other educator or by a trained paraprofessional. Hand scoring is necessary, but it is easy to master. Analyses are conducted via the computer tracking system. Raw scores may be transformed into percentiles, age and grade equivalents, and standard scores (see Chapter 5 for an explanation of these scores) and may be referenced in graph form to data showing an error line, goal line, and trend line. Benchmark assessments are administered three times a year, and typically, systems determine a criterion score to be used for assigning "at-risk" status to students. For example, students who score in the bottom 10 percent of other students in the system (or school) may be designated "at risk." The progress of the at-risk students is assessed more frequently; the progress monitoring probes of AIMSweb are administered once per week. In addition to low performance (i.e., scores in the bottom 10 percent), a second criterion may be added to define which students go on to more focused and presumably more powerful instruction. For example, those students whose rate of progress (slope) falls within the lowest 25 percent and who still score within the lowest 10 percent of the class may be considered eligible for a Tier 2 intervention. Systems may use continued progress monitoring to determine which students are targeted for consideration for special services, including special education eligibility.

Using the scenario created for determining Tier 1 and Tier 2 eligibility (mentioned earlier), those who continue to fall short based on the criteria—including those who continue to score within the lowest 10 percent of all students at the school and show a rate of progress consistent with the lowest 25 percent—may be referred for more in-depth academic, cognitive, or social/emotional assessment to rule out or rule in problems such as mental retardation, emotional disturbance, and learning disabilities.

Content.   AIMSweb materials are designed to provide two levels of assessment specificity for reading fluency, reading comprehension (using a maze or cloze procedure, described in Chapter 3), early numeracy (oral counting, identifying numbers, missing numbers, and quantity), math computation (facts and calculation), early literacy (letter and nonsense word naming, letter sound fluency, phoneme segmentation, (with a similar Spanish version)) spelling, and written expression. First, benchmark materials that are designed to be administered three times per year provide a global assessment. Benchmark data are appropriate for screening in the academic areas. Progress monitoring probes that are designed to be administered once a week are useful for tracking more specific skill acquisition. These measures tap skills that are similar to those taught in the classroom, but the particular skills measured are not tied directly to any particular curriculum. Consequently, even though probe data are more specific than benchmark data, probes will not inform instruction in a direct manner. Even though the AIMSweb system sometimes is touted as a curriculum-based assessment device, the data generated are not likely to align with a particular teacher's classroom goals and may not correspond closely to end-of-the-year, norm-referenced achievement test scores.

Usefulness.   The AIMSweb system has been adopted by many school systems across the country, presumably because it provides methods for universal screening and tracking progress to conform to the No Child Left Behind mandates and related legislation, such as the Individuals with Disabilities Education Improvement Act (IDEA 2004). The ultimate utility of the system remains to be seen. On the surface at least, the data generated can be helpful to system personnel as they track system-wide student gains and at-risk student progress. It can be implemented system wide, on a school-by-school basis, or even by individual teachers or tutors. To obtain maximum use of the system, considerable assessment time and management expertise are required. For example, just ordering the materials needed for a particular school or system is somewhat daunting, requiring a solid familiarity with the components. Systems considering adopting AIMSweb must be prepared to invest significant time and energy in training, assessment, and management.

Psychometric integrity.   Although the origin of the AIMSweb system can be traced back to work of Germann and colleagues in the 1970s, and more recently Shinn (see the AIMSweb site for related literature), the current application is relatively new. Even so, its developers have not ignored the need to support its use by generating psychometric data. For example, for oral reading fluency, authors report inter-rater reliability coefficients in the high .90s; test-retest reliabilities (from 2 to 10 week periods) ranging from .84 to .97; alternate forms reliabilities (with tests administered one week apart) ranging from .84 to .94; and concurrent validity data with correlations ranging from .26 to .91 with various tests of reading, such as the Woodcock Reading Mastery Test (Woodcock 1987/1998) and the Gates-MacGinitie Reading Test (MacGinitie, MacGinitie, Maria, and Dreyer 2000) (www.aimsweb.com/research/). These data are impressive; however, they were collected using a wide variety of sources for the reading passages.

The origin of data specifically used to generate AIMSweb psychometric estimates is not easy to find on the Web site. As the system becomes increasingly popular, independent data will be generated by practitioners and researchers. Some recent research has addressed the need to provide more sophisticated psychometric data for confident interpretation of trend line scores that use repeated measures (i.e., probes). For example, Poncy, Skinner, and Axtell (2005) demonstrated that multiple probes are necessary before trend lines can be interpreted confidently. This is necessary because of the error associated with each probe. As you may remember from our earlier discussion of reliability, there is some error contained in every score and when examiners use multiple scores to make decisions, the error rate is compounded. Thus, to overcome this limitation, many measures are required.

In summary, although initial data are encouraging, further independent research will be helpful in ensuring confident use of the AIMSweb system. Further, the academic tasks in the various screening and probes tend to represent somewhat discrete academic skills, but they do not give teachers specific information about what to teach next, as does the BRIGANCE®. Rather, they simply provide information about a child's performance in a particular area defined by the authors (such as oral reading fluency), show comparability to that of peers, and track changes over time as a function of instruction.

Although the AIMSweb system offers school systems several advantages, implementation is expensive and time intensive. Administrators will need to evaluate whether their particular school system can afford the time required of school personnel to generate the massive and ongoing database produced by the multiple probes, and in fact, whether the system requires such an extensive database.

The Dynamic Indicators of Basic Early Literacy Skills

The Dynamic Indicators of Basic Early Literacy Skills, or DIBELS (Good and Kaminski 2002; https://dibels. uoregon.edu/) provide direct assessment of prereading and reading skills of students in kindergarten to sixth grade. Originally conceptualized as a curriculum-based measure, DIBELS continues to be updated and includes measures that can be aligned with the areas of reading targeted by the National Reading Panel (NRP, National Institute for Child Health and Human Development [NICHD] 2000):

- Phonemic awareness—Initial Sounds Fluency (ISF) and Phoneme Segmentation Fluency (PSF)
- Phonics—Nonsense Word Fluency (NWF)
- Fluency—Letter Naming Fluency (LNF) and Oral Reading Fluency (ORF)
- Comprehension—Retell Fluency (RTF)
- Vocabulary—Word Use Fluency (WUF)

Although not all measures are administered to all ages, the measures can be used to: (a) identify children at risk for reading failure, (b) monitor progress as students acquire literacy skills, and (c) evaluate intervention effectiveness. Two types of measures are available, including benchmark tasks which can be administered to all students three times per year, and progress monitoring tasks which can be administered more frequently.

Structure.   All measures are designed to be administered in one minute. The benchmark materials consist of scoring booklets, reusable student stimulus materials, and examiner scoring and recording forms. Progress monitoring probes include examiner forms and twenty alternate forms of student material per measure. A manual describing administration and scoring is available. All these materials are free and downloadable from the DIBELS Web site given earlier. Alternately, they are available for purchase from Sopris West Publishing Company. Examiners must supply a clipboard and colored pen for administering the Retell Fluency and Word Use Fluency tasks.

Content.   All seven DIBELS measures are described in Table 4.3. As is obvious from reading these descriptions, students are expected to produce a product, hence the use of the term "fluency" as part of the name of every measure. For example, students must identify one of four pictures that begin with a target sound and produce initial sounds of orally presented words that correspond to the pictures for the Initial Sound Fluency measure. They also must segment words into individual phonemes for the Phoneme Segmentation Fluency measure, name letters for the Letter Naming Fluency measure, call pseudowords for the Nonsense Word Fluency measure, read a passage for the Oral Reading Fluency measure, retell a passage for the Retell

TABLE 4.3   Description of DIBELS Measures by NRP Domains

NRP Domains	Phonemic Awareness	Phonics	Fluency	Vocabulary	Comprehension
Measure(s) and Grade-Level Guides	Initial Sound Fluency (K) Phoneme Segmentation Fluency (K–1)	Nonsense Word Fluency (K–2)	Letter Naming Fluency (K–1) Oral Reading Fluency (grades 1–6)	Word Use Fluency (grades 1–6)	Retell Fluency (grades 1–2)
Units of Measure	Number of onsets correct per minute for the set of picture probes Number of correct phonemes in 1 minute	Number of correct letter sounds in one minute	Number of correct letter names in one minute Number of correct words in one minute; median of three passages	Number of words in correct utterances in one minute	Number of relevant words provided in one minute
Skills Targeted	Phonemic awareness	Connecting letters with sounds Recoding phonologically	Knowledge of alphabet Reading ongoing text with accuracy and fluency	Semantic usage	Recalling and recounting ideas from oral reading

Note: Adapted from Rathvon, N. (2004). *Early Reading Assessment: A Practitioner's Handbook.* Description of the DIBELS Measures by Domain, p. 208. New York: The Guilford Press.

Fluency measure, and use a word in a sentence for the Word Use Fluency measure. For students whose first language is Spanish, there is a Spanish version, *Indicadores dinámicos del éxito en la lectura.*

Administration and scoring.   Probes are administered individually and take three to five minutes each. Administration of the complete set of benchmark measures takes about ten to twenty minutes. DIBELS authors recommend that probes be administered as frequently as two times per week or as needed to monitor progress. Teaching items typically are provided, as are discontinue rules. Smooth administration requires careful attention to detail (such as pacing of stimuli, determining correctness of responses, recording scores, and timing latency to response), so practice is required. Fluency measures are scored (e.g., number of correct initial sounds and words read correctly per minute). Scoring can be somewhat difficult. For example, on some tasks, students are given three seconds to respond, and on others, they are given five seconds. To aid the examiner, specific guidelines are provided to help in determining errors, such as inaccuracies, omissions and substitutions, mispronunciations, and so on, but each task has its own set of complexities. Examiners should engage in several practice sessions before administering

DIBELS for classroom use. To ease the burden of scoring and reporting, computer software is available to convert raw scores to percentiles and to provide a summary of the meaningfulness of the scores obtained.

DIBELS can be used for making comparisons using local norms based on at least three administrations per year: fall, winter, and spring. If local norms are used, a categorizing system of at-risk status is suggested. Students who perform below the twentieth percentile are considered to be "at risk"; those who perform between the twentieth and fortieth percentile are considered to be at "some risk." Those scoring above the fortieth percentile are assumed to be at low risk. Based on group performance, some performance indicators have been generated for teachers to use as rough measures of acceptable progress. Benchmark goals and risk indicators for the measures used in grades Kindergarten through six are available on the Web site https://dibels.uoregon.edu/. It is important to note that these benchmarks are updated periodically.

Usefulness. According to its authors, DIBELS is not intended to be a comprehensive or diagnostic battery, but rather a set of quick, efficient, indicators of literacy development, which are particularly valuable for monitoring progress. The materials were developed with several criteria in mind. Some of the most important include brevity, ease of administration, and sensitivity to growth. Many school systems across the country have adopted DIBELS, in part because the authors were successful in meeting their criteria (for development of the instrument), but also, in part, because the instrument is inexpensive to acquire (downloads are easily accessible online and free of charge). Because alternate forms are available and the system is sensitive to assessing a continuum of reading skills, it has been adapted for use in screening for at-risk status and then used to monitor responsiveness to intervention. DIBELS appears to be well suited for these goals, and the data generated are readily available not only for use by classroom teachers but they may also be assimilated for determining classroom, school, and even system-wide accountability. Finally, the DIBELS authors relate the results to a five-step problem-solving model with direct implications for intervention (Kaminski and Good 1998). DIBELS measures can be administered by licensed/certified teachers or other trained personnel and screening data can be obtained for a classroom within a short time.

Psychometrics. Much of the DIBELS technical adequacy data have been generated by the authors and their colleagues (Good and Kaminski 2002) and are available on the DIBELS Web site, though specific reliability and validity information is somewhat cumbersome to find. And, according to Rathvon (2004), these data are somewhat limited (e.g., some studies were conducted with older versions of some tasks, some studies do not show sample sizes, and there is limited evidence for intra-rater reliability). In her review of the reliability evidence, Rathvon noted reliabilities from .72 to .99, and concluded that the reliabilities vary considerably as a function of task and type. Similarly, concurrent validity indexes vary, with values typically ranging from the mid-.30s to mid-.70s when the DIBELS tasks are correlated with similar tasks or subtests, for example with subtests taken from the Stanford Diagnostic Reading Test (Karlsen, Madden, and Gardner 1985), the Woodcock-Johnson Psycho-Educational Battery-Revised (Woodcock and

Johnson 1989), and with teacher ratings. Others have found similar correlations; for example, Elliot, Lee, and Tollefson (2001) report correlations ranging from .60 to .70 between the DIBELS and standardized measures of phonological awareness and teacher ratings of achievement.

DIBELS authors report that most measures are sensitive to grade and age changes, as expected, and the more academically sophisticated students become, the higher their scores become. DIBELS is sensitive also to the regression in scores as a function of summer layoffs (e.g., lower scores are obtained from a fall grade 1 administration, relative to the spring of the kindergarten year; similar declines are found for the higher grades). Finally, some of the tasks show floor effects for some students (for example, PSF for fall and winter administrations for kindergarten students and ORF for many first-graders). **Floor effects** occur when a measure does not have sufficient items to tap lower- or beginning-level skills for weak students. According to Rathvon (2004), the instrument simply seems too hard for these students, in part because of insufficient experience with the content at those ages.

Limitations of DIBELS.   Despite positive features of the DIBELS measures (such as short assessment time and low cost), they are not without critics. It is important to note that although DIBELS has achieved wide use for progress monitoring of reading, some experts including Pressley, Hilden, and Shankland (2006) have questioned the psychometric integrity of DIBELS. In fact, Brunsman and Shanahan, in a 2006 review of the test, indicated that "documentation of reliability of scores and evidence of validity for the described purposes of the DIBELS is woefully inadequate" (Comment Section, ¶ 1). Some experts question its utility for informing instruction (McGill-Franzen, personal communication, June 9, 2006). For example, when teachers administer the Letter Naming Fluency measure to kindergartners, teachers learn how quickly students can name letters but they do not learn what letters students do and do not know. DIBELS has been used as the evaluation tool in many federally-funded Reading First initiatives. However, some of the individuals involved in administering these programs have been accused of pressuring states and systems to use DIBELS (Grunwald 2006; "Two Inquiries" 2005/2006). And, Goodman (2006), along with several colleagues, has written a critical review of DIBELS questioning its reliability and usefulness. A criticism is that because DIBELS scores are based on timed performance, their use may pressure teachers to focus instruction too heavily on reading rate at the expense of other skills, particularly comprehension. Educators are encouraged to observe DIBELS in use before making decisions about adopting it in their own systems.

Interestingly, DIBELS is included in a comprehensive reading program called the Voyager Universal Literacy System (www.voyagerlearning.com/literacy/overview.jsp), but is referred to within the Voyager system as the Vital Indicators of Progress (VIP). According to information in the Assessment and Progress Monitoring section on the Voyager Web site, VIP is equivalent to DIBELS but is designed to assess progress specifically within the Voyager curriculum.

Adequacy of Progress Monitoring Systems

Advocates of the multitiered model of instruction and RTI argue that these approaches will meet the needs of a majority of students (Fletcher, Coulter, Reschly, and Vaughn 2004). Assessment plays an integral role, identifying those students who successfully respond to instruction by comparing student performance to typical performance in specific skill areas. However, not all students respond positively to intervention. Further, there are many technical and practical challenges associated with large-scale implementation of RTI. Some questions that must be addressed if RTI is to be implemented successfully include:

a. Who will administer the assessments?
b. Who will be responsible for scoring, graphing, and managing the data generated from the assessments?
c. Specifically how will the information from the assessments be tied to instruction?
d. How can assessment be scheduled to minimize disruption of student instruction?

A drawback to the use of progress monitoring is the limited amount of information provided. For example, a teacher may learn that a student is below benchmark expectations based on his or her reading fluency rate. However, this information does not tell the teacher exactly where to focus instruction. Consequently, it is likely there will be an ongoing need for criterion-referenced testing as described in the first section of this chapter and in Chapter 3.

■ COMPUTER-BASED ASSESSMENT OF READING

Computers are a part of everyday life. Many children in the United States use computers before entering school (Judge, Puckett, and Bell 2006). Consequently, students (and their teachers) are becoming technologically savvy and increasingly are able to take advantage of the incredible efficiency of computer learning programs, related computer peripherals, and the World Wide Web. Currently, it is possible to obtain a reading assessment using computers. But from a teacher's perspective, how does a computerized assessment help? Is computerized assessment efficient; in other words, does it free the teacher to do other things? Does it provide information unobtainable from other sources? Does it provide the specificity needed to guide instruction? Are the psychometric properties of computerized assessments acceptable? As you might guess, the answers change as a function of the partticular question asked, but in general, many questions such as these can be answered with a qualified "yes." Consequently, teachers and administrators are motivated to investigate the possible benefits of computerized assessment. In the following section, we provide answers to some of the important questions teachers ask about computerized assessment of reading and we focus on the results this type of assessment generates, rather than on the use of the computer to track student and classroom progress from pencil-and-paper administration. Examples of computerized tracking systems were discussed in earlier sections of this chapter (e.g., AIMSweb).

Is computerized assessment efficient?   Obviously, no innovation comes without cost. So the answer to this question is not as straightforward as it first appears. Any new technique requires not only money (to acquire it), but also time (to learn to use it effectively). Computerized assessment is no different. In order to use computerized assessment, teachers must learn how to help their students engage the computer programs. The particulars vary by product. Some computerized assessments are completely Web-based and can be accessed without having to purchase additional software, hardware, or printed materials (such as Total Reader, a Web-based benchmarking system using the Lexile framework, by EdGate 2006), which can be found online at: www.totalreader.com/index.php?fuseaction=home.faq.

Total Reader can be accessed from any computer with Internet capability and can be used for students in grades 3 through 12; it provides an individual record for progress monitoring using content-appropriate materials and allows students to access a variety of reading materials independently. Each student's level of reading is determined by an initial diagnostic test, the results of which can be printed in a report format. The report produces a Lexile measure, a score ranging from 200 (beginning reading) to 1,700 for advanced readers. This system can be used to track reading progress for an individual student's entire school career. Reading materials are provided based on that information. These passages are aligned to Lexile scores using two indicators of passage difficulty: semantic difficulty related to frequency of use and syntactic complexity related to sentence length. Using this system, students can read fiction or nonfiction passages taken from appealing real-world sources at the appropriate level. The authors of Total Reading claim that it can be used to help track students' adequate yearly progress (AYP) required by the NCLB legislation because student progress can be compared to the progress of peers within a school or system. Once students have been taught to use the Total Reader system, they can work relatively independently and teachers can use the report generated to gauge progress. Consequently, this system does provide efficient assessment and can save the teacher time once its use is automated within the classroom.

The Total Reader system is only one of several computerized assessment systems that may be used to increase efficiency in reading assessment. One of the most widely used computerized assessment systems—STAR Reading (2006; Renaissance Learning; www.renlearn.com/starreading/software/) also provides an efficient assessment of reading. STAR combines measures of vocabulary and comprehension to yield an index of student reading levels. In the "Vocabulary In-Context" section, students read a short sentence with a missing word and select the missing word from a set of four choices, as in Figure 4.7, which was taken directly from the STAR Reading Web site.

Using a similar assessment strategy for the "Authentic Text" sections, students read a passage with a missing word and select the missing word from a set of four choices, as shown in Figure 4.8, also taken from the STAR Reading Web site.

According to information provided on the Web site, any student with a reading vocabulary of one hundred words or more can take the STAR assessment. Based on the data generated, a report is produced, which includes information about the skill level of the particular student assessed

FIGURE 4.7 STAR Reading Vocabulary

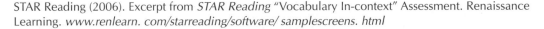

Vocabulary In-context Questions

Deck Braided!   2/25

My big brother is two years _older_ than I am.

1. better

2. larger

3. older

4. faster

The student must actually interpret the meaning of (in other words, comprehend) the sentence in order to choose the correct answer because all of the answer choices "fit" the context sentence either semantically or syntactically.

STAR Reading (2006). Excerpt from *STAR Reading* "Vocabulary In-context" Assessment. Renaissance Learning. *www.renlearn. com/starreading/software/ samplescreens. html*

and an assessment of that student's level compared to peers (e.g., percentile ranks and grade equivalents). In Chapter 5, we describe in detail how these scores should be interpreted; but for now, just realize that they allow comparisons with classmates and same-grade peers across the country. In addition, the STAR Reading Diagnostic Report also includes narratives describing strengths and weaknesses, as well as recommendations. We reproduce an example of a STAR report in Figure 4.9 (p. 156).

Renaissance Learning also publishes computerized assessments of early literacy (STAR Early Literacy). The areas of general readiness, graphophonemic knowledge, phonemic awareness, phonics, comprehension, structural analysis, and vocabulary are assessed.

Computerized assessment is also provided by the "Let's Go Learn" and the Diagnostic Online Reading Assessment system, or DORA (2006; www.letsgolearn.com/). As the name of the system implies, it allows online assessment and generates a report. Scores are provided as grade-level equivalents for a number of reading assessments in the following areas: graphophonics; high-frequency words; word recognition (phonetically irregular words); phonics (ability to sound out words); phonemic awareness (ability to manipulate sounds); spelling; and semantics, including oral vocabulary **(receptive vocabulary)** and reading comprehension (comprehension of silently read passages). DORA provides a rather extensive narrative describing these areas, along with recommendations.

As is probably apparent, there are many computerized assessments available, with accompanying and related intervention packages. In addition to those already mentioned, several others are designed for specific populations

FIGURE 4.8 STAR Authentic Text

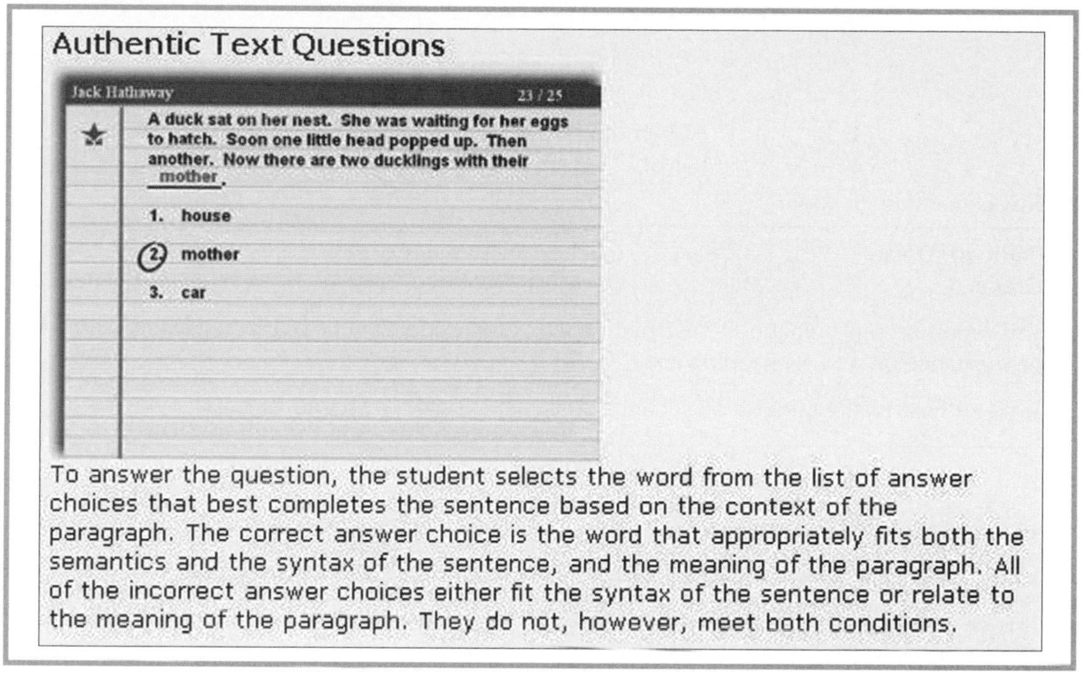

Authentic Text Questions

Jack Hathaway   23 / 25

A duck sat on her nest. She was waiting for her eggs to hatch. Soon one little head popped up. Then another. Now there are two ducklings with their _mother_.

1. house

(2) mother

3. car

To answer the question, the student selects the word from the list of answer choices that best completes the sentence based on the context of the paragraph. The correct answer choice is the word that appropriately fits both the semantics and the syntax of the sentence, and the meaning of the paragraph. All of the incorrect answer choices either fit the syntax of the sentence or relate to the meaning of the paragraph. They do not, however, meet both conditions.

STAR Reading (2006). Excerpt from *STAR Reading* "Authentic Text" Assessment. Renaissance Learning. *www.renlearn.com/starreading/software/samplescreens.html*

and are focused on specific skill areas via the Internet, including the Lexia Program, designed specifically for teachers who provide phonics-based literacy instruction to students with dyslexia and other learning difficulties (www. lexianet.org/). Read 180 (http://teacher.scholastic.com/products/read180/ overview/) is described as an intensive reading program that helps educators confront the problem of adolescent illiteracy on several fronts. Also, the Northwest Evaluation Association (NWEA) uses several state-aligned computerized adaptive assessments (Measures of Academic Progress, for example) to determine the instructional level of students and measure growth over time (www.nwea.org/assessments/).

Can computerized assessment guide instruction? As is apparent by now, computerized assessment systems provide information about the reading skills of students, and in some cases, the information is very specific (e.g., measurement of beginning sounds via assessment of graphophonics from the DORA). So in some cases the information is specific enough to provide teachers with helpful information to guide instruction, much like information that could be obtained from the administration of tests such as those described earlier in this chapter (e.g., BRIGANCE® Inventories). However, in some cases, the information obtained is not linked to any specific reading curriculum and therefore may not be specifically related to classroom goals. In other cases, such as Total Reader, the assessments are an integrated part of a total reading program. Hence, the answer to the question "can computerized assessment guide instruction?" is a qualified "yes."

FIGURE 4.9 STAR Diagnostic Report

STAR Reading®
Diagnostic Report
Monday, December 12, 2005 3:27:15 PM
Test Date: December 12, 2005 3:18:30 PM

East Elementary School

Callicutt, Dylan   **Teacher: DeMarco, Corey**
Grade: 3   **Class: Mr. DeMarco Class B**   **ID: dcalli**

This report presents diagnostic information about the student's general reading skills, based on the student's performance on a STAR Reading test.

Time for First Part: 4 minutes 45 seconds   Time for Second Part: 2 minutes 38 seconds

SS	GE	PR	PR Range	Below Average	Above 50	Above Average	NCE	IRL	ZPD
372	3.1	46	34–59		——◆——		47.9	3.2	2.6–3.7

This student's Grade Equivalent (GE) score is 3.1. His or her reading skills are therefore comparable to those of an average third grader after the first month of the school year. Dylan also achieved a national Percentile Rank (PR) of 46. This score is in the average range and means that Dylan scored greater than 46% of students nationally in the same grade. The PR Range indicates that, if this student had taken the STAR Reading test numerous times, most of his or her scores would likely have fallen between 34 and 59. It reflects the amount of statistical variability in a student's PR score.

These scores indicate that Dylan is likely starting to place less emphasis on identifying words and more emphasis on understanding what he or she reads. Students at this level select fewer picture books for their own reading. They start to challenge themselves with longer picture and chapter books. Dylan is also probably aware of his or her abilities and interests in choosing books to read. He or she is increasingly able to select books and take tests independently.

For optimal reading grown, Dylan needs to:

* Practice reading independently every day
* Continue reading aloud and reading with others
* Develop additional strategies for acquiring vocabulary in context

Dylan's Zone of Proximal Development (ZPD) for independent reading is 2.6–3.7. If Accelerated Reader® reading management software is being used in your classroom or school, Dylan should be encouraged to select books with book levels in the ZPD. These books will provide optimal reading challenge without frustration. The ZPD, however, is approximate. Success at any book level also depends on the student's interest and prior knowledge of a book's content.

The following techniques will also help ensure Dylan's continued growth in reading:

* Guide reading practice so that Dylan maintains an average score of 85 percent or higher on Accelerated Reader Reading Practice Quizzes.
* Use the Accelerated Reader Diagnostic Report and Student Record Report for more detailed information about the student's reading practice.
* Teach Dylan how to select books throughout his or her ZPD.
* Help Dylan establish a minimum book level, minimum percent correct, and point goals for each marking period.

STAR Reading (2006). Sample Report from the *STAR Reading* Assessment. Renaissance Learning.
www.renlearn.com/starreading/software/samplescreens.html

Does computerized assessment provide unique information? As before, the answer to this question is a qualified "yes." Some of the computerized systems offer somewhat unique results. For example, the STAR Reading Diagnostic Report provides information that is uniquely linked to the Accelerated Reader (Renaissance Learning 2006). In other words, the STAR Report yields a grade-level reading range, which describes the examinee's instructional level. This range of appropriate materials is described in terms of grade-level equivalents and is called the Zone of Proximal Development (ZPD). The ZPD of Dylan Callicult, the example shown in Figure 4.9, is 2.6 to 3.7. The report encourages Dylan's teacher to help him select books with these levels. Of interest, the ZPD is based on Vygotsky's social development theory (1978) that to-be-learned content can be optimally matched to the sophistication level of the student. This idea is akin to a similar principle advanced by other developmental psychologists (such as the "problem of the match" by Hunt 1972) acknowledging the importance of providing instruction consistent with the readiness level of the learner, a rule well known by all successful teachers.

Lexiles

Another increasingly valuable contribution offered by some computer-based/ Web-based assessment packages, including for example, the Total Reader system, is the "Lexile Framework." The Lexile Framework is a system that allows scores, called Lexiles, to be generated via the computer allowing teachers and administrators to gauge an examinee's reading ability and success across the examinee's school career. These scores range from 200 to 1,700, typically. Although they can be used to characterize a student's reading ability, the scores are not like traditional reading level scores; that is, they do not refer to grade-level performance nor can they be compared meaningfully to a psychometric scale with the population mean set to a familiar value, such as 100.

If Lexiles reference an unfamiliar scale, how can they be used? Consider, for example, a second-grader who may earn a score of 325; this score can be compared to a score earned by the same student as a ninth grader, say 990. These scores, at both grades, can be compared to Lexile means generated by the system to determine how the examinee compares to others in the school system. In addition, teachers eventually develop knowledge of how these scores are arrayed in their school across grade levels. Consequently, suppose one of Dr. Charles' high school students, Emilio, earns a Lexile score of 490. Dr. Charles, who is familiar with the range of Lexile scores, realizes that such a score is typical of middle fourth-graders. This information lets him know that Emilio likely will have trouble reading the high school biology text independently.

Perhaps the most useful feature of the Lexile Framework is that the scores provide a built-in strategy for helping teachers match students to books along the same continuum of Lexile scores. As mentioned earlier, Lexiles are assigned to the performance of a particular reader based on reading ability; Lexiles are also assigned to a text, based on the difficulty of the text. In this manner, a common language is created for students, teachers, and parents to use, not only to characterize or order the student's reading ability but also to match that ability to the difficulty of books. The difference between a reader's Lexile and a particular text's Lexile can be used to predict the reader's level of comprehension with that text. Many standardized tests yield Lexile scores—and not only those administered via computer. Further, many basal readers and trade books have been assigned Lexiles.

In order to use the Lexile Framework, a tool called the Lexile Calculator has been created. The Calculator predicts a reader's level of comprehension on a particular text and is used as follows: If a reader with a Lexile of 1,000 is given a text with a Lexile of 1,000, the reader is predicted to read that text with 75 percent comprehension. In this case, the difference between the ability of the reader and the text difficulty is "0." This relationship (and the 75-percent difficulty level set to a difference score) was chosen purposely because it is presumed to be somewhat optimal for instruction. A comprehension rate of 75 percent assures that the reader can follow the theme of the text, but still requires that the student work to acquire meaning (from the text). When the Lexile difference between the text calibration and the ability of the reader is −250, the text is more difficult than the reader is capable of reading, and the rate of predicted comprehension falls to 50 percent. On the other hand, if the Lexile rate is 250, the reader is more capable than the text is difficult, and the rate of anticipated comprehension increases to 90 percent. If a teacher wishes to use reading materials that a particular reader can comprehend at the 85 percent level, the teacher would select the material based on a Lexile difference of 150 points; that is, the material would show a Lexile score of below the Lexile established by the reader. The general relationship between predicted comprehension rate relative to the reader-text difference (in Lexiles) is expressed in Figure 4.10.

How are Lexiles determined for text material? Obviously, Lexiles are based on difficulty level, and as you know by now, difficulty level of a passage may be established by determining the semantic sophistication (difficulty and frequency of the vocabulary words) and the syntactic complexity (average sentence length). Lexiles reflect these influences and can be created by a specific computer program called a Lexile Analyzer. Once any text is typed or scanned into the Analyzer (minus headings, titles, etc.), Lexiles can be

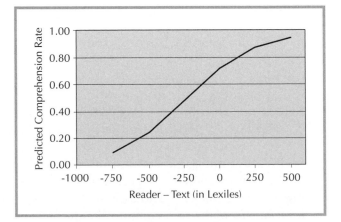

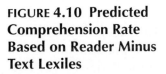

FIGURE 4.10 Predicted Comprehension Rate Based on Reader Minus Text Lexiles

generated. Teachers can access this program by simply logging on to www.lexile.com/EntrancePageHtml.aspx?1, registering at the site, and (without charge) determining within seconds the Lexile level of a text. Lexile levels of many textbooks are already available on this site, and others can be added quickly. Researchers have investigated the relationships between standardized test scores and Lexiles and between basal readers and Lexiles (Stenner 1996). The relationships reported in these studies provide support for the use of Lexiles.

In summary, most of the computerized assessment systems have somewhat unique features, but many of those features are not truly new for the most part and may not be unique just to computerized administered tests; hence, the appropriateness of the qualified "yes" in response to the question, "Does computerized assessment provide unique information?"

Are the psychometric properties of computerized tests acceptable?   Again, the answer is a qualified "yes." Just as do authors of pencil and paper tests, some authors of computerized tests take seriously the need to provide psychometric data to users. And some do not. So it is not always easy for educators to find data supporting the use of a particular computerized assessment system. In other cases, the data are more accessible. For example, for the STAR Reading system reliability and validity data are available from Renaissance Learning. Reliability data include split-half and test-retest correlations that are generally acceptable, ranging from .70s to .90s. Concurrent validity data obtained from correlations of STAR Reading components with other tests are generally acceptable (e.g., ranging from .40s to .80s). Similarly, data from the STAR Early Literacy measures are available from the authors from a sample of approximately 11,000 children in grades K–3 from 84 school districts in the United States and Canada. Measures of split-half and test-retest range from .68 to .90. Standard errors of measurement are also reported and are generally acceptable. We are not aware of any independent studies showing psychometric properties of the STAR, and such studies are needed, not only for the STAR Reading system but for all the computerized systems. As with every other test, the user must take responsibility for determining whether or not the instrument is supported by reliability and validity data. (AERA 1999). Obviously, this process is facilitated by authors and publishers who make psychometric data readily available, as well as by independent researchers and other users who generate psychometric data.

The psychometric adequacy of the Lexile system was evaluated by a committee commissioned by the National Center for Educational Statistics (2001). In general, the committee indicated the system has technical adequacy for determining an individual's reading capacity, though the report focused primarily on issues related to assigning Lexiles to reading material of different types and levels. Interested readers can find detailed information about technical aspects of Lexiles at www.lexile.com.

Reliability and validity information for DORA is available online at www.letsgolearn.com/. Though moderate-to-strong correlations are reported between subsections of DORA and several well-known measures of reading, the sample size is small (e.g., twenty students) and the data used in some of the calculations appear to be taken from various versions of the DORA. So it is unclear how this reliability and validity information relates to versions currently in use.

■ SPECIAL CONSIDERATIONS FOR ADULT AND ENGLISH LANGUAGE LEARNERS

We conclude the discussion of progress monitoring and hybrid assessments with particular suggestions for adult learners and for ELL students. These are presented in Boxes 4.1 and 4.2, respectively.

BOX 4.1 Progress Monitoring Assessment Tips for Adult Learners

1. Assess adult learners' educational histories, background experiences, and interests as well as specific reading skills.

2. Because criterion-referenced and progress monitoring measures focus on mastery of specific skills and generally are not normed, some criterion-referenced measures, such as the BRIGANCE® Inventories, may be appropriate for adults.

3. Consider using instruments that assess functional and workplace literacy skills, such as the BRIGANCE® Diagnostic Life Skills Inventory and

BRIGANCE® Diagnostic Employability Skills Inventory.

4. When using materials designed for younger students with adult learners, ensure that the reading material is age-appropriate.

5. Use of computerized assessments may be appropriate for adults, assuming the reading material is age-appropriate.

6. Because most adult learners have limited time to spend on academic tasks, monitor progress frequently to ensure instructional strategies are effective.

BOX 4.2 Progress Monitoring Assessment Tips for English Language Learners

1. Because of the nature of progress monitoring assessments, such assessments may be more appropriate for ELL students than formal, standardized tests.

2. Frequent progress monitoring is especially important for ELL learners.

3. Be sure to establish rapport and put ELL learners at ease before beginning assessment.

4. At times, it may be helpful to assess ELL students' native language proficiency.

5. Consider using native language assessments, such as the BRIGANCE® Diagnostic Comprehensive Inventory of Basic Skills–Revised Spanish Edition and/or the Spanish language measures from AIMSweb or DIBELS, for students whose first language is Spanish.

Summary

In this chapter, we described tests that incorporate some aspects of informal and formal assessment, tests that typically are given within the context of either a general or special education classroom, and that are used primarily to monitor progress. First, we discussed commercially available criterion-referenced measures not tied to a specific curriculum, in particular the BRIGANCE® Inventories, which are used extensively in special education to determine progress and to set instructional goals. Next, we described hybrid assessments that have roots in teacher-generated curriculum-based methods described in Chapter 3. However, these hybrids are not actually rooted in a particular curriculum; rather, they measure discrete skills (including oral reading fluency of letters, words, and passages) and provide scores that can be compared to benchmarks to determine whether students are making adequate progress. Two of the most widely used hybrids (AIMSweb and DIBELS) include computer management systems that allow students' progress to be graphed and compared to the performance of other students and to the individual student's own progress over time. Despite increasingly widespread use, both tests have been criticized for limited evidence of reliability and for lack of usefulness for planning instruction. Finally, we addressed computerized assessment, some of which use sophisticated, but user-friendly, Lexile systems to track student progress over time and to link students to appropriate level texts. Unlike the BRIGANCE® Inventories, DIBELS, and AIMSweb, these assessments are administered and managed via computer. We expect computerized assessment to become increasingly available and integrated into traditional instruction.

Before concluding this chapter, let us think again about the Literacy Instruction Pie presented in Appendix C. How can measures from this chapter help you construct such a Pie for a class or for an individual student? The progress monitoring tools focus heavily on fluency but also can provide information about word analysis skills and comprehension, at least in a limited way. The computerized assessments provide measures of word analysis and vocabulary and comprehension. And the BRIGANCE® Inventories provide a wide variety of information depending on the sections administered. Teachers and specialists should keep a folder on each student, as well as classroom summaries, such as the types available with AIMSweb and most other computerized assessment and management systems. These data can be combined with more informal data (discussed in Chapter 3), as well as more formal data (discussed in Chapters 5 and 6) to construct Instruction Pies for their classes and individual students.

A summary of characteristics of some of the most commonly used progress monitoring and criterion-referenced assessments and the specific areas of reading assessed by each are presented in Table 4.4 on page 163. Information on technical qualities (such as reliability and validity) and types of scores are presented in Table 4.5 on page 164. In Chapter 5, we turn our attention to norm-referenced, individually-administered measures that typically are used to assess performance in reading and compare that performance to peers.

mylabschool™

Where the classroom comes to life!

MyLabSchool is a collection of online tools for your success in this course, your licensure exams, and your teaching career. Visit www.mylabschool.com to access the following:

- *Online Study Guide*
- *Video cases from real classrooms*
- *Help with your research papers using Research Navigator*
- *Career Center with resources for:*
    Praxis exams and licensure preparation
    Professional portfolio development
    Job search and interview techniques
    Lesson planning

TABLE 4.4   Informal Reading Assessment 1: Characteristics of Informal Assessment and Progress Monitoring Measures

Name of Technique or Measure	Publisher/Source/Date	Grades/Ages	Administration Time	Administration Format	Basic Reading Skills — Sight Recognition	Basic Reading Skills — Phonics/PA	Basic Reading Skills — Fluency	Reading Comprehension — Vocabulary	Reading Comprehension — Comprehension
Criterion-Referenced Assessments (non–curriculum-based)									
BRIGANCE® Diagnostic Inventory of Early Development, 2nd ed.	Curriculum Associates, 2004	Age Birth–6	Varies depending on measures given	Individual	X	X			
BRIGANCE® Diagnostic Comprehensive Inventory of Basic Skills–Revised	Curriculum Associates, 1999	PreK–9	Varies depending on measures given	Individual (includes some group screening tests)	X	X		X	X
Hybrids									
AIMSweb	Edformation, 2006	K–8	Series of 1 minute assessments	Individual	X	X	X		X
Dynamic Indicators of Basic Early Literacy Skills, 6th ed. (DIBELS–6)	University of Oregon, 2005	PreK–6	Series of 1 minute assessments	Individual	X	X	X		X
Computerized Assessments									
Diagnostic Online Reading Assessment (DORA)	Let's Go Learn	PreK–12	Varies depending on measures given	Individual	X	X		X	X
STAR Early Learning	Renaissance Learning	PreK–3 and above	Varies depending on measures given	Individual	X	X		X	X
STAR Reading	Renaissance Learning	1–12	10 minutes	Individual	X			X	X
Total Reader	EdGate	3–12	Varies	Individual		X		X	X

Note: PA = Phonemic Awareness.

Information is based on a combination of published and online materials (including independent test reviews, content from tests and test manuals, and publisher/author promotional materials). Strenuous efforts were made by authors to ensure accuracy but information may contain errors and omissions due to updates in the tests reviewed, errors in published materials, and conflicts in reported information. Lists are not exhaustive.

TABLE 4.5   Informal Reading Assessment 2: Psychometric Properties of Informal Assessment and Progress Monitoring Measures

Name of Measure or Technique	Reliability Reported				Validity Reported			Type of Scores
	IC	TT	AF	IR	CON	PRE	CNC	
Criterion-Referenced Assessments (non-curriculum-based)								
BRIGANCE® Diagnostic Inventory of Early Development, 2nd ed.	X	X	X		X		X	Criterion-referenced; grade equivalents
BRIGANCE® Diagnostic Comprehensive Inventory of Basic Skills–Revised	X	X	X	X	X	X	X	Criterion-referenced; grade equivalents
Hybrids								
AIMSweb	X	X	X	X	X		X	Reading rate
Dynamic Indicators of Basic Early Literacy Skills, 6th ed. (DIBELS–6)	X	X	X		X	X	X	Reading rate
Computerized Assessments								
Diagnostic Online Reading Assessment (DORA)		X			X	X	X	Grade equivalents
STAR Early Learning	X	X					X	Grade equivalents; percentiles
STAR Reading	X	X					X	Grade equivalents; percentiles
Total Reader					X		X	Lexiles

Note: IC = Internal consistency; TT = Test/retest; AF = Alternate forms; IR = Inter-rater; CON = Content; PRE = Predictive; CNC = Concurrent.

Information is based on a combination of published and online materials (including independent test reviews, content from tests and test manuals, and publisher/author promotional materials). Strenuous efforts were made by authors to ensure accuracy but information may contain errors and omissions due to updates in the tests reviewed, errors in published materials, and conflicts in reported information. Lists are not exhaustive.

CHAPTER 5

Formal Assessment of Reading: Individualized Assessment

Teachers, educational diagnosticians, reading specialists, and school psychologists spend a considerable portion of their time assessing reading and related skills. Administrators spend time determining whether instruction is effective and in choosing instructional materials; typically these decisions are based on assessment data. Historically, classroom teachers have spent more time administering informal instruments, such as those discussed in Chapters 3 and 4, and less time using formal measures. Formal measures are characterized as norm-referenced because they yield information about average or typical performance, which can be used to compare a particular student's performance with same-age or same-grade peers (Overton 2006). And, most

teacher-based assessment occurs in the classroom. The reverse is true for educational diagnosticians and school psychologists who, traditionally, have used formal measures more frequently than informal ones outside the classroom, primarily to help determine eligibility for special education or other special services; that ratio may be changing as school decision makers experiment with using new eligibility criteria. For example, implementation of responsiveness-to-intervention strategies to help determine eligibility for learning disabilities may require school psychologists and diagnosticians to administer more informal assessment. Nonetheless, teachers, educational diagnosticians, and school psychologists need to know about informal *and* formal measures, as do other professionals (for example, administrators).

Informal and formal norm-referenced reading tests are widely used and have been discussed in previous chapters of this book, particularly informal measures. The primary purpose of this chapter is to provide more detailed information about a variety of formal assessment instruments, particularly those that measure the areas of reading identified by the National Reading Panel (NRP, National Institute of Child Health and Human Development [NICHD] 2000). A secondary goal is to present a context for understanding the scores derived and how the scores can be used to help students. We focus on the most commonly available and widely used measures and provide information to help guide the selection and use of instruments for traditional and special populations.

Perhaps the best way to build context for understanding the goals associated with formal reading assessment is to refer back to the *Inclusive Model of Reading* presented in Chapter 2 (and reproduced in Appendix B). As is clear in that model, reading comprehension is the ultimate purpose for students engaged in the process of reading. But there are many subskills of reading. For example, subskills may include phoneme manipulation, decoding, automaticity, prosody, and so on. Acquisition of these skills is influenced by cognitive underpinnings of reading such as auditory processing, auditory and **visual memory,** and processing speed. Other less directly related though still important influences may include personality and noncognitive variables such as attention, motivation, and interests. Finally, there are important environmental influences, such as parental support, classroom and school climate, and appropriateness of instructional materials. Many of these influences can be assessed, informally or formally. As shown in Appendix B, all of the influences contribute to successful comprehension and they form a complex equation, with the components interacting over settings and time.

In the beginning of Chapter 5, we describe how formal reading tests are developed and we explain the nature of the scores they yield. This information leads to a powerful understanding of the scores the tests generate and how the scores can be used. In this context, we also discuss how particular types of scores may be used in real-world situations. Next, we describe excerpts from popular tests that provide measures of important areas of reading. As you know by now, no test is perfect—some tests even have serious flaws—nor are tests always wisely used. So we discuss some of the major potential problems and remedies in a section called **test bias.** As in previous chapters, we conclude the chapter with a table listing some of the most commonly used norm-referenced measures of reading; we indicate the areas of reading assessed by each, describe for whom the test is appropriate, give practical information such as administration time and publisher, and identify some of their psychometric properties.

■ DEVELOPMENT OF FORMAL READING MEASURES

As with any cognitive or academic area, development of a formal measure of reading begins with careful consideration of the area to be assessed. The ultimate goal of reading instruction is to promote comprehension; we can infer that students are comprehending and mastering related necessary skills by observing them performing certain behaviors. The first task of any author interested in developing a test of reading is to decide which aspects of reading are to be assessed, such as automatic word recognition, decoding of nonsense words, fluency and vocabulary development, or comprehension. Usually, tests measuring subdomains are referred to as subtests, subscales, or scales; often, subtest or subscale scores are combined to comprise an overall test composite or full scale score. Once authors determine the areas of interest, they express this interest in the form of assessment goals. After these goals are established, a test blueprint, sometimes called a **table of specifications,** can be developed. A **test blueprint** is a graphic representation that summarizes behavioral outcomes and content of a well-defined unit of knowledge, such as an instructional unit in a classroom assessment context. The blueprint typically contains two dimensions. For example, the broad areas of reading might comprise one dimension consisting of phonics, fluency, vocabulary, and comprehension and another of cognitive complexity. Cognitive complexity might be defined as level of knowledge, such as knowledge of facts at a low level versus application of knowledge (an advanced level). We presented a test blueprint very much like the one just described (in Figure 4.2 of Chapter 4), and this blueprint guided the construction of a formal test we developed with a colleague to measure teachers' knowledge of reading instruction.

Once a test blueprint has been established, particular items are written to assess the domain or subdomains along the dimensions expressed in the blueprint. For example, a student's vocabulary can be assessed simply by asking for definitions. So a vocabulary test *could* consist of a list of words to be defined, with a corresponding key (correct acceptable answers), along with a scoring guide (for example, one point for each correct definition). This kind of item taps factual and recall knowledge. A second type of vocabulary item could be written to test another dimension of the blueprint. Suppose we refer to the blueprint example used earlier but now want to assess a higher level of cognitive complexity for vocabulary, we might write multiple-choice items that required application of knowledge. For example, the student might be asked to choose one of four vocabulary words that correctly completed a sentence. To summarize the process, the domain of knowledge is determined, other dimensions of interest are chosen, the blueprint is developed, and items are written. Typically, formal test items are developed by experts in the field who have been asked to create them based on the blueprint and other criteria of interest, such as age-appropriateness of content and ease of administration, scoring, and interpretation.

Once a pool of items has been developed, items are arrayed in logical order in a **developmental version** of the test. Typically, the items then are administered to a small sample of individuals during a process referred to as **pilot testing** or **field testing.** The scores generated are subjected to various logical and statistical analyses to determine the best items. These analyses are guided by particular questions of interest, such as "Is the item too easy or too hard?" and "Do the strongest students (those who know the most about the content) answer the item correctly and do the weakest students miss it?" Once the best items are chosen, they are arrayed into the **standardization version.**

In order to compare a student's score to same-age or same-grade peers, it is necessary to obtain scores on the test from these peers within some geographic area of interest, typically within a given country, state, or region. Of course, it is not possible to collect scores from every student in the country, so a representative sample is chosen. Often, it is one that reflects the percentages within the entire population based on the actual percentages of students who exist within the geographic regions (southeast, northeast, midwest, southwest, northwest); gender category (male, female); race (African American, Euro-American, Hispanic American, Asian American); age (typically by yearly intervals); school-based exceptionality (regular education, type of special education designation); and so on. The number of the students in the sample may range from a few hundred to a few thousand. The important consideration is that the sample mirror as closely as possible the total population of students within the country of interest, in our case, the United States.

Once the standardization sample has been chosen, the test is administered to each student in the sample and the **raw score** is obtained. A raw score represents the number of items the student got correct on a given test. Raw scores are converted into other scores that are more amenable to inter-student comparisons, such as **percentile ranks,** grade or age equivalents, or standard scores with a mean set to some value of interest to the test author, say 50, 100, or 500. The transformation from raw scores to other scores is necessary whenever educators are interested in comparing the performance of one student to that of other students.

TYPES OF SCORES

As implied earlier, raw scores provide only a gross estimate of mastery. They can be converted into percentage of mastery by dividing the total number of possible correct answers into the number correct obtained by a particular student. Teachers do this type of conversion routinely with tests and quizzes; this conversion allows a slightly more informed decision about relative mastery. For example, remember Jesse and Misha from Ms. Crockett's first-grade class? Ms. Crockett has administered a unit test accompanying the basal reading series; one of the tasks has thirty items and requires students to match beginning sounds with pictures of objects and to match pictures of words that rhyme. Jesse earned a raw score of 27, which converts to a mastery score of 90 percent correct and Misha earned a raw score of 15, which converts to 50 percent correct. Based on this information, Ms. Crockett has a pretty good idea that Jesse's phonological awareness skills are more proficient than Misha's. However, these scores tell Ms. Crockett nothing about how either student compares to the typical first-grader. Other scores are required for that purpose.

Grade and Age-Equivalent Scores

Grade and age-equivalent scores are fairly easy to derive. For age-equivalent scores, the average number of items correct can be calculated for each age in the standardization sample, typically by month. For example, for a particular test of reading vocabulary, the average raw score for students who are eight years, three months (expressed as 8–3) might be 29; the average score for students one month older, 8–4, might be 31, and the average score for those one year older, 9–3, might be 47. Once these relationships are established, any student's raw score can be transformed to an age equivalent. Take Misha's raw score of 15, for example; it might be converted to an age equivalent score of 5–6; Jesse's raw score of 27 might covert to an age equivalent of 6–4. The same procedure holds for determining grade equivalents. For example, Misha's raw score of 15 might convert to a grade equivalent of K.7, while Jesse's score of 27 might be transformed to a grade equivalent of 1.5.

Limitations of Age and Grade Equivalents

Age and grade equivalent scores are intuitively appealing; parents seem to understand the idea that their child is making progress consistent with the progress of the typical child at a given age or grade level. For example, Misha's parents are likely to understand that she is performing much like a student at the end of kindergarten, even though she is in the middle of the first-grade year. But they are less likely to be aware that comparisons to "typical" are often based on what is typical for the nation, and this comparison may be misleading when comparing her performance to those in Misha's particular class. So even though Misha is performing below expectation based on national norms, she may not be as far behind relative to peers in her school if they are performing below the national average.

There are other limitations of equivalents. For example, the conversion from raw scores to equivalent scores is not linear; that is, raw score increments of one point may yield three months of age equivalent score change at the extreme ages within a year but may yield only one month change within mid-year ranges. This occurs because students are less likely to obtain extreme scores than scores that fall in the middle of the distribution, and any change at these extremes reflects more of an impact. Also, grade and age equivalents can be misleading. Many test consumers believe that a student is performing at the given grade or age level assigned by the test. What these scores really mean is that the student got the same number correct as the average score for the students in the given age or grade level of the norm or standardization sample. Importantly, scores can be obtained in various ways. That is, a raw score of 27 may convert to a grade equivalent of 1.5, but a typical first-grader may have a very different pattern of performance than an older student with the same grade equivalent score. For example, a typical first-grader may complete successfully most lower level items and get most higher level items incorrect. But an older student with a learning disability might miss easy items intermittently and get some relatively harder items correct. Finally, another relatively minor limitation occurs because age equivalents and grade equivalents are reported on different scales. Grade equivalents are reported in decimals because grade scores are based on a school year, which is roughly ten months. Age scores are based on the calendar year, which is twelve months in length and uses a hyphen instead of a decimal.

Age Equivalent	Grade Equivalent
6–1	1.2
Six years/One month	First grade/Second month

Percentiles

Educators also use percentile ranks to assess progress of their students relative to peers. Percentile ranks (unlike a simple mastery-based percentage score) convey how well a student performs when compared to others in the same grade or at the same age, depending on whether test authors used age- or grade-based norms, but they do not tell the extent to which particular content is mastered. As an example, we might transform Misha's raw score of 15 to a percentile rank using a table created by test authors based on the standardization sample. In this case, we can assume the raw score of 15 transfers to a percentile rank of 16. This means that Misha performed better than 15 percent of those her age in the standardization sample, and by inference the entire country, and as well as those at her specific rank (16th percentile). So again we have evidence that Misha's performance is weak relative to peers. On the other hand, let's assume that Jesse's raw score of 27 converts to a percentile rank of 80; so he performed better that 79 percent of his peers, and as well as the 1 percent who earned his exact score. He is excelling, relative to peers.

Limitations of Percentiles

Percentiles are relatively easy to understand—they tell how many students achieved a score equal to, above, or below the score of a particular student. But they can also be misleading in a couple of ways. First, many people, including some educators, make the mistake of thinking of percentiles as percent correct. As you can see from the scores from Misha and Jesse, this is not the case:

	Misha	Jesse
Percentage mastery	50	90
Percentile	16	80

Percentage mastery means the percent correct and is not related to the percentile that describes the rank of a student's score compared to a set of scores. Second, because percentiles are a way of ranking scores, they cannot be added or subtracted. As we discussed earlier, most people achieve scores somewhere in the middle of the group. So lots of people get scores between the 40th and 60th percentiles, but not many people get scores at the 99th percentile or at the 1st percentile. Consequently, many experts prefer standard scores for making comparisons; we discuss standard scores in the following section.

Standard Scores

Authors often calculate standard scores to convey progress. Most teachers are familiar with IQ scores, and IQ scores represent one type of standard score. By convention, the average or mean IQ score is 100. Other standard score scales use other values as the mean; for example, 50 or 500. The particular mean of a standard score is completely arbitrary and can be set by the test author. Virtually all U.S. college students are familiar with either the Scholastic Aptitude Test (SAT; www.collegeboard.com/splash/) or the American College Test (ACT; www.act.org/). When these tests were developed, the authors set the mean of these tests to 1,000 and 18, respectively. After authors make this decision, they work backward in a sense and the mean raw score obtained from the standardization sample (by age or grade) is set to the standard score mean desired. Early authors of IQ tests set the mean to 100, and that score is now convention. All modern IQ test authors follow that rule, and many test authors follow the same rule when they develop individualized **standardized** academic achievement tests; that is, they use a mean of 100. In the area of personality assessment, authors more often use a scale such that the mean is set to 50. In summary, the mean raw score of any distribution of scores can be converted to the standard score mean of choice.

How are other properties of the standard scores determined?   Not only do authors have to convert the raw score mean to a standard score mean, they also have to convert the raw score **standard deviation** to a standard score standard deviation. So, if the raw score standard deviation is 29, it is converted to some value that remains a constant; typically, for tests that adopt a standard score mean of 100 the standard score standard deviation is set to 15. Although use of a population mean set to 100 and standard deviation set to 15 is very common for many of the reading tests you may use, there are other scales that you already know about. For example, the American College Test (ACT) test authors adopted a standard score mean of 18 and a standard score standard deviation of 6; the Scholastic Aptitude Test (SAT) authors adopted a mean of 500 and a standard deviation of 100 for the sections. Knowing this information helps you put in perspective a score you may have earned on one of these tests.

As mentioned, the choice of a value to represent the population mean and standard deviation is arbitrary. What is not arbitrary is the raw score mean and standard deviation; these are obtained from the actual standardization sample—the group of students on which the test is being normed. So the raw score mean and standard deviation are used as starting points in the conversion process. Most teachers know how to calculate a mean or average. Teachers, particularly those in middle and upper grades, determine grades by adding scores on student assignments and tests and determining the average. The standard deviation is less intuitive than the average and more difficult to calculate. However, the standard deviation is an important value in its own right and is a vital component of many more sophisticated statistical formulas. But teachers typically do not learn to value or calculate a standard deviation unless they have taken a formal measurement or statistics class. In brief, the standard deviation is a number resulting from a multistep formula that expresses the variation of a distribution of scores. Learning to calculate the standard deviation is beyond the scope of this book, but we will provide a brief discussion to facilitate a conceptual understanding. Conceptually, the standard deviation reflects the typical amount that scores vary within a distribution (of scores) relative to one another. In other words, the standard deviation is (roughly) a number that reveals the average amount that scores in a given group vary among themselves.

If the standard deviation is small, the scores within a distribution do not vary much; that is, the scores of students in the group are similar. In this case, the underlying assumption is that the ability assessed is similar for all the students whose scores comprise the distribution. Conversely, if the standard deviation is large, it means the scores of students in the group (and presumably the ability or skill being measured) vary widely. For example, if Ms. Crockett assesses oral reading fluency level in her classroom at the end of the academic year and finds the mean to be 51 words correct per minute (wcpm) and three words correct per minute to be the standard deviation, we would conclude that most students in the room have a similar fluency rate. Most students read between 48 and 54 wcpm one standard deviation below and above the mean, respectively. Suppose a colleague down the hall, Mr. Alverez, assesses fluency for his first-grade class and finds the same mean wcpm but a standard deviation of 9. Most of his students read between 42 and 60 wcpm, and he has more extreme scores. We would conclude that his students vary more than those of Ms. Crockett; that is, Mr. Alverez has more slow and fast readers than Ms. Crockett, even though the average is the same for both classes.

In the context of developing a formal test, once the raw score standard deviation for a particular population of interest has been calculated (for example, all first-grade students from the standardization sample), it is converted to a predetermined standard score standard deviation (perhaps 15). The conversion is relatively simple and relies on a simple statistical formula. In fact, once the simplest type of standard score has been calculated, the so called **z score,** any standard score can be determined easily and the relationship between one type and another is immediately obvious. *Z* scores have a mean of 0 and a standard deviation of 1 and are expressed as standard deviation units; in fact, all the most common standard scores are based ultimately on standard deviation units.

You can understand the relationship between any standard score and the most primitive standard deviation unit of the *z* score distribution easily by considering Figure 5.1. Notice how this figure shows the relationship between *z* scores, various other standard scores, percentile ranks, and the frequency with which all these scores occur in the population. This frequency of occurrence is based on the fact that many abilities and skills of interest are presumably normally distributed, such as intelligence, academic aptitude, motivation,

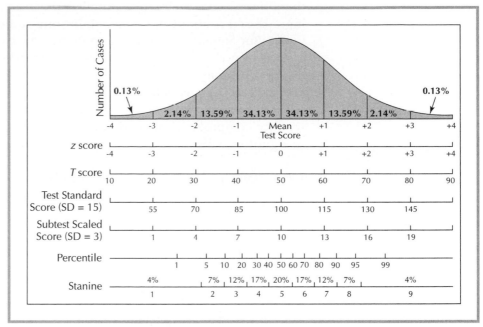

FIGURE 5.1 Relationships among Different Types of Scores in a Normal Distribution

MCLOUGHLIN/LEWIS, *ASSESSING STUDENTS WITH SPECIAL NEEDS,* 5th Edition, © 2001, p. 71. Reprinted by permission of Pearson Education, Inc., Upper Saddle River, NJ.

and so on. Most students have an average amount of these abilities—some have very little, others have significantly more—and we might call the students on the high end of the distribution advanced, gifted, highly motivated, and so on, depending on the particular attribute assessed. Many human characteristics are assumed to fall along the normal curve, so please consider Figure 5.1 carefully. This is an extremely important point. If you understand it well, you will understand the essence of formal measurement. However, a caveat is in order here. There are times when scores of a particular group of students may not occur in a normally distributed fashion. For example, a group of students identified as gifted and talented may exhibit more high scores on a test of reading comprehension than would be expected based on a bell curve. But in general, when considering scores of large groups of students, scores tend to be distributed in the manner shown in Figure 5.1.

Why are standard scores preferred? Standard scores can be used to compare performance of students to that of peers and to themselves in other areas. For example, recall Saimah and Shelby from Mr. Haywood's special education class. When administered a formal test that included measures of both word recognition and reading comprehension, they achieved the following standard scores:

	Word Recognition	**Reading Comprehension**
Shelby	85	85
Saimah	95	70

Assume this test has a mean set to 100 and standard deviation of 15. Both students are performing below average, as compared to peers and as is typical for students receiving special education services. But also note the differences in their scores. Shelby's performance in both areas of reading assessed is about the same, about one standard deviation below her peers. But Samiah shows a different pattern. Her word recognition skills are not so weak compared to peers (standard score of 95, compared to mean of 100), but her reading comprehension skills are much weaker (two standard deviations below average). Assuming these scores are accurate (for example, not due to error), Saimah needs extensive work to build her reading comprehension skills and less focus on building automatic word recognition skills.

Use of Standard Scores in Special Education

Standard scores are used in determining eligibility of students for special education. Federal special education law, specifically the Individuals with Disabilities Education Improvement Act of 2004 (IDEA 2004), defines thirteen areas of disability. For a student to be determined eligible for special education services, the law requires a nondiscriminatory, comprehensive, individual educational evaluation. Specific assessment criteria for the various disability categories are determined by federal, state, and district law and policies and may vary somewhat, especially from state to state. Nonetheless, to be eligible for special education, students in most of the disability categories must undergo an individual, comprehensive assessment that typically includes measures of intelligence and academic achievement, and, often, behavior and social skills. For example, in order to identify a student as having mental retardation, most states use a cutoff IQ score of 70 and similarly low scores on measures of adaptive behavior, or the "ability to adapt to the world in different situations" (Overton 2006, 256). If you look at the normal curve in Figure 5.1, you will see that a standard score of 70 falls two standard deviations below the mean and that only about 3 percent of the population earns scores this low or lower. In other words, the IQ score of 70 falls at about the 3rd percentile. Conversely, in order to identify a student as intellectually gifted, many states require that the student achieve an IQ score of 130, two standard deviations above the mean and at the 97th percentile, along with similarly high scores on academic achievement measures.

Use of Standard Scores to Identify a Learning Disability

In a somewhat more complex and controversial procedure, many states determine whether a student has a learning disability by comparing an IQ score to scores on academic achievement testing. Essentially, standard scores from achievement tests (such as a measure of word recognition or a measure of reading comprehension) are subtracted from the IQ standard score; a difference of one or more standard deviations is considered evidence that the student's achievement is below expectations and is, thus, evidence of a learning disability. This practice is referred to as the IQ-achievement discrepancy procedure, which we discussed in Chapter 2, and as you will remember, its use is somewhat controversial. In any case, the use of standard scores is integral to this process. Because standard scores (those using the same mean and standard deviation, typically 100 and 15, respectively) can be added and subtracted, they can be used to determine whether a student's progress in one or more academic areas lags significantly below expected achievement levels, based on the IQ score. See the following examples:

	Saimah	Shelby
Standard score IQ	94	103
Reading comprehension	− 70	− 85
	24	18

For Saimah and Shelby the discrepancy scores are quite large and probably sufficient large to meet learning disability criteria in most states. As mentioned in Chapter 2, this process has been criticized and IDEA 2004 allows an alternative—the responsiveness-to-intervention procedure—which was discussed in Chapter 1. Nonetheless, individualized achievement tests that yield standard scores provide useful information about students' performance relative to peers and allow intra-individual comparisons among various types of achievement skills. For example, using these scores it is possible to compare Saimah's word recognition skills to her reading comprehension.

Limitations of Standard Scores

Standard scores are designed to reduce confusion and error associated with using raw scores and percentage mastery scores. In addition, they are superior to percentiles in that they can be compared, added, and subtracted. Nonetheless, because the choice of a given standard score mean is arbitrary, some test publishers choose different metrics for different tests (a mean of 100, standard deviation of 15, vs a mean of 50, standard deviation of 10; see Figure 5.1). We suggest you make a copy of Figure 5.1 and keep it on hand for reference when you need to read and understand such scores (for example, when you receive a psychoeducational report on a student referred for special education).

Stanines

Stanine is a term coined from combining two words, **standard nine,** and is a holdover from early computer days when computer space was at a premium and test authors needed a one-column number to express the whole range of scores along the normal curve. Stanines express the entire range of scores by dividing the distribution of scores into nine categories. The middle stanine, 5, contains 20 percent of the distribution, with four stanines on either side. With the exception of stanines 1 and 9, all are equally distributed along the normal curve, although the percentages of individuals within each stanine change because of the shape of the normal curve. Stanines are gross representations of performance and are only used when crude approximations are appropriate.

Normal Curve Equivalents

Normal curve equivalents, or NCEs, frequently are reported for group achievement tests. These scores have characteristics of percentiles and standard scores. For example, the NCE distribution has a mean of 50, similar to percentiles. However, NCEs are actually standard scores and can be added and subtracted. NCEs have a standard deviation of 21.06. NCEs are often used by researchers when investigating relationships among variables such as socioeconomic status and achievement. They can also be used as a basis for evaluating relative gain in academic performance across time for students in a classroom, school, or district. Look at Figure 5.1 to see how NCEs compare to percentiles and other types of standard scores.

■ ADMINISTRATION AND SCORING OF FORMAL TESTS

Now that you know about the types of scores generated by formal tests, you may wonder how those scores are generated. In order to generate useful scores, formal tests must be administered carefully, in a prescribed or *standard* manner, and according to a script. Only then can the scores be used comparatively. In other words, the examiner is expected to administer a particular test in the same way each time so that the characteristics of the administration process accurately tap what students know and can do. If uneven or improper administration contributes directly to scoring inequities, error is introduced into the resulting score and comparing two or more scores is less meaningful. For example, if the examiner allows too much time, gives hints, or reads items aloud that were not read aloud to the students in the standardization group, students taking the test with this particular examiner are likely to score better than those in the standardization sample, but not based on what they actually know and can do. A concise summary of tips for administration of standardized tests is presented in Figure 5.2.

Standard Error of Measure

Formal tests allow users to evaluate the error within the scores by providing a statistic called the **standard error of measure.** This value is related directly to the reliability of the test, and once reliability is known, the standard error of measure can be calculated easily. We discussed reliability in Chapter 4; it is related directly to the error a test contains (i.e., error is defined as $1 -$ reliability). Consequently, the more reliable a test is, the less error it contains and the smaller the standard error of measure. When an examiner obtains a score from a formal test, the standard error of measure is used to establish a range of scores existing below and above the obtained score that contains the student's true score with a certain probability. For example, if we convert Misha's raw score of 15 to a standard score of 85 (16th percentile rank) and see in the manual of the test used to obtain this score that the standard error of measure is three, then we would report Misha's score as follows: Chances are two out of three that the range of scores from 82 to 88 contains Misha's true score. We know the probability because errors are normally distributed, as are raw scores, and we can think of the standard error of measure as a score representing one standard deviation on either side of the score obtained. We can tell from looking at the normal curve depicted in Figure 5.1 that approximately two-thirds of the population (two out of three) falls within one standard deviation below and one standard deviation above the population mean. (Importantly, in the context of understanding the band of error around one score, you must think of the score, 85 in this case, as representing the mean of a distribution of scores like Misha's). The point is that formal measurement yields an estimate of error, which is one of the primary benefits of using such this type of measure. We can contrast this situation to the typical classroom-based informal assessment. In the classroom, error is rarely known; teachers do not find it useful or time-efficient to go to the great lengths required to calculate the statistics needed to estimate error.

FIGURE 5.2 Tips for Administering Standardized Tests

- Become familiar with the test manual, particularly the instructions for administration.
- If possible, observe someone administering the test.
- Practice administering and scoring the test.
- Have a reliable and easy to use stopwatch.
- Pay particular attention to subtests or items which must be timed. Timed items are often marked with a symbol such as a clock in the test manual and test protocol. If not, it is a good idea to highlight or otherwise mark them.
- Gather all materials needed for testing prior to administration.
- Carefully calculate and double check chronological age (CA). Some children do not know their birthdates, particularly the year. Consult a reliable source. Serious errors may result from using the wrong CA.
- Adhere to test manual guidelines. Giving extra time, answering student questions or prompting may produce invalid results.
- Be familiar with test manual instructions re: how to handle students' questions about their performance or requests for more information.
- In general, do not prompt students or give corrective feedback unless the test manual specifies it is permissible to do so.
- Instead, praise students for working hard, for trying to complete tasks, etc.
- When students do not respond, it is generally permissible to say "Give it a try" or "Do you want to make a guess?' Consult test manual for how to score failure to respond and specific prompts that may be given.
- Students often give ambiguous responses. Many tests allow examiners to say something like "Tell me more about it". Consult test manual for specific prompts that may be given.
- Record student responses on the test protocol. Consult test manual re: how to mark the protocol. For example, some tests require the examiner to circle a preprinted response; some are indicated with a 1 or 0 and others require the examiner to write in the student's repose verbatim, then compare that response to sample correct and incorrect responses in the test manual.
- Learn the start and stop rules for the given age or grade level of students to whom you will administer the test.
- Learn the basal and ceiling rules. Many tests use a rule of 5 in a row correct to establish basal and 5 in a row incorrect to establish ceiling but this rule varies between tests and even between subtests on the same test, so always consult the test manual. When in doubt during an actual test administration, it is better to give additional items to ensure an adequate basal or ceiling.
- Once you have administered the test, you must determine the raw score. For tests in which students attempt all the items, this is easy. Count the number correct. For tests with basals and ceilings, this is more complicated. The raw score is the number correct, but items below the basal are counted as correct. Forgetting to count those items is a common mistake of inexperienced examiners.
- Once you have chronological age and raw scores calculated, you are ready to determine derived scores, such as standard scores, percentiles, and age and grade equivalents. For most tests, this means consulting a norms table and finding derived scores based on the student's chronological age and raw score. Increasingly, computer scoring is available.
- Once you have your derived scores, record them in the appropriate places on the test protocol. In many cases, computer scoring programs provide a report of scores which can be printed or saved in an electronic file.
- Finally, look at your scores. Do they make sense with what you know about the student's performance? If not, double check for errors in the process. Is CA correct? Is date of testing correct? Are raw scores calculated correctly?
- The most important guideline: Consult the test manual!

Establishing Basals and Ceilings

One of the strategies test authors use to reduce error, beyond the standardized assessment procedures discussed earlier, is to limit testing time and reduce the associated fatigue. In order to administer a test in the most efficient manner, teachers should not make students answer too many easy questions and perform too many easy tasks or answer too many hard questions and perform too many hard tasks. This requires determining a **basal** (point in the test below which a student should be able to answer correctly all items) and a **ceiling** (point in the test above which a student should miss all items). This process is part of a strategy sometimes referred to as **adaptive testing.** If, for example, a test has 90 items, the experienced examiner would start at some point in the test beyond item 1 to avoid administering all 90 items. Perhaps for a third-grade student, the examiner would begin by administering item 20, based on some probability (of successful completion of all the easier items) established during standardization of the test. The basal rule might require that five consecutive items be answered correctly. So if items 20 through 24 are answered correctly but item 25 was missed, the examiner assumes that the student knows all the content expressed on the easier items. In this case, a basal would have been established at item 24. But if the examiner had started at item 20 and the student had missed it, the basal rule might require that testing proceed in reverse order until five consecutive items are answered correctly, at which point the examiner moves back to item 21 and continues testing until a ceiling is reached. The ceiling is obtained in the same fashion as the basal, except in reverse; that is, the examiner must administer items until the student misses some number of consecutive items, perhaps five. (Again, criteria required to establish a basal and ceiling are based on the standardization data, which determines probabilities associated with getting items correct below the basal and wrong above the ceiling.) The total number of correct items below the ceiling is typically considered the raw score for the test and can then be converted to a standard score by using tables provided by the author. Figure 5.3 shows snippets of example **test protocols** similar to those used in many individualized achievement tests. A test protocol is the "response sheet or record form used by the examiner to record the students' answers" (Overton 2006, 234). These sections of test protocols, shown in Figure 5.3, depict the application of basal and ceiling rules when the directions require administering all the items in a given group or cluster, typically, items that appear on a single page.

DETERMINING CHRONOLOGICAL AGE

How does the examiner know where to enter the norms table? One piece of essential information is chronological age (CA) or month in grade. Typically, tables are built by test authors to allow comparisons based on age, grade, or both. Figure 5.4 presents an excerpt from an example norm table.

Obviously, the examiner can determine the grade level of the student easily by just counting the months in the academic year and converting those to a decimal. If the student is in third month of the third grade, the appropriate entering point is 3.3. But determining CA is a little more daunting, and most test booklets have spaces provided for calculating CA. Typically for calculating age, months are assumed to have thirty days, and CA is rounded up for fifteen or more days. The following examples show application of the steps for calculating

	Word Recognition	Vocabulary
	Basal rule: 3 in a row correct. Ceiling rule: 3 in a row incorrect.	Basal rule: All items in a set correct. Ceiling rule: All items in a set incorrect.

Word Recognition

Basal rule: 3 in a row correct.
Ceiling rule: 3 in a row incorrect.

    1. ___
    2. ___
    3. ___
→ 4. _1_
    5. _1_
    6. _1_
    7. _1_
    8. _1_
    9. _1_
  10. _0_
  11. _0_
  12. _0_

Note: Starting point for this student indicated by the →

Vocabulary

Basal rule: All items in a set correct.
Ceiling rule: All items in a set incorrect.

    1. ___
    2. ___
    3. ___
    4. ___
    5. ___

→ 6. _1_
    7. _1_
    8. _1_
    9. _1_
  10. _1_

  11. _0_
  12. _0_
  13. _0_
  14. _0_
  15. _0_

Note: Starting point for this student indicated by the →

FIGURE 5.3 Sample Reading Subtests Showing Basal and Ceiling Rules

Raw Score Conversion Table for Reading Comprehension Test				
Age: 8 years, 9 months				
Raw Score	Standard Score	Percentile	Grade Equivalent	Age Equivalent
↑				
15	95	37	2.1	7–6
16	96	39	2.4	7–9
17	97	42	2.7	7–11
18	98	45	2.9	8–3
19	99	47	3.2	8–6
20	100	50	3.5	8–9
↓				

Note: Examiners calculate the raw score for the test, then look up derived scores (standard scores, percentiles, grade- and age-equivalents) based on the examinee's chronological age.

FIGURE 5.4 Sample Excerpt from a Norm Table for an Individually Administered Reading Comprehension Test for Students Age 8 years, 9 months

the age of Shelby and Saimah, the fifth graders who receive help in reading from their special education teacher, Mr. Haywood. The first case is straightforward; the child is 10–1. The second scenario is a little more complex.

Shelby

Date of test	2008	11	25
Date of birth	− 1998	10	19
Chronological age	10	1	6

Saimah

Date of test	2008(2007)	11(10)(22)	25(55)
Date of birth	− 1998	12	29
Chronological age	9	10	26 or 9–11

To calculate Saimah's age, thirty days must be borrowed from the month category, because twenty-nine days cannot be subtracted from twenty-five days; similarly, twelve months cannot be subtracted from ten months, so a year (twelve months) is borrowed and moved into the month column before the calculations can be executed. Because twenty-six days are more than fourteen, the month category is rounded up, leaving a CA of 9–11, rather than 9–10. Importantly, although many test authors use only years and months in the calculation of tables, some are starting to use years, months, and days to eliminate the need to round months. In our experience, teachers tend to think of calculating CA as easy and they often make mistakes. Because making a mistake has serious consequences, we urge you to practice calculating and checking your answers. First, try the two examples shown in Table 5.1 (correct answers are given at the end of this chapter). Then, for practice, calculate your CA.

■ INDIVIDUALIZED VERSUS GROUP TESTS

Formal tests may require either individualized or group administration. Most of the content discussed so far in Chapter 5 has focused on individualized assessment. However, some formal tests may be administered in groups and even to all the students in a particular classroom. Many of the characteristics of individualized testing also apply to formal group testing. For example, administration should be standardized and typically will adhere to a script. There may be timed elements or components within both, but

TABLE 5.1 Calculation of Chronological Age (CA)

	Example 1	
2007	08	28
−1997	04	07

	Example 2	
2008	07	14
−1998	07	30

there may be differences as well. Often, in group administrations, all items are administered to all students and no effort is made to establish a basal or ceiling. Group testing, sometimes called **high-stakes testing** because important decisions are made based on the results, is discussed in Chapter 6.

■ HOW DO INDIVIDUALIZED, NORM-REFERENCED MEASURES ASSESS READING?

In this section, we describe how different areas of reading are measured by the achievement tests most frequently used by school psychologists and educational diagnosticians (Bell, McCallum, and Burton 2006). Most individualized achievement tests are broad in that they frequently cover several academic areas, such as reading, mathematics, and written expression (such as the Wechsler Individual Achievement Test-II or WIAT-II; Psychological Corporation 2001). However, some focus only on one academic area (such as the Woodcock-Johnson Diagnostic Reading Battery; W-J III DRB; Woodcock, Mather, and Schrank 2004; Woodcock Reading Mastery Test, Revised; WRM TR; Woodcock 1987/1998; Key Math-Revised; Connolly 1988/1998). These are considered **diagnostic tests** because they provide in-depth information about one academic area, such as reading. The W-J III DRB has ten subtests, each measuring a different type of reading or reading-related skill. Diagnostic reading tests may provide separate measures of phonics, automatic word recognition, reading fluency, reading vocabulary, and reading comprehension. Other tests are less in-depth and actually are considered **screening tests** (such as the Wide Range Achievement Test-4; WRAT4; Wilkinson 2006; Woodcock-McGrew-Werder Mini-Battery of Achievement; Woodcock, McGrew, and Werder 1994). Screeners typically assess only one or two areas of a given domain; for example, the WRAT4 assesses reading with one measure of word recognition and one measure of comprehension (a modified cloze procedure). The Woodcock-McGrew-Werder Mini-Battery of Achievement contains three measures including letter and word identification, reading vocabulary, and reading comprehension.

Overton (2006) provides a thorough review of individual norm-referenced tests and consistent with the language above, differentiates them as follows: tests that provide numerous measures of several domains are considered **achievement tests;** tests that provide numerous measures of one domain are considered diagnostic tests; and tests that provide only one measure of a given domain are considered screening tests. As Overton makes clear, "screener" tests should not be used to determine eligibility for special education; it is possible to miss important information about a student's performance when only a screener is used. Achievement and diagnostic tests typically can be used to determine special education eligibility because they provide more thorough information about a student's performance in a domain such as reading. In the following section, we provide examples of assessments in the major areas of reading, those identified by the NRP and an additional area, automatic word recognition, widely recognized as an important and somewhat distinct skill from phonemic awareness and phonics. Note that in many cases, the same construct or subdomain (such as reading fluency) is measured in different ways by different tests. Flanagan, Ortiz, Alfonso, and Mascolo (2006) provide a

FIGURE 5.5 Variations in Task Characteristics of Basic Reading Skill/Reading Fluency Skills Tests

BATTERY Subtest	Regular Words	Pseudo- words	Isolated Stimuli (letters, words)	Connected Stimuli (sentences, paragraphs)	Timed
DAB-3					
Alphabet/Word Knowledge	✓		✓		
Phonemic Analysis			✓		
KTEA-II					
Phonological Awareness	✓		✓		
Letter and Word Recognition	✓		✓		
Nonsense Word Decoding		✓	✓		
Word Recognition Fluency	✓		✓		✓
Decoding Fluency		✓	✓		✓
Naming Facility			✓		✓
PIAT-R/NU					
Reading Recognition	✓		✓		
WIAT-II					
Word Reading	✓		✓		
Pseudoword Decoding		✓	✓		
W-J III					
Letter-Word Identification	✓		✓		
Reading Fluency	✓			✓	✓
Word Attack	✓	✓	✓		
Sound Awareness	✓		✓		
TOCL					
Knowledge of Print	✓			✓	
Word Recognition	✓			✓	
WRAT-Expanded					
Reading	✓		✓		
YCAT					
Reading	✓		✓	✓	
GDRT-2					
Letter/Word Recognition	✓		✓		
Phonetic Analysis	✓	✓	✓		
Reading Vocabulary	✓		✓		
Rapid Naming	✓		✓		✓
Phonological Awareness	✓		✓		
CORT-4					
Rate, Accuracy, Fluency	✓			✓	✓
PRT					
Decoding		✓	✓		
Fluency	✓			✓	✓
RAN/RAS			✓		✓
Objects			✓		✓
Colors			✓		✓
Numbers			✓		✓
Letters			✓		✓
RAS 2-Set			✓		✓
RAS 3-Set			✓		✓

Flanagan, D. P., Ortiz, S. O., Alfonso, V. C., & Mascolo, J. T. (2006). *The Achievement Test Desk Reference: A Guide to Learning Disability Identification* (2nd ed). Hoboken, NJ: John Wiley & Sons.

FIGURE 5.6 **Variations in Task Characteristics of Reading Comprehension Tests**

BATTERY Subtest	Cloze Format	Open-Ended Questions	Multiple Choice	Literal Questions	Inferential Questions	Silent Reading	Oral Reading	Examiner Reads	Examinee Reads	Examiner/ Examinee Read	Timed	Examinee Can Refer Back to Test
DAB-3												
Reading Comp.		✓		✓	✓	✓						
KTEA-II												
Reading Comp.		✓		✓	✓	✓			✓	✓		✓
PIAT-R/NU												
Reading Comp.		✓	✓	✓	✓	✓			✓			✓
WIAT-II												
Reading Comp.		✓		✓	✓	✓			✓	✓		✓
W-J III	✓											
Passage Comp.				✓		✓			✓			
Reading Vocabulary				✓	✓	✓			✓			
HAMAT												
Reading		✓	✓	✓	✓	✓			✓			✓
TOCL												
Word Recognition				✓		✓				✓		
Reading Comp.		✓				✓			✓	✓		
WRAT-Expanded												
Reading		✓	✓	✓	✓	✓			✓			
GDRT-2												
Reading Vocabulary			✓			✓			✓			
Meaningful Reading						✓			✓			
GORT-4												
Comprehension			✓	✓	✓		✓			✓		
GSRT												
Silent Reading Comp.			✓	✓	✓	✓			✓			✓
PRT												
Comprehension		✓	✓	✓			✓			✓		✓
SRI-2												
Vocabulary in Context			✓	✓	✓	✓			✓			✓
Passage Comp.		✓	✓	✓	✓	✓	✓		✓			
TERA-3												
Meaning	✓	✓	✓	✓	✓		✓		✓			
W-J III DRB												
Passage Comprehension	✓					✓			✓			✓
Reading Vocabulary				✓	s				✓			
WRMT-R/NU												
Passage Comp.	✓					✓			✓			✓
Word Comprehension						✓			✓			
ITPA-3												
Sentence Sequencing			✓			✓		✓				✓

Flanagan, D. P., Ortiz, S. O., Alfonso, V. C., & Mascolo, J. T. (2006). *The Achievement Test Desk Reference: A Guide to Learning Disability Identification* (2nd ed.). Hoboken, NJ: John Wiley & Sons.

FIGURE 5.7 **Tasks Similar to Those from the Sound Awareness Subtest from the Woodcock-Johnson III Tests of Achievement.** Woodcock, R. W., McGrew, K. S., & Mather, N. (2001). Itasca, IL: Riverside Publishing.

RHYMING:	"What rhymes with no?"
DELETION:	"Say snowman without saying snow"
SUBSTITUTION:	Change /m/ in man to /p/.
REVERSAL:	"Listen to the sounds in the word /t/ /i/ /p/. Now you say the sounds backward."

comprehensive review of different achievement tests, and they explicitly address how different areas of achievement are assessed by different achievement tests; their reviews of measures of basic reading/fluency skills and reading comprehension are reproduced in Figures 5.5 and 5.6.

Phonemic Awareness

Most of the current major individual achievement tests include measures of phonemic awareness, reflecting the extensive amount of research conducted on this topic since 1990. The Kaufman Tests of Educational Achievement-II (Kaufman and Kaufman 2004) has a Phonological Awareness subtest that assesses a student's ability to engage in rhyming, sound matching, blending, segmenting, and deletion. The Wechsler Individual Achievement Test-II's (WIAT-II; Psychological Corporation 2001) Word Reading subtest assesses rhyming, sound matching, and blending but does not provide a separate measure of phonemic awareness. The W-J III Tests of Achievement provide a measure of phonemic awareness via a subtest called Sound Awareness. (Interestingly, phonological awareness measures are also included on the W-J III Tests of Cognitive Ability; Woodcock, McGrew, and Mather 2001). The Sound Awareness subtest requires the student to use rhyming, deletion, substitution, and reversal to manipulate sounds in words. Figure 5.7 presents phonemic awareness tasks similar to those from the W-J III. In addition to broad achievement tests, several diagnostic measures assess only or primarily phonemic awareness, including the Comprehensive Test of Phonological Processing (Wagner, Torgeson, and Rashotte 1999).

Phonics

The W-J III (Word Attack subtest), the KTEA-II (Nonsense Word Decoding subtest) and the WIAT-II (Pseudoword Decoding subtest) require the student to read aloud a list of nonsense words designed to mimic the phonetic structure of words in the English language. Figure 5.8 shows a sample of nonsense words typical of these tests.

Automatic Word Recognition

The KTEA-II Letter Word Recognition subtest requires the student to point to or name various letters, sounds, and words. The WIAT-II Word Reading tasks vary depending on student age. Tasks include identifying letters, identifying beginning and ending sounds of words, identifying rhyming words, and

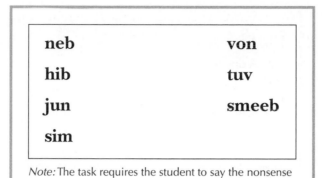

FIGURE 5.8 Sample Set of Items from a Typical Nonsense or Pseudoword Subtest

Note: The task requires the student to say the nonsense words aloud to the examiner.

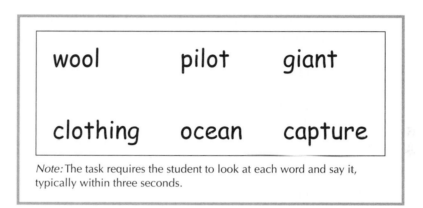

FIGURE 5.9 Sample Set of Items from a Typical Word Identification Subtest

Note: The task requires the student to look at each word and say it, typically within three seconds.

reading words from a word list as quickly as possible. The W-J III Letter-Word Identification subtest requires students to read letters and then words. The goal of most word recognition measures is to measure students' *automaticity*, or instantaneous recall and recognition of words. Consequently, words that are commonly used and somewhat irregular in their spelling (such as *there*, *here*, and *weigh*) often are represented heavily on word recognition tests. In addition, students are frequently timed, at least informally, so that words not pronounced within one to three seconds are scored as incorrect. Figure 5.9 presents a sampling of words typical of individualized achievement measures.

Fluency
Several measures of fluency are available. The Test of Silent Word Reading Fluency (Mather, Hammill, Allen, and Roberts 2004) can be administered either individually or in a group format. (Group administered measures are considered in Chapter 6.) The KTEA-II provides several timed measures including a Decoding Fluency subtest in which students read nonsense words and are timed. Another KTEA-II subtest, Word Recognition Fluency, requires students to read words from a word list while being timed. Another timed measure, available on the WIAT-II, is called Associational Fluency and Naming Facility and is described as a measure of rapid automatic naming, which was discussed in Chapter 2. The WIAT-II requires the examiner to time the student as he or she orally reads passages from the Reading Comprehension

FIGURE 5.10 **Items Similar to Those from the Reading Fluency Subtest of the Woodcock-Johnson III Tests of Achievement.**

Woodcock, R. W., McGrew, K. S., & Mather, N. (2001). *Woodcock-Johnson III. Tests of Achievement.* Itasca, IL: Riverside Publishing.

1. A fish can fly	Y	N
2. A dog is a blue	Y	N
3. Ants are large	Y	N
4. A bike has four wheels	Y	N
5. Ice is hot	Y	N

Note: After completing six practice items, the student reads a series of simple sentences and circles Y for yes and N for no. The subtest is timed for three minutes and scores are based on number of items correct.

subtest. And, the W-J III uses yet a different format. Students read as many sentences as they can within a three-minute period, responding to each sentence by circling "Y" for true and "N" for false. Figure 5.10 shows a sampling of items similar to those from the WJ-III Reading Fluency subtest.

Vocabulary

The WRMT-R and the W-J III Tests of Achievement provide a measure of reading vocabulary called, appropriately enough, Reading Vocabulary. In this subtest, the student is required to state orally synonyms and antonyms for printed words and orally complete analogies that are presented to them to read. Figure 5.11 provides a sample of tasks similar to those from the WRMT-R and

FIGURE 5.11 **Items Similar to Those from the Reading Vocabulary Subtests from the Woodcock-Johnson III Tests of Achievement and the Woodcock Reading Mastery Tests Revised.**

Woodcock, R. W., McGrew, K. S., & Mather, N. (2001). *Woodcock-Johnson III Tests of Achievement.* Itasca, IL: Riverside Publishing and Woodcock Reading Mastery Tests Revised. Woodcock, R. W. (1987/1998); Woodcock Reading Mastery Tests Revised/Normative Update. Circle Pines, MN: American Guidance Service.

Synonyms

large
Correct: big, huge

speak
Correct: talk

Antonyms

top
Correct: bottom

stop
Correct: go, start

Analogies

feather bird   scale_____

Correct: fish

brush canvas   pen_____

Correct: paper

Note: For each task, students are presented with a sample item and given feedback; then they independently read words from the three lists and give a word that means opposite, the same, or they complete an analogy.

the W-J III. The nature of these tasks ensures that these words are in students' reading vocabulary; that is, students must be able to both read the word and provide appropriate information. The W-J III also provides a measure of oral vocabulary, called Picture Vocabulary. In this case, the student looks at pictures of common objects, such as a shoe, water faucet, and light switch and identifies them by name.

Comprehension

The WIAT-II provides a measure of reading comprehension, the aptly named Reading Comprehension subtest. In this subtest, younger students identify pictures and corresponding words and older students are required to read short sentences or passages and to respond orally to comprehension questions. Acceptable and unacceptable answers are provided in the test manual. See Figure 5.12 for a sample reading passage similar to those presented in the WIAT-II. Both the WRMT-R and the W-J III Tests of Achievement measure reading comprehension via a subtest called Passage Comprehension. Younger students look at pictures and point to words that correspond to the pictures. Older students read sentences of increasing length and complexity and fill in a missing word. This procedure is called *cloze* (see Chapter 3).

FIGURE 5.12 Sample Reading Passage Typical of Passages Designed to Assess Reading Comprehension

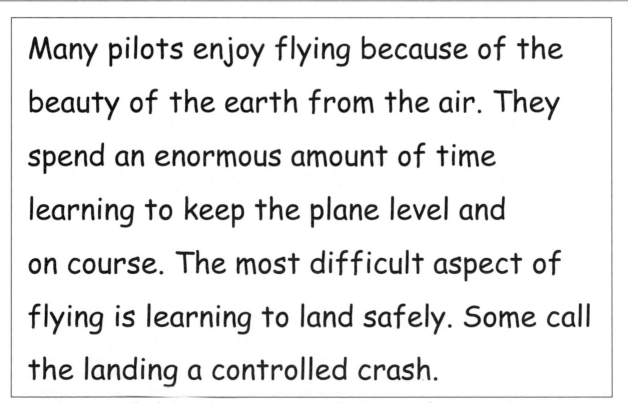

Many pilots enjoy flying because of the beauty of the earth from the air. They spend an enormous amount of time learning to keep the plane level and on course. The most difficult aspect of flying is learning to land safely. Some call the landing a controlled crash.

Note: Students are typically asked to read a series of increasingly difficult passages and answer comprehension questions. Sometimes a distinction is made between inferential and literal questions and between items tapping vocabulary.

◼ TEST BIAS

Teachers want to use sound, reliable tests so that they, their students, and parents can have confidence in the scores the tests generate. More to the point, teachers want tests that are fair for all who use them—for those from low socioeconomic levels; from different races, ethnic groups, and cultures; from ELL classes (English language learners); and for those with disabilities. To use a technical term, tests should not be *biased*. In particular, the scores from the test should not provide a systematic advantage to a particular group or subgroup based on irregularities in test content, administration, or interpretation (see Boxes 5.1 and 5.2 at the end of this chapter for suggestions on using formal tests with adult learners and ELL students). When a test produces such an unfair advantage, it is said to be *biased* against the group that is disadvantaged (Payne 2003).

What evidence do test experts look for when they consider test bias? Some pertinent questions might include:

- Does the test assess the same content for all the groups using it?
- Are the constructs that are being assessed by the test measured consistently for all groups using it?
- Does the test predict later achievement or ability equally for all the groups using it?
- Does the test provide equally useful instructional information for all groups using it?

These questions can be answered in part by having experts and users examine the items and make judgments about the cultural, racial, and gender fairness of the items. Such an expert panel can help flag items that may not be fair.

In addition to expert judgment, several more sophisticated empirical and quantitative tests of fairness can be applied. For example, the ability of a test to predict comprehension skills may be given to males and females, and if the test predicts less well for males, as determined by a statistical index called the correlation coefficient as discussed in Chapter 1, specific test items should be evaluated further to determine the ones that have less predictive capability based on gender. These quantitative procedures can be very sophisticated and time consuming but necessary in order to prevent test bias and increase test fairness.

One cautionary note should be kept in mind. Sometimes, test users assume that a test is biased against a particular group if the average or mean score on that test is lower for one group than another. This mean difference does raise a red flag and the difference might mean that the test is biased against the lower scoring group. But, this is not always the case. Some groups perform less well on some measures than on others. For example, young girls tend to score higher on verbally-laden tests than young boys; that is, girls tend to acquire language earlier than boys. Many indicators show that this outcome is true. So if a verbally-laden test produces this information, we simply acknowledge that another piece of evidence for this finding has been uncovered. We would not conclude that the test is biased against boys. But, when this finding occurred for the first time, it sparked intense scrutiny of the tests involved; the tests were considered suspect until massive additional evidence confirmed the finding.

Most of the standardized tests referred to in this handbook have been examined for test bias during their development by the authors and publishers. Test manuals address this point and if you are considering purchasing a particular reading test, you should look for this kind of information in the test manual.

Keep in mind that a test can be misused, even when it is psychometrically sound and assumed to be fair or unbiased. For example, a test may be administered to a group of individuals that was not represented in the standardization sample. In this country, highly verbally-laden IQ tests have been developed (and standardized) for English-speaking students. It would not be fair to administer to a highly verbal IQ test to a student who had just arrived in this country from China and who spoke only limited English. We could not expect the test to assess the student's IQ fairly using a English language loaded test.

SELECTING FORMAL, INDIVIDUALIZED INSTRUMENTS

Various professional organizations have developed standards for test selection and best practices. Payne (2003) lists a number of them, particularly those with implications for students with limited English or English as a second language. Some of the more salient standards include:

- Before administering a test, consider the examinee's age, race, gender, ethnicity, socioeconomic status, and cultural background.
- Consider the match between test demands and characteristics of examinees, such as language, speed/pacing requirements, and motivation.
- Consider whether persons (or groups) who use a different language should be tested in their native language, in a second language, or both. The answer to this question will depend on the comparison group of interest.
- Consider whether the test manual contains adequate information to judge the appropriateness of a test for linguistically diverse examinees.
- Reliability and validity should be established for translated tests within the target population.
- Establish rapport and use effective and sensitive administration practices for novice examinees.
- Consider the potential effects of different examiner-examinee racial, ethnic, gender, and cultural characteristics and how those differences may affect test performance.
- Testing should minimize threats to reliability and validity for non–English-speaking or non–standard English-speaking examinees.
- Any linguistic test-taking modifications allowed by the test author and publisher should be clearly stated in the test manual.
- Examiners should not administer or interpret tests for which they have not been adequately trained nor should they assess an examinee with special needs unless they have been trained to do so.
- If special equipment, such as a computer, is needed to assess, the examiner should ensure that examinees from diverse groups have adequate access, support, and training to use those devices.
- Examiners should take into account diverse backgrounds when building a context for the test.
- Examiners should ensure that examinees are represented appropriately

in the standardization sample or they should state clearly the limitations associated with using a test that does not exhibit an examinee-standardization match.

Others (McCallum 1998; McCallum, Bracken, and Wasserman 2001) provide cautions about the use of verbally-laden tests with certain populations of students; some of those recommendations are general and apply to users of reading tests. We have included some of the relevant recommendations in Boxes 5.1 (for adults) and 5.2 (for ELL students).

When selecting a formal instrument, educators should consider its characteristics and the extent to which it is better (or worse) than others. Once educators determine specifically what they want to assess, they should consider the choices and make decisions based on the needs of specific children, classrooms, schools, or systems. Criteria for evaluating and selecting tests—formal and informal, group and individual—are presented in Chapter 7.

In Chapter 6, we expand our discussion of formal measures by describing instruments developed for group administration of reading skills. Both similarities and differences exist between individualized and group-administered

BOX 5.1 Tips for Formal Assessment of Adult Learners

1. Assess adult learners' educational histories, background experiences, and interests, as well as specific reading skills.

2. Assume that multiple assessments will be needed to provide complete information about adult learners' reading strengths and weaknesses.

3. Ensure that the test used with adults is standardized for that population.

4. Put adult learners at ease. Be sure to establish rapport and a purpose before launching into formal testing.

5. Limit use of grade-equivalent scores (and to a lesser extent, age-equivalent scores) because these scores can be easily misinterpreted

6. Include item content appropriate for adults, as opposed to young students, even though the difficulty level of the content may be low in order to achieve a reasonable test floor.

7. Consider entering your test data and using the instructional skills profile available from the Adult Reading Components Study Web site (www.nifl.gov/readingprofiles/) to find instructional recommendations.

BOX 5.2 Tips for Formal Assessment of English Language Learners (ELL)

1. Follow standards set for test administration, scoring, and interpretation in general, as well as for ELL and other diverse learners, as developed by experts. Many of these standards are reproduced in the section on test bias in this chapter; some of the most relevant are reproduced in this box in abbreviated form.

2. Be aware that an ELL examinee's formal test scores typically will be compared to other students in the United States who may not resemble the ELL examinee in background, culture, knowledge, and the like.

3. Be aware that an ELL examinee's scores on formal tests may be lower because of cultural, linguistic, and knowledge differences.

4. Avoid administering a language-loaded test to ELL examinees unless the language content in the test *is* the focus of assessment.

5. Ensure that the test does not contain item content that may be offensive toward the ELL examinee's home country, race, or culture.

6. Ensure that the reliability and validity of the test have been established for ELL learners.

7. Evaluate recommendations from expert panels to ensure that the items are not biased against ELL learners.

8. Examine evidence from statistical techniques designed to determine bias to ensure that items are not biased against ELL learners.

9. When possible, establish rapport and aid in administering the test by using an examiner who can communicate in the ELL examinee's native language.

10. Be aware that an ELL examinee's progress in learning a second language and his or her ability to understand the demands of the test may be limited by negative transfer from the native language.

11. Reduce importance of quick performance on tests; some cultures do not value quickness.

12. Ensure that the test only measures what you intend to measure (i.e., specific types of reading skills) and not other irrelevant content.

13. Be particularly sensitive to group mean differences and ensure that if mean differences occur, the differences are not the result of bias.

14. Use ample teaching items to ensure that ELL learners understand the task demands.

15. Be aware that use of grade-equivalent scores (and to a lesser extent, age-equivalent scores) can be problematic because it is easy to misinterpret the scores.

---

formal tests. For example, both allow peer comparisons, but individualized measures allow more response options for students. In Chapter 6, we describe the salient characteristics of group measures and discuss the relevant comparisons to individualized measures.

Summary

In this chapter, we described individualized formal tests. In most cases, formal tests are administered by school psychologists, educational diagnosticians, and special education educators. Occasionally, classroom teachers and reading specialists administer them. Typically they are administered to provide comparative information; that is, they show the relative performance of a particular student compared to peers and the relative performance within a student on subdomains of reading. Various types of scores show these relationships, such as age or grade equivalents (scores equal to those of the norm group at a particular age or grade), percentile ranks (scoring that indicates the percentage of students scoring below the examinee), and standard scores (a score with a set mean, or average, and standard deviation to allow comparisons across different tests and different students). These scores typically are obtained for a particular student by converting raw scores using tables provided in test manuals based on standardization data and collected to reflect the performance of all students in the country. Standard scores are considered superior to other types of derived scores because they can be added and subtracted to make comparisons between students and for the same student on different tests. Standard scores on individual achievement tests have been used for years to obtain diagnostic information and to determine whether students are eligible for identification as having a learning disability.

Authors of formal tests usually show evidence of the quality of these instruments in the test manuals by reporting reliability (consistency) and validity (accuracy) data, obtained either from the standardization sample or from other samples collected for these purposes. Unlike teacher-made informal tests, formal tests provide gross measures and the content is not tied specifically to any particular classroom or curriculum. Consequently, formal tests are not likely to help teachers plan instruction, except in a crude manner. Also, unlike teacher-made informal tests, formal instruments are likely to be administered in a standardized manner and according to a script. There are numerous formal, individualized tests that assess reading and reading-related skills. We discussed several of the more commonly used measures to assess automatic word recognition, phonemic awareness and phonics, fluency, vocabulary, and comprehension. Some tests are normed only for school-age students, while others are designed for preschool students or adults.

It is interesting to note the various ways in which the same reading skill may be assessed. For example, reading fluency may be assessed orally or silently. Reading comprehension may be assessed via a cloze technique or by requiring examinees to respond to multiple-choice questions. Teachers will want to be aware of how the various reading skills were assessed before setting instructional goals based on assessment results. The chapter concludes with a special section on test bias, which represents a growing concern because of the increasing use of formal tests for the ELL population. It is important to keep in mind the purpose of testing when trying to decide whether a test is biased against a particular group. Increasingly, reading tests are available in other languages, particularly Spanish. If we want to know how well an ELL student reads in English, it is appropriate to administer an English-language reading test. However, conclusions should be limited to specifically what was assessed. Tips for assessing ELL and for adults with low literacy levels are presented in Boxes 5.1 and 5.2.

Before leaving the topic of formal, individualized testing, recall the Literacy Instruction Pie presented in Chapter 2 (also Appendix C). How can measures from this chapter help you construct such a pie—for a class or for an individual student? Formal assessment helps teachers pinpoint the relative performance of their students in any area of reading. And, if a particular student shows very high performance in one particular area (for example, fluency) but a low score in another area (perhaps comprehension), the student's teacher may choose to spend more time focusing instruction on building comprehension strategies for that student. For example, the teacher may spend more time helping the student learn to use question generation techniques, graphic organizers, and comprehension monitoring strategies, and less time using fluency building activities such as repeated reading of familiar text and partner reading.

Typically, individualized formal measures allow administration of particular subtests designed to assess specific elements of reading depicted on the Pie, including fluency, vocabulary, and comprehension. In fact, some tests are limited because they offer assessment of only one or two of the areas; others offer measures of all these areas of reading depicted on the Pie, and more. Formal measures offer indexes of relative performance across these areas, and in a sense, they provide a global assessment of progress.

In closing, Tables 5.2 and 5.3 on pages 194–198 provide specific information about a variety of individual tests to help teachers and others make informed decisions. We focus primarily on instruments that measure one or more of the five major areas of reading identified by the NRP (NICHD 2000), including phonemic awareness, phonics, fluency, vocabulary, and text comprehension. We also include automatic word recognition because of its important contribution to building fluency. Table 5.2 provides basic information including test name, publisher, publication date, and administration time, and it identifies the areas of reading assessed. Table 5.3 provides information about the psychometric characteristics of the measures, including reliability and validity and types of scores available.

Correct Answers to Table 5.1

      Example 1:   10 years, 4 months, 21 days or 10–5
      Example 2:   9 years, 11 months, 14 days or 9–11

mylabschool™
Where the classroom comes to life!

MyLabSchool is a collection of online tools for your success in this course, your licensure exams, and your teaching career. Visit www.mylabschool.com to access the following:
- *Online Study Guide*
- *Video cases from real classrooms*
- *Help with your research papers using Research Navigator*
- *Career Center with resources for:*
    Praxis exams and licensure preparation
    Professional portfolio development
    Job search and interview techniques
    Lesson planning

TABLE 5.2 Characteristics of Formal, Individualized, Norm-Referenced Assessments of Reading

Test Name	Publisher/Source/Date	Grades/Ages	Purpose	Administration Time	Basic Reading Skills		Fluency	Reading Comprehension	
					Word Recognition	Phonics/PA		Vocabulary	Comprehension
Durrell Analyses of Reading Difficulty, 3rd Ed.	Harcourt, 1980	1–6	To screen for reading problems	35–50 minutes	X	X	X	X	X
Early Reading Diagnostic Assessment-Revised (ERDA-R)	Harcourt, 2002	K–3	To assess achievement levels, to monitor reading progress, to aide in instructional planning, and to link assessment with intervention	15–20 minutes for screener; 45–60 minutes for battery	X	X	X	X	X
Gray Diagnostic Reading Tests, 2nd Ed. (GDRT-2)	PRO-ED, 2004	Ages 6–13	To assess students who have difficulty reading continuous print and who require an evaluation of specific abilities and weaknesses	45–60 minutes	X	X	X	X	X
Gray Oral Reading Tests 4th Ed. (GORT-4)	PRO-ED, 2001	Ages 6–18	To measure growth in oral reading and an aid in the diagnosis of oral reading difficulties	20–30 minutes	X	X	X		X
Kaufman Tests of Educational Achievement II (KTEA-II)	Pearson, 2004	Ages 4.6–25	To measure achievement in reading, mathematics, written language, and oral language	30–85 minutes	X	X	X	X	X
Peabody Individual Achievement Test, Revised/Normative Update (PIAT-R/NU)	Pearson 1989/1998	Ages 5–22	To provide an efficient individual measure of achievement	60 minutes	X			X	X

Test	Publisher, Year	Ages	Purpose	Administration Time					
Process Assessment of the Learner: Test Battery for Reading and Writing (PAL-RW)	Harcourt, 2001	K–6	To assess the development of reading and writing processes in children	30–60 minutes	X	X	X	X	X
Standardized Reading Inventory— Second Edition (SRI-2)	PRO-ED, 2001	Ages 6–14.6	To assess children's independent, instructional, and frustration reading levels in word recognition and comprehension skills	30–90 minutes	X	X		X	X
Test of Early Reading Ability—Third Edition (TERA-3)	PRO-ED, 2001	Ages 3.6–8.6	To identify children who need interventions, to identify strengths and weaknesses, to monitor progress, to serve as a research tool, and to serve as a companion test.	15–45 minutes	X	X		X	X
Test of Word Reading Efficiency (TOWRE)	PRO-ED, 1999	Ages 6–24	To measure ability to pronounce printed words accurately and effectively	5–10 minutes			X	X	
Wechsler Individual Achievement Test— 2nd Ed. (WIAT-II)	Harcourt, 2001	Ages 4–85	To assess achievement skills, for learning disability diagnosis, special education placement, curriculum planning, and clinical appraisal for preschool	45 minutes (PreK–K) 90 minutes (grades 1–6) 90–120 minutes (grades 7–16)	X	X		X	

(Continued)

TABLE 5.2 (Continued)

Test Name	Publisher/Source/Date	Grades/Ages	Purpose	Administration Time	Basic Reading Skills			Reading Comprehension	
					Word Recognition	Phonics/PA	Fluency	Vocabulary	Comprehension
Wide Range Achievement Test, 4th Ed. (WRAT-4)	Psychological Assessment Resources, 2006	Ages 5–94	To assess achievement in three broad areas: reading mathematics, and spelling	15–45 minutes	X				X
Woodcock-Johnson III Diagnostic Reading Battery (W-J III DRB)	Riverside, 2004	Ages 3–90+	To assess reading achievement and important related abilities	60 minutes	X	X	X	X	X
Woodcock Johnson-III (W-J III) Tests of Achievement	Riverside, 2001	Ages 2–80+	To provide a co-normed set of tests for measuring general intellectual ability, specific cognitive abilities, scholastic aptitude, oral language, and academic achievement	35–115 minutes	X	X	X	X	X
Woodcock-McGrew-Werder Mini Battery of Achievement	Riverside, 1994	Ages 4–90	To provide a brief wide-range test of basic academic skills	25–30 minutes	X			X	X
Woodcock Reading Mastery Tests—Revised/Normative Update (WRMT-R/NU)	Harcourt, 1989/1998	Ages 5–75	To provide an individually administered, norm-referenced assessment of key areas of reading	30–45 minutes	X	X		X	X

Information is based on a combination of published and online materials (including independent test reviews, content from tests and test manuals, and publisher/author promotional materials). Strenuous efforts were made by authors to ensure accuracy but information may contain errors and omissions due to updates in the tests reviewed, errors in published materials, and conflicts in reported information. Lists are not exhaustive.

TABLE 5.3 Psychometric Properties of Formal, Individualized, Norm-Referenced Assessments of Reading

Test Name	Reliability			Validity				Scores
	IC	TT	AF	IR	CON	PRE	CNC	
Durrell Analysis of Reading Difficulty, 3rd Ed.	X				X		X	Standard scores, grade equivalents
Early Reading Diagnostic Assessment-Revised (ERDA-R)	X	X		X	X	X	X	Percentile ranges
Gray Diagnostic Reading Test, 2nd Ed (GDRT-2)	X	X	X	X	X	X	X	Standard scores, age equivalents, grade equivalents, and percentiles
Gray Oral Reading Tests-4th Ed. (GORT-4)	X	X	X	X	X	X		Standard scores, percentiles, normal curve equivalents, T-scores, z scores, and stanines
Kaufman Tests of Educational Achievement II (KTEAII)	X	X	X	X	X			Standard scores, percentiles, age equivalents, grade equivalents (fall/spring norms), error analysis
Peabody Individual Achievement Test, Revised/Normative Update (PIAT-R/NU)	X	X			X	X	X	Standard scores, percentiles, stanines, normal curve equivalents, age equivalents, grade equivalents
Process Assessment of the Learner: Test Battery for Reading and Writing (PAL-RW)	X	X		X	X	X	X	Deciles
Standardized Reading Inventory-Second Edition (SRI-2)	X	X	X	X	X	X	X	Reading quotient standard score, grade equivalents
Test of Early Reading Ability—Third Edition (TERA-3)	X	X	X		X	X	X	Standard scores, percentiles, stanines, normal curve equivalents, age equivalents, grade equivalents
Test of Word Reading Efficiency (TOWRE)		X	X					Standard scores, percentiles, stanines, normal curve equivalents, age equivalents, grade equivalents

(Continued)

TABLE 5.3 (Continued)

Test Name	Reliability			Validity				Scores
	IC	TT	AF	IR	CON	PRE	CNC	
Wechsler Individual Achievement Test—2nd Ed. (WIAT-II)	X	X	X					Standard scores, percentiles, quartiles, deciles, stanines, normal curve equivalents, age equivalents, grade equivalents, and reading rate
Wide Range Achievement Test, 4th Ed. (WRAT-4)	X	X	X		X		X	Standard scores, percentiles, stanines, normal curve equivalents, age equivalents, grade equivalents
Woodcock-Johnson III Diagnostic Reading Battery (W-J III DRB)	X	X			X	X	X	Standard scores, percentiles, stanines, normal curve equivalents, age equivalents, grade equivalents
Woodcock-Johnson III (W-J III) Tests of Achievement	X	X	X	X	X	X	X	Standard scores, percentiles, stanines, normal curve equivalents, age equivalents, grade equivalents
Woodcock-McGrew-Werder Mini-Battery of Achievement	X	X			X		X	Standard scores, percentiles, age equivalents, grade equivalents
Woodcock Reading Mastery Tests—Revised/Normative Update (WRMT-R/NU)	X		X		X		X	Standard scores, percentiles, age equivalents, grade equivalents

Note: IC = Internal consistency, TT = Test/Retest, AF = Alternate forms, IR = Inter-rater, CON = Content, PRE = Predictive, CNC = Concurrent User Qualifications www.pearsonassessments.com

Information is based on a combination of published and online materials (including independent test reviews, content from tests and test manuals, and publisher/author promotional materials). Strenuous efforts were made by authors to ensure accuracy but information may contain errors and omissions due to updates in the tests reviewed, errors in published materials, and conflicts in reported information. Lists are not exhaustive.

CHAPTER 6

Formal Group Assessment: Focus on Accountability

In this chapter, we build on the information in Chapter 5 by describing characteristics of group administered standardized tests. First, we describe the characteristics of group tests used primarily to inform instruction and monitor progress. Next, we discuss some of the issues and controversies surrounding high-stakes testing. High-stakes testing informs teachers and administrators about their performance; allows comparisons among teachers,

schools, systems, even states; and often helps to establish accountability. Because the consequences of high-stakes testing can be significant, educators must guard against potential abuses in test preparation practices (and we discuss some of these here). Then, we describe characteristics of high-stakes tests (and other formal group achievement tests), followed by a discussion of two well-known examples of formal group instruments that shape public policy—the National Assessment of Educational Progress (NAEP 2006) and the National Assessment of Adult Literacy (NAAL, National Center for Educational Statistics 2006). Finally, we provide examples of measures commonly used to assess the various areas of reading. The chapter concludes with a table providing specific information about some of the most widely used group tests.

■ CONTEXT FOR FORMAL STANDARDIZED ASSESSMENT

As mentioned above, assessment data from formal, group-administered achievement tests primarily are used to determine accountability for students, teachers, and administrators. The bottom line question that these tests are designed to answer is: Are schools providing effective instruction so that students make adequate progress? Data from group-administered formal tests can be used to meet a wide variety of accountability-related goals. These goals might include comparing the performance of students to their peers; comparing the performance of classrooms, schools, systems, and even states to like entities; evaluating the performance of teachers based on the performance of their students; determining the readiness of students for entry into educational and career opportunities; and providing information about levels of performance that can be used to determine the need for further, individual, and more targeted assessment.

What goals are least likely to be achieved by collecting formal group data? Norm-referenced group data typically do not help teachers plan instruction, at least not with much specificity. The information is usually too general, typically not directly tied to curriculum, and in some cases, not available until several months after test administration. Individualized and group-administered informal tests (those discussed in Chapter 3) are best suited for informing instruction because they provide relevant classroom information. Formal group tests also are not ideal for progress monitoring because they typically do not measure small changes in growth or progress adequately as do the progress-monitoring measures described in Chapter 4. Finally, group-administered formal test results typically cannot be used to make special education eligibility decisions. Those decisions typically are based on individualized formal tests such as those described in Chapter 5, because the psychometric properties of individualized tests are often more robust than the group tests; that is, they tend to have less error and greater validity.

Despite limitations, group formal tests are useful in some important ways. To get additional context for understanding the usefulness of group-administered testing, take a look back at the Inclusive Model of Reading depicted in Chapter 2 (also Appendix B). Remember one caveat about testing in general—most any skill or construct can be assessed formally or informally. So many of the reading-relevant skills shown in the Inclusive Model can be

assessed using group-administered formal instruments. Measures of reading vocabulary and comprehension, in particular, lend themselves to group assessment. Also, group-administered tests are typically more efficient than individually administered ones; they can provide useful important information without taking a lot of teacher and student time. Finally, group tests can be useful for screening, that is, for providing general estimates of reading level. And, because they are typically norm-referenced, they provide some objective information about how students are progressing relative to other students.

■ CHARACTERISTICS OF GROUP FORMAL STANDARDIZED TESTING

As with individualized, standardized tests, group formal tests are administered according to strict procedures—teachers typically read the instructions verbatim and adhere to time limits set by the test authors. In fact, much of the information describing individualized standardized tests in Chapter 5 also applies to group testing. The essential difference is that group tests were designed for, and normed on, groups of students rather than individuals. An obvious advantage of group tests is that they require less time than individual testing; that is, they can efficiently provide information about groups of students. An obvious implication of group assessment is that student responses generally are limited to written responses of some type while individualized testing can allow oral responses and even manipulation of materials. In the context of reading assessment, this means that group tests will not provide teachers the opportunity to hear students read, attempt to sound out words, think aloud about their reading, retell what they have read, or respond to test directions by moving their limbs or manipulating objects. Group testing relies on written responses and often requires use of some type of scan form for ease of scoring. However, a distinction needs to be made here between tests designed to be used in the classroom and scored by the teacher for instructional planning or progress monitoring—such as the Gates-MacGinitie (MacGinitie, MacGinitie, Maria, and Dreyer 2000); the Gray Silent Reading Tests (Wiederholt and Blalock

2000); or the Test of Silent Word Reading Fluency (Mather, Hammill, Allen, and Roberts 2004)—and group achievement tests used to determine accountability, such as the Iowa Tests of Basic Skills (ITBS, Riverside Publishing Company 2003) or the Stanford Achievement Test (Harcourt 2002). The latter typically are administered near the end of the school year and sent by the district for scoring (often by an agency contracting with the state's department of education). In the case of tests designed for classroom use, hand scoring is often available and the format of students' responses can be more varied (for example, circling correct answers, writing words to demonstrate spelling skills, or writing short answers to questions following reading). Further, many group achievement tests now include a writing sample that is scored according to a prescribed set of criteria, or rubric, such as the writing assessment in the Tennessee Comprehensive Assessment Program (TCAP).

Tips for Administering and Scoring Formal Group Tests

In general, most of the tips for administering tests presented in Figure 5.2 (shown in Chapter 5) also apply to group formal testing. The primary point to remember is to follow the procedures in the manual or directions. Specific time limits, instructions, and materials needed typically are presented clearly in the examiners' materials. For some group tests, you will need to calculate chronological age (CA) to determine a score. Procedures for calculating chronological age are presented in Chapter 5. (Remember, once you have mathematically calculated chronological age, double check it to make sure it makes sense.) Also, group formal tests yield many of the same types of scores as individualized formal tests, including percentile ranks, age and grade equivalents, and normal curve equivalents. Some formal group tests, particularly those designed for the classroom, will also yield a standard score with a mean of 100 and standard deviation of 15. As discussed in Chapter 5, standard scores are the best unit of measure to use when comparing scores across students, which are inter-individual comparisons—distinct from comparing scores of a specific student over time (intra-individual comparisons). Figure 6.1 depicts the front page of the protocol from the Test of Silent Contextual Reading Fluency (TOSCRF; Hammill, Wiederholt, and Allen 2006) for Sammy, a third-grader with reading difficulties. Note the place to compute his chronological age and record his percentile, standard score, age and grade equivalents, as well as a descriptive rating determined by the test authors. Sammy is in Ms. Porter's third-grade class and, along with several other students in her class, has been referred to the Individual Education Program (IEP) team because of poor performance in reading. Dr. James, the school psychologist, administered the TOSCRF to all the students in Ms. Porter's class and obtained the scores shown in Figure 6.1 for Sammy.

Refer back to Figure 5.1 to see how various types of scores relate to one another along the normal curve and to determine how Sammy's scores compare to those of his peers. Sammy's performance on the TOSCRF is consistent with other things we know about his performance—his word analysis skills are weak for his age and grade. In fact, his raw score of 29 yielded an age equivalent score of below 7 (< 7–0), a grade-equivalent score of 1.2, a percentile rank of 18, standard score of 87, and a stanine score of 3. These scores show that Sammy is performing well below his peers, and in fact, the

TOSCRF

Test of Silent Contextual Reading Fluency

Student Record Form A

Section 1. Identifying Information

Name _Sammy_   Female ☐   Male ☒   Grade _3_

	Year	Month	Day
Date Tested	2006	10	28
Date of Birth	1998	5	22
Age*	8	5	6

School _Coffee County_
Examiner's Name _Greg Haywood_
Examiner's Title _Special Education Teacher_

*For normative purposes, use years and months. Do not round up.

Section 2. Record of Normative Scores

Raw Score	%ile Rank	Standard Score	SEM	Descriptive Rating (from Table 3.1)	Age Equivalent	Grade Equivalent
29	18	87	6	below average	<7	1.2

Section 3. Interpretation and Recommendations

Sammy held the pencil tightly; he erased a few times. He seemed to try hard, and stayed focused. He sighed several times during the 3 minutes.

t score = 41   z score = -.90   stanine = 3

Section 4. Student Responses

Example 1.   YOUGO

Example 2.   LOOKHERE

© 2006 by PRO-ED, Inc.
1 2 3 4 5   10 09 08 07 06

Additional copies of this form (#12237) may be purchased from
PRO-ED, 8700 Shoal Creek Blvd., Austin, TX 78757-6897
800/897-3202, Fax 800/397-7633, www.proedinc.com

FIGURE 6.1 Scored Protocol from the *Test of Silent Contextual Reading Fluency, Form A* for Sammy, a 3rd-Grader

Hammill, D. D., Wiederholt, J. L, & Allen, E. A. (2006). *Test of Silent Contextual Reading Fluency.* Austin, TX: PRO-ED. Used by permission.

descriptive rating provided in the TOSCRF manual labels him *below average.* The IEP team will review these scores and the scores from a number of other group-administered (end-of-year ITBS scores, for example) and individually administered tests (such as reading subtests from the Woodcock-Johnson-III Tests of Achievement, W-J III). Typically, the individually administered standardized tests are given by the school psychologist and scores written into a report used by the IEP team to make a decision about instructional help and special education eligibility. This is the situation for Sammy.

In addition to age and grade equivalents, percentiles, and standard scores, formal group tests often use a scaled score, which is a unique type of standard score. For example, the publishers of the Iowa Test of Basic Skills (ITBS; Riverside 2003) anchor its developmental scaled scores at 200, equivalent to the fourth-grade median score, and 250, equivalent to the eighth-grade median. Also, many group tests provide Lexiles (described in Chapter 4), which give teachers a good numerical system for matching students' reading ability to reading materials along a single score continuum, ranging from 200 to 1700. All these scores allow educators to document student progress over time within a given subdomain, such as reading comprehension. For example, see the ITBS scores in Figure 6.2 from a group of third-grade students. Note the various types of scores provided, including the designation *SS* for scaled scores.

As noted in Chapter 5, as test makers, technology, and statistical software packages get more sophisticated, so do tests. We typically think of group formal testing as standardized and norm-referenced. However, some group formal tests also provide criterion-referenced information. For example, beginning in 2004–2005, the TCAP provided not only data used for accountability, but also for grades 3–8, the test items were linked directly to grade-level achievement standards set by the Tennessee State Department of Education (TCAP 2006). Content validity refers to the extent to which a test is tied to content from a given curriculum, as discussed in Chapter 4. The linking of test items with actual achievement standards for students strengthens the content validity of a test. Figure 6.3 shows academic achievement scores of a fifth-grader taken from an end-of-the-year group-administered test. This student, Maddie, is the older sister of Jesse, the first-grade student we discussed in previous chapters. As does Jesse, she reads well relative to grade-level peers. In fact, her overall standard score for the Reading/ Language Arts category is 115 (84th percentile) and is described as "advanced"; the percentiles that describe her scores are all above 80. As is apparent, she is performing well in other areas, too. These consistently high scores across the board simply corroborate the finding that students who read well often perform well in other academic areas. This end-of-the-year test is similar to other tests that provide both norm-referenced and criterion-referenced information; for example, the Test of Adult Basic Education, or TABE (CTB/McGraw-Hill 1994).

FIGURE 6.2 Excerpt from Sample Class Report from the *Iowa Tests of Basic Skills*

THE IOWA TESTS

LIST OF STUDENT SCORES
Iowa Tests of Basic Skills® (ITBS®)

Class/Group: Ness
School: Longfellow
District: Dalen Community
Order No.: 002-A70000028-0-002

Test Date: 04/2002
Report Date: 04/26/02
Norms: Spring 2000
Page: 1
Grade: 3

Student (Gender / Birth Date / Age / Program / Form)	Score	Reading Vocab	Reading Comp	Reading Total	Word Analysis	Listening	Lang Spelling	Lang Capitalization	Lang Punctuation	Lang Usage/Express	Lang Total	Math Concepts/Estimate	Math Problems/Interp	Math Computation	Math Total	Core Total	Social Studies	Science	Maps/Diagrams	Ref Materials	Sources Total	Composite
Andrews, Jamie (F) 09/92 / 09-06 / AB / A — 0000141452	SS	204	188	196	196	179	203	214	196	215	207	182	193	172	188	196	179	186	204	228	216	197
	GE	5.0	4.0	4.5	4.5	3.4	5.1	5.8	4.5	5.8	5.3	3.6	4.4	3.2	4.0	4.5	3.4	3.9	5.0	6.9	5.9	4.5
	NS	7	5	6	6	4	7	7	6	7	7	5	6	5	5	6	4	5	6	8	8	6
	NPR	81	55	67	64	39	82	83	67	82	81	44	63	22	55	68	39	51	79	97	91	69
Benevides, Alicia (F) 03/93 / 09-01 / A — 0000157073	SS	172	198	185	172	198	182	147	184	180	173	175	189	176	182	180	188	183	193	190	192	184
	GE	3.0	4.6	3.8	3.0	4.6	3.6	1.7	3.7	3.5	3.1	3.3	4.1	3.4	3.7	3.4	4.0	3.6	4.2	4.1	4.2	3.7
	NS	4	6	5	4	6	5	2	5	5	4	5	5	5	5	4	5	5	6	6	6	5
	NPR	31	71	53	31	71	48	9	52	44	30	35	59	35	48	42	58	49	67	63	65	50
Catts, Jim (M) 11/92 / 09-04 / A — 0000146255	SS	°152	°147	°150	°146	°147	°152	°155	°181	°146	°158	°146	°134	°159	°140	°149	°165	°150	°157	°163	°160	°154
	GE	°1.8	°1.7	°1.8	°1.5	°1.7	°1.9	°2.1	°3.6	°1.5	°2.2	°1.5	°1.0	°2.5	°1.2	°1.7	°2.6	°1.8	°2.2	°2.6	°2.4	°1.9
	NS	°1	°1	°2	°1	°2	°2	°3	°5	°2	°3	°1	°1	°3	°1	°1	°3	°2	°3	°3	°3	°2
	NPR	°8	°4	°5	°2	°4	°5	°15	°46	°6	°10	°2	°1	°8	°1	°2	°19	°6	°12	°13	°12	°4
Easterday, Ona (F) 11/92 / 09-04 / A — 0000173431	SS	157	####	####	168	142	150	178	154	142	158	158	169	168	164		159	139	151	181	166	
	GE	2.1			2.8	1.3	2.3	3.4	2.0	1.3	2.2	2.3	2.9	2.8	2.6		2.4	1.2	1.8	3.5	2.7	
	NS	3			3	2	3	4	3	2	3	3	4	3	3		3	1	1	5	3	
	NPR	11			20	4	10	42	10	4	10	10	26	20	17		12	1	8	46	19	
Fossil, Graham (M) 09/92 / 09-06 / A — 0000146937	SS	152	160	156	151	165	159	147	165	174	161	179	173	182	176	164	168	163	151	175	163	164
	GE	1.8	2.3	2.1	1.8	2.6	2.3	1.7	2.6	3.2	2.4	3.4	3.1	3.7	3.3	2.6	2.8	2.5	1.8	3.1	2.5	2.5
	NS	2	3	2	2	3	3	2	3	4	3	5	4	5	5	3	4	3	2	4	3	3
	NPR	8	15	9	8	21	10	9	21	34	14	43	33	49	37	15	24	19	8	34	15	14
Friday, Leticia (F) 07/93 / 08-08 / A — 0000143196	SS	132	167	150	158	153	150				151	153	158	155	156	152	159	163			154	156
	GE	K.9	2.8	1.8	2.2	2.0	1.8				1.8	2.0	2.2	2.3	2.3	1.9	2.4	2.5			2.0	2.0
	NS	1	4	2	3	2	2				2	2	2	3	2	1	3	3			2	2
	NPR	1	24	5	13	6	4				5	6	13	4	8	3	12	19			6	5
Hernandez, Claire (M) 03/93 / 09-01 / A — 0000163173	SS	218	232	225	224	214	192	214	215	260	220	224	250	199	237	227	220	202	249	235	242	224
	GE	6.1	7.3	6.7	6.6	5.8	4.2	5.8	5.9	9.8	6.3	6.6	8.8	4.7	7.6	6.8	6.2	4.9	8.7	7.5	8.2	6.4
	NS	8	9	9	9	7	6	7	7	9	8	8	9	7	9	9	8	7	9	9	9	9
	NPR	95	96	96	98	85	69	85	86	99	93	98	99	84	99	99	95	77	99	99	99	98
Johnson, Eliot (M) 03/93 / 09-01 / A — 0000145652	SS	180	147	164	147	180	185	193	196	178	188	177	185	180	181	178	165	163	168	170	169	172
	GE	3.5	1.7	2.5	1.7	3.5	3.8	4.3	4.5	3.4	4.0	3.3	3.8	3.5	3.6	3.3	2.6	2.5	2.8	2.9	2.8	3.0
	NS	5	2	3	2	5	5	6	6	5	5	4	5	5	5	4	3	3	4	4	4	4
	NPR	45	4	18	4	45	54	65	70	40	57	38	53	44	46	38	19	19	22	26	23	27
Lee, Adam (M) 09/92 / 09-07 / GT / A — 0000157073	SS	210	194	202	197	197	188	256	235	250	232	180	197	186	188	207	192	183	189	190	190	198
	GE	5.4	4.3	5.0	4.6	4.6	4.0	9.4	7.5	8.8	7.3	3.5	4.6	3.9	4.0	5.3	4.2	3.6	4.0	4.1	4.1	4.6
	NS	8	6	7	6	6	6	9	8	9	9	5	7	5	5	7	6	5	6	6	6	6
	NPR	89	66	78	72	72	61	99	94	98	98	45	72	59	59	85	64	49	61	63	61	74
Mondavi, Kara (F) 11/92 / 09-04 / GT / A — 0000157074	SS	183	194	188	228	215	201	214	235	215	216	237	213	203	225	210	192	186	204	228	216	204
	GE	3.7	4.3	4.0	6.9	5.8	4.9	5.8	7.5	5.8	5.9	7.7	5.7	5.2	6.7	5.5	4.2	3.9	5.0	6.9	5.9	4.9
	NS	5	6	5	9	7	7	7	8	7	7	9	7	7	9	8	6	5	7	8	8	7
	NPR	50	66	58	98	84	82	85	94	84	91	99	87	89	98	89	64	54	81	98	92	82

SS=Standard Score   GE=Grade Equivalent   NS=National Stanine   NPR=National Percentile Rank   o=Excluded from group averages by school request   #=Student did not meet completion criteria   *Not included in Totals and Composite

Riverside Publishing A HOUGHTON MIFFLIN COMPANY

Iowa Tests of Basic Skills® (ITBS®) reproduced with permission of The Riverside Publishing Company.

FIGURE 6.3a Test Results from a Proptypical State-Mandated Group Achievement Test for Maddie, a High Achieving Fifth-Grader

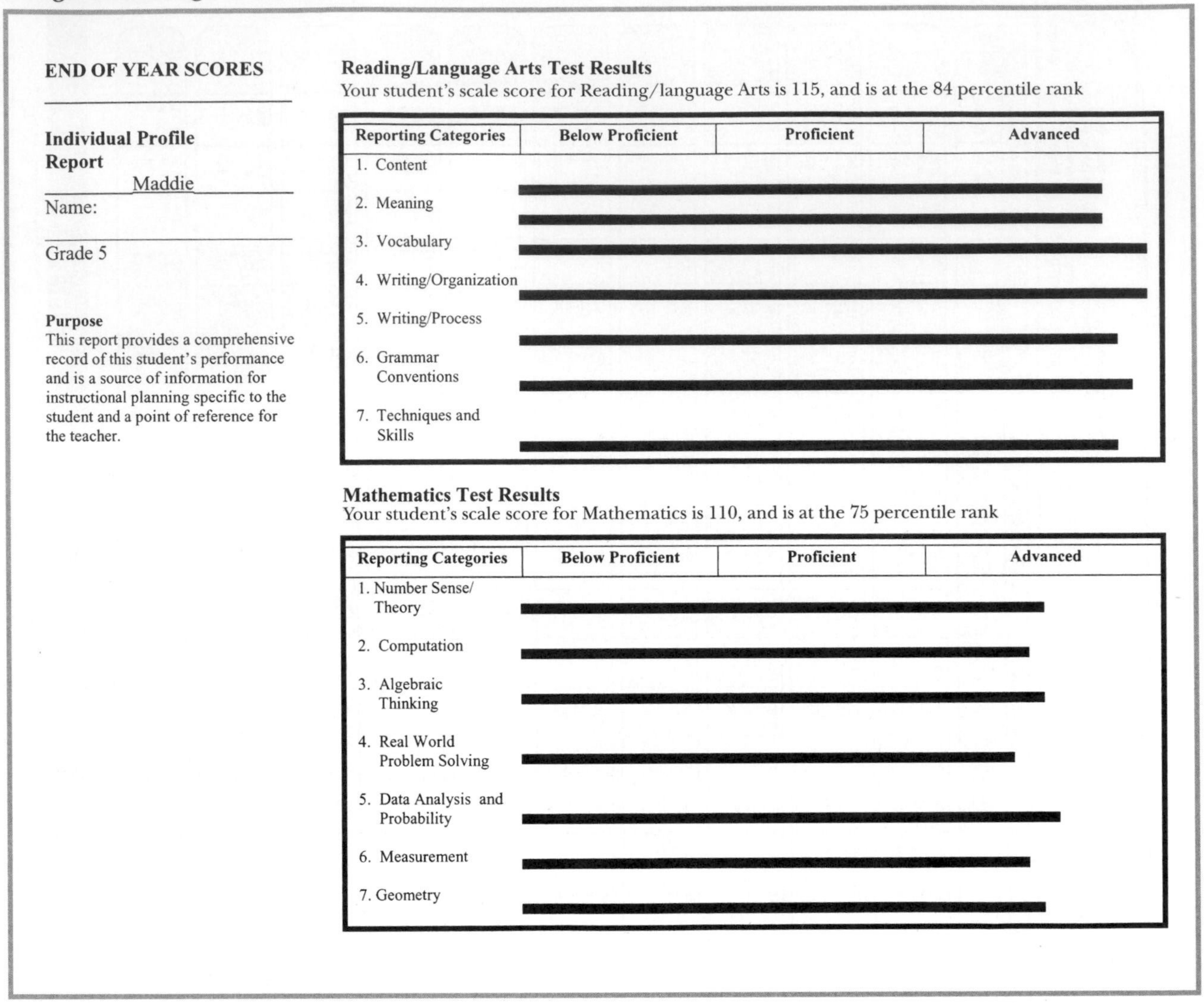

END OF YEAR SCORES

Individual Profile Report

Name: _____Maddie_____

Grade 5

Purpose
This report provides a comprehensive record of this student's performance and is a source of information for instructional planning specific to the student and a point of reference for the teacher.

Reading/Language Arts Test Results
Your student's scale score for Reading/language Arts is 115, and is at the 84 percentile rank

Reporting Categories	Below Proficient	Proficient	Advanced
1. Content			
2. Meaning			
3. Vocabulary			
4. Writing/Organization			
5. Writing/Process			
6. Grammar Conventions			
7. Techniques and Skills			

Mathematics Test Results
Your student's scale score for Mathematics is 110, and is at the 75 percentile rank

Reporting Categories	Below Proficient	Proficient	Advanced
1. Number Sense/ Theory			
2. Computation			
3. Algebraic Thinking			
4. Real World Problem Solving			
5. Data Analysis and Probability			
6. Measurement			
7. Geometry			

■ GROUP ACHIEVEMENT TESTS FOR INSTRUCTIONAL PLANNING AND PROGRESS MONITORING

Despite concerns noted earlier, formal group tests can be useful for a variety of purposes, including gross progress monitoring, instructional planning, and screening. And, as students get older and develop more sophisticated reading skills, it is possible to get fairly specific information about particular reading strengths and weaknesses from group tests. In fact, educators have a long history of using group achievement tests to help determine students' instructional levels (such as the Gates-MacGinitie Reading Test just mentioned). Some more recent tests allow teachers to quickly assess a whole class and determine which students might benefit from further assessment. For example, even brief tests such as the TOSCRF and a related test called the Test of Silent Word Reading

FIGURE 6.3b (Continued)

END OF YEAR SCORES	Science Test Results

Science Test Results
Your student's scale score for Science is 109, and is at the 73 percentile rank

Individual Profile Report

Name: Maddie

Grade 5

Purpose
This report provides a comprehensive record of this student's performance and is a source of information for instructional planning specific to the student and a point of reference for the teacher.

Reporting Categories	Below Proficient	Proficient	Advanced
1. Structure & Function of Orgs			
2. Ecology			
3. Life Cycles and Bio Change			
4. Space Weather and Climate			
5. Earth's Features & Resources			
6. Motion & Forces			
7. Matter			

Social Studies Test Results
Your student's scale score for Social Studies is 133, and is at the 99 percentile rank

Reporting Categories	Below Proficient	Proficient	Advanced
1. Economics			
2. Governance & Codes			
3. Geography			
4. US Hist Per 2 (1801-1900)			
5. US Hist Per 3 (1890-Pres)			

Fluency (TOSWRF; Mather, Hammill, Allen, and Roberts 2004) are designed to be given either individually or in groups to students reading at first-grade level and up and can provide good screening data. The tests require only three minutes each and rely on the word chain technique (see Figure 6.4) in which students make a mark between each word; both tests provide a number of scores (including grade/age equivalents, percentiles, and standard scores). The authors cite evidence of strong reliability and validity for both tests, and there is some independent evidence as well (Bell, McCallum, Burton, Gray, Windingstad, and Moore 2006; Windingstad, Choate, Bell, and McCallum 2007). These tests have alternate forms so they can be used in a gross way to monitor progress; however, because they are standardized across a wide age span and are very brief, they cannot show instructional gains made over a relatively short period of time.

The Gates-MacGinitie is a popular reading test, now in its fourth edition, that has been used for classroom, school, and district monitoring of progress

FIGURE 6.4 Excerpt from the Protocol from the *Test of Silent Word Reading Fluency, Form A,* Depicting the Word Chaining Technique

Mather, N., Hammill, D. D., Allen, E. A., & Roberts, R. (2004). *TOSWRF: Test of Silent Word Reading Fluency.* Austin, TX: PRO-ED. Used by permission.

straightwildgrewaboveswimtrouble/
setdrivequickkickrollbottlejollysky/
fewdesertfaultgazepressrootcrept/

on|at|get|run|car|is|fun|blue|big|like|back/
each|much|three|zoo|apple|far|fly|would/
way|under|bird|found|egg|lunch|yard|live/
stay|girl|cake|ofbutpetroomlightvery/

and for grouping students for instruction. As with many other group tests, the Gates-MacGinitie has various levels, appropriate for kindergarten through adult literacy. Test items for students in grades 3–8 tap vocabulary and comprehension and take about an hour to administer. Both vocabulary and comprehension are assessed via a multiple-choice format. Scoring can be done via computer or by hand, and a report of results in Lexiles is available. In addition, a manual titled *Linking Testing to Teaching: A Classroom Resource for Reading Assessment and Instruction* is available to help educators use assessment results for instructional planning (www.riverpub.com/products/gmrt/index.html). Specific descriptions of the vocabulary and comprehension items from the Gates-MacGinitie are presented later in the chapter.

Some group tests target older students specifically. The Nelson-Denny is designed for high school and college-age students and contains measures of reading rate (a one-minute timing of silent reading), vocabulary, and comprehension, and it takes about forty minutes to administer. This test might be used by the high school biology teacher, Dr. Charles (mentioned in earlier chapters), to obtain a measure of reading comprehension for his students. As you will remember, the students in his class exhibited wide variation in reading ability, and we proposed a strategy for determining students' levels using a brief individually-administered assessment. But, a group test can also provide similar information. Knowledge about how each performs could help Dr. Charles find and assign supplemental but relevant reading materials from other biology texts or trade books. As you might expect from the longer administration time, the Nelson-Denny provides more information than the TOSWRF or TOSCRF. An estimate of rate and measures of reading vocabulary and reading comprehension are available.

Other tests are available to assess older students. For example, Ms. Sanchez, the teacher of adult basic education introduced in Chapter 1, might use the TABE. The TABE is commonly used in adult education settings across the United States and provides a measure of reading comprehension. The TABE is multilevel; teachers are encouraged to first administer a locator test to help determine the most appropriate level of administration for entering students. For students who struggle on the Nelson-Denny or TABE, teachers should consider giving an individualized test or perhaps a CBM assessment that taps more basic reading skills, such as word analysis and fluency skills. Information about individualized tests and the specific areas they address were described in Chapter 5.

Though not especially useful for specific instructional planning, progress monitoring, or determining eligibility for special education, some type of large-scale group testing is probably necessary to determine and ensure accountability. Research suggests that some schools do not provide even minimally adequate instruction unless some mandatory accountability testing is in place (Bell 1984; Payne 2003). Further, norm-referenced group testing can provide information about the progress of students in particular groups of interest, including students with disabilities, students in certain ethnic or racial groups, and students with varying socioeconomic status.

■ HIGH-STAKES TESTING

Some formal, group-administered tests are referred to as high-stakes testing because the scores lead to decisions about accountability of classrooms, schools, systems, and even states. These data may have implications for accreditation, funding, and in some cases, even for determining which students may be promoted or allowed to graduate. Overton (2006) cites U.S. Department of Education statistics from the year 2000, noting that at least twenty-six states use results of statewide testing programs to make determinations about graduation and six use these data to determine promotion (of individual students). Other states use statewide testing data to evaluate the quality of teaching, based on their students' progress, including the value-added assessment system used in Tennessee based on TCAP scores. Clearly, high-stakes testing is pervasive in the United States. But how did this state of affairs develop? What is the origin of high-stakes testing? The brief answer is that high-stakes testing is politically motivated, and controversial, as we discuss next.

How did high-stakes testing originate? One of the first significant political movements to influence the development of high-stakes assessment in this country occurred in 1946, when the U.S. Chamber of Commerce called for an assessment system to ensure that schools prepared well-qualified workers for the post–World War II era (Fine 1947). Additional impetus came during the Cold War era of the 1950s, 1960s, and 1970s, when unflattering international comparisons of student performance, combined with the fear of losing U.S. scientific and military superiority, fueled a frenzy of educational reform (Postlethwaite 1985). Two additional motivating influences added to the growing support for high-stakes testing to demonstrate accountability of student and teacher performance in the late 1960s and 1970s—the interest of state governments to provide evidence of teacher accountability and a growing number of lawsuits brought by parents of semiliterate graduates against school systems for not properly educating their children (Conley 2005). More recent data from international comparisons showing that U.S. students perform less well than students in several other developed countries in reading and math continue to create anxiety about the level of preparedness of U.S. students (National Center for Educational Statistics 1999, as cited in Conley 2005). These influences combine to stimulate political discourse and action and result in additional impetus for accountability.

Why is high-stakes testing controversial?   As you might suspect, using national or state-based assessment data as evidence of accountability is controversial. However, some of the criticisms against the use of tests have more to do with the way the data are used than the technical limitations of the instruments. For example, according to Conley (2005), high-stakes standardized tests are best at providing a snapshot of current performance, a one-time assessment of what students can do at a moment in time, and they are not very good at providing growth-oriented assessment. But as test authors and scholars use increasingly sophisticated measurement techniques, this criticism becomes less appropriate. For example, the Lexiles used on a number of tests provide scale scores in different academic and content areas that allow growth estimates within a given area over several years of schooling. Other critics suggest that high-stakes testing demoralizes educators, parents, and students who receive low scores; encourages teaching to the tests rather than a broader more appropriate curriculum; fails to include enough low-end content for low functioning and special needs students; and tends to encourage cheating because of high-stakes outcomes. Although all these can be problematic, most of the criticisms are related to user abuses, not to the tests themselves.

Guidelines for High-Stakes Testing

In response to the criticisms of high-stakes tests, certain guidelines have been developed. For example, Elliott, Braden, and White (2001) provide suggestions for using high-states testing, calling for systems to tie assessment to predetermined goals, to rely on multiple measures, and to ensure that instruments are reliable and valid for the purposes intended. The American Educational Research Association (AERA) in 2000 adopted a set of technical and policy guidelines for using high-stakes testing based on standards described in the Standards for Educational and Psychological Testing (American Educational Research Association 1999). These are reproduced in Table 6.1.

As you can see from this table, the first guideline admonishes school system personnel to align the test to the curriculum. This is a crucial goal, but for years critics charged that there was little correspondence between the content tapped by high-stakes tests and that from the school-based curriculum. System educators often used misaligned or poorly aligned test data to make inferences about the educational performance of students, and, by extension, teachers in the system. Of course, this problem is related more to the lack of planning and abuse of the test data than it is to the quality of the test itself. On the other hand, educators also need to be wary of focusing instruction too heavily on the test items, more commonly referred to as **teaching to the test,** a phenomenon that occurs when educators teach content and test format that inappropriately mirrors actual test content. (Clearly, this phrase could be used positively to only mean focusing instruction in a general way on the test content, but it is not typically used in this manner.) Popham (2002) provides two general test prepara-

TABLE 6.1   Standards for Educational and Psychological Testing (Joint Committee, 1999)

Standard Condition	Description
Alignment between the test and the curriculum	Assessments should be specific to all dimensions of the instructional treatment and have multiple forms.
Validity of passing scores and achievement levels	Standard-setting procedures must accompany the use of any "cut-scores" or proficiency categories.
Opportunities for meaningful remediation for examinees who fail high-stakes tests	Remediation should focus on the knowledge skills assessed. Reasonable time should exist between retests.
Appropriate attention to language differences among examinees	If the student lacks proficiency in the language used in the assessment, the assessment becomes a language test. Accommodations may be necessary for English spoken as second language (ESL) students.
Careful adherence to explicit rules for determining which students are to be tested	Uniformity in inclusion rules relates to comparability in meaningfulness of data.
Protection against high-stakes decision based on a single test	No life-determining decision should be made on the basis of test data alone. There are multiple opportunities to perform well and, when necessary, alternate assessment approaches should be taken.
Adequate resources and opportunity to learn	Particularly when testing for accountability and certification, ensure that students have had equal opportunity to learn and that the curriculum is relevant.
Validation for each separate use	Assessments and their interpretations are not valid in general but for specific applications. The projected use needs to be "validated."
Full disclosure of likely negative consequences of high-stakes testing programs	All consequences of test use need to be made known to the public.
Sufficient reliability for each intended use	Acceptable reliability is necessary for all groups and scores used to report results about individual students, classrooms, schools, or districts.
Ongoing evaluation of intended and unintended effects of high-stakes testing	It is necessary to monitor the extent to which assessment meets user needs as well as what might be some unintended effects, if any.

Payne, D. A. (2003). *Applied Educational Assessment 2nd ed.* (2003). Belmont, CA: Wadsworth/Thomson Learning. Reprinted with permission.

tion guidelines and some detailed recommendations for appropriate and inappropriate test preparation practices. Popham refers to the two general guidelines as: (1) the professional ethics guideline (no test-preparation practice should violate ethical norms of the education profession) and (2) the educational defensibility guideline (no test-preparation practice should increase students' test scores without also increasing mastery of the domain assessed). He uses these two general guidelines to evaluate the appropriateness of five test-preparation practices. Following his lead, we describe briefly the five practices below and ask you to provide your best guess as to the appropriateness of each based on your awareness of the two general guidelines. Then, we share with you Popham's view regarding the appropriateness of these practices.

1. **Previous-form preparation** allows students to practice test-taking with items from old, out-of-print versions of a current test.

2. **Current-form preparation** allows students to practice on items taken directly from a currently used version of a test.

3. **Generalized test-taking preparation** allows simulation of test administration using a variety of test-preparation strategies to fit a variety of test formats, such as helping students schedule time optimally, modeling good calculated guessing strategies, and encouraging students to read the stem carefully before looking at the options of multiple-choice questions.

4. **Same-format preparation** allows students to practice responding only to items that represent the content of the actual test and mirror the format of the items from the test.

5. **Varied-format preparation** allows students to practice responding to items that represent directly the content of the actual test using a variety of item formats.

How did you respond? In your opinion, which of these practices abide by Popham's two general guidelines, if any? According to Popham, only practices 3 and 5 are clearly appropriate; practice 2 violates both guidelines and practices 1 and 4 violate the educational defensibility guideline.

Not all experts and agencies are quite as restrictive as the criteria cited by Popham. In fact, the policy of the National Assessment of Educational Progress (NAEP; National Assessment of Educational Progress; National Center for Educational Statistics, U.S. Department of Education (http://nces.ed.gov/nationsreportcard/itmrls/), a government agency established to assess national academic progress in basic areas, is to release previous questions from nearly all subject areas. These questions are available to teachers and parents at the NAEP Web site, and students may review them to get a sense of specific question format. (Obviously, the particular released items will not be reused.) But becoming familiar with the format can be helpful. Based on the literature, Guthrie (2002) concludes that 10 percent of the differences in high-stakes test scores (between students) can be attributed to test-wiseness and format familiarity. Guthrie (377) recommends a 10-week study period before administration of a high-stakes test during which, "approximately 10 percent of the time should be spent on format practice so the students are familiar with the types of items and questions."

Problems and Solutions Associated with High-Stakes Testing

As you are aware, high-stakes testing continues to attract both praise and criticism, especially the massive standardized testing of high school students over the past few decades; see Payne (2003) for more discussion. High-stakes testing of high school students is related to school-based goals of awarding of scholarships and preparing students for college admissions testing. Because of the extensive testing of this population, Payne developed a set of common criticisms and related solutions for externally developed standardized tests. We reproduce those in Table 6.2, in part because these criticisms and recommended solutions are relevant for all high-stakes testing, not only to the testing of high school students. The table effectively summarizes the

TABLE 6.2 External Testing Programs: Criticisms and Solutions

Criticism of External Testing	Response or Possible Solution
1. Not all important outcomes are measured.	1. Those variables of primary importance to college work are assessed. If important variables are ignored, they may not have been defined clearly enough.
2. Only facts and knowledge are measured.	2. Within the past several years external tests have stressed the ability to use information. Command of useful knowledge is important.
3. External tests are unfair to some students.	3. Measuring instruments are fallible. Common essential outcomes are emphasized. Great care is made to control bias.
4. The use of objective (for example, multiple-choice) items is discriminatory.	4. If these items are relevant to the criterion of college success, they are valid. Choice making is an aspect of all human activities.
5. External tests adversely influence curriculum innovation and educational change.	5. There is danger that this will be the case. Test developers work with curriculum experts and educators in establishing objectives.
6. Tests do no predict perfectly.	6. Tests, as well as individuals, are fallible. Successful predictions far outnumber mispredictions. It is impossible to assess all relevant variables in advance.
7. There is too much duplication of testing.	7. Development of general-purpose equivalency tables that allow equating of results from different tests would help.
8. Too much time and money are expended on tests.	8. Considering the potential payoff and the importance of the decisions to be made, the investment is minimal.
9. The advantaged can secure coaching that helps ensure success on tests.	9. Research indicates that coaching has, on the whole, only a modest effect. If coaching also improves school performance, so much the better. The validity of the test is not undermined. The opportunity for coaching should be made available to all.
10. The use of external tests invites insidious comparisons between schools.	10. Scores should be reported only to target institutions and individual students.
11. Exposure to external testing situations adversely affects students' emotional stability and mental health.	11. There is little or no evidence that this is true.
12. External test scores determine college entrance.	12. Nothing could be further from the truth. An entrance decision is made on the basis of a collection of a variety of relevant data, never on a single test score.

Payne, D. A. (2003). *Applied Educational Assessment 2nd ed.* (2003). Belmont, CA: Wadsworth/Thomson Learning. Reprinted with permission.

criticisms. Payne addresses each in a thoughtful and measured manner, based on his considerable experience and expertise.

In spite of the limitations of some standardized tests and the abuse of the scores they yield, most educators recognize their value, or at least the need for them. In fact, their use has been tied to the very fabric of our modern democratic society, which requires that massive numbers of individuals be evaluated and rewarded based on their mastery of relevant content. Clearly, objective, fair, and unbiased assessment is needed to determine mastery. The goal of the United States has been to encourage growth of a "meritocracy," a society that rewards knowledge acquisition and those who produce, rather than a society that rewards its members based on race, gender, birthright, and related family influence. As Angoff and Anderson noted in 1963:

> No other method that we know of today can provide measurement for the tremendous numbers of individuals who demand objective consideration of their talents. Certainly no other method that we know of today can accomplish this measurement as equitably as the standardized test (cited in Payne 2003, 56).

Nothing has happened to change the mind of many experts regarding the use of standardized tests since Angoff and Anderson offered their observation. In fact, testing has increased, in part because test results typically are considered to be more objective than the recommendation of parents, teachers, and related professionals, particularly given the extensive scrutiny tests have undergone in the last few decades. During the 1970s in particular, many tests were described as biased against racial and minority group members, in large part because they tended to yield lower scores for members of these minority groups than for the majority population. Since that time, test experts and users have gotten more sophisticated in several ways. First, tests are reviewed routinely for bias and potentially discriminatory items before they are published. Second, experts and consumers are more aware of the meaning of mean differences; in essence, differences in scores exhibited by members of different groups. They now recognize that although mean differences trip a red flag and trigger further scrutiny into possible bias, these differences do not *necessarily* convey bias. Other sophisticated technical criteria must be evaluated, such as the extent to which test content and constructs are measured in the same way for minority and nonminority group members and the extent to which a test predicts equally well for both groups. Mean differences probably have more to do with socio-economic status, access to educational opportunity, parental and community support for education, and school climate than racial or minority status. In fact, differences between groups are now considered evidence of a failure in our educational system, which is one of the driving forces behind No Child Left Behind (NCLB 2001). Test bias was addressed in some depth in Chapter 5.

High-Stakes Testing of Students with Disabilities and English Language Learners (ELL)

The use of high-stakes standardized tests is still more controversial for some students than others, and particularly for those with disabilities or those who are from culturally or linguistically diverse backgrounds. Individuals with Disabilities Education Improvement Act (IDEA 2004) and NCLB require that almost all students participate in accountability testing, but accommodations and alternate assessments may be allowed for some students. In fact, NCLB requires that the progress of students with disabilities, those with low socio-economic status, those in various ethnic/racial groups (such as Black and

Hispanic), and English language learners (ELL) be disaggregated and evaluated separately. The goal is to be certain that students from various settings and with various backgrounds make adequate yearly progress (AYP); that is, to close the achievement gap between students who are white with a middle-to-upper socioeconomic status (and without disabilities) and students in typically lower-achieving groups.

Group testing of students with disabilities and those whose first language is not English is especially tricky. The percentage of students with disabilities who can be exempted from taking state accountability tests has decreased; IDEA 2004 requires that all but those with the most profound disabilities (lowest performing 1 to 3 percent) must participate in state accountability testing. In Tennessee, for example, students with disabilities may (a) take the same accountability tests as other students and in the same manner; (b) take the same tests but with accommodations such as extended time, alternative setting, flexible scheduling, assistance of a scribe, large-print, and so on; or (c) take an alternative assessment focusing on more functional skills. The IEP team, consisting of parents, teachers, and others involved in the students' education, decides the most appropriate assessment option for students with disabilities. In general, accommodations on the test should reflect instructional accommodations the student routinely receives during the school day. Recall Shelby and Saimah in Mr. Haywood's special education class? Both are fifth-graders with reading difficulties. They take the state-mandated group achievement test, but Mr. Haywood tests them in the resource room setting and reads orally all sections but the reading section because they receive help with content area reading in the classroom and this help is documented on their IEPs.

A number of accommodations may be considered for students with disabilities who are taking the state group achievement test. For example, the following accommodations are typically considered and allowed. Others are allowed under certain conditions and for certain academic areas, if consistent with the IEP or 504 Plan. Those that are typically allowed include:

a. Large print
b. Oral instructions
c. Calculators/mathematical tables
d. Flexible setting (for example, individual versus small group versus study carrel);
e. Visual/tactile aids
f. Multiple testing sessions (within the same day)
g. Flexible scheduling
h. Use of a scribe/recording device
i. Test booklet marking
j. Oral self-reading

Other accommodations, sometimes referred to as "special accommodations," include:

a. extended time
b. read aloud internal test instructions/items

  c. prompting, upon request
  d. use of an interpreter
  e. use of manipulatives for math tests
  f. use of assistive technology

Of course, care and common sense must be used when planning and implementing test accommodations. Scores derived from standardized tests are based on norms derived under prescribed standardized testing conditions. To the extent these conditions are changed, we have less confidence in what the score means. For example, we are aware that some systems make a practice of advising teachers to read the reading portion of standardized tests to some students with disabilities. This practice ensures that the score cannot be considered a measure of reading skill, but rather more of an assessment of listening comprehension. Although teachers who read (the reading portion) of tests to their students are well intentioned, administering tests in this way makes the scores invalid as measures of reading.

Students for whom English is a second language are also no longer exempt from state accountability testing. ELL students must take the same state-mandated tests as other students; however, there are provisions for having directions and other portions read aloud. Specific provisions vary from state to state.

■ FORMAL GROUP ACHIEVEMENT TESTING FOR ACCOUNTABILITY: TWO WELL-KNOWN EXAMPLES

In the following sections, we turn the attention away from tests designed for classroom use to two group-administered achievement tests, commissioned by the U.S. government, that have a strong influence on public policy and opinion: the NAEP 2006, introduced earlier, and the NAAL 2006 (National Center for Educational Statistics). We discuss the reading-related goals of these assessment strategies, the guidelines that influenced their development, the characteristics of the standardization samples used, the types of scores they produce, and their technical properties and common uses.

NAEP

Since 1969, NAEP has provided a nationally representative and continuing assessment of what students know and can do in various subject areas and typically is referred to as "the nation's report card." Specifically, assessments occur at grades 4, 8, and 12 in reading, mathematics, science, writing, U.S. history, civics, geography, and the arts, but scores are not reported for individual students or schools. Since 1990, performance is reported for the nation as a whole, by state, and can be broken down by gender and race/ethnicity. So even though student or school comparisons are not possible, other comparisons are available. The standardization sample is large. For example, in 2005 more than 165,000 fourth-grade students and 159,000 eighth-grade students participated nationally.

NAEP reports performance in two primary ways: scaled scores and benchmarks or levels. First, scores are reported on a scale of from 0 to 500. These scores allow certain comparisons. The overall average scores for the nation's public schools were 215, 212, and 215 for fourth-grade students for the years 1992, 1994, and 1996, respectively; these scores can be compared to the average scores of states. For example, Tennessee scored just below the national mean in 1992 (212), just above in 1994 (213), and just below in 1996 (212). Change scores are also reported. As an example, the state of Texas showed an average gain of six points from 1992 (to 2005) in fourth-grade reading scores, but an average decrease of three points in eighth grade scores from 1998 (to 2005). A second strategy for reporting performance is based on somewhat arbitrary but useful "benchmarks" for three levels: Basic (partial mastery of prerequisite knowledge and skills considered fundamental for proficient work); Proficient (competency of challenging content, including subject-matter and analytical skills, and appropriate application to real-world situations), and Advanced (superior performance). Table 6.3 provides descriptions of the three NAEP performance levels for fourth-, eighth-, and twelfth-grade students in reading.

TABLE 6.3   National Assessment of Educational Progress Performance Descriptions

Achievement-level policy definitions	
Basic	Partial mastery of prerequisite knowledge and skills that are fundamental for proficient work at each grade.
Proficient	Solid academic performance for each grade assessed. Students reaching this level have demonstrated competency over challenging subject matter, including subject-matter knowledge, application of such knowledge to real-world situations, and analytical skills appropriate to the subject matter.
Advanced	Superior performance.
Fourth grade	
Basic	Fourth-grade students performing at the Basic level should demonstrate an understanding of the overall meaning of what they read. When reading text appropriate for fourth-graders, they should be able to make relatively obvious connections between the text and their own experiences and extend the ideas in the text by making simple inferences.
Proficient	Fourth-grade students performing at the Proficient level should be able to demonstrate an overall understanding of the text, providing inferential as well as literal information. When reading text appropriate to fourth grade, they should be able to extend the ideas in the text by making inferences, drawing conclusions, and making connections to their own experiences. The connection between the text and what the student infers should be clear.
Advanced	Fourth-grade students performing at the Advanced level should be able to generalize about topics in the reading selection and demonstrate an awareness of how authors compose and use literary devices. When reading text appropriate to fourth grade, they should be able to judge text critically and, in general, to give thorough answers that indicate careful thought.
Eighth grade	
Basic	Eighth-grade students performing at the Basic level should demonstrate a literal understanding of what they read and be able to make some interpretations. When reading text appropriate to eighth grade, they should be able to identify specific aspects of the text that reflect overall meaning, extend the ideas in the text by making simple inferences, recognize and relate interpretations and connections among ideas in the text to personal experience, and draw conclusions based on the text.
Proficient	Eighth-grade students performing at the Proficient level should be able to show an overall understanding of the text, including inferential as well as literal information. When reading

(Continued)

text appropriate to eighth grade, they should be able to extend the ideas in the text by making clear inferences from it, by drawing conclusions, and by making connections to their own experiences—including other reading experiences. Proficient eighth-graders should be able to identify some of the devices authors use in composing text.

Advanced	Eighth-grade students performing at the Advanced level should be able to describe the more abstract themes and ideas of the overall text. When reading text appropriate to eighth grade, they should be able to analyze both the meaning and the form of the text and support their analyses explicitly with examples from the text; they should be able to extend text information by relating it to their experiences and to world events. At this level, student responses should be thorough, thoughtful, and extensive.

Twelfth grade	
Basic	Twelfth-grade students performing at the Basic level should be able to demonstrate an overall understanding and make some interpretations of the text. When reading text appropriate to twelfth grade, they should be able to identify and relate aspects of the text to its overall meaning, extend the ideas in the text by making simple inferences, recognize interpretations, make connections among and relate ideas in the text to their personal experiences, and draw conclusions. They should be able to identify elements of an author's style.
Proficient	Twelfth-grade students performing at the Proficient level should be able to show an overall understanding of the text which includes inferential as well as literal information. When reading text appropriate to twelfth grade, they should be able to extend the ideas of the text by making inferences, drawing conclusions, and making connections to their own personal experiences and other readings. Connections between inferences and the text should be clear, even when implicit. These students should be able to analyze the author's use of literary devices.
Advanced	Twelfth-grade students performing at the Advanced level should be able to describe more abstract themes and ideas in the overall text. When reading text appropriate to twelfth grade, they should be able to analyze both the meaning and the form of the text and explicitly support their analyses with specific examples from the text. They should be able to extend the information from the text by relating it to their experiences and to the world. Their responses should be thorough, thoughtful, and extensive.

Adapted from McKenna, M.C. & Stahl, S.A. (2003). *Assessment for Effective Reading Instruction.* New York: Guilford Press, p. 34.

NAEP uses a reading framework to guide assessment. Specifically, NAEP assesses three contexts for reading, including reading for literacy experience (exploring events, characters, and plots and actions within novels, stories, and poems), reading for information (exploring textbooks, essays, speeches, and magazines), and reading to perform a task (exploring maps, bus and train schedules and directions for making repairs). Students are assessed on four different aspects of reading: general understanding, interpretation, making connections, and critical appreciation of content/organization/ structure/humor. Both short-term and long-term trends are reported.

General Trends

What can NAEP tell us about reading performance of students in the nation over the past few years? We will not attempt to summarize the overall results, but some interesting findings are apparent. National averages were two points higher in 2005 than in 1992 at grades 4 and 8, the first year certain scores were available nationwide. Between 1992 and 2005, there was no significant change in the percentage of fourth-grade students who per- formed at or above the Basic level, but the percentage performing at or above Proficient increased during this time. The percentage of eighth-grade students performing at or above Basic was higher in 2005 (73 percent) than in 1992 (69 percent), but there was no significant change in the percentage scoring at or above Proficient between these same years. In general, overall performance has remained the same.

Racial and Ethnic Trends

On a more molecular level, scores for fourth-grade Asian/Pacific Islanders, Blacks, Hispanics, and Whites increased between 1992 and 2005. In general, fourth-grade Whites score higher on average than their Black and Hispanic counterparts, but the White-Black and White-Hispanic score gaps narrowed from 2003 to 2005. Consideration of short-term trends show that Black and Hispanic students scored higher in 2005 than in 2003. In 2005, fourth-grade students who were eligible for free or reduced lunch showed a two-point gain from 2003 to 2005. Allington (2006) helps put the racial/ethnic differences in perspective. He notes that gains have been made by all groups, especially minority students, but because of population shifts (i.e., increasing large numbers of minority students), overall performance has remained about the same. Also, he notes that most of the significant gains made by Blacks and Hispanics occurred between the early 1970s and 1990; consequently, more needs to be done to continue to narrow the achievement gap between Whites and others.

Gender Trends

In 2005, fourth-grade females scored higher their male counterparts, although the male students' scores increased by three points from 1992 to 2005. Similar trends were observed for eighth-graders; that is, average scores increased between 1992 and 2005 (Perie, Grigg, and Donahue 2005). One of the most important findings from the NAEP data was reported in 2006 by Klecker; she shows gender comparisons from 1992 to 2003 in reading scores for fourth-, eighth-, and twelfth-grade students. There are strong gender effects, with females outperforming males at every grade and year; however, perhaps the most telling trend shows how the differential performance widens as students age, particularly from the fourth to eighth grade. **Effect size** differences (a measure of the mean difference between the two groups in standard deviation units) range from .13 to .27 for fourth-graders, from .27 to .43 for eighth-graders, and from .22 to .44 for twelfth-graders. The average effect sizes were .21, .36, and .37 for grades 4, 8, and 12, respectively. Klecker suggests that school reform efforts, including NCLB, should focus initially on meaningful disaggregation of the NAEP data in order to uncover troubling trends such as this one, then to address the cause and remediation of this particular gender-based discrepancy. This finding is probably not news to many teachers who see a more molecular version of this discrepancy play out in the classroom every day and must focus a disproportionate amount of their energy on motivating underachieving boys. We address the extremely important link between motivation and reading in Chapter 7.

NAAL

NAEP provides a good data base for evaluating the U.S. school-age population. But how much do we know about reading skills of the adult population? There is a database available to help answer this question. Sponsored by the

National Center for Educational Statistics, NAAL provides a periodic and comprehensive assessment of adult literacy (http://nces.ed.gov/naal/). It was administered in 2003 to a representative sample of more than 19,000 adults (16 years of age and older). Participants came from all fifty states and the District of Columbia, and even included approximately 1,200 inmates of federal and state prisons. Not only does NAAL provide a snapshot of English literacy among American adults, it also provides an indicator of progress because current results can be compared to previous assessments. There are considerable data available showing progress from the 1992 assessment to one conducted in 2003 in the three literacy areas:

- **Functional literacy** or **prose literacy**—the ability to search, comprehend, and use continuous text sources such as newspapers, brochures, and instructional materials
- **Document literacy**—the ability to search, comprehend, and use noncontinuous text sources such as job applications, payroll forms, maps, tables, and labels
- **Quantitative literacy**—the ability to identify and perform computations required to balance a checkbook, calculate tips, and to use numbers embedded in printed orders

It is possible to compare average scores from 1992 and 2003 to obtain trends. Scores exist on a scale of 0 to 500. Importantly, there were no statistically significant changes in scores in prose and document literacy between 1992 and 2003, but the differential increase in quantitative literacy was significant—from 275 to 283. Adults in 2003 showed better skills in this area than those assessed in 1992, a promising finding. In addition, there were fewer adults in the lowest level (of four) of English language literacy (i.e., below Basic Level) in 2003 in both document and quantitative literacy, 14 percent versus 12 percent and 26 percent versus 22 percent, respectively. Conversely, slightly more adults were found in one or more of the three higher levels in the 2003 sample for the two prose areas: Basic, Intermediate, and Proficient. In 2003, thirty million adults (14 percent) performed at the lowest Below Basic level (they answered either none or only the most simple and concrete items), sixty-three million (29 percent) were able to answer simple and everyday literacy-based questions, ninety-five million (44 percent) were able to participate in moderately challenging literacy activities, and twenty-eight million (13 percent) could perform complex and challenging literacy activities. Data from NAAL show how average NAAL scores and prose reading levels are related to education. The relationship is obvious: those with less than or some high school produced an average score of 207; those with a high school education produced an average score of 262; and, those who graduated from college produced an average score of 314.

Because the NAAL database is large, other comparisons are possible. For example, eleven million adults in 2003 were considered nonliterate in English. Seven million could not answer the simple test questions because of cognitive or academic limitations, and four million adults could not take the test because of language barriers. Important changes occurred within certain racial or ethnic groups from 1992 to 2003. For example, White adults increased by an average of nine points in quantitative literacy, Black adults increased on average six points in prose, eight points in document, and sixteen points in quantitative. Asian/Pacific Islander adults increased sixteen points in prose; on the other hand, Hispanic adults decreased eighteen points in prose and fourteen points in document, perhaps related to the more rapid influx of non- or limited English-speaking Hispanics into the United States. Literacy increased among age cohorts 25–39, 50–64, and 65+ from 1992 to 2003, and the trend was strongest within the oldest two cohorts.

Data from NAAL, just as those from NAEP, can be disaggregated and used to inform educators regarding trends and trouble spots. In this case, the decision makers who use the NAAL data are educators and administrators of adult education programs; these educators have the responsibility of devising instructional programs and practices that will benefit adults with low levels of literacy. Research-based support for interventions for adults are described in the adult literacy literature (Kruidenier 2002), and an assessment tool recently has been developed and standardized to assess the extent to which teachers of adults know this literature, the Assessment of Reading Instructional Knowledge-Adult form (ARIK-A; Zeigler, Bell, McCallum, in press). The instrument, developed under the auspices of the National Institute for Literacy, is designed to be used as a professional development tool to assess knowledge of teaching adult reading in the areas of phonemic awareness/phonics, fluency, vocabulary, comprehension, and reading assessment. Based on the results of the ARIK-A, teachers may determine that they should spend time improving their knowledge base in one or more of areas of reading instruction in order to provide the most effective instruction.

HOW DO GROUP NORM-REFERENCED MEASURES ASSESS READING?

In this section, we continue to explore strategies to apply data from norm-referenced group tests. We address in particular the ability of some of these measures to assess the areas of reading described by the National Reading Panel (NRP, National Institute for Child Health and Human Development [NICHD] 2000) as well as automatic word recognition. We describe how reading is measured by group-standardized assessments, which are typically administered by classroom teachers. Group achievement tests come in many shapes and sizes. Some, such as the TOSWRF and TOSCRF described earlier, have only one level; these tests are designed to be appropriate for a group of students across a wide age and grade span. Others, such as the Gates-MacGinitie and the TABE, provide various levels—depending on the age, grade, and/or estimated skill level of the students who will be taking the test. This is also the case with most group tests used for accountability purposes, such as the Iowa Test of Basic Skills (ITBS) (kindergarten through grade 8), the related Iowa Test of Educational Development (ITED) (grades 9–12), and the Stanford Achievement Test (Harcourt 2002). Table 6.4 presents a scope and sequence chart for the ITBS and ITED in the area of reading. You will note that vocabulary is measured at all levels, word analyses at lower levels only, and reading (comprehension) at first-grade and up. Teachers and administrators should be aware of what is being measured in the tests they use; the scope and sequence chart provides a concise visual summary.

TABLE 6.4 Scope and Sequence Chart

Skills Tested	ITBS										ITED		
Level	5	6	7	8	9	10	11	12	13	14	15	16	17/18
Grade	K–1	K–1	1–2	2–3	3	4	5	6	7	8	9	10	11/12
Vocabulary													
General vocabulary	■	■	■	■	■	■	■	■	■	■	■	■	■
Word analysis													
Printed letters	■	■	■										
Letter-sound correspondences	■	■	■										
Rhyming sounds	■	■	■	■									
Initial sounds	■	■	■	■	■								
Letter substitutions		■	■	■	■								
Word building		■	■	■	■								
Vowel sounds		■	■	■	■								
Silent letters			■	■	■								
Affixes			■	■	■								
Reading													
Cues for word recognition	■	■											
Cues for word identification	■	■	■	■									
Construct factual meaning	■	■	■	■	■	■	■	■	■	■	■	■	■
Construct inferential meaning	■	■	■	■	■	■	■	■	■	■	■	■	■
Construct evaluative meaning	■	■	■	■	■	■	■	■	■	■	■	■	■
Interpret nonliteral language				■	■	■	■	■	■	■	■	■	■

Content

The Reading tests measure how well students construct meaning from reading passages of varying lengths, difficulties, and genres. The content measured is a developmentally appropriate continuum of reading skills designed to reflect students' learning processes from Kindergarten through high school. An overview of the tests included in the battery is provided in the Scope and Sequence chart above.

In addition to having various levels, many group tests provide alternate or parallel forms to allow for flexibility of use. For example, tests may be used in a pretest/posttest manner (e.g., to assess the effectiveness of a new reading intervention); in this case, use of alternate forms reduces the likelihood of **practice effect,** an improvement in scores caused by familiarity with specific test content. Also, alternate forms are sometimes used to help maintain test security and to decrease the temptation to teach to the test as we discuss earlier in this chapter. Finally, in some cases, alternate forms can be used to help monitor progress, assuming they contain enough content to be sensitive to relatively small changes in student achievement. For progress monitoring and when tests are given relatively close in time, it is especially important to guard against practice effects.

In the following sections, we provide examples from some commonly used tests to measure various areas of reading. As we noted in Chapter 5, different subdomains of reading are measured in different ways by different tests. We point out a few examples in the following sections, but administrators and teachers will want to carefully peruse information provided by test publishers and authors when selecting tests. Further, such an awareness is necessary for knowledgeable interpretation and appropriate use of results. If the tests are to be useful, consumers need to know what they measure and how. Note that the descriptions are not intended as comprehensive views of the tests cited. The examples are intended merely as that—examples—to help you think about how different tests actually measure aspects of reading.

Measures of Phonemic Awareness, Phonics, and Automatic Word Recognition/Orthography

Word skills (phonemic awareness, phonics, and automatic word recognition/orthography) are more likely to be lumped together on group tests than on individual tests, particularly those designed to span a wide age range. One reason is that group testing requires primarily written responses; students typically cannot respond orally. However, phonemic awareness increasingly is represented in group achievement tests for the early grades. For example, the Basic Early Assessment of Reading (BEAR, Riverside 2002) designed for individuals, groups, or classrooms and, according to its authors, yields criterion-referenced information about student performance in phonemic awareness and phonics as well as other areas of reading identified by the National Reading Panel for students in kindergarten through grade 3. The tenth edition of the Stanford Achievement Test, a popular norm-referenced achievement test, includes a Sounds and Letters subtest. According to information from the publisher, the content reflects heavier emphasis (than in previous editions) on phonemic awareness and phonics, in accordance with research supporting their importance (Harcourt 2002). And the ITBS, also norm- referenced, has a Word Analysis subtest for students in kindergarten through grade 3; the Word Analysis subtest taps phonemic awareness (including rhyming), phonics (including letter-sound correspondence) and word analysis skills (including affixes). Figure 6.5 depicts a sample from the Word Analysis subtest from the ITBS.

The TABE, like many other group norm-referenced tests, provides several levels of tests depending on the estimated literacy level of the adult

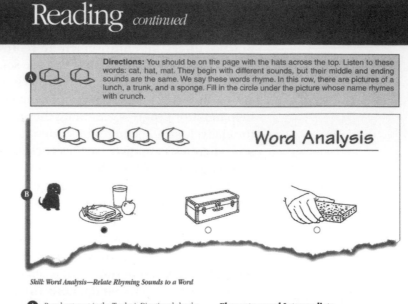

FIGURE 6.5 Sample from the *Iowa Tests of Basic Skills* (Riverside, 2003). Word Analysis Subtest

Excerpt from the Word Analysis Practice subtest from the *Iowa Tests of Basic Skills®* *(ITBS®)* reproduced with permission of The Riverside Publishing Company.

students being assessed. The lowest level (L for Literacy) provides measures of prereading skills for adults with low literacy skills via the following subtests: Matching Letters, Recognizing Letters, Ending Sounds, and Middle Sounds; these tests have time limits ranging from two to four minutes. At the lowest level, the TABE provides a measure of word recognition, Recognition of Signs, a five-minute test.

Measures of Fluency

Several tests measure reading fluency, though group administration requires that students read silently. However, the BEAR includes an oral reading fluency measure, which unlike the rest of the test, must be administered individually so the teacher/examiner can hear the child read. Fluency assessments, particularly group-administered silent ones, tend to measure speed and, in some cases, accuracy, but not prosody or inflection, which are also important aspects of fluency. The TOSWRF and TOSCRF, both of which are described earlier in this chapter, rely on the word-chaining technique (in which students make a mark to separate strings of letters into words). In the TOSWRF, words are unrelated while the TOSCRF uses words in context. Authors report relatively high correlation coefficients (for example, .80s) between the two but note that they appear to measure slightly different skills. Reportedly, the TOSCRF is more highly correlated with reading comprehension because of the contextual nature of the presentation of the words. Refer back to Figure 6.4 to see an excerpt from the TOSWRF.

Another group test that yields a measure of reading rate is the Nelson-Denny. On this test, the reading rate assessment is embedded in the comprehension assessment. Students are instructed to begin reading and put a mark at their place at the end of one minute. Numbers are provided to the right of the passage; the student's reading rate is determined by the number of words in the passage up to the sentence he or she stops reading. Figure 6.6 shows the directions for the reading rate and comprehension portion of the Nelson-Denny.

Measures of Vocabulary

Most group achievement tests have measures of vocabulary, but considerable variability exists in how vocabulary is assessed. Recall the distinction between oral vocabulary and reading vocabulary? *Oral* vocabulary refers to the vocabulary students understand when listening and talking. *Reading* vocabulary refers to the vocabulary students can read independently and understand. Some tests provide measures of both. Young children or older students with low literacy levels will have a limited or nonexistent reading vocabulary, but may have relatively well-developed oral vocabulary. The ITBS provides measures of both oral and reading vocabulary but in different ways at different levels of the test. For example, measures of listening vocabulary for students in kindergarten and grade 1 require no reading. For older students, reading vocabulary is assessed in two ways: (1) students "select one of four words that best describes an accompanying picture" and (2) students "choose one of four words to complete a sentence" (Riverside 2003, 25). On the other hand, the Gates-MacGinitie, for grades 3 through 8, presents a definition and a set of five words; the student is to choose the word that best matches the definition. Figure 6.7 presents an excerpt from the Gates-MacGinitie Vocabulary subtest.

The TABE uses yet a different approach; it provides measures of vocabulary in its lowest level via subtests called Context Meaning and Phrase and Sentence Meaning. For the higher levels, assessment of vocabulary is subsumed in one test called Reading. In both cases, examinees are presented with words in the context of a sentence and choose the correct meaning from a set of multiple-choice options. As you can see, vocabulary can be measured in a variety of ways. In addition to measures in reading tests, numerous language and cognitive tests contain measures of vocabulary, which attest to

PART II.   COMPREHENSION TEST

DIRECTIONS

A. Please do not turn this page of the test booklet until directed to do so.

B. There are seven reading passages in the Comprehension Test. Read completely through a passage; then answer the questions following that passage. For Passage One only, you must hold the book open to read the passage and the items. For all the following passages, you may fold the book over. You may look back at the material you have read, but do not puzzle too long over any one question. When you have completed the questions for one passage, go immediately to the next one. Continue working until you have answered all of the questions or until you are told to stop. Your score is based on the number of *correct* responses. Since there is no penalty for incorrect answers, it is to your advantage to mark every question you read.

C. The first minute of the time you spend on this part of the test will be used to determine your Reading Rate. The examiner will call "Mark" when one minute has elapsed. At that time you are to record on your answer sheet the number printed to the right of the line you are reading. If, as in the example below, you were reading the line with the number 076 printed next to it, you would record that number in the appropriate place on your answer sheet.

Sample Reading Selection

One of the most important jobs of the priests in Babylonia and in Egypt   008
was watching the sun and the moon. These ancient astronomers   021
regularly observed the visible heavenly bodies in their daily movements   029
across the sky. Both of these groups had written languages by 3500 B.C.,   041
and they very carefully recorded the actions of these "gods." They were   053
especially interested in eclipses, which they interpreted as one god   064
devouring the other. We owe much to these scientists of the past for their   076 ←
careful observations and accurate record keeping.   088

D. Wait for the signal to turn this page.

E. Now listen carefully to the examiner for further instructions.

MAKE NO MARKS ON THIS TEST BOOKLET

Page 7

FIGURE 6.6 Directions from the *Nelson-Denny Reading Test, Part II Comprehension, Form G.* (1993)

Nelson-Denny Reading Test, Part II Comprehension, Form G. (1993). Itasca, IL: Riverside Publishing Company. Reproduced with permission

the importance vocabulary plays in literacy development and academic achievement in general.

Measures of Comprehension
Reading comprehension is a complex and multifaceted skill that develops across the life span. All the elements in the Inclusive Model in Appendix B contribute to comprehension. You may recall from Chapter 1 that Calkins characterizes reading as "thinking guided by print" (2001, 359). Not surpris-

Vocabulary

V-1. a big garage

- Ⓚ place for cars
- Ⓛ machine
- Ⓜ sidewalk
- Ⓝ covered porch
- Ⓞ cloth sack

V-2. They will close it.

- Ⓟ stay near
- Ⓠ begin
- Ⓡ make
- Ⓢ shut
- Ⓣ go past

STOP

FIGURE 6.7 Excerpt from Reading Vocabulary Subtest from the Gates-MacGinitie *Reading Tests,* *4th* **edition**

MacGinitie, MacGinitie, Maria, & Dreyer (2000). *Reading Tests, 4th edition.* Itasca, IL: Riverside Publishing Company. Reproduced with permission.

ingly, then, reading comprehension can be measured in a variety of ways. You may recall from the discussion of the Qualitative Reading Inventory (Leslie and Caldwell 2006) in Chapter 3 the importance of presenting students with both expository and narrative text and with assessing both factual and inferential understanding. Most test developers agree on the importance of tapping comprehension along a continuum of cognitive complexity. That is, some test items assess only factual knowledge, while others require the examinee to analyze or evaluate the content. For example, developers of the ITBS (2003) describe a continuum with critical thinking on one end and factual recall on the other. They note that the ITBS include a variety of item types to balance assessment between items requiring higher-order and lower-order thinking skills. The Gates-MacGinitie provides a measure of reading comprehension across its various levels; fiction and nonfiction selections from published works are used as the stimulus passages. Test developers indicate that items are designed to tap *explicit* content and *inferred* content. Students read passages and answer questions presented in a multiple-choice format. Younger students write directly in test booklets, while older students respond on scan forms. Figure 6.8 depicts a sample comprehension question from the Gates-MacGinitie Reading Comprehension subtest.

The TABE provides a measure of reading comprehension in its lowest-level test called Passage Meaning. For the higher levels, reading is assessed via one fifty-minute subtest called Reading. Examinees must read passages and answer factual and inferential questions presented in a multiple-choice format. Similarly, the Nelson-Denny provides a twenty-minute measure of

FIGURE 6.8 Excerpt from the Reading Comprehension Subtest from the Gates-MacGinitie *Reading Tests, 4th edition*

MacGinitie, MacGinitie, Maria, & Dreyer (2000). *Reading Tests, 4th edition.* Itasca, IL: Riverside Publishing Company. Reproduced with permission.

Comprehension

Sometimes—not very often—we get two full moons in one month. That second full moon is called a "blue moon." <u>No one knows</u> why. Now we say "once in a blue moon" to mean "once in a long time."

C-1. To be a "blue moon," the moon must be

Ⓘ dark.

Ⓙ long.

Ⓚ blue.

Ⓛ full.

C-2. What is it that <u>no one knows</u>?

Ⓜ What the name is.

Ⓝ Who uses the name.

Ⓞ Where the name came from.

Ⓟ What the name means.

🛑 STOP

reading comprehension; students read passages of expository material and answer questions in a multiple-choice format on a scan form. The questions can be classified as interpretive or literal.

SPECIAL CONSIDERATIONS FOR ADULT AND ELL LEARNERS

We conclude the discussion of formal group assessment of reading with particular suggestions for adult learners and for ELL students. These are presented in Boxes 6.1 and 6.2 respectively.

BOX 6.1 Formal Group Assessment Tips for Adults

1. Assess adult learners' educational histories, background experiences, and interests as well as specific reading skills.

2. Provide further skill assessment for those adults who score below an eighth-grade level on the Test of Adult Basic Education (TABE).

3. Use numerous measures to gain a complete assessment of adult learners' strengths and weaknesses.

4. Ensure that tests used for adults are normed for adults.

5. Because adult learners may feel particularly conscious of their performance in a group testing situation, take special care to put them at ease and ensure confidentiality of scores.

6. Refer to the Adult Reading Components Web site to plug in scores and get educational recommendations for adult learners: www.nifl.gov/readingprofiles/

BOX 6.2 Group Formal Assessment Tips for ELL Learners

1. Because NCLB requires that ELL students participate in group achievement testing for accountability purposes, be familiar with the accommodations allowed in your state and school district. For example, some states allow directions to be read in the students' native language, some allow for flexible grouping, and the like.

2. Prepare ELL students for group assessment by providing practice sessions. Address their questions or concerns to relieve anxiety. (We like what one of our children's teachers told her class—"This test is to show if I did a good job this year as

   your teacher. Just do your best and don't worry about it.")

3. Work with bilingual and English as second language instructors to inform parents about the purposes of group achievement testing, to relieve anxiety, and to ensure parental support.

4. Be aware of the limitations of testing students in a second language when interpreting assessment results.

5. Also refer to Text Box 5.2. Many of the issues related to test bias and other suggestions there are relevant for formal group assessment as well.

Summary

When selecting formal, group assessments of reading, educators should be aware of what they measure, the specific manner in which these skills are measured, and the adequacy of the instrument to measure these skills consistently and accurately. In some cases, educators will have a choice in the assessments being used, particularly those for instructional or progress monitoring. They typically have little or no choice about state-mandated accountability tests. Nonetheless, knowledge of the types of testing tasks, the ways in which skills are assessed, and the types of scores and other information provided can empower teachers and reduce the intimidation they may feel from high-stakes testing. Tables 6.5 and 6.6 present critical information about some of the most commonly used and recently normed formal group assessments of reading. Table 6.5 provides basic information including test name, publisher, publication date, administration time and whether there are aspects that can be administered individually (also identifies the areas of reading assessed). Table 6.6 provides information about the psychometric characteristics of the measures, including reliability and validity, and types of scores available.

Now that you have an understanding of reading assessment, you should have an appreciation of the progression of assessment—from simple classroom worksheets to formal, state-mandated tests—and hopefully, a better understanding of their relative strengths and weaknesses and what they can and cannot do. Think again about the Literacy Instruction Pie in Appendix C. With the information in Chapters 3–6, you should be able to identify various types of assessments for each area of the Pie. In Chapter 7, we address how to pull together the various types of assessment information to make informed decisions about how much emphasis each piece of the Pie warrants for a class or given student.

(mylabschool™
Where the classroom comes to life!

MyLabSchool is a collection of online tools for your success in this course, your licensure exams, and your teaching career. Visit www.mylabschool.com to access the following:
- *Online Study Guide*
- *Video cases from real classrooms*
- *Help with your research papers using Research Navigator*
- *Career Center with resources for:*
    Praxis exams and licensure preparation
    Professional portfolio development
    Job search and interview techniques
    Lesson planning

TABLE 6.5 Characteristics of Formal, Group, and Norm-Referenced Assessment of Reading

Test Name	Publisher/ Source/Date	Grades/ Ages	Purpose	Administration Time	Administration Format	Word Recognition	Phonics/P.A.	Fluency	Vocabulary	Comprehension
						Basic Reading Skills			Reading Comp.	
Adult Basic Learning Examination	The Psychological Corporation, 1986–1987	Adults with less than 12 years of formal schooling; LE-3	To measure the educational achievement of adults who may or may not have completed twelve years of schooling . . . also useful in evaluating efforts to raise the educational level of these adults	SelectABLE–15 minutes Level 1 130–155 minutes Level 2 and 3 175–215 minutes	Group				X	X
Basic Early Reading Assessment (BEAR)	Riverside, 2002	Grades K–3	To assess reading and language arts skills at the beginning of the year, evaluating strengths and weaknesses, assessing progress, and monitoring oral reading fluency development	30–40 minutes per subtest 90 minutes for screener	Group or Individual Oral Reading Fluency must be individual	X	X	X		
California Achievement Test (CAT) (5th ed.)	Macmillan-McGraw-Hill, 1957–1993	Grades K–12.9	To measure achievement in basic skills taught in schools throughout the nation	87–330 minutes	Group				X	X
Comprehensive Testing Program III	Educational Testing Service Pub., 1974–1996	Grades 1–12	To measure attainment of major educational objectives regardless of particular curriculum programs and methods	155–330 min per level	Group				X	X
Comprehensive Test of Basic Skills	CTB-McGraw-Hill, 1996	Grades K–12	To measure achievement in reading, language, spelling, mathematics, study skills, science, and social studies	4 hours–5 hours 20 minutes (depending upon grade level)	Group	X	X		X	X

(Continued)

TABLE 6.5 (Continued)

Test Name	Publisher/Source/Date	Grades/Ages	Purpose	Administration Time	Administration Format	Basic Reading Skills			Reading Comp.	
						Word Recognition	Phonics/P.A.	Fluency	Vocabulary	Comprehension
Gates-MacGinitie Reading Tests (GMRT) (4th ed.)	Riverside, 2000	K–12; adults	To assess student achievement in reading	55–100 minutes	Group	X	X		X	X
Gray Silent Reading Tests (GSRT)	PRO-ED, 2000	Ages 7–25	To assess silent reading comprehension	15–30 minutes	Group or Individual					X
Iowa Tests of Basic Skills (ITBS)	Riverside, 2001, 2003	Grades K–8	To provide a comprehensive assessment of student progress in major content areas	30 minutes	Group	X			X	X
Multilevel Academic Survey	The Psychological Corporation, 1985	K–12 with reading or math deficits	To make decisions about student performance in reading and mathematics	10–35 minutes for grade level tests; 1–5 minutes per curriculum level test	Group					X
National Achievement Test (2nd ed.)	American Tetronics, 1980–1990	Grades K–12; LE–12: A–L	To measure student achievement in the skill areas commonly found in school curricula	134–351 minutes; varies by level	Group	X	X		X	
Nelson-Denny Reading Test	Riverside, 1993	Ages 9–16, Adult	To assess student achievement and progress in vocabulary, comprehension, and reading rate	35 minutes for standard administration; 56 minutes for extended-time administration	Group			X	X	X
Predictive Reading Profile (PRP)	Lingui Systems, 2001	Grades K–1	To identify children at risk for reading failure and to identify instructional needs	2–2.5 hours	Group or Individual	X	X		X	

Test Name	Publisher/ Source/Date	Grades/ Ages	Purpose	Administration Time	Administration Format	Basic Reading Skills - Word Recognition	Basic Reading Skills - Phonics/P.A.	Basic Reading Skills - Fluency	Reading Comp. - Vocabulary	Reading Comp. - Comprehension
Richmond Test of Basic Skills Edition #2	NFER-Nelson Pub., 1975–1988	Ages 8–0 to 13–11	To provide comprehensive continuous measurement of growth of an individual child in the fundamental skill	60 minutes per test	Group				X	X
SRA Achievement Series Forms 1, 2, and Survey of Basic Skills Forms P & Q	Macmillan-McGraw Hill, 1978–1987	K.5–12.9	To assess broad areas of knowledge, general skills and their application	135–278 minutes	Group	X	X		X	X
Stanford Achievement Test-Abbreviated (8th ed.)	The Psychological Corporation, 1989–1992	Grades 1.5–12	To measures student achievement in reading, mathematics, language, spelling, study skills, science, social science, and listening	95–160 minutes partial battery; 119–180 minutes basic battery; 155–233 minutes complete battery	Group	X			X	X
Stanford Early School Achievement Test (3rd ed.)	The Psychological Corporation, 1969–1989	Grades K.0–1.5	To measure school achievement	Level 1: 90 minutes over 9 sessions; Level 2: 225 minutes over 9 sessions	Group	X	X			
Test of Academic Performance	The Psychological Corporation, 1989	Grades K–12	To assess the achievement in four curriculum areas: Mathematics, Spelling, Reading, and Writing	Varies according to test	Individual and Group	X				X

(Continued)

TABLE 6.5 (Continued)

Test Name	Publisher/Source/Date	Grades/Ages	Purpose	Administration Time	Administration Format	Word Recognition	Phonics/P.A.	Fluency	Vocabulary	Comprehension
						Basic Reading Skills			Reading Comp.	
Test of Achievement & Proficiency Forms K, L, & M	Riverside Publishing, 1978–1996	Grades 9–12	To provide a comprehensive and objective measure of student's progress in high school curriculum	90–275 minutes	Group				X	X
Test of Adult Basic Education (TABE)	CTB/McGraw-Hill, 1994	Adults	To assess basic educational skills in an adult population	2 hours–3.5 hours	Group	X	X		X	X
Test of Reading Comprehension (3rd ed.) (TORC-3)	PRO-ED, 1995	Ages 7–0 through 7–11	To assess a student's general silent reading comprehension	30 minutes per subtest; 120 minutes total	Group or Individual				X	X
Test of Silent Contextual Reading Fluency (TOSCRF)	PRO-ED, 2006		To measure a student's ability to recognize printed words in context accurately and efficiently	3–10 minutes	Group or Individual	X		X		
Test of Silent Word Reading Fluency (TOSWRF)	PRO-ED, 2004	Ages 6–6 through 7–11	To measure a student's ability to recognize printed words accurately and efficiently	3–10 minutes	Group or Individual	X		X		

Note: Information is based on a combination of published and online materials (including independent test reviews, content from tests and test manuals, and publisher/author promotional materials). Strenuous efforts were made by authors to ensure accuracy but information may contain errors and omissions due to updates in the tests reviewed, errors in published materials, and conflicts in reported information. Lists are not exhaustive.

TABLE 6.6 Psychometric Properties of Formal, Group, Norm-Referenced Assessment of Reading

Test Name	Reliability Reported			Validity Reported			Types of Scores
	IC	TT	AF	IR	CON	PRE	CNC	
Adult Basic Learning Examination	X							Percentile ranks, stanines, normal curve, grade equivalent, and scale scores
Basic Early Reading Assessment (BEAR)		X						
California Achievement Test (CAT) (5th ed.)	X				X			"Pattern scoring" contrasted with number correct and raw score
Comprehensive Testing Program III	X				X			Full-scale norms for Fall and Spring, percentile rank, stanines, and normed scores
Comprehensive Test of Basic Skills	X							Normal curve equivalents, percentiles, grade equivalents, stanine, grade mean equivalent for class, and scale scores
Gates-MacGinitie Reading Tests (GMRT) (4th ed.)	X	X	X		X			Lexiles: normal curve equivalents, national and local percentiles and stanines, grade equivalents
Gray Silent Reading Tests (GSRT)	X	X	X	X	?	X		Standard scores, age equivalents, grade equivalents, and percentiles
Iowa Tests of Basic Skills	X				X			Percentile ranks; performance across grades
Multilevel Academic Survey	X	X						Placement scores
National Achievement Test (2nd ed.)								Scale scores, percentile, and stanines; normal curve equivalent
Nelson-Denny Reading Test	X		X			X		Percentile ranks, grade equivalents, standard scores, and stanines
Predictive Reading Profile (PRP)						X		Raw scores, cluster scores, percentiles, stanines, descriptive classifications
Richmond Test of Basic Skills Edition #2		X				X		

(Continued)

TABLE 6.6   (Continued)

Test Name	Reliability Reported				Validity Reported			Types of Scores
	IC	TT	AF	IR	CON	PRE	CNC	
SRA Achievement Series Forms 1, 2, and Survey of Basic Skills Forms P & Q			X					
Stanford Achievement Test-Abbreviated (8th Edition)								Stanines, grade equivalents, and normal cuvre equivalents; raw scores, percentile rank, scaled scores
Stanford Early School Achievement Test-3rd								
Test of Academic Performance		X						Grade equivalents
Test of Achievement and Proficiency Forms K, L, & M								
Test of Adult Basic Education (TABE)	X	X	X		X	X	X	Locator score, grade equivalents
Test of Reading Comprehension (TORC-3)								Standard scores, percentiles, composite reading comprehension quotient
Test of Silent Contextual Reading Fluency (TOSCRF)		X	X	X	X		X	Raw scores, standard scores, percentiles, and age and grade equivalents
Test of Silent Word Reading Fluency (TOSWRF)		X	X	X	X		X	Raw scores, standard scores, percentiles, and age and grade equivalents

Note: IC = Internal consistency, TT = Test/retest, AF = Alternate forms, IR = Inter-rater, CON = Content, PRE = Predictive, CNC = Concurrent

Information is based on a combination of published and online materials (including independent test reviews, content from tests and test manuals, and publisher/author promotional materials). Strenuous efforts were made by authors to ensure accuracy but information may contain errors and omissions due to updates in the tests reviewed, errors in published materials, and conflicts in reported information. Lists are not exhaustive.

Using Informal and Formal Assessment to Inform Teaching

Information in Chapter 7 will help readers of this handbook "pull it together," a phrase sometimes used to characterize problem-solving based on the ability to consider a wealth of information, to bring together what appear to be disparate bits of information, and to focus this information on creating a solution for a particular problem. In this case, the "problem" to be resolved can be summarized in this question, "How can I, as an educator, ensure the best possible reading instruction?" This question may be applied to a single student or to an entire class, and because good instruction depends upon good assessment, we provide a set of criteria for use when selecting and evaluating assessment instruments. Next, we discuss assessment of writing, an

important aspect of both the Inclusive Model of Reading and the Literacy Instruction Pie. We follow with a description of some within-the-student variables that interact with teacher and classroom influences either to promote or discourage reading success, namely reading-related attitudes, motivation, interests of students, and cognitive correlates of reading. Next, we discuss how teachers can use the Instruction Pie introduced in Chapter 2 to organize their assessment data, problem solve, plan instruction, and help evaluate their own effectiveness. In the final sections of the chapter, we describe how educators can integrate assessment and instruction and we present several case studies illustrating the assessment-instruction link and the Individual Education Program (IEP) used for special education students. Finally, we close with a worksheet that allows teachers to summarize assessment data, strategies, and resources.

In this final chapter, you will be cued to reflect on content in the previous chapters. By doing so, you will realize how much you now know about reading and assessment of reading. You know about critical areas of reading as identified by the National Reading Panel (NRP, National Institute for Child Health and Human Development [NICHD] 2000) and others. You know about several models of reading. Although the specifics of the models differ, they all address how a combination of cognitive and academic skills such as phonology, orthography, semantics, and vocabulary culminate in reading with comprehension. Also, you have become familiar with several of the most commonly used formal and informal tests—those appropriate for group *and* individual administration.

In summary, you know that pulling it all together requires that you think about assessment purposes and activities in a broad context. One of the most important contextual variables is teacher knowledge, knowledge *about* selecting and administering tests, related academic and nonacademic variables that have an impact on reading, assessment challenges posed by special populations, and so on. Related to teacher success is awareness of *how* to implement this knowledge, including administration and interpretation of tests and application of resulting information to instruction. This chapter helps build these two knowledge bases—declarative and procedural knowledge, respectively—needed to use assessment data to effectively teach reading. We begin by providing guidelines to help you think about selecting the most effective tests, followed by a discussion of the crucial relationship between reading and writing instruction and assessment.

■ SELECTING AND EVALUATING ASSESSMENTS

Although you have internalized a significant body of reading assessment knowledge, you may be uncertain about the specific criteria required to guide selection of particular reading assessment instruments and techniques. Specifically, if you are asked to help select a reading test for a student, class, school, or district, how will you decide? Because the field of reading continues to be plagued by controversy, it is important that educators have the wisdom and expertise to make informed decisions, to be able to assess critically for themselves the conflicting information available from experts in the field. For example, educators should not rely solely on claims of publishers and their representatives to guide informed decision making about selection of assessment instruments.

To begin the test evaluation and selection process, each user should ask a series of questions:

- Will the assessment results be used to help teachers plan instruction?
- Will the results be used to monitor progress?
- Will they be used to determine eligibility for special educational services?
- Or will they be used for accountability?

Of course, you now know that some tests can serve more than one purpose, and, hopefully, they all yield at least a little information useful for instructional planning. Unfortunately, tests too often are used for purposes other than the ones for which they were designed. For example, a single measure, particularly a brief screener, should not be used to determine whether a student is eligible for special education.

Knowing the purpose of assessment will help you decide the type of test you need. For example, if you are a classroom teacher who wants to know more about the general level of reading comprehension of your entire class, you will probably select a group-administered measure of reading comprehension such as the Gates-MacGinitie or the Gray Silent Reading Tests described in Chapter 6. If you are a reading specialist working with individual students who struggle in reading or who are new to your school, you may want to administer a comprehensive individualized assessment such as the Qualitative Reading Inventory described in Chapter 3. If you are a primary teacher or a special education teacher in a school that is using a response-to-intervention model (RTI), you will probably be expected to measure oral reading fluency. In that case, you may be asked to use an individually administered oral fluency measure, perhaps using a curriculum-based measurement (CBM) format or one of the progress monitoring measures described in Chapter 4. If you are an educator of adults, you will likely use the Test of Adult Basic Education (TABE) or a similar measure; but because the TABE provides only a measure of silent reading comprehension, you will want to supplement with other tests normed on adults if your student performs poorly on it. If you are an administrator with the responsibility of selecting or giving input into the selection of accountability measures, you will need to select a group-standardized test with strong reliability and validity and with a good match to your district's reading curriculum and standards. The Iowa and the Stanford tests, discussed in Chapter 6, are examples of assessment instruments used to establish accountability.

Once you know the purpose for assessment, you need to determine what area or areas of reading you want to assess. Some measures are unidimensional, such as the Test of Silent Word Reading Fluency (assesses only silent reading fluency) and the Gray Silent Reading Test (measures only comprehension); both are described in Chapter 6. If you want to obtain measures of several areas of reading, you may have to administer more than one instrument or a comprehensive battery such as the Qualitative Reading Inventory (described in Chapter 3) or the Woodcock Reading Mastery Test and Woodcock-Johnson III Diagnostic Reading Battery (both described in Chapter 5). The tables in Chapter 3–6 provide specific information about a variety of tests, their psychometric properties, and the areas of reading assessed by each. But keep in mind that these lists are not exhaustive. Not all good tests are included, and some of the tests included are not accepted universally by reading experts. Rather, the tests listed represent the most commonly used and most recently developed assessments.

To aid you in making informed test selections or in evaluating test quality, we present a Test Review Criteria form (Figure 7.1) that provides helpful criteria for reviewing and judging test quality. These criteria focus on psychometric characteristics and administration and scoring features. Because there are hundreds of tests that measure reading and reading-related skills, and because tests are continually being revised, it is not possible to provide an exhaustive, comprehensive, and current list of tests and test properties here; consequently, we encourage you to use this form when selecting or evaluating any test. As you consider the questions in the Test Review Criteria form, remember that many of the answers can be found in the test manuals of the test under consideration. Additional sources for answering the Test Review Criteria questions can be found by reading test reviews. Reviews can be found in the Buros Mental Measurements Yearbook, available online via most university libraries. In some cases, measurement-related journals contain reviews, including the *Journal of Psychoeducational Assessment,* published by Sage Journals Online (http://online.sagepub.com/). Reviews from the Buros and Sage sources are particularly helpful because they are independent, which is to say, they are not written by the test authors or publishers. Therefore, these and other independent reviews are considered more objective than test manuals or other materials promulgated by test publishers. In addition, some texts provide reviews of tests and are considered good sources because of their independence (see Salvia and Ysseldyke 1998; Sattler 2002; Rathvon 2004; Flanagan, Ortiz, Alfonso, and Mascolo 2006; Overton 2006).

As you have gathered by now, this text provides information about quite a number of reading and reading-related tests. Using various sources of data, you can answer questions on the Test Review Criteria form, which will lead you either to selection or rejection of particular tests. In previous chapters, we provided specific guidelines for making judgments about test quality, including minimally acceptable statistical values associated with reliability and validity back in Chapter 4. Other sources that provide even more detailed guidelines for determining quality include perhaps the best single source—a publication authored in 1999 by a joint commission of assessment experts representing the American Psychological Association (APA), American Educational Research Association (AERA), and the National Council on Measurement in Education (NCME) called *Standards for Educational and Psychological Testing* (AERA 1999). This document provides extensive descriptions of test characteristics, and the most discriminating test users will become familiar with this information before making decisions about test quality.

■ ASSESSMENT OF WRITING: A RELATED SKILL

Why is it important to consider students' writing proficiency in a reading assessment text? Perhaps the most practical reason is that when students write, they apply skills they learn in reading. Consequently, good writing instruction improves reading and vice versa. We know that when students

FIGURE 7.1 Test Review Criteria

Background Information and Psychometrics

Full Name of Test: _____

Cost: _____   Date of Publication: _____

Publisher's address: _____

_____

What is (are) the purpose(s) of the test according to the authors?

_____

_____

For whom is the test appropriate (what population of learners)?

Ages: _____   Gender: _____

Race: _____   Ethnicities: _____

Is the standardization sample representative of the intended populations?

Yes _____ No _____

(Check the manual to find the match of the standardization data to U.S. population; fit of standardization data to U.S. Census data should be within a few percentage points.)
If not, explain.

_____

What is the date of the standardization? _____

(Generally should not be more than 15 years old)

Does the test have components or subtests? If so, name and briefly describe the subtests:

_____

_____

_____

_____

Is the test reliable? Provide ranges for types of reliability:

(Typically, use .90 as minimum for eligibility decisions, .80 for screening decisions, and .60 for research purposes.)

Test retest coefficients range from   _____ to _____.

Internal consistency coefficients range from   _____ to _____.

Inter-rater reliability coefficients range from   _____ to _____.

Intra-rater reliability coefficients range from   _____ to _____.

Other reliabilities range from   _____ to _____.

Is the test valid? Provide ranges for validity coefficients:

(Typically, good tests yield construct/concurrent validity coefficients from .50 to .90 and predictive validity coefficients from .40 to .70; occasionally, coefficients are higher.)

Evidence of Content validity: Expert review:

Yes _____   No_____

(Continued)

Figure 7.1 (Continued)

Other evidence (e.g., factor structure) _____

Construct validity coefficients range from _____ to _____.

Concurrent validity coefficients range from _____ to _____.

Predictive validity coefficients range from _____ to _____.

Other coefficients reported (e.g., treatment) range from _____ to _____.

Test Administration and Scoring

Is the test individually or group administered? (Underline one or both.)

Is the test user friendly? _____

Why or why not? _____

How long does it take (typically) to administer the test?
Approximately _____ minutes

Does the test require a standardized administration? That is, are directions scripted?
Yes _____ No_____

Is the format forced choice, such as true–false, multiple-choice, matching, or free response?
(Underline all that apply.)

Does the test require the examinee to respond by using a pencil?
Yes _____ No_____

Does the test require the examinee to manipulate materials?
Yes _____ No_____

Does the test require the examinee to orally identify or read symbols, words, sentences, paragraphs, or other text? (Underline all that apply.)

Is the test scored by hand, by computer, or some combination of both?
(Underline all that apply.)

What type of scores does the test yield?
Age equivalents, grade equivalents, percentage correct, percentiles, standard scores,
stanines, or normal curve equivalents
(Underline all that apply.)

What type of information does the test yield?
Curriculum-based, progress monitoring, peer comparisons, or intra-individual comparisons?
(Underline all that apply.)

Is computerized interpretation available?
Yes _____ No_____.

Is computerized report writing available?
Yes _____ No_____

Are results helpful for guiding classroom instruction?
Yes _____ No_____ Sometimes _____

What examiner qualifications are required?
_____

For this review, did you use the manual, independent sources (such as *Buros Mental Measurement Yearbook*), or professional journals? (Underline all that apply.) Name of journal if applicable _____

Name of reviewer _____ **Date** _____

learn new words, writing them and using them in context helps cement both their spelling and their meaning (Beck, McKeown, and Kucan 2002). Highlighting the reciprocal relationship between reading and writing, Allington (2005) has called the reading/writing connection one of the "other" pillars of reading not addressed by the National Reading Panel.

Many experts consider the dichotomy between reading and writing to be artificial, that we cannot obtain a complete literacy picture without considering writing. Like reading, writing is a sophisticated process that draws on cognitive, linguistic, and sociocultural variables and is intimately connected with one's reading proficiency, interests, and attitudes. Also like reading, writing involves several types of related but somewhat different skills, including spelling, orthography, and vocabulary. In addition, planning and working memory are especially important in writing. And, for most students, handwriting is an important aspect of writing proficiency.

Writers must apply their reading-related knowledge and skills as they translate symbols into meaning on the page through motoric movements (typically by handwriting but increasingly by typing). Sophisticated writers plan and monitor their writing, similar to sophisticated readers as they apply comprehension monitoring strategies. Think back to the discussion of declarative and procedural knowledge in Chapter 2. Effective writing requires knowing *about* (declarative knowledge) how letters are formed and spelled, meaning and use of punctuation, word meanings, and so on *and then* applying this knowledge (procedural knowledge) to create meaning on the page. This distinction is important when we consider student strengths and weaknesses. For example, a student with **cerebral palsy** may have the declarative knowledge necessary for proficient writing but be unable to type or to hold a pencil firmly enough to write. In another case, a student with **autism** may have intact handwriting skills but may lack knowledge of semantics and syntax required to create meaningful communication. Assistive technology, such as voice-to-text software, may be an appropriate accommodation for the student with cerebral palsy while the student with autism may need enhanced language instruction.

How are the various aspects of writing assessed?   A fair and thorough answer to this question is well beyond the scope of this text. In fact, the question warrants an entire text of its own. Nonetheless, we will provide some basic information. Many of the aspects of writing (and mathematics for that matter) can be assessed in the various ways we describe in Chapters 3–6 of this text. Consider informal assessment of writing via work samples. In early grades, teachers focus on handwriting, spelling, and the ability to convey basic ideas. In later grades, teachers tend to focus on composition skills. Most of us are familiar with traditional language arts exercises in which students identify parts of speech. More recently, educators are encouraged to emphasize authentic writing experiences with embedded opportunities to practice grammar and spelling skills and to deemphasize worksheets focusing on discrete skills. For example, Allington and Cunningham (2002) call for a better balance in the classroom between real reading and writing and skills-oriented seatwork. Authentic writing creates many opportunities for assessment. Numerous rubrics have been developed to help teachers evaluate writing (Calkins 1983; Allington and Cunningham 2002; Medina 2006). Student writing provides numerous opportunities for assessment of basic writing skills and higher-level composition skills, including handwriting, grammar, punctuation, spelling, vocabulary, creativity, fluency, and the ability to write in certain genres (such as stories and persuasive letters).

In addition to informal, classroom assessment of writing, some criterion-referenced and hybrid measures (as described in Chapter 4) are also available. Several of the BRIGANCE® Inventories introduced in Chapter 4 include assessments of specific writing skills. For example, the BRIGANCE® Diagnostic Comprehensive Inventory of Basic Skills (1999) includes measures of spelling, handwriting, and mechanics for kindergarten through grade 9. Further, the AIMSweb progress monitoring program includes measures of spelling and written expression. Spelling is assessed when students write words from graded word lists. Written expression is assessed via three-minute writing samples that students generate in response to age-appropriate story starters.

Writing can also be assessed via formal, individualized measures such as those described in Chapter 5. In fact, many of the measures described there contain subtests measuring writing. For example, the Woodcock-Johnson III (2001) contains a spelling measure (with dictated words), a writing samples subtest (in which students write descriptive sentences based on picture prompts and specific cues), a writing fluency subtest (a timed subtest in which students write short, simple sentences containing three key words), an editing subtest (in which students identify and correct errors in short passages, such as spelling, capitalization, punctuation, and word use), a punctuation and capitalization subtest (in which students must write words and phrases that are dictated and provide correct punctuation and capitalization), and several handwriting measures. In addition, there are individualized measures devoted solely to writing (such as the Test of Written Language, Third Edition; TOWL-3; Hammill and Larson 1996). The TOWL-3 includes eight untimed subtests with equivalent forms. The TOWL-3 assesses writing in a spontaneous (authentic) format; students write an essay in response to a picture prompt. The essay is evaluated based on the writer's ability to use writing conventions in context (spelling, capitalization, and punctuation), language in context (vocabulary, syntax, and grammar), and story construction (plot, development of character, and general composition). The TOWL-3 also includes a contrived format, focused on specific skills such as the ability to form letters into words, capitalization and punctuation, word usage, and knowledge of syntax necessary to write conceptually sound sentences.

Finally, many group formal tests, the "high-stakes" tests, now include writing samples, in recognition of the importance of writing in overall literacy. For example, the Tennessee Comprehensive Assessment System includes a writing sample given several times throughout the elementary grades. Students write a short essay in response to a prompt or query. The writing prompts are administered under standard conditions, as are other high-stakes tests. However, rather than the typical norm-referenced scores associated with most group formal tests, this essay is scored by experts according to a rubric. Scores can range from 1 to 6. In addition, many group achievement tests include measures of spelling; often the format requires the student to choose a correctly spelled word from a series of four or five choices. Some also include measures of proofing skills by asking students to read writing samples and indicate what is wrong (such as missing or incorrect punctuation or capitalization). For example, the Iowa Tests of Basic Skills for students in grades 3 through 8 includes items assessing students' capitalization, punctuation, and usage and expression skills. According to the Interpretive Guide (2003, 38), items on the usage portion "require students to make decisions about the application of the grammatical conventions of standard written English. In the expression portion, the skills deal with reducing ambiguity, conveying intended meaning and presenting written ideas in logical order."

As you might imagine, establishing reliability and validity of writing tests is tricky, particularly for authentic writing samples. Most formal tests (group and individual) require training to ensure that the scores are consistent across scorers (inter-rater reliability as discussed in Chapter 4). The Buros Mental Measurements Yearbook and professional journals are good sources of information about writing assessments. Some of the resources in Appendix D may also be useful for writing assessment. And, finally, the Test Review Criteria presented earlier in this chapter can also be applied to selecting writing assessments.

■ MOTIVATING STUDENTS TO READ

Teachers need to know how to motivate their students to read, about reading **self-efficacy** (an individual's belief regarding his or her ability to be successful), and about how to assess reading interests. These motivational components are depicted in the Inclusive Model of Reading in Appendix B and influence reading significantly (see the review by Guthrie and Humenick 2004), though indirectly. In other words, affective variables do not contribute directly to discriminating initial sounds in words nor to the appreciation of conceptually similar vocabulary words. But these variables do contribute to the tendency of students to approach reading material, to engage in reading for recreational and academic purposes, to think about the meaning embedded in print, and, in short, to profit from the reading experience.

As the double-ended arrows in the Inclusive Model of Reading show, affective variables interact with other variables that more or less directly impact comprehension—the ultimate goal of reading. For example, context variables shown in the Inclusive Model contribute to motivation to read in a variety of ways. If parents or other caregivers have the time and opportunity to read to young children, to model reading for pleasure, and to make books available, children will be more motivated to read on their own. Later in their development, students are more likely to read for pleasure when they have friends who do so. And one thing that all teachers agree on, reading begets reading; that is, students who read often develop better reading skills than those who read less often, all other things being equal. And the better that students read, the better they feel about their ability to extract meaning from print, and in turn, the better their reading self-efficacy.

Self-efficacy was first described by Bandura (1977; 1978; 1986) and refers to an individual's beliefs about his or her ability to perform a task successfully. Students with strong reading self-efficacy choose to read more often for recreation and for information than those with poorer reading self-efficacy. Teachers can use instruments such as the ones described next to assess students' motivation to read, interests related to reading, and reading self-efficacy. These instruments are user friendly for the examiner and examinee. Teachers can add this affective information to more direct assessment data on reading and reading-related skills to create a composite, leading to a more complete understanding of their students' reading practices. Also, information from affective assessments can be combined with other data to develop recommendations teacher and parents can use to promote development of reading skills.

Relative Influence of Motivation

Some educators, those who consider themselves strong visual learners, may conceptualize (and visualize) successful reading instruction as consisting of many multiple components, like a giant jigsaw puzzle with interlocking pieces, all contributing, more or less, to development of a good reader. Other educators, those with a more quantitative bent, might conceptualize or visualize successful teaching of reading as a mathematical equation, with differential influences from various sources integrated into a formula. Both of these conceptualizations can be represented through the Literacy Instruction Pie introduced in Chapter 2 and reproduced in Appendix C. As you will remember, the Literacy Instruction Pie encourages educators to evaluate the relative importance of the pieces for an entire class or for a particular student at any point in time, and the equation, or relative size of the pieces, changes as student needs change. However, one component that remains a constant across age, grade, student readiness level, and sophistication—one that permeates the entire reading process—is reading motivation. We show the pervasive influence of motivation on all aspects of literacy instruction by the addition of the diagonal lines drawn across the entire Pie, as depicted in Figure 7.2.

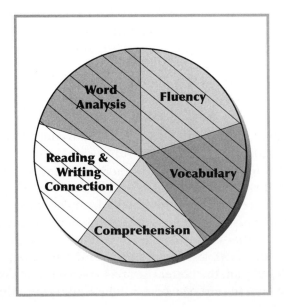

FIGURE 7.2 Literacy Instruction Pie Showing Influence of Motivation

The fact that motivation is important to successful reading instruction was apparent to the philosopher Rousseau, who speculated in 1762 that any method of teaching reading would be successful given adequate learner motivation (McKenna and Kear 1999). In all likelihood, modern-day teachers would not agree with such a sweeping generalization; but the point is important to keep in mind. Through the years, other experts have weighed in on the importance of motivation. For example, the Commission of Reading summarized the existing research in 1995 and noted the link between skilled reading and the reader's interest in the content (Anderson, Hiebert, Scott, and Wilkerson 1985). Others make even stronger statements. Smith (1988, 177) concluded that, "the emotional response to reading . . . is the primary reason most readers read, and probably the primary reason most nonreaders do not read."

After a review of the relationship between motivation and successful reading instruction, Guthrie and Humenick (2004, 351) concluded that, "a motivated reader is not likely to automatically gain these complex cognitive competencies independently. The unmotivated reader, however, is quite unlikely to gain these reading competencies at all." These researchers define motivation to mean **engagement,** and they further describe it as a cognitive commitment toward reading to learn and to extend the reader's aesthetic experience. This commitment produces relevant energy and direction to the reading process and is not isolated from the overall language experience or cognitive activity underlying the act.

Because there is little research available focusing on the role of motivation in acquiring single words, Guthrie and Humenick targeted for study primarily the relationship between motivation and acquisition of comprehension skills. They noted, following the work of Wigfield and Guthrie (1997), that motivation for reading is not a unitary attribute, but rather is multifaceted. In fact, Wigfield and Guthrie identified twelve dimensions of motivation for reading. In an extension of their research, Guthrie and Humenick categorized the influence of these twelve dimensions within three more general types of motivation: external motivation, internal motivation, and self-efficacy. Externally motivated readers put forth effort to gain incentives such as points, grades, gold stars, money, and "free time." On the other hand, internally motivated readers engage in reading to obtain information that satisfies their curiosity. Presumably, internally motivated readers have interests and desires that are satisfied by the new knowledge gained from reading. The third motivational attribute, self-efficacy, refers to students' beliefs in their capacity to read well, their attitudes about anticipated success or failure. Confident students are more likely to engage in reading and to learn from text.

Guthrie and Humenick (2004) reviewed twenty-two experimental or quasi-experimental studies in an effort to determine how external motivation, internal motivation, and self-efficacy influence reading outcomes. They identified several instructional practices that positively influenced reading motivation, interest, and time, including: (a) creating knowledge goals that emphasize learning content consistent with background knowledge, interests, and connections to larger goals; (b) allowing student choices regarding reading content and reading time; (c) assigning interesting texts based on students interests, use of illustrations, and consideration of relevance to background knowledge; and (d) allowing social collaboration based on joint assignments.

McKenna and Stahl (2003) summarize some of the relevant research informing teachers about how students' reading related beliefs, attitudes, and interests are formed and maintained. Apparently, these are formed directly from interactions with reading content itself and from interactions with models that may influence perceptions regarding the reading process, such as parents, peers, and teachers. In addition, reading attitudes are influenced by instructional methods and by gender (girls have more positive attitudes toward reading than boys), but not much by ethnicity. Reading attitudes tend to worsen over time, and particularly for poor readers. According to the research literature, the number of reading interests declines with age and the influence of gender increases with age, but girls are more likely to read "boy's books" than boys are to read "girl's books." Typical male interests include science, machines, sports, and action/adventure, while typical female interests include interpersonal relationships and romance; males *and* females seem interested in humor, animals, and the unusual (McKenna and Stahl 2003).

While the generalizations from the research literature can be helpful to teachers in choosing motivating reading materials, it is still helpful to gain information firsthand from students regarding sources of interest and motivation. There are a number of techniques and tools teachers and other practitioners can use to determine attitudes, beliefs, interests, and self-efficacy, including classroom observations, reading journals, interviews, sentence completions forms, interest inventories, surveys, and the thought-bubble technique. As with all assessment techniques, pros and cons are associated with each.

Classroom Observations

Most teachers are consummate observers. They observe their students all day participating in different settings and responding to various task demands, not the least of which is reading. Classroom observations may be as simple as informal or **anecdotal** notes that a teacher makes regarding a student's interests or self-efficacy. This would occur when, for example, Ms. Crockett writes about one of her students: "Jesse told me today that he really likes to read about animals" or "Jesse noted today that he gets in trouble at home because he doesn't like to listen to his Mom read to him and his sister." Teachers should keep notes in students' portfolios, being careful to *describe* behaviors rather than to *label* them. For example, Sammy, the third-grader who struggles with reading, tends to avoid reading during free time. His teacher, Ms. Porter, notes in his reading portfolio that during free time, Sammy chooses to build with blocks and work at the art center rather than go to the reading rug. She avoids labeling this behavior as "lazy" or "uninterested in learning." An interview, which we discuss in a following section, will help her determine why Sammy avoids going to the reading rug.

In addition to anecdotal observations that most teachers make, observations can be very systematic, direct, and structured. This type of observation relies on a set of fairly rigid rules. The observer, often a special education teacher or school psychologist, observes for a specified period looking for specifically defined behaviors, such as the number of times a student verbally expresses an interest or the number of times students choose to engage in a particular activity when given free time. In addition, notes from the observation are documented at the time the behavior occurs, not from memory at a later time. The most frequent type of direct observation requires a **frequency count.** The observer, in consultation with the teacher, decides what behaviors are important to observe, often after the teacher takes anecdotal notes as described earlier. It is important to note that a direct classroom observation by someone other than the classroom teacher is required as part of the assessment process for determining students' eligibility for special education. A simple, generic observation form is provided in Figure 7.3. We have used variations of this form over the years in numerous classrooms. We copy the two sides of the form back to back for ease of use. Side 1 provides space for anecdotal or narrative observation, descriptive only, not evaluative or judgmental. Side 2 provides space for frequency counting. Even more systematic observations can be taken. The strategies required to create these very systematic observations are beyond the scope of this discussion, but these details can be found in textbooks describing behavioral observation techniques (Sattler 2002).

Reading Journals

Reading journals can be used for a variety of purposes, one of which is to help teachers determine students' reading interests and self-efficacy. Some teachers make extensive use of journals and require students to make routine entries, including a running record of books read, dates of reading, range of pages read each time, origin of the book (such as from the library, as a gift, or from a friend), and so on. These entries can be used to provide a good context for teaching writing skills, as well as to determine students' perceptions about their reading assignments or choices.

The information shared in journals can provide to the teacher a sense of students' reading self-efficacy. For example, if Shelby, one of Mr. Haywood's students, writes "I hate reading time every day," Mr. Haywood will need to spend some extra time devising creative strategies for motivating her, based on her particular interests and reading level. One particular caveat is important—don't let the routine reading journal entries turn into book reports with rigorous requirements for completion. Students may learn to dislike assigned reading material if it always serves as a precursor to effortful writing activities (McKenna and Stahl 2003), and as teachers know, writing is a very complex and difficult activity for many children and adolescents (and some adults as well). Teachers have an obligation to help students learn to appreciate the act of reading because of the information and satisfaction it provides. As most teachers know, reading can reduce curiosity and pique it at the same time, which can lead to vicarious enjoyment of activities that are out of reach of most students and can help the student create knowledge for later discussion with peers about common interests.

Sentence Completion Forms

Educators and clinicians have used sentence completion forms for years to obtain useful information about students' mental health, self-efficacy, and interests. Students who can write reasonably well can complete the sentence stems—or young or special needs students can have them presented orally by a teacher

FIGURE 7.3 Classroom Observation Form, Anecdotal and Systematic Recording

CLASSROOM OBSERVATION FORM
(ANECDOTAL OBSERVATION) SIDE 1

Student: _____   School: _____

Observed by: _____

Grade/Class: _____   Teacher: _____

Date: _____   Time: To: _____   From: _____

Floor Plan of Classroom: (Include Teacher and Student Seating)

Anecdotal Observations:

_____
_____
_____
_____
_____
_____
_____
_____
_____
_____
_____
_____
_____
_____
_____
_____
_____
_____
_____
_____
_____
_____
_____
_____
_____

CLASSROOM OBSERVATION FORM
(SYSTEMATIC OBSERVATION) (On the Count*) SIDE 2

On Task   +   Off Task   –

Out of Seat   0   Talking Out   t

Other (DEFINE): _____

S = Target Student   T = Teacher P_1, P_2 = Peer 1, Peer 2

---

*On the count refers to recording what the student is doing every minute or every thirty seconds. Use a combination of symbols and short notes to describe student behavior that occurs "on the count." Suggested minimum time for observation is twenty minutes.

and completed orally by the student. For example, sentence completion stems sometimes are used by school psychologists to determine motivation for and attitudes about school and might begin with one of the following:

"The best thing about school is _____."
"My teacher helps me _____."
"The thing I hate most about school is _____."

This strategy can be tailored very easily to fit a variety of needs, and students may offer information not only about school but about home life, peers, and so on. Classroom teachers may use this strategy to determine their students' perceptions about specific aspects of instruction, such as reading, by using stems such as:

"I like to read about _____."
"When I am older I want to read about _____."
"My friends think reading is _____."
"My favorite book is _____."
"The thing I hate most about reading is _____."

The appeal of this procedure is obvious to teachers who want to know more about their students' perceptions regarding reading and their students' reading self-efficacy. Teachers and specialists can create specific stems to suit particular goals.

Thought-Bubble Technique

In addition to the sentence completion technique, psychologists and educators have used drawing techniques for years to gain rapport with students and to obtain sensitive information that students might not reveal in more straightforward verbal exchanges (Goodenough 1926; Flavell, Green, and Flavell 1993). For example, some children who have trouble with peer relationships may be asked to draw themselves and their peers engaged in some activity. Interpretation may be based on how many peers are drawn, how close the peers are to the student, which peers are closest, what their relative sizes are, and so on. The drawing produced from the activity sometimes is used as a point of departure for talking with a student about interpersonal relationships. Variations may include family drawings and the like.

Zambo (2006) describes briefly the history and characteristics of a variation of the drawing technique—the thought-bubble technique—that seems capable of motivating some students to reveal their perceptions regarding the act of reading. This technique shows a student reading, as in a cartoon, with an empty bubble drawn above the head of the student; the student's face is also empty. The student is asked to draw the face of the reader and write comments in the bubble. Zambo provides simple scoring guidelines leading to a conclusion about whether the student likes and appreciates the reading process, feels neutrally toward reading, or feels negatively toward reading. Points are assigned for features of the drawing, including words, facial characteristics of the eyes and mouth, and use of symbols such as hearts, daggers, and question marks. Positive or negative numbers are assigned to the features based on the positive or negative affect they convey. For example, comments such as "I love reading" would be assigned a positive 1, and "I hate

FIGURE 7.4 Thought Bubble Technique from Zambo

Taken from Zambo, Debby. (2006, May). Teaching Tips: Using thought-bubble pictures to assess students' feelings about reading. *The Reading Teacher, 59(8),* 798–803.

reading" a negative 1. Likewise, the use of a heart showing appreciation of the reading process would be scored a positive 1, and a sword battling a book would be a negative 1. See Figures 7.4 and 7.5, taken from Zambo's article showing two very different responses to the picture of a girl reading. She suggests strategies for ensuring the reliability and validity of this technique, but the data obtained should be considered only a crude indication of perceptions regarding reading nonetheless.

FIGURE 7.5 Thought Bubble Technique from Zambo

Taken from Zambo, Debby. (2006, May). Teaching Tips: Using thought-bubble pictures to assess students' feelings about reading. *The Reading Teacher, 59(8),* 798–803.

Interest Inventories

Interest inventories typically take the form of a list of topics that may hold appeal for students. Teachers use these inventories to determine the kinds of things or activities students will work for. Then, teachers can use the information to reward their students for engaging in instructional activities. McKenna and Stahl (2003) provide an example of such a form, which we have reproduced here in Figure 7.6. The directions simply inform students to

FIGURE 7.6 **Interest Inventory**

Tell Me What You Like!

Name _____

Which topics do you like most? Pretend you're a teacher and give each one of these a grade.
Give it an *A* if you really like it, a *B* if you like it pretty well, a *C* if it's just OK, a *D* if you don't like it, and an *F* if you can't stand it!

If I've missed some topics you really like, please write them on the lines at the bottom of the page.

_____	sports	_____	monsters
_____	animals	_____	horses
_____	magic	_____	detectives
_____	jokes	_____	love
_____	exploring the unknown	_____	famous scientists
_____	sharks	_____	ghosts
_____	camping	_____	other countries
_____	UFOs	_____	dogs
_____	spiders	_____	cooking
_____	the jungle	_____	the ocean
_____	drawing, painting	_____	music
_____	riddles	_____	science fiction
_____	friendship	_____	cats
_____	snakes	_____	families
_____	the wilderness	_____	the desert
_____	fishing	_____	computers

What other topics do you really like? Write them here:

_____

_____

_____

_____

McKenna, M. & Stahl, S. (2003). Taken from McKenna, M.C. & Stahl, S.A. (2003). *Assessment for Reading Instruction.* New York: Guilford Press, p. 213.

provide a rating for some thirty-two topics based on the typical grading scheme. For example, students are told to assign an "A" to a topic they really like, a "B" to one they like pretty well, and so on. Topics include sports, animals, fishing, cooking, and others. As is apparent from observation of this form, there is an open-ended question asking students to add any other topics of interest. Of course, teachers may make up this kind of interest inventory and can keep adding topics of interest as the topics are introduced. McKenna and Stahl provide some guidelines for using interest inventories by advising teachers to:

1. Include only topics for which materials are available
2. Include a wide range of topics for both boys and girls
3. Include nonfiction and fiction topics
4. Refrain from mentioning reading when administering the inventory to preclude a negative mindset on the part of students who may dislike reading already
5. Keep completed inventories handy

Attitude Inventories

Several reading attitude inventories are available. These are intended to provide teachers with information about the reading self-efficacy and motivation of their students and will help a teacher determine the extent to which students find reading appealing. Teachers may use these once or multiple times to gauge attitudinal changes over the year. We describe a couple of the most appealing inventories in the following sections.

Elementary Reading Attitude Survey (ERAS)

The ERAS was developed by McKenna and Kear (1990) to determine student attitudes toward recreational and academic reading activities. To increase the likelihood that students will find it appealing, the test authors kept it short (only 20 items) and used images of the fictional cartoon character Garfield (created by ERAS co-developer Jim Davis) to anchor a four-point scoring scale ranging from very happy to very upset. Students are to indicate how the short questions about reading make them feel, not how the questions might make Garfield feel. The first ten items inquire about students' perceptions regarding recreational reading, such as free reading choices and reading versus playing, and the second ten inquire about perceptions regarding academic reading, such as reading for information and reading school books. The ERAS is characterized by other appealing features as well—it can be administered quickly and has a large national database against which scores can be compared and percentiles generated. In addition, there is some evidence supporting the psychometric adequacy of the ERAS.

ERAS authors report reliability estimates calculated for each grade level, for both subscales, and for the composite score. Coefficients ranged from .74 to .79. Evidence of validity was established in a number of ways; for example, high-ability readers, on average, earned scores significantly higher than low-ability readers. In a second comparative study, students who voluntarily checked out books from the school library earned scores significantly higher than those who did not. Interested practitioners can obtain the entire instrument and scoring directions from McKenna and Stahl (2003) or McKenna and Kear (1990; 1999); full citations are provided in the References section of this handbook.

The Reader Self-Perception Scale (RSPS)

This scale was developed by Henk and Melnick (1995) to assess how students feel about themselves as readers. It consists of thirty-three items along four dimensions of self-efficacy: progress, observational comparison, social feedback, and physiological states. Progress items are designed to determine the students' perceptions of their reading ability relative to the past; observational comparison items require students to make comparisons between their performance and the performance of peers; social feedback items require students to characterize how others perceive their reading ability; and physiological states items require students to characterize how reading makes them feel inside. Rating is based on a five-point scale from strongly agree to strongly disagree. The authors provide some comparative data showing interpretation of raw scores into High, Average, and Low categories for each scale. Also, Henk and Melnick (1995) and others describe the development of the scale and some basic psychometric properties. From a sample of 1,479 middle school children, they report evidence for internal consistency reliability (scale indexes ranged from .81 to .84), statistical evidence (from factor analytic data) showing that the items were placed appropriately onto the specific scales, and "moderate yet significant relationships . . ." with the Elementary Reading Attitude Survey (McKenna and Kear 1990), as well as a variety of standardized reading achievement measures (Henk and Melnick 1992; 1993, as cited in Henk and Melnick 1995).

Interviews

Teachers, reading specialists, educational diagnosticians, or school psychologists may interview students to determine their reading-related interests and motivation. Obviously, the interview is driven by the particular kind of information sought, and practitioners may devise questions to meet more general or specific goals. One general rule practitioners should observe about creating interview questions is initially to ask questions that are more general, followed by increasingly specific questions, as needed. The idea is to allow the student to contribute as much information as possible spontaneously. This strategy increases the likelihood of obtaining unanticipated but useful information—content that might be stifled by too many questions focusing on specific directions.

Using Affective Information

Once assessment of motivation, interests, and attitudes has been completed, how can educators use this information? As with many assessment tools, those designed to obtain affective information related to reading can be used for more than one purpose. For example, some inventories yield scores allowing either peer or norm-based comparisons, mastery-based percentages, or both. But perhaps the most important information these instruments yield is descriptive and qualitative. The specific answers to items can inform teachers and others about the topics that most interest students, the aspects of reading that most appeal to them, the aspects of the reading environment that might most motivate them, and importantly, their reading self-efficacy. In some cases, information from these inventories can help teachers choose instructional materials; the affective information should be especially helpful in selecting reading material on topics that will interest individual students. In addition, some students may reveal specific difficulties through their self-disclosures within the inventories, including slow reading, forgetting what is read, or having trouble paying attention when reading.

Other Within-the-Individual Variables: Cognitive Correlates of Reading

The information on affective assessment just presented, combined with information in previous chapters, provides a relatively complete presentation of within-the-individual reading variables. But when you look at the Inclusive Model in Appendix B, you can see a host of other variables we have not addressed with specificity. First, consider other within-the-individual factors that are not direct reading skills, the cognitive correlates of reading: auditory processing, rapid automatic naming, processing speed, working memory, long-term memory, and others. As discussed in Chapter 2, these variables have an impact on an individual's reading abilities and typically are assessed (usually by a school psychologist) when a student is referred for evaluation for a learning disability or other exceptionality, such as language impairment or mental retardation.

A number of cognitive/IQ tests provide measures of cognitive and processing variables. For example, the Wechsler Intelligence for Children-IV (Wechsler 2003) provides measures of verbal, performance (visual-spatial), memory, and processing speed abilities. The Woodcock-Johnson III Tests of Cognitive Abilities (Woodcock, McGrew, and Mather 2001) provides measures of a number of abilities including verbal comprehension, fluid reasoning (ability to perceive relationships nonverbally), auditory processing, processing speed, and short-term and long-term memory. And the Universal Nonverbal Intelligence Test (UNIT; Bracken and McCallum 1998), an intelligence test designed to be culturally fair, is administered nonverbally to eliminate low scores resulting from language barriers and to provide measures of memory, reasoning, and symbolic and nonsymbolic (abstract) processing. The UNIT is particularly appropriate for ELL students. These tests typically are administered by school psychologists, but teachers and administrators should have basic familiarity to enable them to communicate effectively when a student is assessed for special education eligibility. As we have suggested in previous chapters, scores on IQ tests usually are reported in standard scores (with a mean of 100 and standard deviation of 15) and percentiles, so we recommend that you keep a copy of Figure 5.1 handy for future reference to aid in interpretation.

When are assessments of cognitive processing variables appropriate?   Although we acknowledge the important influence of cognitive variables on reading abilities, we do not recommend a cognitive assessment for most students, at least not initially, even for those who struggle in reading. Cognitive assessments are time-consuming and their results do not lead directly to instructional suggestions, as discussed in Chapter 2. Consequently, we encourage classroom teachers to hone their reading assessment and instruction skills, to directly assess the reading skills of students who continue to struggle, and to document results of different instructional approaches. When the teacher is "stumped," we suggest consulting with the reading specialist, special education teacher, school psychologist, or all three to determine the next steps. Occasionally, teachers will encounter a seemingly capable student who just cannot seem to learn to read and spell; this inconsistency may be characteristic of dyslexia, as discussed in Chapter 2. To read successfully, students with dyslexic tendencies typically require more in-depth assessment and more intensive instruction than do other students. Toward the end of that chapter, we considered characteristics of Sammy, a third-grade student with dyslexic tendencies.

Another situation that may require individualized assessment occurs when a student whose first language is not English has considerable difficulty with either acquiring basic academic skills in English or in acquiring content. Recall Saimah from India, a fifth-grader in Mr. Haywood's school, whose first language is not English. Her family moved to the United States so her father could work as a consultant in a computer firm; both parents are college-educated and Saimah was exposed to some English in school in India in the primary grades. She began second grade in the United States but continues to have difficulty academically, particularly with reading. To avoid misidentifying English Language Learners (ELL) as learning disabled or as having other exceptionalities, experts recommend assessment that is culturally fair and nondiscriminatory (Overton 2006). Saimah was administered the UNIT (the nonverbal intelligence test described earlier) by the school psychologist. Her Full Scale IQ score of 94 was in the average range, but she had relatively more difficulty with symbolic material than abstract material; symbolic reasoning is associated positively with verbal facility. In addition, an interview indicated that she was delayed in talking in her native language, that she had a history of ear infections, and that there was a family history of language and learning problems on the maternal side. Consequently, the Individual Education Program (IEP) team determined that Saimah's learning difficulty was not the result of issues related to acquiring a second language; that is, the IEP team determined that her difficulties were not attributable to second language acquisition-associated phenomena (SLAAP; Brown 2004), but rather to within-the-individual learning difficulties and that she would benefit from special education services designed to enhance her reading skills.

So armed with a variety of assessment techniques and the occasional help of specialists, teachers should be equipped to plan, implement, and interpret comprehensive reading assessment. But take a look at the Inclusive Model in Appendix B once again. What are the influences from contextual variables, including the teacher, instructional materials, home life (including literacy richness), peers, school, and community? Having gotten this far through this handbook, ideally you are a dedicated teacher/practitioner or an enthusiastic administrator willing and able to make such analyses.

Teacher Self-Assessment

In addition to assessing students' reading skills and motivation, we challenge teachers to self-assess. We recommend using the Sentence-Completion technique and starting with the following questions:

"My classroom is attractive because _____."
"I encourage students to read by _____."
"Good things happen in my class when _____."
"I hold students accountable (nonpunitively) for reading by _____."
"When I model reading behavior, students _____."
"When I encourage weak readers to read more, they _____."
"When I encourage good readers to try new genres, they _____."
"When I allot students time to read, they _____."
"When I ask students to read with one another, they _____."
"When I organize the class so that reading is promoted, my students _____."
"When I read aloud to my students, they _____."
"When I encourage parents to provide literacy experiences at home, my students _____."

Teachers can use the Literacy Instruction Pie to organize their thoughts about self-assessment and instruction. As printed in Figure 7.2, the Pie has pieces of equal size, and all the components are influenced by motivation. As suggested in an earlier chapter, one way to use the Pie is to match the available assessment data with the Pie slices. Teachers should ask themselves, "What type of data do I have?" "What additional data do I need?" "What do the data tell me about the instructional needs of my students?" And, finally, "What resources do I have or need to have in order to meet the identified instructional needs?" Teachers may modify the "size" of the Pie slices to accommodate student needs, signifying the time allotted to each instructional component.

■ GATHERING AND EVALUATING DATA

Teachers of grades 4 through 8 are likely to have group achievement test data giving norm and criterion-referenced scores for students' performance in various academic areas. Teachers of kindergarten through grade 3 may not have group achievement data available; many states do not require accountability testing until the end of grade 3, in accordance with No Child Left Behind (NCLB 2001), guidelines. Increasingly, K–3 teachers have access to progress monitoring data, such as AIMSweb or DIBELS. Although quite different from group accountability testing, the progress monitoring data yields information about general levels of performance. High school teachers have access to students' cumulative records, with group achievement data and grades. Most states require testing in content areas such as English, biology, history, and algebra. So depending on the grade of the student, high school teachers have access to these data. Adult educators typically have limited records on their students but will probably have information from a test such as the Test of Adult Basic Education (TABE) that gives grade equivalents as well as norm-referenced information for performance in basic academic areas.

Group data are limited in specificity, but they provide a starting point. In addition to group data, most teachers have access to other data. For example, Ms. Crockett routinely assesses progress in word analysis, vocabulary, and comprehension using unit tests and worksheets from the basal reading series used in her system. Mr. Haywood uses the BRIGANCE® to identify specific strengths and weaknesses across all areas of reading. And, in both schools, the Qualitative Reading Inventory is used as a supplement to classroom assessment. Dr. Charles, the high school biology teacher, begins his class each semester assessing oral reading fluency and accuracy in the textbook; in addition, the reading specialist for his system provides assessment of reading with tests such as the Nelson-Denny and the Qualitative Reading Inventory (QRI) for students who struggle with reading the textbook. This provides Dr. Charles with more information about his students' reading rate, word attack, automatic or sight vocabulary and comprehension. Finally, Ms. Sanchez supplements the TABE with several measures including the Test of Silent Word Reading Fluency (for a fluency measure) as well as word recognition and word decoding tasks from the Woodcock-Johnson III Diagnostic Reading Battery.

We suggest teachers keep an assessment folder with group data for the entire class. This allows the teacher to see overall trends, strengths, and weaknesses. In addition, teachers should keep an individual folder on each student; this folder can be part of the student's reading portfolio, along with student work samples and anecdotal notes or observations, results of interest or attitude surveys, and other relevant information. Once teachers gather all available data, they should note students' progress, and strengths and weaknesses in the major areas of reading. A worksheet for summarizing reading assessment data is presented at the end of this chapter.

Classroom teachers have the challenge of meeting a wide range of needs. Most reading instruction still relies on the basal reader (Schumm 2006). Fortunately, most current basal series have supplemental reading material that is both harder than and easier than the primary reading materials. In addition, the instructors' guides are filled with activities designed to strengthen each of the areas of reading. The challenge for the teacher is to find enough time to choose wisely and to plan activities in accordance with student needs. For teachers using a literacy approach such as the Four Blocks (Cunningham, Hall, and Sigmon 1999), each of the major areas of reading is addressed—phonemic awareness, phonics, and sight words/orthography in the Working with Words block, fluency in the Self-Selected Reading block, vocabulary and comprehension in the Guided Reading block; all are reinforced in the Writing block. Nonetheless, teachers must ensure that students are getting enough explicit instruction in areas of need.

Use of the Literacy Instruction Pie makes the assessment-instruction link more explicit. Teachers should consider how much time they actually spend each day doing activities that lead to learning in each of the areas. (Keep in mind that the areas are not mutually exclusive and that many types of reading activities will lead to gains in more than one area of reading). Several researchers have found that some classrooms provide surprisingly little time for students to actually read and write (Durkin 1984). We challenge teachers and administrators to use the Pie—to note the instructional time each day that is devoted to reading activities—and to keep in mind that seatwork is often not engaging. Students learn best when actively engaged in reading, writing, listening, and talking.

Increasingly, teachers use technology to help them provide instruction. Edyburn (2006) reviews computer hardware and software available for this purpose. These tools can be extremely useful, but in our view, they should not be considered a substitute for providing direct reading instruction by the teacher. Even older students who struggle with reading continue to need direct and explicit instruction in reading, along with instruction in content areas. One way to address this challenge is to use content-area (for middle and high school students) and career/domestic-oriented (for adults) reading materials that expose students to important content and allow students to build fluency.

There are many excellent books on reading instruction and several that combine assessment and instruction. See Appendix D for a list of assessment and instruction resources. Our goal in this book is to focus primarily on assessment, to allow readers with either nonassessment or nonreading backgrounds to become more knowledgeable about the continuum of assessments related to reading. Nonetheless, we want to emphasize the importance of connecting assessment to instruction; without doing so, assessment is useless.

■ PULLING IT ALL TOGETHER!

In the following sections, we consider some specific cases of students reading—first from an entire class, then individual students. We examine assessment data, share instructional suggestions, and present a problem-solving plan for use when students struggle.

Assessment-to-Instruction for an Entire Class

How can a teacher make use of formal and informal test data to help improve reading instruction for an entire class? In the section that follows, we discuss how group data can be considered by a teacher to help plan reading instruction from the Iowa Tests of Basic Skills (ITBS). The ITBS yields a Group Primary Reading Profile, which provides a comprehensive collection of all the reading and reading-related information available from the ITBS administration. In Figure 7.7, we show an example of a Class Primary Reading Profile for a third-grade class from the ITBS manual (Riverside 2001).

Clearly, classwide data show an overall reading score for the class—the Reading Profile Total. For this class, the National Percentile Rank (NPR) is 70, which indicates performance above the national average (recall that the 50th percentile is average). But when the scores are broken down by particular skill area, spelling is shown to be weak, compared not only to the rest of the nation (NPR

FIGURE 7.7 Class Primary Reading Profile from the Iowa Tests of Basic Skills

THE IOWA TESTS

CLASS PRIMARY READING PROFILE
Iowa Tests of Basic Skills® (ITBS®)

Class/Group: Ness
Building: Longfellow
System: Dalen Community

Form/Level: A/9
Test Date: 04/2002
Norms: Spring 2000
Order No.: 002-A70000028-0-002
Page: 1
Grade: 3

A student's ability to read is related to success in many areas of schoolwork. This Reading Profile combines information from the reading and reading-related skills measured by various tests in the *Iowa Tests of Basic Skills®*.

The Vocabulary test measures knowledge of words important in the comprehension of all kinds of reading materials. This test is also the best single measure of general verbal ability in the entire test battery. Vocabulary development contributes to a student's understanding of spoken and written language encountered both in and out of school.

The Word Analysis test measures a student's awareness of sound-to-symbol relationships that play an important role in early literacy development. It also tests a student's ability to identify and analyze word parts. Word Analysis is a particularly useful part of the Reading Profile for students whose comprehension-related skills in reading and/or listening are relatively weak.

The Spelling test measures a student's understanding of how the sounds of spoken English are encoded into written words. Weaknesses in spelling can provide insight into aspects of the reading process that involve word attack skills or the ability to sound out and comprehend unfamiliar words.

The Listening test measures many of the same comprehension skills as a reading test, but for spoken rather than written language. These comprehension skills range from understanding factual details in a story to making inferences, predicting outcomes, and understanding sequences or new concepts. The Listening test is an especially useful indicator of comprehension skills for students whose ability to decode written language is limited.

The Reading Comprehension test measures the ultimate goal of reading: the understanding of written language in a variety of fiction, nonfiction, and poetry. Factual details as well as inferences and generalizations based on stories are tested.

Reading Profile Summary

TESTS	N	NPR
Vocabulary	23	80
Word Analysis	23	64
Spelling	23	39
Listening	23	83
Reading Comprehension	23	55
READING PROFILE TOTAL	23	70

The shaded portion above highlights the class's overall reading performance.

NATIONAL PERCENTILE RANK (NPR)

Tests and Skills	Total No. Items	No. Att.	%C Class	%C Nat.	Diff.
Vocabulary					
Vocabulary	29	29	86	62	24
Word Analysis					
Phonological Awareness and Decoding	11	11	91	71	20
Initial Sounds	4	4	100	76	24
Medial Sounds	4	4	100	69	31
Final Sounds	3	3	67	69	-2
Identifying and Analyzing Word Parts	24	24	71	67	4
Silent Letters	4	4	75	71	4
Initial Syllable	5	5	100	67	33
Final Syllable	5	5	76	62	14
Suffixes	5	5	82	67	15
Compound Words	5	5	62	68	-6
Spelling					
Vowels	9	9	52	67	-15
Consonants	8	8	64	68	-4
Vowel/Consonant Combinations	4	4	59	81	-22
Affixes	3	3	63	55	8
Correct Spelling	4	4	75	76	-1

Difference* Class - Nation

Tests and Skills	Total Items	No. Att.	%C Class	%C Nat.	Diff.
Listening					
Literal Comprehension	16	16	81	74	7
Literal Meaning	4	4	77	81	-4
Following Directions	4	4	70	67	3
Visual Relationships	3	3	90	89	1
Sustained Listening	5	5	79	65	14
Inferential Comprehension	15	15	82	65	17
Inferential Meaning	4	4	71	53	18
Concept Development	3	3	87	75	12
Predicting Outcomes	3	3	79	71	8
Sequential Relationships	5	5	78	65	13
Reading Comprehension					
Factual Understanding	17	17	73	61	12
Inference and Interpretation	12	12	62	61	1
Analysis and Generalization	8	8	58	48	10

Difference* Class - Nation

* A plus sign (+) or a minus sign (-) in the difference graph indicates that the bar extends beyond +/- 20.

No. Att. = Number Attempted   %C = Percent Correct

Riverside Publishing A HOUGHTON MIFFLIN COMPANY

Taken from The Iowa Tests Interpretive Guide for Administrators, Riverside Publishing, 2001.

of 39), but also relative to the other areas within this class. Reading comprehension is not a weakness compared to the performance of all third-grade students in the nation (NPR of 55), but it is lower than the other reading-related areas within this particular class. Based on these results, this third-grade teacher might choose to spend more time providing instruction in spelling (reading-writing connection on the Literacy Instruction Pie), and perhaps comprehension. And even though word analysis is very strong for this class (NPR of 64), one subskill is *relatively* weak—breaking down compound words. Consequently, the teacher may want to address how to attack these words more effectively (word analyses on the Instruction Pie). Within the spelling area, students performed poorest when trying to incorporate vowels and vowel/consonant combinations into words. In the comprehension area, students performed poorest when making inferences and interpretations. More specific information advising teachers about the use of this information is available in the Iowa Tests Interpretive Guide for Teachers and Counseling (Riverside 2003). Other group standardized tests provide similar information.

Information from group tests (and from an aggregate of data from individually administered test) can be informative. Teachers may obtain gross information about the performance of their students relative to similar classrooms within the same school or system and from across the state and nation. NPRs, stanines, and standard scores can provide this type of information. (Remember, keep a copy of Figure 5.1 handy to aid in interpretation.) In addition, as just discussed more specific information sometimes can be obtained, showing relative strengths and weaknesses within reading and reading-related areas, such as word analyses versus comprehension, or even within specific reading areas, such as initial versus medial versus final sounds, within the word analysis section of the assessment.

In addition to providing adequate specific skills instruction, it is important that teachers provide students with time just to read. Although research findings on the effectiveness of **sustained silent reading** (SSR) are controversial, there is some research support for encouraging students to read as teachers monitor their progress (Stahl 2004). In this whole-class strategy, the teacher models reading behavior. Such an activity emphasizes the importance of the teacher as a model for reading behavior (Yoon 2002).

Because teachers face so many factors in and out of the classroom that are out of their control, their tendency sometimes is to fail to realize what a significant impact they can make as models. For example, teachers who model a love of books can create an infectious atmosphere. Consequently, teachers should create an inviting classroom with lots of books on the shelves. One study recommends a minimum of ten books per student with the books varied in terms of topic, such as fiction, nonfiction, and various **genres**, and levels of difficulty (Schumm and Argulles 2006). Most challenging is to find low readability books that are interesting and that do not appear immature. Several book-leveling systems (for example, Fountas and Pinnell 2006) make this task easier. Providing incentives (external motivation) combined with modeling and subtle praise ("I see you chose a book on ghosts; let me know if it is scary!" or "I think it is neat that you picked a poetry book this time") helps motivate students to read.

TABLE 7.1   Summary of Assessment Data for Jesse, a Beginning First-Grader

Test	Score		Interpretation
Qualitative Reading Inventory-4			
Word Lists: Words Read with Automaticity	Preprimer Primer Level 1	90% 70% 36%	Jesse is reading preprimer material at the independent level; his instructional level appears to be primer level.
Passage Comprehension—Percent Questions Correct	Preprimer Primer Level 1	100% 67% 75%	
Words Correct Per Minute	Preprimer Primer Level 1	71 36 28	
Miscue Analysis	Total miscues = 11 45% omissions 27% self-corrections 27% retains meaning		Typical errors for primer-level reader
DIBELS			
Oral Reading Fluency	46 wcpm (53rd percentile)		Acceptable progress for early first-grade student

Assessment-to-Instruction for Individual Students

In the sections below we describe first how a teacher may facilitate instruction for a typically performing student. Then we focus on strategies for a student who is struggling.

Assessment-to-Instruction for a Typically Performing Student

In this section, we present test data gathered by a first-grade teacher, Ms. Crockett, early in the school year on her student Jesse. Some of the information available about Jesse is reproduced in Table 7.1. As is apparent, Jesse is making good progress and his scores are consistent with expectations for a beginning first-grade student. In his case, there is no reason to require standardized test data; that is, he is not at risk for reading problems. Most of Ms. Crockett's students earn QRI and DIBELS scores similar to Jesse.

How can Ms. Crockett use test information to inform reading instruction for Jesse? Ms. Crockett currently uses the Scott Foresman reading series, and she uses it effectively. The pattern of miscues from the QRI does not reveal any unusual problems. In other words, the errors Jesse made are typical for a student reading at his level. As is obvious from his pattern of performance, many of his errors are adaptive. For example, although he miscalled several words (eleven miscues in all for the passage assessed), several of the miscalled words actually began with the correct sound, ended with the correct sound, and retained meaning. He was less successful with medial vowel sounds, and a goal should be made to give him more instruction targeting that skill. Significantly, almost one-half of his errors resulted from omissions, which is typical of impulsivity. Ms. Crockett should observe Jesse's problem-solving attack strategies for other indicators of impulsivity; if impulsivity is a pattern for Jesse, she may need to provide special attention to help him focus. For example, she might encourage him to monitor his comprehension as he reads by asking himself "Does this make sense?"

Like all good teachers Ms. Crockett evaluates her performance as a teacher based in part on the academic gains of her students. As part of this process, she considers how well her time has been spent and, perhaps, how her time has been spent relative to the components of the Literacy Instruction Pie, although in all likelihood, not in a formal way. Let's assume Ms. Crockett also uses a more systematic computerized assessment and tracking system, such as the Northwest Evaluation Association's (NWEA) Measures of Academic Progress (introduced in Chapter 4); she might find that 75 percent of her students have met their target growth rate in reading. Further, based on NWEA feedback and other assessment data, she might discover that Jesse's skills place him in this portion of the class, and that his skills, as with most students in the class, are about equally developed in all the areas of the Pie: word analysis, fluency, vocabulary, comprehension, and the reading-writing nexus. (Although she has not made systematic comparisons of Jesse's writing thus far, she has observed that his skills are typical). Ms. Crockett might assume that her time with Jesse (and the rest of the class) has been well spent and would choose not to alter the percentage of time she routinely allots to each of the components of the Pie for general instruction. However, she likely will provide as much unique help to her students as possible. For example, she has noted that Jesse likes to read about animals and will help him look for books of interest at the appropriate reading level. She can also use this information to pair him for partner reading and for writing activities. Further, based on anecdotal notes she has learned that he does not like to read with his mother and his sister Maddie, who is a fifth-grader and a strong reader. She will discuss this observation with his mother and suggest that his mother spend some one-on-one reading time with Jesse, with the caveat that she choose books he likes. Now that Ms. Crockett has discovered how many students have not met their target reading growth rates, has determined who these students are, and has discerned their particular weaknesses, she likely will choose to spend a significant portion of her time with those students. Because many of these students have not acquired fundamental reading skills, she probably will focus more instructional time with these students on the two basic reading building blocks of the Pie—word analysis and vocabulary building.

Assessment-to-Instruction for Students Who Struggle

Even though a teacher may provide the best possible reading instruction for the entire class, often one or two (or even a few) students will not make satisfactory progress. What can a teacher do for a particular student who is struggling? We have one piece of advice with many positive implications—adopt a systematic problem-solving approach. When researchers want to know how or why something occurs, they look for cause-effect relationships, as we discussed in the section on scientifically-based reading research in Chapter 1.

Now, we present some guidelines for applying a problem-solving approach to students' reading difficulties. For example, it is possible to show that certain reading-related problems can be caused by a variable the teacher can control—ineffective instruction. (Obviously, lack of reading progress can be influenced by a number of internal within-the-individual and contextual variables; however, teachers can control the external variables more readily, and consequently, we focus on those.) If a teacher is interested in evaluating whether an instructional strategy being used is "causing" progress or contributing to a lack of it, whichever the case may be, the teacher can devise a strategy to test this relationship. How? We will describe the general steps of a generic problem-solving model that can be applied to any problem in any classroom by any teacher, and we will illustrate briefly how the model could be used to address the reading difficulties of three students: Todd, Emilio, and Sammy.

DATA-BASED PROBLEM-SOLVING

Several general problem-solving models are built on sound scientific principles (Batsche and Knoff 1995; Shinn 1998), and we use one that has been described in the literature (McCallum 1991). This model, called the **Data-Based Problem-Solver Model** (DBPS), is universal, which means it can be applied to any challenging situation or behavior. We use it to explain reading challenges and solutions. It requires that the teacher follow four simple steps:

1. Problem solution/identification
2. Problem solution/plan development
3. Problem solution/plan implementation
4. Problem solution/evaluation

The first step of the DBPS model requires that the teacher frame the question in logical language that could apply to any problem, specifically, "What is the relationship between X and Y?" This "What is the relationship between X and Y" format is necessary to set up a testable hypothesis about the nature of two unknowns—X and Y—and assumes that the problem-solver, in this case the teacher, can identify both unknowns. In this scenario, the teacher defines the reading problem in observable, measurable terms (for example, lack of instruction or inappropriate instruction), which is the X in the relationship question. She then thinks about the aspect of behavior affected by that problem (for example, fluency and comprehension), which is the Y part of the question.

Case Study: Todd

Let us consider a real example. Suppose our special education teacher, Mr. Haywood, has a child who has not made acceptable progress according to oral reading fluency measures. We know that Mr. Haywood has been brainstorming ways to help one of his students, Todd. Todd is a fourth-grader who has been served by Mr. Haywood since the end of his third-grade year. He has made steady progress in word decoding and sight-word recognition, but he still reads very slowly and without inflection. Mr. Haywood recently attended a professional development workshop with a focus on reading fluency and learned that when teachers structure time for students to get plenty of practice reading material at an appropriate readability level, their fluency and comprehension tend to increase. A recommended strategy for increasing fluency includes partner reading, in which students take turns reading material to one another—a strategy that affords students more reading time than traditional instruction in which they read only with the teacher or take turns in a reading group. And, compared to independent reading, the strategy is superior because it ensures that students are more likely actually reading. With this information, Mr. Haywood can fill in the X and the Y of the relationship question, and he might follow the specific steps of the DBPS model as outlined by McCallum (Figure 7.8). The question might be as follows: What is the relationship between a particular type of instructional strategy (partner reading in this case) and reading fluency?

Step 1 in the DBPS model includes not only the relationship question, but also the development of a hypothesis—a when-then proposition: When Todd participates in an effective instructional strategy (partner reading for twenty minutes a day from familiar text material at his reading level), fluency (as defined by wcpm) will increase by at least 10 wcpm after four weeks. In Step 2, Mr. Haywood determines the particulars of the instructional strategy (for example, specific partner, time of day, and time per day). In Step 3, the intervention begins, and the data collected are compared to baseline data. **Baseline** data are gathered over a brief period, perhaps two or three weeks before the intervention phase and measured as wcpm. Although he could use a variety of techniques to do this, including the QRI, running records (timed), DIBELS or AIMSweb, or a more traditional standardized test such as the Test of Silent Contextual Reading Fluency TOSCRF, perhaps the most appropriate would be CBM conducted as Todd reads from leveled readers. Todd's baseline rate then can be compared to any gains that might occur later during Step 3 (intervention). Step 4 requires evaluation, comparison of the baseline data collected during Step 1 to data collected during the intervention, or Step 3. If the intervention is producing adequate gains, perhaps it should be continued as is. If there is lack of adequate progress, then the intervention should be changed in some way to make it better (such as monitoring partner reading to be sure students are engaged, finding more motivating books, increasing reading time, changing time of day, or introducing use of a reinforcer to motivate Todd).

FIGURE 7.8 Data Based Problem Solver Model

Student's Name: _____   Age: _____   Grade: _____

Initial Referral Problem
Describe the student's behavior of concern objectively.

_____

_____

_____

Step 1: Problem Identification
Describe the problem in scientific language (What is the relationship between X and Y?).

_____

_____

_____

Step 2: Solution Development (Hypothesis)
Represent the problem as a hypothesis; state it as an if-then proposition.

_____

_____

_____

Step 3: Intervention Implementation (Make a Prediction)
Develop a When/Then prediction that can be answered either *yes* or *no*.

_____

_____

_____

Step 4: Plan Evaluation
After implementation, answer the When/Then question.

_____

_____

_____

Adapted from McCallum, R.S. (1991). Do training models influence school psychology training? *Council of Directors of School Psychology Programs Press, 10 (1)*, 1–3.

Case Study: Emilio

We can use the DBPS model to illustrate yet another case, this time from a tenth-grade classroom in Dr. Charles' school. This student, Emilio, has poor reading skills, with particularly poor comprehension. His math skills are relatively stronger, but he struggles in most subjects that are reading-intensive. Emilio transferred into Dr. Charles' school early this school year, and Dr. Charles has learned very little about his background. He has noticed that Emilio says very little in class and that his English language skills appear to be limited. Apparently, Emilio and his parents came into this country a few years ago; his father currently works in a local canning factory. Dr. Charles has access to a Lexile score (490) from the Total Reader computer assessment system as well as Iowa Tests of Educational Development (ITED) scores from his previous school. End-of-the-year ITED scores show problems in reading, though math scores are near grade level. A copy of Emilio's available scores is displayed in Table 7.2.

Scores from the ITED show an NPR of 16 and Scaled Score (SS) of 225 on the Vocabulary scale and an NPR of 17 (SS of 213) on Comprehension. Emilio's performance within the Comprehension section was not uniform. His Factual Understanding rank is higher than his ranks in the Inference and Integration and Analyses and Generalization areas. Related Language Arts scores were also low, though slightly higher than the reading scores. His Spelling NPR is 38 (SS of 248) and Revising Writing NPR is 42 (SS of 249). In order to understand Emilio's standard scores, be aware that they can be compared to those from the standardization sample. The publisher sets the median score obtained by all fourth-grade students in the Spring administration to 200, the median score obtained in the spring by eighth-grade students to 250, and the median score obtained in spring by tenth-graders to 268. Dr. Charles also requested that the reading specialist in the school administer the Nelson-Denny to obtain additional information about Emilio's reading skills. He obtained percentile ranks (PR) of 18, 16, and 12 for the Vocabulary, Comprehension, and Reading Rate subtests, respectively.

Dr. Charles and the reading specialist are familiar with the DBPS model, and both suspect that Emilio's poor comprehension is related to his lack of English proficiency, particularly vocabulary. Consequently, they phrased the DBPS Step 1 relationship question as follows: What is the relationship between implementing an English language vocabulary development instructional strategy and reading comprehension? This question allows them to generate a when-then hypothesis they can test; namely, when Emilio is provided with vocabulary instruction by his content teachers (including preteaching vocabulary and root-word strategies) for thirty minutes per day

TABLE 7.2   Summary of Assessment Data for Emilio, a Tenth-Grader

Test	Score			Interpretation
Total Reader	490			Approximately third-grade level
Iowa Tests of Educational Development	**National Percentile Rank (NPR)**		**Scaled Score**	
Vocabulary	16		225	Well below average
Comprehension	17		213	Well below average
Spelling	38		248	Below average
Revising writing	42		249	Below average
Nelson-Denny	**National Percentile Rank (NPR)**	**Stanine**	**Normal Curve Equivalent**	
Vocabulary	18	3	31	Well below average
Comprehension	16	3	29	Well below average
Reading rate (words per minute)	12	3	25	Well below average

for three months, their comprehension scores will increase by five NCE points on the Nelson-Denny. Step 2 of the DBPS model requires the selection of particular elements of a vocabulary development program by his content teachers and the ELL teacher (including a preview and prediction drill developed by content area, with guidance from the ELL expert). Step 3 requires implementation of the program. Finally, after three months an alternate form of the Nelson-Denny will be administered to check progress (and to address the hypothesis generated in an earlier step of the DBPS model). If Emilio does not progress as anticipated, other questions could be addressed using the DBPS model. For example, because Emilio shows significant vocabulary and comprehension weaknesses, a DBPS plan could be developed specifically to address the relationship between Emilio's use of graphic organizers and his reading comprehension. This strategy may be implemented to supplement the ongoing vocabulary development instruction based on the assumption that poor vocabulary development is only a partial explanation for poor comprehension.

Case Study: Sammy

We use the DBPS model to illustrate a final case—this time from a third-grade classroom in Mr. Haywood's school. This student, Sammy, has been referred by his teacher (Ms. Porter) and his parents for a **comprehensive evaluation** because of poor reading skills. He is making adequate progress in other academic areas (including mathematics), although his writing skills are considered only minimally acceptable. Ms. Porter and Sammy's parents believe Sammy may have a learning disability. Sammy is in the third grade and has a history of special help and an enriched home life, including repeating kindergarten, attending summer school after the first and second grades, and engaging in routine reading time with his parents at home. Nonetheless, his reading skills continue to lag behind most of his peers. Ms. Porter administered the ERAS and found that his attitude toward recreational and academic reading is poor. In an interview with Ms. Porter, she confirmed the findings from the ERAS; Sammy simply does not like to read.

Additional data are provided by the schoolwide reading screening process using oral reading probes on AIMSweb. Sammy's scores are at the 8th percentile rank—below the cutoff for at-risk status set to capture the lowest 10 percent. His progress over the most recent six weeks of the third-grade year is at the 21st percentile rank (also below the cutoff score for at-risk status, set to a rate of progress equal to the student at the 25th percentile). Also available are scores from the school's group test, the ITBS. Scores from all academic tests show problems in reading, though math scores are near or just above grade level. Selected ITBS scores for Sammy are presented in Table 7.3.

Scores from the ITBS show an NPR of 18, a stanine score of 3, and a grade-equivalent score (GE) of 2.5 on the Reading Profile Total, and similarly low NPR, GEs, and stanines for word analysis and spelling. His comprehension score is somewhat better, and his listening score is even better. Specific word analysis scores revealed particular weaknesses in subskill areas assessing awareness of medial and final sounds and identifying and analyzing final syllables, suffixes, and compound words. Sammy shows some weaknesses in all three comprehension subskill areas: factual understanding,

TABLE 7.3   Summary of Assessment Data for Sammy, a Third-Grader

Test/Assessment	Score		
Iowa Tests of Basic Skills	**National Percentile Rank (NPR)**	**Stanine**	**Grade Equivalent (G.E.)**
Reading Total	18	3	2.5
Vocabulary	45	5	3.5
Comprehension	24	4	2.8
Spelling	10	2	2.3
Word Analysis	4	2	1.7
Listening	45	5	3.5
Mathematics Total	59	5	4.0
Woodcock-Johnson III Diagnostic Reading Battery*	**National Percentile Rank (NPR)**	**Standard Score**	**Grade Equivalent (G.E.)**
Word Attack	13	83	1.4
Letter-Word Identification	23	87	2.2
Reading Vocabulary	27	89	2.7
Passage Comprehension	37	95	3.0
Elementary Reading Attitude Scale (Garfield)	**Total: 5 NPR**	**Recreational: 26 NPR**	**Academic: 13 NPR**
Qualitative Reading Inventory-4	Miscue analysis: Errors indicate weak word attack skills, misread 46 of 175 words at Level 2		

*Note: Standard score mean for Woodcock Diagnostic Reading Battery = 100; standard deviation = 15.

inference and interpretation, and analysis and generalization. In addition, he shows a significant weakness in one specific spelling subskill area: vowel/consonant combinations and relatively weak performance on the other spelling areas (such as affixes). Finally, Sammy's language subskills are on or above grade level except for usage/expression (NPR = 40; GE 3.4); his mathematics score is slightly above average (NPR = 59; GE 4.0). Sammy's reading-related and spelling ITBS stanine scores ranged from 2 (word analysis and spelling) to 5 (vocabulary and listening). All his reading-related grade-equivalent scores were weak, ranging from 1.7 to 3.5. Mr. Haywood administered the Woodcock Diagnostic Reading Battery; Sammy's standard scores ranged from 83 to 95. All are weak compared to his peers. Word attack scores are the lowest and are consistent with the low word analysis scores from the ITBS. Finally, his scores from the TOSCRF are also low (including a percentile rank of 18).

It is helpful to consider Sammy's environment in order to understand his pattern of scores. Because Sammy has an enriching home life, it is not surprising that his vocabulary and listening skills are relatively well developed and are near the national average; however, his performance on word analysis, spelling, and reading comprehension tasks is relatively weak. Sammy participates in and appears to understand class discussions. He seems especially interested in science and gets along well with peers. Ms. Porter suspects the reading difficulties are related to his difficulties in decoding, which has a negative impact on his reading fluency and comprehension. She is considering referring Sammy for an assessment by the school psychologist to determine whether he has a learning disability in reading. Ms. Porter has increased the time she spends helping Sammy master word analysis skills, so that slice of the Literacy Instruction Pie is relatively larger when Ms. Porter plans for and instructs Sammy.

Steps of the DBPS model can be used to provide direction in developing instructional options for Sammy. A reasonable question for Step 1 might be: What is the relationship between Sammy's word analysis instructional time and his reading fluency skills? Given that Sammy's comprehension skills are also poor, another question may be posed: What is the relationship between his use of comprehension building strategies, such as question generation and use of text structure, and his reading comprehension? Clearly, one or more of the questions could provide direction for Ms. Porter, and conceivably, both could lead to development of a DBPS plan, depending on resources and time. For now, we will choose one question and show how it could lead to development of a DBPS plan for Sammy.

Because Sammy's phonemic awareness and phonics skills are poor, we might choose to address the first relationship question: What is the relationship between Sammy's word analysis instructional time and his reading fluency skills? Data from the QRI-4 show that he struggled with passages at the second- and third-grade levels. For example, on the Level 2 passage, he misread 46 out of 175 words and could answer only one of the comprehension questions following the passage. His errors included frequent vowel sound substitutions, and he often miscalled medial and final sounds of words. Although most of his errors resulted from poor phonics skills, he made several semantic errors, saying "dad" for the word "mom." Given this information, there is good evidence to support the need to investigate the relationship between Sammy's phonemic awareness and phonics skills (or lack of) and his poor reading fluency and comprehension. Consideration of the relationship question leads to development of a specific hypothesis: When Sammy spends thirty minutes per day engaged in specific strategies designed to strengthen his word analysis skills, including using Making Words (Cunningham and Hall 1994), Elkonin blocks, and the computer software program Headsprout (www.headsprout.com), then his reading fluency as measured by AIMSweb will increase to a rate commensurate with the rate of the student at the 30th percentile after six weeks.

Development of the DBPS plan requires in Step 2 that details be determined, such as negotiating who will instruct Sammy in Making Words and use of Elkonin blocks (i.e., small manipulatives that represent sounds), which days Sammy will spend on the computer, what time of day will be assigned to which task, where the computer will be placed, and so on. Step 3 of the DBPS model requires implementation and someone to monitor implementation. Finally, the success of the intervention will be determined, in this case from the AIMSweb scores that are available from probes taken routinely at the school. The scores showing rate of progress after six weeks of intervention can be compared to preintervention scores.

Because Sammy shows significant comprehension weaknesses as well, a DBPS plan could be developed specifically to address the relationship between teaching understanding of text structure and reading comprehension. In this case, Ms. Porter, in consultation with the reading specialist, first chooses to provide more instructional time on word analysis. For most third-graders and above, word analysis is deemphasized relative to other areas of reading, especially vocabulary and comprehension. So, as we mentioned earlier, she must adjust the size of the Literacy Instruction Pie for Sammy relative to her other students, but she will need to continue to provide adequate vocabulary- and comprehension-building experiences.

Data-Based Problem-Solving and Multitiered Instruction

Use of the DBPS plan can help teachers and support personnel address student difficulties in a systematic manner. Teachers who may be in the midst of orienting to a new model for screening and addressing reading problems, particularly those who are now using a multitier model of instruction, may be wondering how the DBPS plan fits in. The short answer is that the DBPS plan will be most appropriate for children who fail to make adequate progress even though the teacher uses sound instructional practices that are effective for most of the students in the class—students who will get referred for additional "tiers" of instruction under the multitiered model. These students are good prospects for the kind of systematic and intensive problem-solving guided by the DBPS plan. And, as part of the consideration of the problem phase of the DBPS plan, teachers may think of the components of the Literacy Instruction Pie for guidance; that is, when formulating the problem statement in the DBPS plan (the "what is the relationship between X and Y?" question), it may be helpful to consider which element of the Pie is most limited. This component, perhaps it is "vocabulary" may then become the Y element in the relationship question.

Remediation versus Compensation

When assessment data show academic weaknesses, teachers are expected to take action. However, it may be difficult to determine whether the action should require remediation (additional instructional time devoted to going over the same content in the same or similar fashion), use of additional or novel instructional approaches, or compensation (use of strategies or technologies that minimize the student's limitation). Several writers have indicated that these (or similar) questions should be addressed early to maximize instructional efficiency (Edyburn 2006; King 1999). Presumably, teacher preparation programs, in-service and continuing education activities, and professional resources (including books and journals) provide teachers with the skills to address these questions, particularly the first one. In our experience, as teachers become more experienced, they develop greater skill at knowing when (and how) to reteach, and they grow increasingly familiar with alternative strategies for teaching particular skills. Appendix D provides a wide range of resources for enhancing instruction in particular skill areas. As a general rule, teachers know less about how to choose and use assistive and related technologies than they do about traditional instructional approaches. For teachers and teachers-to-be who may need help in this area,

Edyburn provides some suggestions for relating student limitations to compensatory technologies. These include the use of audiobooks and text-to-speech software to build fluency, use of electronic word tools to build vocabulary, and use of multimedia reading materials to build decoding skills.

Most students with disabilities (and those who need compensatory interventions) will exhibit reading difficulties. Once identified as eligible for special education, as a result of a learning disability or some other disability such as mental retardation or speech-language impairment, a group that includes parents and general and special education teachers (the Individualized Education Program or IEP team) works together to develop the IEP. Although the IEP has evolved into a somewhat complex legal document, the essence is that the identified student needs something different or in addition to general instructional practices in order to make adequate progress. These differences are documented in the IEP.

Individual Education Program (IEP)

According to the U.S. Department of Education Web site (www.ed.gov/index.jhtml), the IEP is a written document that must be developed for every student with an identified disability. It contains very prescribed content; the most important content is arguably the statement of educational goals for the student. Progress toward these goals must be monitored routinely and reported to parents or guardians. At the heart of the IEP is a description of specific information about the types of special education and supplemental services; accommodations or modifications to be provided; frequency of those services, accommodations, or modifications; as well as where they will be offered, including beginning dates and duration. An **accommodation** is a support or service provided to help a student fully access instruction and content and demonstrate what he or she knows. An accommodation does not significantly change what the student is expected to learn or do, and it does not substantially alter the content, performance expectations, or standards. In contrast, a **modification** is a change in curriculum or instruction to help the student participate and make progress in the general curriculum. A modification does alter what the student is expected to learn or do and substantially alters the content, performance expectation, or standard. A curriculum modification is made when a student either is taught the same content or information as the rest of the class but at a different level of complexity or is taught something different entirely from the rest of the class.

In addition to identifying services, accommodations, and modifications, present levels of academic achievement and functional performance are included on the IEP, with particular attention paid to describing how the student's disability affects involvement and progress in general education. These present levels of performance are taken directly from assessment data. Other components of the IEP include:

1. A statement of measurable annual goals, to include short-term objectives for the lowest functioning 1 to 3 percent of students who take alternate assessments in lieu of federal and state-mandated group achievement tests
2. A description of how the student's progress will be assessed

3. A timetable describing when periodic progress reports will be due
4. A description of transition services for students aged 16 and older
5. A statement acknowledging that the student's rights have been explained (not later than one year before the student reaches the age of majority)

Assessment is most related to IEP development in three ways. First, assessment information should be used to determine the student's present levels of academic functionality. Based on these levels, achievement goals are set for the following year. Second, accommodations, modifications, or both that are needed for the student to experience success are indicated. Assessment results help determine the extent and nature of accommodations and modifications. For example, suppose Matt, a tenth-grade student with a learning disability, performs at the fourth-grade level on a test of reading comprehension. The IEP team might recommend that Matt have access to his textbooks on audiotape and use of computer reading software that will allow him to listen to, rather than read, content in his subject area classes. Finally, assessment data help determine test accommodations. The IEP must document whether the student with a disability will take the general state-mandated group achievement test or an alternative assessment. Students whose reading and other academic skills are significantly below that of peers may be candidates for the alternative testing. But NCLB and IDEA allow only 1 to 3 percent of students to take the alternative tests. Consequently, most students with disabilities will take the general group assessments, with their accommodations documented on the IEP. Common types of testing accommodations were discussed in Chapter 6.

We close the discussion of IEPs by providing examples for Shelby and Saimah, two of Mr. Haywood's students who have IEPs. First, based on assessment data, annual goals are developed. An annual goal for Shelby reads as follows: *Shelby will demonstrate one year's progress in automatic word recognition as measured by the Kaufman Tests of Educational Achievement-II Letter Word Recognition subtest and/or the BRIGANCE® Diagnostic Comprehensive Inventory of Basic Skill–Revised Basic Sight Vocabulary subtest. An annual goal for Saimah is: Saimah will demonstrate one year's progress in reading vocabulary as measured by the Woodcock-Johnson III Reading Vocabulary subtest and by the Qualitative Reading Inventory-4.* Second, special services, accommodations, and modifications are listed. Shelby and Saimah participate in reading in their regular classrooms but also receive supplemental help forty-five minutes per day with Mr. Haywood—all of which is documented on the IEP. In addition, they will have access to computerized software in the general classroom that "reads" content area materials to them. And Saimah gets additional instruction twice a week from the system's English-as-Second-Language (ESL) instructor. These accommodations and services are noted on the IEP. Neither Shelby nor Saimah have modifications because the goal is for them to be successful without having the essence of the curriculum altered. Finally, the IEP contains documentation of test accommodations that mirror the accommodations students receive during daily instruction. Both Shelby and Saimah participate in the general education group achievement testing. However, their IEPs contain information about test accommodations that include flexible scheduling and a change in setting. They take the test with Mr. Haywood who reads directions to them as well as test items in math and content areas, but he does not read the reading content.

■ ASSESSMENT TO INSTRUCTION

Assessment data are useless unless educators apply them to inform instruction and to improve the quality of life of students. How can assessment information inform instruction? By now, you may have many examples in mind. These may derive, in part, from cases provided in previous chapters of this handbook and, of course, from your own educational experiences. To aid you in thinking about the assessment-to-instruction link, we have created a worksheet to summarize assessment data from the components identified in the Inclusive Model of Reading (Appendix B) and the Literacy Instruction Pie (Appendix C). This worksheet is presented in Figure 7.9. On it, teachers can document assessment information for their students. Also, on the worksheet are spaces to make notes about student performance in the various areas of reading. Teachers can make shorthand notes about assessment data, including test scores, whether the data indicate a strength or an area of need, and materials or strategies to be used. Keep in mind that even strong readers need good instruction; the worksheet can be used to identify instructional needs of readers at all levels. Because the worksheet is inclusive, use of it prompts teachers to consider aspects of reading that may be overlooked.

How can a teacher use the worksheet to identify specific weaknesses and strengths and to plan instruction? It is possible to determine whether a score or performance level on any assessment represents a strength or weakness based on two essential elements: (a) how well the student performs (relative to peers) and (b) the teacher goals or expectations for the student. Typically, informal assessment measures provide teachers with qualitative and quantitative indicators of performance level, including the number and type of miscues and words correct per minute. On the other hand, formal measurements provide only a few qualitative indicators of performance. Rather, formal measures produce standard scores and percentiles based on functioning relative to peers nationwide. So a score of one standard deviation below average (such as a standard score of 85 and a percentile rank of 16) will often signify a weakness, but one standard deviation above the mean (for example, 115 and a percentile rank of 84), a strength. (Refer to Figure 5.1 for interpretive relationships among formal scores.) Ultimately, the meaningfulness of scores depends on the context. For example, a grade-equivalent score (GE) of one-half year below grade level represents weak performance for a first-grade student, but is much less significant for a ninth-grade student. Figure 7.10 on pages 280–281 shows a completed worksheet for Shelby, the fifth-grade student introduced in Chapter 3. Take a look at the worksheet to get a sense of how assessment data can be linked to particular instructional strategies. Choice of particular instructional strategies will depend on the teacher's knowledge base and the types of resources available. There are many excellent texts describing reading instruction strategies and resources for specific skill instruction, some of which are listed in Appendix D. In addition, a brief set of reading instructional tips is

FIGURE 7.9 Assessment-Instruction Worksheet
Teachers can determine whether a score or performance level represents a strength or weakness based on how the student performs (relative to peers) and based on teacher goals for the student. See text for explanation.

Assessment-Instruction Worksheet					
Name: _____ Date: _____ Grade: _____ Other Information: _____					
Reading or Related Skill	**Assessment or Test**	**Performance Level or Score**	**Strength (S), Adequate (A), or Weakness (W)**	**Next Steps**	**Materials and Strategies**
Reading Composite/Overall Reading					
Word Analysis — Phonemic awareness					
Word Analysis — Phonics					
Word Analysis — Word recognition/orthography					
Fluency — Rate (wcpm)					
Fluency — Accuracy					
Fluency — Inflection or prosody					
Vocabulary — Oral					
Vocabulary — Reading					
Comprehension: Literal, Inferential					
Reading/Writing — Composition					
Reading/Writing — Spelling					
Motivation and Interests					
Cognitive or Other Related Scores — Auditory processing					
Cognitive or Other Related Scores — Rapid automatic naming					
Cognitive or Other Related Scores — Memory: Working/short-term; long-term					
Cognitive or Other Related Scores — Other (such as IQ; other academics)					

presented in Appendix E. Importantly, completed worksheets can be stored in the classroom to help track progress, along with copies of subsequent classroom assessments; work samples; additional formal group and individual assessment results; and summaries of interviews, observations, and surveys.

Summary

In closing, we echo the recommendation by Walpole and McKenna (2006) that educators develop a "comprehensive assessment toolkit" (59). The information presented in this text will provide educators with information they need to make informed choices about the tools they put in their assessment toolkits. The primary theme of this chapter is "pulling it together," because educators must be able to synthesize information from numerous sources in order to create effective instruction for students, either individually or collectively. The primary goal is to provide knowledge about linking assessment to instruction, with evaluation of many contextual elements that must be considered in order to maximize instruction. We began the chapter by providing test review guidelines to help educators make wise decisions about assessment instruments. Next, we focused attention on aspects of the Inclusive Model of Reading not previously addressed, including writing; reading self-efficacy; and reading-related interests, motivation, and attitudes. Educators must motivate their students to read, particularly those students who consider reading an aversive activity. Some students enter school with a very positive attitude toward reading and will voluntarily engage in reading and reading-related behaviors, but others will not. How can these students become engaged readers? Educators need to consider intrinsic and extrinsic sources of motivation and be ready to take advantage of a number of assessment tools and strategies to help determine current levels of student motivation as well as activities available to increase motivation, as needed. In addition, we provided data from tests administered to a class of students and described how classwide data can influence instruction. Next, we presented test data on three students and explained how the data clarify the students' performance relative to peers. Then, we described the link between the scores and instruction using a generic problem-solving model. This model, called the Data-Based Problem-Solver Model, offers a four-step process for conceptualizing the relationship between reading problems and possible causes and solutions (for example, instructional needs). We closed the chapter by discussing how teachers can modify the time they spend providing instruction for students (depicted by the Literacy Instruction Pie) based on student needs, as identified by assessment results from informal and formal tests and computerized tracking systems. Finally, we noted that teachers may be able to determine the most effective intervention strategies by deciding whether the student's limitation requires reteaching, the reorienting of instructional goals and strategies, or the application of compensatory technologies and techniques.

We hope that in reading this chapter, you have found helpful information for "pulling it all together." Remember, your instructor will be the most important catalyst (and resource) in facilitating your progress. We do have one additional tip for making that happen, and we are indebted to one of the anonymous reviewers of an early draft of this book for the suggestion. The suggestion is based on the adage that two (or more) heads are better than one, and it requires that you share assessment information with one or more colleagues. By working with a partner and using assessment data from each person's classroom or other setting, you should be able to help each other analyze and interpret student data, which in turn should lead to helpful classroom recommendations.

mylabschool™
Where the classroom comes to life!

MyLabSchool is a collection of online tools for your success in this course, your licensure exams, and your teaching career. Visit www.mylabschool.com to access the following:
- *Online Study Guide*
- *Video cases from real classrooms*
- *Help with your research papers using Research Navigator*
- *Career Center with resources for:*
    Praxis exams and licensure preparation
    Professional portfolio development
    Job search and interview techniques
    Lesson planning

FIGURE 7.10 Assessment-Instruction Worksheet Completed for Shelby

Assessment-Instruction Worksheet

Name: _Shelby_   Date: _11/25/08_   Grade: _5_   Other Information: _____ wears glasses _____

Reading or Related Skill		Assessment or Test	Performance Level or Score	Strength (S), Adequate (A), or Weakness (W)	Next Steps	Materials and Strategies
Reading Composite/Overall Reading		ITBS	NPR = 18, GE = 3.3	W	Provide supplemental instruction	Core program (multilevel reading instruction) and 45-minutes of supplemental instruction per day (see below)
		W-J III	SS = 85, 3.7 GE	W		
Word Analysis	Phonemic Awareness	W-J III	SS = 97, 5.1 GE	A	Focus on higher-level word skills	N/A
	Phonics	W-J III	SS = 85, 3.1 GE	W	Teach syllable types	Making Words, Phonics They Use
	Word Recognition/ Orthography	QRI-4	Level 2 99 Level 3 90 Level 4 70	S @ Level 2, A @ Level 3, W @ Level 4	Automatize high-frequency words and irregular words	Gunning high-frequency word list (e.g., word games, sight-word association procedure)
Fluency	Rate (wcpm)	CBM	84 (wcpm)	W for grade 5	Increase rate and maintain accuracy	Partner reading, choral reading, reading with computer software
	Accuracy	Not administered				
	Inflection or Prosody	Not administered				
Vocabulary	Oral	ITBS Listening	NPR = 48, 5.3 GE	A	Build on oral vocabulary to improve reading	Provide opportunities for students to use words in various contexts; Relate meaning of new words to familiar words

Reading or Related Skill		Assessment or Test	Performance Level or Score	Strength, Adequate, or Weakness*	Next Steps	Materials and Strategies
	Reading	W-J III Rdg Vocab	SS = 85, 2.9 GE	W	Increase knowledge of roots and endings	Teach meanings of prefixes, suffixes, and word endings and practice applying them
Comprehension: Literal, Inferential		QRI-4	Level 2 90 Level 3 75 Level 4 45	S @ Level 2 A @ Level 3 W @ Level 4	Reading practice at level and interest	Guided reading, comprehension monitoring strategies, sticky notes strategy
		ITBS	NPR = 24, GE = 4.4	W		
Reading/ Writing	Composition	W-J III Writing Samples	SS = 91, 4.1 GE	W	Improve ability to respond to writing prompts	Authentic writing, writing and sharing connections
	Spelling	W-J III Spelling	SS = 87, 3.9 GE	W	Improve consistency in written spelling	Making words, phonics they use
		ITBS Spelling	NPR = 20, 4.2 GE	W		
Motivation and Interests		ERAS	Total: 25 NPR; Recreational: 40 NPR; Academic: 15 NPR		Determine and build on current interests	Practice with interesting reading materials at appropriate instructional level
Cognitive or Other Related Scores	Auditory Processing	W-J III Incomplete Words	SS = 101 5.4 GE	A	Basic auditory skills intact, focus on higher-level word skills	
	Rapid Automatic Naming	Not administered				
	Memory: Working/ Short Term, Long-Term	W-J III STM Cluster	SS = 86, 3.7 GE	W	Build word recall and retrieval	Use multiple strategies
	Other (such as IQ; other academics)	Wechsler	Full Scale IQ = 103	A	Determine and build on current interests	Identify interesting reading materials at appropriate level
		ITBS Mathematics Total`	NPR = 59, GE = 5.7	S	Use math strength to build confidence, as an interest for reading content	

APPENDIX

A

International Reading Association Professional Standards for Reading Assessment: Standard 3 Assessment

Standard 3: Assessment, Diagnosis, and Evaluation

Candidates use a variety of assessment tools and practices to plan and evaluate reading instruction. As a result, candidates:

Element	Paraprofessional Candidates	Classroom Teacher Candidates (plus previous level)	Reading Specialist/ Literacy Coach Candidates (plus previous 2 levels)	Teacher Educator Candidates (plus previous 3 levels)	Administrator Candidates
3.1 Use a wide range of assessment tools and practices that range from individual and group standardized tests to individual and group informal classroom assessment strategies, including technology-based assessment tools.	Administer scripted formal and informal assessments and technology-based assessments under the direction of certified personnel.	Select and administer appropriate formal and informal assessments including technology-based assessments. They understand the requirements for technical adequacy of assessments and can select technically adequate assessment tools. They can interpret the results of these tests and assessments.	Compare and contrast, use, interpret, and recommend a wide range of assessment tools and practices. Assessments may range from standardized tests to informal assessments and also include technology-based assessments. They demonstrate appropriate use of assessments in their practice, and they can train classroom teachers to administer and interpret these assessments.	Prepare and coach preservice candidates and inservice teachers to administer and interpret assessments appropriate for selected purposes. They interpret and critique technical aspects of assessments. They can articulate what makes up an effective assessment plan.	Understand the role of assessment in the delivery of excellent reading instruction. Working with reading professionals, they can develop appropriate building and districtwide assessment plans.
3.2 Place students along a developmental continuum and identify students' proficiencies and difficulties.	N/A	Compare, contrast, and analyze information and assessment results to place students along a developmental continuum. They recognize the variability in reading levels across children in the same grade and within a child across different subject areas. They can identify students' proficiencies and difficulties. They recognize the need to make referrals for appropriate services.	Support the classroom teacher in the assessment of individual students. They extend the assessment to further determine proficiencies and difficulties for appropriate services.	Prepare and coach preservice candidates and inservice teachers to place students along a developmental continuum. They ground this preparation in research.	Know the range of students' reading performance in their building or under their control and know how this range relates to the broader student population. They provide support for an effective assessment plan.

Element					
3.3 Use assessment information to plan, evaluate, and revise effective instruction that meets the needs of all students, including those at different developmental stages and those from different cultural and linguistic backgrounds.	N/A	Analyze, compare, contrast, and use assessment results to plan, evaluate, and revise effective instruction for all students within an assessment/evaluation/instruction cycle.	Assist the classroom teacher in using assessment to plan instruction for all students. They use in-depth assessment information to plan individual instruction for struggling readers. They collaborate with other education professionals to implement appropriate reading instruction for individual students. They collect, analyze, and use schoolwide assessment data to implement and revise school reading programs.	Prepare and coach preservice candidates and inservice teachers to use assessments to plan and revise effective instruction for all students within an assessment instruction cycle. They acknowledge and understand the research supporting different perspectives regarding assessment and instruction.	Support professional uses of assessment data.
3.4 Communicate results of assessments to specific individuals (students, parents, caregivers, colleagues, administrators, policymakers, policy officials, community, etc.)	N/A	Interpret a student's reading profile from assessments and communicate the results to the student, parents, caregivers, colleagues, and administrators.	Communicate assessment information to various audiences for both accountability and instructional purposes (policymakers, public officials, community members, clinical specialists, school psychologists, social workers, classroom teachers, and parents).	Prepare and coach preservice candidates and inservice teachers to be able to communicate for various audiences (policymakers, public officials, community members, classroom teachers, and parents).	Communicate assessment information to various audiences for accountability. They understand how assessment should be used for instructional purposes and demonstrate the ability to use it for the benefit of student growth and development. They can articulate to the public what makes up an effective assessment plan.

Inclusive Model of Reading

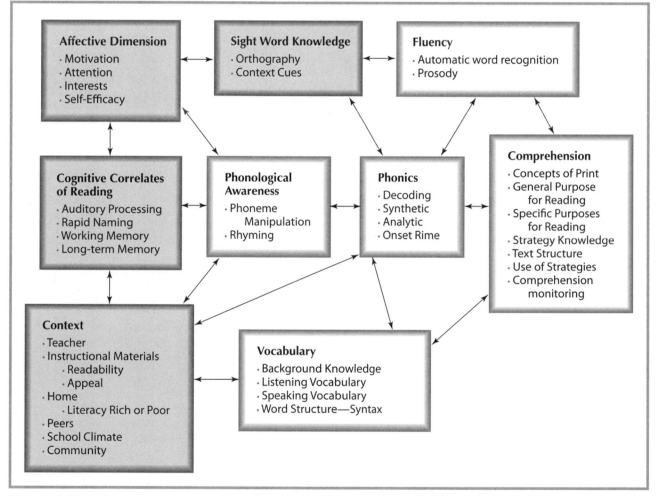

Note: Non-shaded boxes represent areas of reading identified by the National Reading Panel.

APPENDIX

C

Literacy Instruction Pie
with Overlay of Motivation

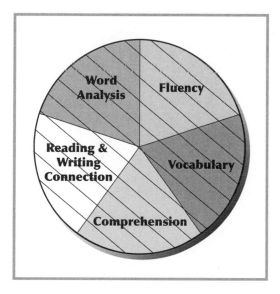

APPENDIX

D

Resources for Assessment and Instruction of Reading

General

Adams, M. (1990). *Beginning to read: Thinking and learning about print.* Cambridge, MA: MIT Press.

Allington, R. L. (2001). *What really matters for struggling readers. Designing research-based programs.* New York: Addison-Wesley Educational Publishers.

Armbruster, B. B., Lehr, F. & Osborn, J. (2001). *Put reading first: The research building blocks of teaching children to read.* Washington, DC: The Partnership for Reading.

Armbruster, B. B., Lehr, F. & Osborn, J. (2003). *A child becomes a reader* (2nd ed.). Washington, DC: The Partnership for Reading.

Barrentine, S. J. (Ed.). (1999). *Reading assessment. Principles and practices for elementary teachers,* 113–117. Newark, DE: International Reading Association.

Biancarosa, G. & Snow, C. E. (2004). *Reading next—A vision for action and research in middle and high school literacy: A report to Carnegie Corporation of New York.* Washington, DC: Alliance for Excellent Education.

Clay, M. M. (2000). *Running records for classroom teachers.* Portsmouth, NH: Heinemann.

Cunningham, P. M. (2005). *Phonics they use: Words for reading and writing* (4th ed). Boston, MA: Pearson Education.

Cunningham, P. M., Hall, D. P. & Sigmon, C. M. (1999). *The teacher's guide to the four blocks: A multimethod, multilevel framework for grades 1–3.* Greensboro, NC: Carson Dellosa.

Daly, E. J., III, Chafouleas, S. & Skinner, C. H. (2005). *Interventions for reading problems: Designing and evaluating effective strategies.* New York, NY: The Guilford Press.

Flanagan, D. P., Ortiz, S. O., Alfonso, V. C. & Mascolo, J. T. (2006). *The achievement test desk reference: A guide to learning disability identification* (2nd ed.). Hoboken, NJ: John Wiley & Sons.

Fountas, I. C. & Pinnell, G. S. (1996). *Guided reading: Good first teaching for all children.* Portsmouth, NH: Heinemann.

Fountas, I. C. & Pinnell, G. S. (2006). *The Fountas & Pinnell leveled book list, K–8* (2006–2008 Edition). Portsmouth, NH: Heinemann.

Henk, W. A. & Melnick, S. A. The reader self-perception scale (RSPS): A new tool for measuring how children feel about themselves as readers. *The Reading Teacher, 48*(6), 470–482.

Hudson, R. F., Lane, H. B. & Pullen, P. C. Reading fluency assessment and instruction: What, why and how? *The Reading Teacher, 58*(8), 702–714.

Inverneizzi, M. A., Landrum, T. J., Howell, J. L. & Warley, H. P. Toward the peaceful coexistence of test developers, policymakers, and teachers in an era of accountability. *The Reading Teacher, 58*(7), 610–618.

Kame'enui, E. J., Fuchs, L., Francis, D. J., Good, R., III, O'Connor, R. E., Simmons, D. C., Tindal, G. & Torgesen, J. K. (2006). The adequacy of tools for assessing reading competence: A framework and review. *Educational Researcher, 35*(4), 3–11.

Kame'enui, E., Simmons, D. C., Cornachione, C., Thompson-Hoffman, S., Ginsburg, A., Marcy, E., Mittleman, J., Irwin, J. & Baker, M. (N. D.) *A practical guide to reading assessments*. Newark, DE: International Reading Association.

Krashen, S. (2004). *The power of reading: Insights from the research*. Portsmouth, NH: Heinemann.

Leslie, L. & Caldwell, J. (2006). *Qualitative reading inventory* (4th ed.). Boston, MA: Pearson Education.

Mariotti, A. S. & Homan, S. P. (2005). *Linking reading assessment to instruction: An application worktext for elementary classroom teachers* (4th ed.). Mahwah, NJ: Erlbaum Associates.

McGill-Franzen, A. (2006). Kindergarten literacy. Matching assessment and instruction in kindergarten. New York: Scholastic.

McKenna, M. C. & Stahl, S. A. (2003). *Assessment for reading instruction*. New York: Guilford Press.

Miller, W. H. (2001). *The reading teacher's survival kit: Ready-to-use checklists, activities, and materials to help all students to become successful readers*. Boston, MA: Houghton Mifflin.

National Institute for Literacy. (2005). *What is scientifically based research?* Portsmouth, NH: RMC Research Corporation.

National Institute of Child Health and Human Development. (2000). *Report of the National Reading Panel: Teaching children to read* (NIH Publication No. 00–4769). Washington, DC: U.S. Government Printing Office.

Pavlak, S. A. (1985). *Informal tests for diagnosing specific reading problems*. West Nyack, NY: Parker Publishing.

Rasinski, T. V. & Padak, N. (2004). *Effective reading strategies: Teaching children who find reading difficult* (3rd ed.). Columbus, OH: Pearson Merrill Prentice Hall.

Rathvon, N. (2004). *Early reading assessment: A practitioner's handbook*. New York: Guilford Press.

Ruddell, R. B. (2002). *Teaching children to read and write. Becoming an effective literacy teacher* (3rd ed.). Boston: Allyn & Bacon.

Schumm, J. J. (Ed). (2006). *Reading assessment and instruction for all learners*. New York: Guilford Press.

Shaywitz, S. E. (2003). *Overcoming dyslexia. A new and complete science-based program for reading problems at any level*. New York: Alfred A. Knopf.

Stanovich, P. J. & Stanovich, K. E. (2003). *Using research and reason in education: How teachers can use scientifically based research to make curricular and instructional decisions*. Portsmouth, NH: RMC Research Corporation.

Strickland, D. S., Ganske, K. & Monroe, J. K (2002). *Supporting struggling readers and writers. Strategies for classroom intervention 3–6*. Portland, NM: Stenhouse Publishers.

Temple, C., Ogle, D., Crawford, A. & Freppon, P. (2005). *All children read. Teaching for literacy in today's diverse classrooms*. Boston: Pearson.

Walker, B. J. (2004). *Diagnostic teaching of reading: Techniques for instruction and assessment* (5th ed.). Upper Saddle River, NJ: Pearson Education.

Word Analyses

Adams, M. J., Foorman, B. R., Lundberg, I. & Beller, T. (1998). *Phonemic awareness in young children: A classroom curriculum*. Baltimore, MD: Paul H. Brookes Publishing.

Cunningham, P. M. & Hall, D. P. (1994). *Making words*. Parsipanny, NJ: Good Apple.

Greene, J. F. (1997). *Sounds and letters for readers and spellers: Phoneme awareness drills for teachers and speech/language pathologists*. Longmont, CO: Sopris West.

Hendricks, C. & Rinsky, L. A. (2007). *Teaching word recognition skills* (7th ed.). Upper Saddle River, NJ: Pearson Education.

Moats, L. C. (2005). *LETRS (Language essentials for teachers of reading and spelling)*. Longmont, CO: Sopris West.

Leu, D. J., Kinzer, C. K., Wilson, R. M. & Hall, M. (2006). *Phonics, phonemic awareness, and word analysis for teachers: An interactive tutorial* (8th ed.). Upper Saddle River, NJ: Pearson Education.

Fluency

Fountas, I. C. & Pinnell, G. S. (2006). *Teaching for comprehension and fluency*. Portsmouth, NH: Heinemann.

Rasinski, T. V. & Padak, N. (2005a). *Three-minute reading assessments: Word recognition, fluency & comprehension, grades 1–4*. New York: Teaching Resources.

Rasinski, T. V. & Padak, N. (2005b). *Three-minute reading assessments: Word recognition, fluency & comprehension, grades 4–8.* New York: Teaching Resources.

Stahl, S. A., (2004). What do we know about fluency? Findings of the National Reading Panel. In P. McCardle & V. Chhabra (Eds.). *The voice of evidence in reading research* (pp. 187–211). Baltimore, MD: Paul H. Brookes.

Vocabulary

Beck, I. L. & McKeown, M. G. (2001). Text talk: Capturing the benefits of read-aloud experiences for young children. *The Reading Teacher, 55*(1), 10–20.

Beck, I. L., McKeown, M. G. & Kucan, L. (2002). *Bringing words to life: Robust vocabulary instruction.* New York: Guilford Press.

Kamil, M. L. (2004). Vocabulary and comprehension instruction. In P. McCardle & V. Chhabra (Eds.). *The voice of evidence in reading research* (pp. 213–234). Baltimore, MD: Paul H Brookes.

Comprehension

Calkins, L. M. (2001). *The art of teaching reading.* New York: Longman.

See Kamil, M. L. (2004) in the **Vocabulary** section.

See Fountas, I. C. & Pinnell, G. S. (2006) in the **Fluency** section.

Reading/Writing

Calkins, L. M. (1983). *The art of teaching writing.* Portsmouth, NH: Heinemann.

Miller, W. H. (1995). *Alternative assessment techniques for reading and writing.* Normal, IL: Center for Applied Research in Education.

Rego, A. M. P. (2006). The alphabetic principle, phonics, and spelling. In Schumm, J. J. (Ed). *Reading assessment and instruction for all learners* (pp. 118–162). New York: Guilford Press.

Wooten, D. A. (2000). *Valued voices: An interdisciplinary approach to teaching and learning.* Newark, DE: International Reading Association.

Motivation

Guthrie, J. T. & Humenick, N. M. (2004). Motivating students to read: Evidence for classroom practices that increase reading motivation and achievement. In P. McCardle & V. Chhabra (Eds.). *The voice of evidence in reading research* (pp. 329–354). Baltimore, MD: Paul H. Brookes Publishing.

Special Education

Bos, C. S. & Vaughn, S. (2006). *Strategies for teaching students with learning and behavior problems* (6th ed.). Boston, MA: Pearson.

Bursuck, W. D. & Damer, M. (2007). *Reading instruction for students who are at risk or have disabilities.* Boston, MA: Pearson Education.

Daly, E. J., Chafouleas, S. & Skinner, C. H. (2005). Interventions for reading problems: Designing and evaluating effective strategies. New York: The Guilford Press.

Edyburn, D. L. (2006). Reading difficulties in the general education classroom: A taxonomy of text modification strategies. *Closing the Gap, 21,* 1–5.

Fletcher-Janex, E. & Reynolds, C. R. (Eds.). (2006). *The special education almanac.* Hoboken, NJ: John Wiley & Sons.

Gibb, G. S. & Dyches, T. T. (2007). *Guide to writing quality individualized education programs* (2nd ed.). Boston, MA: Pearson Education.

Overton, T. (2006). *Assessing learners with special needs: An applied approach.* (5th ed.). Upper Saddle River, NJ: Pearson Prentice Hall.

Reschly, D. J. & Grimes, J. P. (2002). Best practices in nondiscriminatory assessment. In A. Thomas & J. Grimes (Eds.). *Best practices in school psychology IV* (pp. 1337–1350). Bethesda, MD: National Association of School Psychologists.

English Language Learners

Freeman, Y. S. & Freeman, D. E. (1997). *Teaching reading and writing in Spanish in the bilingual classroom.* Portsmouth, NH: Heinemann.

Helman, L. A. (2005). Using literacy assessment results to improve teaching for English-language learners. *The Reading Teacher, 58*(7), 668–677.

Peregoy, S. F. & Boyle, O. F. (1993). *Reading, writing & learning in ESL: A resource book for K–8 teachers.* White Planes, NY: Longman.

Peregoy, S. F. & Boyle, O. F. (2004). *Reading, writing & learning in ESL: A resource book for K–12 teachers* (4th ed.). Needham Heights, MA: Allyn & Bacon.

Adults

Kruidenier, J. (2002). *Research-based principles for adult basic education reading instruction.* Washington, DC: National Institute for Literacy.

McShane, S. (2005). *Applying research in reading instruction for adults: First steps for teachers.* Washington, DC: National Institute for Literacy.

Online Resources

Adult Reading Components Study (ARCS)
www.ncsall.net/fileadmin/resources/research/brief_strucker2.pdf

The British Dyslexia Association
www.bdadyslexia.org.uk/

Council for Exceptional Children
www.cec.sped.org/

International Dyslexia Association
www.cec.sped.org//AM/Template.cfm?Section=Home

International Reading Association
www.reading.org/

Learning Disabilities Association of America
www.ldaamerica.org/

National Center on Student Progress Monitoring (Review of Progress Monitoring Tools)
www.studentprogress.org/chart/chart.asp#

National Center for the Study of Adult Learning and Literacy
www.ncsall.net/?id=25

National Institute for Literacy
www.nifl.gov/

Northwest Evaluation Association
www.nwea.org/

Southwestern Educational Development Laboratory
www.sedl.org/

What Works Clearinghouse
www.whatworks.ed.gov/

APPENDIX
E

Instructional Tips

General

Provide adequate time for reading and writing every day.

Provide 90 minutes on average of reading per day (Allington 2006).

Provide 30–45 minutes on average of writing per day (Allington 2006).

Provide access to lots of books and other materials students *can* and *want to* read.

Allow students to have choices about what they read.

Provide opportunities for students to read with peers and talk about their reading with peers.

Collect and use assessment data to determine student strengths, weaknesses, and interests and to target instruction appropriately.

Provide instruction in all areas of reading.

Provide a balance between authentic reading-writing activities and specific skills-building instruction.

Word Analyses

Use a sequential and systematic approach balanced with embedded practice to learn words.

Use predictable books with young children.

Teach young children or beginning readers to count or clap words in a phrase, syllables in a word, and finally, phonemes in a word.

Do rhyming activities, sing songs, tell nursery rhymes, and play games with young children.

Use students' names as a basis for teaching letters and sounds.

Play word games, such as *change a hen to a fox,* and lead students to change *hen* to *fox* by changing one letter of the word at a time (Cunningham 2005).

Use word walls (posted lists of words) to build automatic word recognition.

Use high-frequency words in the word wall.

Use words that can be decoded analytically in the word wall (words with common rimes).

For higher grades, use words from subject area texts in word walls.

Do "Making Words" activities—guide students to make small words from bigger words (Cunningham and Hall 1994).

Teach common patterns in words by having students identify and create rhyming words.

Teach phonics by analogy—students use words they know to decode new words.

Teach six syllable types—(c = consonant, v = vowel):

Closed—cvc (*cat*)

Open—cv (*go*)

Double vowel—cvvc (*read*)

Vowel-consonant-E—vce (*write*)

R-controlled—cv + r (*car*)

Consonant-le—C + le (*candle*) (Bos and Vaughn 2006)

Teach meanings of prefixes, suffixes, and word endings and practice applying them.

Fluency

Provide opportunities for choral reading—have a group read together focusing on inflection and rate.

Be sure text is at the appropriate level, neither too difficult nor too easy.

Have students take turns reading with a partner and focusing on inflection and rate.

Provide opportunities for older, struggling students to read easy-level books to younger students.

Provide opportunities for students to reread text to meet a set standard of rate and accuracy.

Allow students to audiotape and time themselves while reading.

Use oral reading fluency norms (in Figure 3.7) as a general guideline to set expectations.

Model fluent reading; read the first few pages of a text, then let students read the rest of the text.

Provide opportunities for echo reading; read a passage and let students read it immediately afterward.

Vocabulary

Discuss the meaning of words before reading text.

Provide opportunities for students to use words in various contexts.

Relate meaning of new words to familiar words.

Teach meanings of prefixes, suffixes, and word endings and practice applying them.

Provide opportunities for students to encounter new words repeatedly in text.

Guide students to determine meaning of vocabulary from text rather then giving them definitions.

Provide opportunities for students to work in groups (such as working with a partner or peer tutor) to learn vocabulary.

Use a variety of methods to promote active engagement (Kamil 2004).

Allow students to act out definitions, make mental pictures, use the words in writing, and attend to context cues to infer meanings (Kamil 2004).

Use vocabulary from children's literature to introduce and use new, more sophisticated words.

Create examples and nonexamples of a given word meaning and have students determine which is which.

Teach students a process for determining meanings of words in context.

Teach vocabulary directly and through multiple, incidental opportunities (wide ranging independent reading, writing, and classroom discussion).

Teach students to use dictionaries and computer resources efficiently and effectively.

Comprehension

Teach young children or beginning readers to guess the covered word in a phrase or sentence.

Teach students to predict what will happen in text.

Teach story structure—teach students how to ask what, why, when, where, who, and the like.

Introduce new reading material by reading and discussing a portion.

Teach comprehension monitoring—students ask, "Does this make sense?"

Use cooperative learning groups to teach reading.

Use reciprocal teaching strategies: predicting, clarifying, questioning, and summarizing (Palincsar and Brown 1984).

Use graphic organizers to aid comprehension. Use teacher-generated graphic organizers to introduce a story or subject-area content. Teach students to develop their own graphic organizer, such as story maps, during and after reading.

Use well-designed questions to promote comprehension.

Teach students to generate and answer their own questions as they read.

Teach students to summarize what they read.

Teach students to use more than one strategy simultaneously to improve comprehension.

Reading/Writing

Teach the same words in reading and spelling.

Provide opportunities for frequent authentic writing during each week.

Provide some extended time for authentic writing a couple of times per week.

Provide time for students to share their writing with peers.

Teach students to use a timeline to develop background knowledge and relate what they read to what they already know (Wooten 2002).

Use literature as a catalyst for student writing.

Use student interests and experiences as catalysts for writing.

Teach students to use sticky notes to mark passages of interest and to write brief notes they can build upon in writing and discussion.

Motivation

Don't assume that students can read grade-level material.

Interview students to determine their interests.

Provide access to a wide variety and types and levels of reading materials.

Match reading content with student interest.

Encourage strong readers to try new genres.

Teach students to self-select books of appropriate interest and reading level.

Teach students the five-finger rule for determining book difficulty (see Chapter 3).

Provide access to lots of books and other materials students *can* and *want to* read.

Involve parents and other family members in literacy experiences.

Provide ample time for a wide range of reading.

Foster students' reading self-efficacy.

Provide opportunities for students to read and write together.

Provide opportunities for buddy reading (when older and younger students read together).

Glossary

Accommodation   a support or service to help students fully access instructional content and demonstrate what they know; learning expectations in an accommodation are not altered

Achievement tests   tests used to assess one or more academic areas

Acquired alexia   loss of the ability to read after a stroke

Action research   inquiry or investigation in an educational or other applied setting used to inform one's practice

Adaptive behavior   ability to communicate, to engage others socially, to take care of hygiene and dressing needs, and in general, to function independently

Adaptive testing   efficient testing strategy that uses probes to determine best starting (basal) and stopping (ceiling) points

Adequate yearly progress (AYP)   consistent with the No Student Left Behind Act of 2001, each state is required to document the progress of subgroups of students in achieving state mandated standards

Adult basic education   delivery of instruction to the population of adults who exhibit low literacy levels in English and do not hold a high school diploma

Age-equivalent scores   scores calculated by averaging the raw scores of students in a sample at a particular age level and thereby providing an approximation of the age-level performance of students who earn similar scores in the future

Aimline   a line on a curriculum-based measurement (CBM) graph showing typical skill acquisition rate and development

Alphabetic principle   expresses the notion that there are systematic and predictable relationships between written letters and spoken words

Alphabetics   a broad term encompassing phonemic awareness and phonics

Alternate forms reliability   consistency of scores between administrations of parallel or equivalent forms of a test at the same time to the same individuals

Anecdotal   written or oral observations of student behaviors

Assessment   a broad range of activities, including observation and testing; collected data are used to monitor progress and plan instruction

Attention deficit hyperactivity disorder (ADHD)   a disorder characterized primarily by impulsivity, excessive activity, and/or inattention

Auditory memory   the ability to recall content previously presented orally

Auditory processing   includes phonemic awareness and enables a person to master phonics

Autism   one of the IDEA disability categories characterized by poor social interaction and communication skills, typically assumed to be caused by a neurological disorder

Automaticity   typically refers to reading a word with little or no conscious effort, although it may reference other skills

Automatic word recognition   quick and effortless recognition of words; sometimes used as a synonym for *sight word recognition*

Awareness   information that is in consciousness

Balanced literacy   a broad reading approach that includes many opportunities for students to read at their instructional level, practice phonics acquisition and other word attack skills, and write; in addition, it includes use of explicit fluency and comprehension strategies that may be more effective than approaches focusing heavily on either phonics or whole language approaches

Basal series   sequential, interrelated materials, including books, designed to build fundamental reading skills

Basal   point in the test below which a student should be able to answer all items correctly

Baseline   brief period before the introduction of an intervention during which data are collected

Basic reading skills   phonetic decoding and sight-word recognition

Basic writing skills   includes punctuation, grammar, editing, and proofreading skills

Benchmarks   established expectations of students' progress in various grades and for various times of the year

Blends   combinations of two or more consonants in a syllable that maintain the sounds of each

Case study   a descriptive report that focuses on only one student and integrates information gleaned from assessment with relevant educational, medical, and developmental history

Ceiling   point in the test above which a student likely will miss all items

Cerebral palsy   a neurologically based disability characterized by inability to control muscle movements

Choral reading   reading together with the teacher or another model

Cloze   type of reading comprehension assessment in which a student must supply missing words from a text from which the teacher has deleted every *nth* word

Code-based   refers to reading programs that emphasize mastery of the sound-symbol relationship

Comprehension   process of constructing meaning from what is read and relies on all reading subskills

Comprehensive evaluation   compilation of various assessment data collected from numerous sources, usually used to make a special education eligibility decision

Concurrent validity   type of construct validity that addresses the relationship between the test of interest and other established measures of the construct under scrutiny

Connected text   written content tied by meaning

Consolidated word recognition   the ability of a reader to recognize chunks or groups of letters automatically

Construct validity   the extent to which a test assesses some phenomenon of interest

Content validity   the extent to which a text reflects some well-defined domain of knowledge

Contextual analysis   use of context to derive meaning

Context cues   using surrounding words and knowledge of the meanings of those words to identify an unknown word

Context processor   one of four major components of Adams' Cognitive Model of Reading that is primarily responsible for determining how a piece of information relates to the context surrounding it to create meaningfulness

Cooperative learning   placing students in working groups to help achieve a set goal with a common payoff

Core program   the overall reading curriculum used by general education classes in a particular school or district

Correlation coefficient   a number ranging from −1.00 to +1.00 that is obtained from a set of calculations to represent the relationship between two variables

Correlational studies   a popular type of scientific study that relies on observation (but not manipulation) of two or more variables that co-occur; typically relies on a calculation of a correlational coefficient to determine strength of the relationship between variables but does not allow cause-and-effect statements

Criterion-referenced   assessments that tell how well a student has mastered a specific skill or objective

Current form preparation   students practice test-taking on items taken directly from a current instrument

Curriculum-based measurement (CBM)   teacher-made assessments measuring mastery of specific instructional objectives, often administered at the end of an instructional unit or period

Data-Based Problem-Solver Model   a four-step process used as a guide to address educational dilemmas; includes problem identification, problem-solution plan development, problem-solution implementation, and problem-solution evaluation

Declarative knowledge   knowing about something or knowing that something is the case

Decode   the process of associating written symbols (e.g., letters) with sounds to create words

Dependent variable   a variable that may change based on the manipulation of another "independent" variable

Developmental version   original edition of a test that is piloted or field tested, then analyzed and edited

Diagnostic tests   tests that provide in-depth information usually about one academic area

Direct instruction   instruction that involves teacher and student interaction, teacher provides modeling and corrective feedback; sometimes used as a synonym for *explicit* instruction; some direct instruction curriculum programs are delivered with a script

Disaggregate   data describing one or more groups taken from a larger base of data

Distracters   in the context of a multiple choice exam, options that are plausible but incorrect

Document literacy   ability to search, comprehend, and use noncontinuous text sources such as job applications, payroll forms, maps, tables, and labels

Dyslexia   a disorder presumed to be neurological in origin characterized primarily by difficulties with accurate/fluent word recognition, decoding, and spelling

Echo reading   oral reading done by following right after the teacher or after a model

Effect size   a measure of the mean difference between the two groups in standard deviation units

Elkonin blocks   small manipulatives that represent sounds

Emergent literacy   a rudimentary awareness that print can communicate meaning and that more advanced literacy abilities are required to extract sophisticated meaning from material; characterized by learning to recognize and say the alphabet, manipulating sounds in words, and understanding the purpose and function of writing

Emotional disturbance   one of the IDEA disability categories; characterized by difficulty learning, difficulty building or maintaining relationships with others, inappropriate behaviors or feelings, an overall mood of unhappiness or depression, or a tendency to develop physical symptoms or fears associated with personal or school problems

Empirical data   information collected by direct observation

Engagement   purposeful and active involvement in a given activity

English language learners (ELL)   students whose first language is not English

Error analysis   technique for determining patterns or reasons for student errors or difficulties

Errors per minute   the number of mistakes a student makes in one minute of oral reading

Etiology   study of the causes of diseases or problems, including reading difficulties

Explicit instruction   an overt and planned teaching strategy in which a teacher models the application of a strategy, explains the procedure directly, provides guided practice, and helps students practice until they can apply the strategy themselves

Expository   nonfiction text

Field testing   the process of administering a developmental version of a particular assessment to a small sample of individuals to determine item functioning; synonymous with *pilot testing*

Floor effects   insufficient number of easy items on a test

Fluency ability to read efficiently, accurately, easily, and with appropriate inflection, rhythm, intonation, and expression

Fluid reasoning the ability to perceive and understand relationships among words, ideas, and spatial entities

Frequency count tally of the number of specified behaviors, usually within a specified timeframe

Full alphabetic coding awareness of each (and all) letters within a word

Functional literacy the ability to use routine reading materials effectively, such as newspapers, brochures, and instructional materials

Generalized test-taking preparation simulation of test administration using a variety of test-preparation strategies to fit a variety of test formats

Genres areas of literature, such as action, romance, and poetry

Grade-equivalent scores scores calculated by averaging raw test scores of students in a sample at particular grade levels, then using these averages to provide an approximation of the grade-level performance of students who subsequently take the test and score at one of those levels

Grapheme letters or combinations of letters

Graphic organizers pictorial depictions of relationships between concepts that help illustrate ideas or concepts and their interrelationships

Guided reading a multistep, teacher-directed reading instruction strategy that focuses on comprehension mastery

Helper-supplied word a word provided by a helper when the reader pauses too long

Hesitation a pause in oral reading that may or may not be long enough to force the helper to supply the word; after three to five seconds, the word is typically provided

High-stakes testing typically refers to group-administered, norm-referenced testing used for accountability of students, teachers, schools, systems, states, and so on; the term also refers to individualized tests used to establish eligibility criteria for special education placement

Implicit strategies that rely on providing nonsalient cues to novice readers, cues that might help them "discover" the importance of structure embedded in text types

Independent variable refers to an activity or intervention that is changed (manipulated) in order to determine whether the manipulation produces a positive effect on another variable such as academic progress

Individual education program (IEP) an instructional plan developed, reviewed, and agreed upon annually by a multidisciplinary team as required by law for students in special education; it is based on relative strengths and diagnosed needs and includes present levels of performance, long-term goals and short-term objectives, criteria for measuring achievement, amount and type of special education and participation in general education, appropriate services, curricular modifications, and dates of initiation and duration of services

Inferential comprehension knowledge gained indirectly by using text-based context cues

Informal reading inventories nonstandardized classroom assessment technique used to evaluate reading rate, types of errors or miscues, and word recognition; used to identify appropriate levels of instruction for students

Information processing model typically, a visual depiction of a set of relationships that denotes how information from the environment enters the sense organs, gets evaluated by the brain, and ultimately guides responses

Insertion a word or phrase that is read but not actually present in the text

Intellectually gifted elevated ability, to the point of requiring special instructional services from educators; typically defined by high academic achievement, such as the 96th percentile or better, and cognitive performance, such as an IQ score of 130 or better

Intelligence   cognitive aptitude required to reason, understand, learn, visualize, problem-solve, and remember

Intelligence quotient (IQ)   a number obtained by cognitive testing used to represent general cognitive functioning and usually expressed as a standard score with a mean of 100 and standard deviation of 15

Internal consistency reliability   consistency between and among items, often determined by comparing scores on two halves of the same test

Inter-rater reliability   consistency of scoring between or among different examiners or raters

Inter-individual comparisons   comparisons of scores between or among students

Intra-individual   within the person

Intra-individual comparison   comparison of scores of the same student over time or through situations

Intra-rater reliability   consistency over time by the same rater

Lack of prosody   reading without regard for inflection and punctuation, such as commas, periods, and question marks

Learning disabilities   one of the IDEA disability categories; characterized by impairment of one's basic psychological processes involved in understanding or using language and resulting in problems in listening, speaking, reading, writing, spelling, or performing mathematical calculations

Leveled readers   books that have been assigned difficulty level based on specified criteria such as sophistication of vocabulary and length

Leveled   refers to reading materials that have been analyzed and categorized according to levels of difficulty and readability

Lexile   score typically ranging from 200 to 1700 that reflects a student's reading level across all grades and ages

Listening vocabulary   type of oral vocabulary consisting of words a student understands when he or she hears them

Logographic   referring to a customary abbreviation or symbol for a common word or phrase

Long-term memory   one of the three components of the memory system; all the information one has stored from experience

Maze   type of reading comprehension assessment in which the teacher has deleted every *nth* word and the student must supply missing words by choosing from a list of possibilities

Meaning-based   refers to reading strategies that rely on discovery learning and whole-language approaches

Meaning processor   one of four major components of Adams' Cognitive Model of Reading that is primarily responsible for determining the meaning of text

Medial letters   letters in the middle of a word

Mediated   process of thinking through a series of steps

Mental retardation   one of the IDEA disability categories; characterized by significantly subaverage general intellectual functioning and deficits in adaptive behavior that negatively affect the student's educational performance, usually defined by IQ scores below 70 with concomitantly low performance in adaptive behavior

Metacognition   ability to consider one's own thinking in order to plan and monitor progress

Miscue analysis   type of error analysis in which a teacher counts the number of times a student makes particular reading errors such as omissions, insertions, substitutions, reversals, helper-supplied words, repetitions, lack of prosody, hesitations, mispronunciations, or self-corrections

Miscues   oral reading errors that are unexpected responses a reader makes to text

Mispronunciation incorrect decoding (sounding out) of a word

Modification a change made to a curriculum or to instruction to help a student participate and make progress in the general curriculum; learning expectations in modifications are altered

Morpheme the smallest unit of meaning in a word

Morphemic analysis deriving meaning by breaking words down into their smallest meaningful parts

Multitiered model of instruction instruction that becomes increasingly intense over time because of inadequate progress

Narrative text fiction

Nondiscriminatory comprehensive educational evaluation a provision of IDEA requiring that assessments to determine special education eligibility must be culturally fair and nonbiased

Norm reference to a peer group

Norm group a sample of individuals upon which a test is initially standardized; scores of examinees who subsequently take the test can be compared to scores obtained by peers in the norm group

Norm-referenced tests refers to comparisons of the performance of one student (or a group of students) to the performance of peers in order to determine relative levels of achievement, intelligence, personality, and so on

Omission skipping a word during oral reading

Operationalization definition of a construct in measurable terms

Oral vocabulary the words a person uses when speaking or understands when listening

Orthographic processor one of four major components of Adams' Cognitive Model of Reading and is primarily responsible for receiving information from the environment in the form of print

Orthography system of printed symbols or marks (such as letters) that represents a spoken language

Partner reading reading strategy whereby students are paired with partners to monitor each other's reading and to help each other when necessary

Peer-reviewed journals professional publications in which the published articles have undergone a thorough (and typically blind) review process during which numerous experts determine the quality, reliability, and acceptability of the articles

Percentile ranks numbering that conveys the relative standing of a student when compared to others in the same grade (or at the same age) by identifying the proportion or percentage of students who took the test and performed worse

Phonemic awareness the ability to appreciate differences in individual speech sounds

Phonics the knowledge of the relationship between sounds and letters

Phonological awareness broad term that includes phonemic awareness and refers to the general ability to determine similarities and differences in sounds

Phonological processor one of four major components of Adams' Cognitive Model of Reading that is primarily responsible for receiving information from the environment in speech or sounds

Pilot testing the process of administering the developmental version of a particular test to a small sample of individuals to determine the quality of items; synonymous with *field testing*

Portfolio collection of work samples, typically used to document progress over time

Portfolio assessment informal classroom assessment technique consisting of a collection of authentic student work and records of student progress; used to document a student's accomplishments or development over time

Practice effect improvement in scores resulting from familiarity with specific test content because of previous testing

Predictable text stories in which certain phrases are repeated

Predictive validity   the extent to which a test predicts success on some variable of interest

Previous form preparation   students practice test-taking with items from old, out-of-print versions of a test currently being used

Primer   early first-grade-level reading material

Problem of the match   using a student's current level of performance to determine how best to match the curriculum to the student's entering skills

Procedural knowledge   knowing how to do something; in reading, knowing how to engage the processes necessary to extract meaning from printed text

Processing speed   the time required to attend and respond to simple task demands

Progress monitoring   routine assessment of a student's progress on certain key indicators, which may be compared to the typical progress of students in the same grade

Prose literacy   ability to search, comprehend, and use continuous text sources such as newspapers, brochures, and instructional materials

Prosody   reading with inflection; raising and lowering one's voice based on whether one is reading a sentence or question and pausing appropriately at punctuation marks

Psychometric   a reference to the branch of measurement that deals with the design, administration, and interpretation of tests

Qualitative study   a scientific study that requires researchers to interview participants in order to obtain their perspectives about some event or process

Quantitative literacy   ability to identify and perform computations required to, for example, balance a checkbook, calculate tips, or use numbers embedded in printed orders

Quasi-experimental study   a type of scientific study that relies on evaluating the result of manipulating or varying some intervention or treatment between or among existing (intact) groups of individuals

Rapid automatic naming   the rapid naming of letters, words, and objects

Raw score   representation of the number of questions correctly answered on a given test

Reading vocabulary   the words a student knows and understands as he or she reads a text

Reading wars   an ongoing debate among educators about how best to teach reading

Reason-based practices   using systematic hypothesis testing to solve problems

Receptive vocabulary   ability to understand the meaning of words when presented orally

Reciprocal teaching   a teaching strategy in which a teacher models and instructs students to ask questions, summarize, clarify, and predict what will come next in text

Recoding   decoding a word based on its phonological cues

Reliability   the extent to which a test yields consistent scores; also known as *true* or *error-free variance*

Repetition   a word repeated unnecessarily during oral reading

Response to intervention (RTI)   a tiered model of educational instruction that requires more intensive intervention when a student fails to make expected progress

Retelling   reciting the events, main ideas, and some details of a story in chronological order

Reversal   a change in the printed word order during oral reading

Rimes   high-frequency spelling patterns, such as /an/

Rubric   scoring system that uses a prescribed set of criteria to evaluate student work

Running records   informal classroom assessment technique requiring a teacher to listen to and score student's oral reading (errors) according to a prescribed set of rules

Same-format preparation   students practice test-taking by responding only to items that represent the content of the actual test and mirror the format of the items from the test

Scaffold   structure of knowledge characterized by increasingly sophisticated connections among content and concepts

Scientifically based reading instruction   methods and strategies of reading instruction that have demonstrated effectiveness based on well-conducted research

Scientifically-based research   rigorous research that can be used to guide teaching practices, usually found in peer-reviewed journals, is corroborated by other studies, is representative of a consensus among experts, and is supported by related and connected studies

Screening tests   brief tests that typically provide minimal assessment of some construct; used to determine whether additional evaluation is necessary

Section 504   a "shorthand" reference to the Section 504 of the Rehabilitation Act, which prohibits entities receiving federal funds from discriminating against individuals with disabilities (because of their disabilities)

Self-correction   rereading a word or phrase a second time within three to five seconds to eliminate an error

Self-efficacy   an individual's beliefs about his or her ability to perform successfully

Short-term memory   one of three components of the memory system; rote recall without transformation of content

Sight vocabulary   the words a student can read automatically

Sight word recognition   quick and effortless recognition of words; sometimes uses as a synonym for *automatic word recognition*

Single-subject design study   type of scientific study using only one student and requires the teacher to vary systematically instruction and to monitor the effects of that variation

Slope   the element of a line graph that shows the rate of change between two variables, typically shown by the steepness of the line

Socioeconomic status (SES)   an individual's position in society based on his or her education level and income (and other factors)

Speaking vocabulary   a type of oral vocabulary that consists of words a person knows how to use when speaking

Speech-language impairment   one of the IDEA disability categories; characterized by a communication disorder, such as stuttering (or other impaired articulation), deficient language usage, or voice production, which adversely affects educational performance

Standard error of measure   a statistic that reflects the band of error around a given score

Standard deviation   the typical amount of variation from the mean in a set of data

Standard nine   the root words that are combined to make the term *stanine*, which expresses the entire range of scores by dividing the distribution of scores into nine categories

Standard score   derived score that is the result of converting raw scores into standard deviation units (z-scores) and that may be converted to a scale with a set mean and standard deviation, such as the IQ scale

Standardization version   the edition of a test that has been field tested and edited and will be used to determine performance of an entire population on some construct of interest

Standardized assessment   testing using a norm-referenced instrument

Standardized   refers to assessments that are administered in the same manner every time (often according to a script); typically, standardized procedures are used to obtain norm-referenced data

Story map   specific type of graphic organizer used to show the sequence of events and structure of a story

Story structure   elements of a story such as character and plot

Substitution   a word that replaces another during oral reading

Subvocalize   saying words silently to oneself as one reads

Summarization   the act of condensing what has been read by deciding what is most important, identifying the main ideas, making generalizations, and paraphrasing

Sustained silent reading (SSR)   extended period in which students choose and read books silently

Syntax   the function of a word or group of words in a sentence

Systematic instruction   teaching content and skills in a prescribed order from less to more complex and sophisticated

Table of specifications   visual summary of the number of test items assessing each category in a particular test; synonym for *test blueprint*

Task analyze   identifying the components of a specific task and organizing them into teachable parts

Teaching to the test   a phenomenon that occurs when educators teach content and test format specifically to reflect content covered on an upcoming test

Test bias   when scores from a test provide a systematic advantage to a particular group or subgroup based on irregularities in test content, administration, or interpretation

Test blueprint   a visual summary of the number of items assessing particular categories on a test synonym for *table of specifications*

Test protocols   student response sheets, test booklets, or record forms

Testing   obtaining a sample of behavior used to determine level of mastery of content or skills

Test-retest reliability   consistency between administrations of the same test twice to the same individuals within a relatively short period of time

Think-aloud   use of questions that prompt a student to stop during reading and describe the thought processes engaged

Three-tier model of instruction   a specific example of a multitiered model of instruction increases in intensity and time along the three tiers depending on student progress

Transactional view   a philosophy of reading instruction that emphasizes the importance of the context in which reading occurs, deemphasizes the within-the-reader variables, and recognizes a wide variety of normal variability in reading skills

Treatment validity   the extent to which a test yields information that informs instruction directly

True experimental study   most powerful type of study used to determine cause and effect; requires random assignment to groups and manipulation of an independent variable (to assess the effect that manipulation has on the dependent variable)

Varied-format preparation   students practice test-taking by responding to items that represent the content of the actual test using a variety of item formats

Visual memory   the ability to recall content previously presented by sight

Vocabulary   the store of individual words that a person knows and understands

Wait to fail   in education, the phrase refers to the time lag necessitated by use of a method of determining a learning disability that requires a significant discrepancy between intellectual ability (e.g., IQ) and a particular measure of achievement, where achievement is lower than the IQ

Whole language   approach to reading that focuses on the idea that learning to read happens naturally as students are exposed to language and reading

Word families   sets of words with common structural elements, such as rimes

Words correct per minute (wcpm)   the number of words a student can read in one minute, minus errors and miscues

Working memory   one of the three components of the memory system in which previously presented information is held and transformed

z score   a score expressed in standard deviation units with a mean of 0 and a standard deviation of 1

References

Abrams, L. M., & Mohn, R. S. (2007). *Understanding research student activities for Slavin: Educational research in an age of accountability.* Boston, MA: Pearson.

Accelerated Reader (2006). Renaissance Learning. Retrieved June 4, 2007, from www.renlearn.com/ar/default.htm

Adams, M. (1990). *Beginning to read: Thinking and learning about print.* Cambridge, MA: MIT Press.

Adams, M., & Treadway, J. (2000). *Informing reading/writing instruction in grades K–3 through assessment.* Workshop presented to the annual convention of the National Association of School Psychologists, New Orleans, LA.

Adams, M. J., & Huggins, A.W.F. (1985). The growth of children's sight vocabulary: A quick test with educational and theoretical implications. *Reading Research Quarterly, 20,* 262–281.

AIMSweb. (2007). San Antonio, TX: Harcourt Assessment. Retrieved June 4, 2007, from www.aimsweb.com

Allington, R. L. (1994). What's special about special programs for children who find learning to read difficult? *Journal of Reading Behavior, 26,* 1–21.

Allington, R. L. (2001). *What really matters for struggling readers. Designing research-based programs.* New York: Addison-Wesley Educational Publishers.

Allington, R. L. (2002). *Big brother and the national reading curriculum. How ideology trumped evidence.* Portsmouth, NH: Heinemann.

Allington, R. L. (2005). The other five pillars of reading instruction. *Reading Today, 22*(6), 3.

Allington, R. L. (2006). *What really matters for struggling readers. Designing research-based programs* (2nd ed.). New York: Addison-Wesley Educational Publishers, Inc.

Allington, R. L., & Cunningham, P. M. (2002). *Schools that work: Where all children read and write* (2nd ed.). Boston, MA: Allyn & Bacon.

American College Test (ACT). Retrieved June 4, 2007, from www.act.org/

American Educational Research Association, American Psychological Association, and National Council on Measurement in Education. (1999). *Standards for educational and psychological testing.* Washington, DC: American Educational Research Association.

Anderson, J. R. (1995). *Learning and memory.* New York: John Wiley & Sons.

Anderson, R. C., Heibert, E. H., Scott, J. A., & Wilkinson, I. A. G. (1985). *Becoming a nation of readers: The report of the Commission on Reading.* Washington, DC: National Institute of Education.

Armbruster, B. B., & Osborn, J. (2001). *Put reading first: The research building blocks of teaching children to read.* Washington, DC: The Partnership for Reading.

Arter, J. A., & Spandel, V. (1992). *Using portfolios of student work in instruction and assessment.* Educational measurement: Issues and practice, *11*(1), 36–44.

Baddeley, A. D. (1979). Working memory and reading. In P. Kolers, E. Wrolstad, & H. Bouma (Eds.), *Processing of visible language.* (Vol. 1). New York: Plenum Press.

Badian, N. A. (1988). The prediction of good and poor reading before kindergarten entry: A nine-year follow-up. *Journal of Learning Disabilities, 21*(2), 98–103.

Bandura, A. (1977). Self-efficacy: Toward a unifying theory of behavioral change. *Psychological Review, 84,* 191–215.

Bandura, A. (1978). Reflections on self-efficacy. *Advances in Behaviour Research and Therapy, 1,* 237–269.

Bandura, A. (1986). *Social foundations of thought and action.* Englewood Cliffs, NJ: Prentice Hall.

Batsche, G. M., & Knoff, H. M. (1995). Best practices in linking assessment to intervention. In A. Thomas & J. Grimes (Eds.), *Best practices in school psychology III* (pp. 569–585). Bethesda, MD: National Association of School Psychologists.

Beck, M. D. (n.d.). Review of the tests of adult basic education, forms 7 and 8. In *Buros Mental Measurements Yearbook, 13.* Retrieved June 5, 2007, from http://web5.silverplatter.com.proxy.lib.utk.edu:90/webspirs/start.ws?customer=c14360anddatabases=S(YB)

Beck, I. L., McKeown, M. G., & Kucan, L. (2002). *Bringing words to life: Robust vocabulary instruction.* New York: Guilford Press.

Bell, S. M. (1984). *Is minimum competency testing a must?* Unpublished manuscript, The University of Tennessee.

Bell, S. M., McCallum, R. S., Burton, B., Gray, R., Windingstad, S., & Moore, J. (2006). Concurrent validity of the test of silent word reading fluency. *Assessment for Effective Intervention, 31*(3), 1–9.

Berninger, V. W., Thalberg, S. P., DeBruyn, L., & Smith, R. (1987). Preventing reading disabilities by assessing and remediating phonemic skills. *School Psychology Review, 16,* 554–565.

Betts, E. A. (1946). *Foundations of reading instruction.* New York: American Book Company.

Bond, G. L., & Dykstra, R. (1967). The cooperative research program in first-grade reading instruction. *Reading Research Quarterly, 2,* 5–142.

Bos, C. S., & Vaughn, S. (2006). *Strategies for teaching students with learning and behavior problems* (6th ed.). Boston, MA: Pearson Education.

Bracken, B. A., & McCallum, R. S. (1998). *The Universal Nonverbal Intelligence Test.* Itasca, IL: Riverside Publishing Company.

Brigance, A. H. (1994). *BRIGANCE® life skills inventory.* N. Billerica, MA: CURRICULUM ASSOCIATES®.

Brigance, A. H. (1995). *BRIGANCE® employability skills inventory.* N. Billerica, MA: CURRICULUM ASSOCIATES®.

Brigance, A. H. (1999). *BRIGANCE® comprehensive inventory of basic skills—revised.* N. Billerica, MA: CURRICULUM ASSOCIATES®.

Brigance, A. H. (2004). *BRIGANCE® inventory of early development* (2nd ed.). N. Billerica, MA: CURRICULUM ASSOCIATES®.

Brigance, A. H. (2005). *BRIGANCE® K and I screen.* N. Billerica, MA: CURRICULUM ASSOCIATES®.

Brigance, A. H. (2005). *BRIGANCE® preschool screen.* N. Billerica, MA: CURRICULUM ASSOCIATES®.

Brigance, A. H. (2007). *BRIGANCE® assessment of basic skills—revised, Spanish edition.* N. Billerica, MA: CURRICULUM ASSOCIATES®.

British Dyslexia Association. Retrieved from June 4, 2007, from www.bdadyslexia.org.uk/

Brown, C. L. (2004). Reducing the over-referral of culturally and linguistically diverse students (CLD) for language disabilities. *National Association of Bilingual Education Journal of Research and Practice, 2*(1), 225–243.

Brown, L. (2003). Test of nonverbal intelligence: A language-free measure of cognitive ability. In R. S. McCallum (Ed.), *Handbook of nonverbal assessment* (pp. 191–221). New York: Kluwer.

Brozo, W. (2002). *To be a boy, to be a reader: Engaging teen and preteen boys in active literacy.* Newark, DE: International Reading Association.

Brunsman, B., & Shanahan, T. A. (n.d.) Review of the dynamic indicators of basic early literacy skills. In *Buros Mental Measurements Yearbook,* 16. Retrieved June 5, 2007, from http://web5.silverplatter.com.proxy.lib.utk.edu:90/webspirs/start.ws?customer=c14360anddatabases=S(YB)

Burton, B., Below, J., Windingstad, S., & Gray, R. (2007). *Informal and formal reading assessment: Who's using what?* Paper presented to the annual convention of the National Association of School Psychologists, New York.

Calkins, L. M. (1983). *The art of teaching writing.* Portsmouth, NH: Heinemann.

Calkins, L. M. (2001). *The art of teaching reading.* New York: Longman.

Catts, H. W., Fey, M. E., Zhang, X., & Tomblin, J. B. (2001). Estimating the risk of future reading difficulties in kindergarten children: A research-based model and its clinical implementation. *Language, Speech, and Hearing Services in Schools, 32,* 38–50.

Chall, J. S. (1967). *Learning to read: The great debate.* New York: McGraw-Hill.

Chall, J. S. (1983). *Learning to read: The great debate.* Updated ed. New York: McGraw-Hill.

Chall, J. S. (1996). *Stages of reading development* (2nd ed.). Fort Worth, TX: Harcourt Brace.

Christiansen, C. A. (2000). Preschool phonemic awareness and success in reading. In N. A. Badian (Ed.), *Prediction and prevention of reading failure.* (pp. 153–178). Baltimore: York Press.

Cizek, G. J. (n.d.). Review of the *BRIGANCE® diagnostic inventory of basic skills.* In *Buros Mental Measurements Yearbook, 14.* Retrieved June 5, 2007, from http://web5.silverplatter.com.proxy.lib.utk.edu:90/webspirs/start.ws?customer=c14360anddatabases=S(YB)

Clay, M. M. (1983). Getting a theory of writing. In B. M. Kroll & G. Wells (Eds.), *Explorations in a development of writing* (pp. 259–284). New York: John Wiley & Sons.

Clay, M. M. (1986). Constructive processes: Talking, reading, writing, art and craft. *The Reading Teacher, 39,* 764–770.

Clay, M. M. (1987). Implementing reading recovery: Systemic adaptations to an educational innovation. *New Zealand Journal of Educational Studies, 22,* 55–58.

Clay, M. M. (1993). *Observation survey of early literacy achievement* (2nd ed.). Portsmouth, NH: Heinemann.

Clay, M. M. (2000). *Running records for classroom teachers.* Portsmouth, NH: Heinemann.

Conley, M. W. (2005). *Connecting standards and assessment through literacy.* Boston, MA: Pearson Education.

Conolly, A. J. (1988/1998). *Key math-revised/normative update: A diagnostic inventory of essential mathematics.* Circle Pines, MN: American Guidance Service.

Cook, T. D., & Campbell, D. T. (1979). *Quasi-experimentation: Design and analysis issues for field settings.* Chicago: Rand-McNally.

Cousin, P. T., Berghoff, B., & Martens, P. (1999). Using retrospective miscue analysis to inspire: Learning from Michael. In S. J. Barrentine. *Reading assessment. Principles and practices for elementary teachers* (pp. 152–159). Newark, DE: International Reading Association.

CTB/McGraw-Hill. (1994). *Tests of Adult Basic Education.* Forms 7 and 8. Monterrey, CA: Author.

CTB/McGraw-Hill. (2000). *Fox in a box: An adventure in literacy.* Monterey, CA: Author.

Cummins, J. (1984). Wanted: A theoretical framework for relating language proficiency to academic achievement among bilingual students. In C. Rivera (Ed.), *Language proficiency and academic achievement.* Clevedon, Avon: Multicultural Matters.

Cunningham, P. M. (2000). *Phonics they use: Words for reading and writing* (3rd ed). New York: Longman.

Cunningham, P. M., & Hall, D. P. (1994). *Making words.* Parsipanny, NJ: Good Apple.

Cunningham, P. M, Hall, D. P., & Sigmon, C. M. (1999). *The teacher's guide to the four blocks: A multimethod, multilevel framework for grades 1–3.* Greensboro, NC: Carson Dellosa.

Curtis, M. E., & Kruidenier, J. R. (2005). *Teaching adults to read: A summary of scientifically based research principles.* Washington, DC: National Institute for Literacy.

Das, J. P., Kirby J. R., & Jarman, R. F. (1979). *Simultaneous and successive cognitive processes.* New York: Academic Press.

Developmental Reading Assessment (DRA). Retrieved June 4, 2007 from www.pearson learning.com/index.cfm?a=37

Diagnostic Online Reading Assessment System (DORA) by Let's Go Learn. (2007). Retrieved June 4, 2007, from www.letsgolearn.com/

Durkin, D. (1984). Is there a match between what elementary teachers do and what basal reading manuals recommend? *The Reading Teacher, 37,* 734–744.

Edformation. Retrieved June 4, 2007, from www.aimsweb.com/index.php

Edyburn, D. L. (2006). Reading difficulties in the general education classroom: A taxonomy of text modification strategies. *Closing the Gap, 21,* 1–5.

Ehri, L. C. (1998). Grapheme-phoneme knowledge is essential for learning to read words in English. In J. L. Metsala & L. C. Ehri (Eds.), *Word recognition in beginning literacy* (pp. 3–40). Mahwah, NJ: Erlbaum.

Ehri, L. C. (2004). Evidence-based practices that teachers are asked to implement. In P. McCardle & V. Chhabra (Eds.), *The voice of evidence in reading research.* (pp. 153–186). Baltimore, MD: Paul H. Brookes.

Elkonin, D. B. (1973). U.S.S.R. In J. Downing (Ed.), *Comparative reading* (pp. 551–579). New York: Macmillan.

Elliott, J., Lee, S. W., & Tollesfson, N. (2001). A reliability and validity study of the dynamic indicators of basic early literacy skills—modified. *School Psychology Review, 30,* 33–49.

Elliott, S. N., Braden, J. P., & White, J. I. (2001). *Assessing one and all: Educational accountability for students with disabilities.* Arlington, VA: Council for Exceptional Children.

Fine, B. (1947). *Our children are cheated: The crisis of American education.* New York: Holt.

Flanagan, D. P., Ortiz, S. O., Alfonso, V. C., & Mascolo, J. T. (2006). *The achievement test desk reference: A guide to learning disability identification* (2nd ed.). Hoboken, NJ: John Wiley & Sons.

Flavell, J. H. (1985). *Cognitive development* (2nd ed.). Englewood Cliffs, NJ: Prentice Hall.

Flavell, J. H., Green, F. L., & Flavell, E. R. (1993). Children's understanding of the stream of consciousness. *Child Development, 64,* 387–398.

Fletcher, J. M., Coulter, W. A., Reschly, D. J., & Vaughn, S. (2004). Alternative approaches to the definition and identification of learning disabilities: Some questions and answers. *Annals of Dyslexia, 54*(2), 304–331.

Fletcher, J. M., & Francis, D. J. (2004). Scientifically based education research: Questions, designs, and methods. In P. McCardle & V. Chhabra (Eds.), *The voice of evidence in reading research* (pp. 59–80). Baltimore, MD: Paul H. Brookes.

Fletcher, J. M., Shaywitz, S., Shankweiler, D. P., Katz, L., Liberman, I. Y., Stuebing, K. K., et al. (1994). Cognitive profiles of reading disability: Comparisons of discrepancy and low achievement definitions. *Journal of Educational Psychology, 86,* 6–23.

Fountas, I. C., & Pinnell, G. S. (1996). *Guided reading: Good first teaching for all children.* Portsmouth, NH: Heinemann.

Fountas, I. C., & Pinnell, G. S. (2006). *The Fountas and Pinnell leveled book list, K–8.* (2006–2008 Edition). Portsmouth, NH: Heinemann.

Fuchs, L. S., & Deno, S. L. (1994). Must instructionally useful performance assessment be based in the curriculum? *Exceptional Children, 61*(1), 15–24.

Fuchs, L. S., & Fuchs, D. (1992). Identifying a measure for monitoring student reading progress. *School Psychology Review, 22*(1), 27–48.

Fuchs, L. S., & Fuchs, D. (2005). Response to intervention as a method of LD identification: four case studies. Retrieved June 5, 2007, from http://tennessee.gov/education/speced/doc/seoperrtifuchcase.pdf

Fuchs, L. S., Fuchs, D., Hamlett, C. L., Walz, L., & Germann, G. (1993). Formative evaluation of academic progress. How much growth can we expect? *School Psychology Review, 22,* 27–48.

Fuchs, D., & Young, C. L. (2006). On the irrelevance of intelligence in predicting responsiveness to reading instruction. *Exceptional Children, 73*(1), 8–30.

Gagne, E. D., Yekovich, C. W., & Yekovich, F. B. (1993). *The cognitive psychology of school learning* (2nd ed.). New York: Harper Collins College Publishers.

Gee, J. P. (2001). Reading as situated language: A sociocognitive perspective. *Journal of Adolescent and Adult Literacy, 44*(8), 714–725.

Gersten, R. (2001). Sorting out the roles of research in the improvement of practice. *Learning Disabilities: Research and Practice, 16*(1), 45–50.

Gersten, R., & Dimino, J.A. (2006). RTI (Response to Intervention): Rethinking special education for students with reading difficulties (yet again). *Reading Research Quarterly, 41*(1), 99–108.

Good, R. H., & Kaminski, R. A. (2002). *DIBELS* Oral reading fluency passages for first through third grades. (Technical report no.10). Eugene, OR: University of Oregon. https://dibels.uoregon.edu/

Goodenough, F. L. (1926). *Measurement of intelligence by drawings.* New York: Harcourt Brace and World.

Goodman, K. S. (1986). *What's whole in whole language: A parent-teacher guide.* Portsmouth, NH: Heinemann.

Goodman, K. S. (2006). *The truth about DIBELS: What it is, what it does.* Portsmouth, NH: Heinemann.

Goodman, Y. (1985). Kidwatching: Observing children in the classroom. In A. Jagger & M. T. Smith-Burke (Eds.), *Observing the language learner* (pp. 9–18). Newark, DE: International Reading Association.

Grunwald, M. (October 1, 2006). Special report: *Reading First* under fire. *The Education Issue: Washington Post,* B01.

Gunning, T. G. (2000). *Creating literacy instruction for all children* (3rd ed). Boston, MA: Allyn & Bacon.

Guthrie, J. T. (2002). Preparing students for high-stakes test-taking in reading. In A. E. Farstrup & S. J. Sammuels (Eds.), *What research has to say about reading instruction* (3rd ed) (pp. 370–391). Newark, DE: International Reading Association.

Guthrie, J. T., & Humenick, N. M. (2004). Motivating students to read: Evidence for classroom practices that increase reading motivation and achievement. In P. McCardle

& V. Chhabra (Eds.), *The voice of evidence in reading research* (pp. 329–354). Baltimore, MD: Paul H. Brookes.

Hammill, D. D., & Larson, S. C. (1996). *Test of written language* (3rd ed). Austin, TX: PRO-ED.

Hammill, D. D., Mather, N., Allen, E. A., & Roberts, R. (2004). *The test of silent word reading fluency.* Austin, TX: PRO-ED.

Hammill, D. D., & Swanson, H. L. (2006). The National Reading Pancl's meta-analysis of phonics instruction: Another point of view. *The Elementary School Journal, 107*(1), 17–26.

Hammill, D. D., Wiederholt, J. L., & Allen, E. A. (2006). *Test of silent contextual reading fluency.* Austin, TX: PRO-ED.

Harcourt (2002). *Stanford achievement tests* (10th ed.). San Antonio, TX: Author.

Hargis, C. H. (1999). *Teaching and testing in reading.* Springfield, IL: Charles C. Thomas.

Hargis, C. H. (2006). Setting standards: An exercise in futility? *Phi Delta Kappan, 87*(5), 393–395.

Harris, A. J., & Sipay, E. (1990). *How to increase reading ability* (10th ed.). White Plains, NY: Longman.

Hasbrouck, J. E., & Tindal, G. (1992). Curriculum-based oral reading fluency norms for students in grades 2 through 5. *Teaching Exceptional Children, 24*(3), 41–44.

Headsprout. Retrieved June 4, 2007, from www.headsprout.com

Henk, W. A., & Melnick, S. A. (1995). The reader self-perception scale (RSPS): A new tool for measuring how children feel about themselves as readers. *The Reading Teacher, 48,* 470–482.

Honig, B., Diamond, L., & Nathan, R. (1999). *Assessing reading: Multiple measures for kindergarten through eighth grade.* Novato, CA: Arena Press.

Hunt, J. McV. (1972). The role of experience in the development of competence. In J. McV. Hunt (Ed.), *Human intelligence.* Brunswick, NJ: Transaction Books.

Individuals with Disabilities Education Act Amendments (IDEA) of 2004, 20 U.S.C. (2004).

International Dyslexia Association. (2003). Definition of dyslexia. Retrieved June 4, 2007, from www.interdys.org

International Dyslexia Association. Just the facts. Definition of dyslexia. Retrieved June 4, 2007, from www.interdys.org/fact%20sheets/Definition%20N.doc

International Reading Association (2003). *Standards for reading professionals revised,* Retrieved June 4, 2007, from www.reading.org/resources/issues/reports/professional_ standards.html

Johnson, G. (1930). An objective method of determining reading difficulty. *Journal of Educational Research, 21,* 283–287.

Johnston, F. R., Invernizzi, M., & Juel, C. (1998). *Book buddies: Guidelines for volunteer tutors of emergent and early readers.* New York: Guilford Press.

Johnston, P. H. (2000). *Running records: A self-tutoring guide.* Portland, ME: Stenhouse.

Judge, S., Puckett, K., & Bell, S. M. (2006, September/October). Closing the digital divide: An update from the Early Childhood Longitudinal Study. *Journal of Educational Research, 100*(1), 52–60.

Kamil, M. L. (2004). Vocabulary and comprehension instruction. In McCardle, P., & V. Chhabra (Eds.), *The voice of evidence in reading research* (pp. 213–234). Baltimore, MD: Paul H. Brookes.

Kaminiski, R. A., & Good, R. H. (1998). Assessing early literacy skills in a problem-solving model: Dynamic indicators of basic early literacy skills. In M. R. Shinn (Ed.), *Advanced applications of curriculum-based measurement* (pp. 113–142). New York: Guilford Press.

Karlsen, B., Madden, R., & Gardner, E. (1985). *Stanford diagnostic reading test* (3rd ed.). San Antonio, TX: The Psychological Corporation.

Kaufman, A. S., & Kaufman, N. L. (2004). *Kaufman tests of educational achievement* (2nd ed.). Circle Pines, MN: American Guidance Service.

Kazdin, A. E. (1981). Behavioral observation. In M. Hersen & A. S. Bellack (Eds.), *Behavioral assessment: A practical handbook* (2nd ed.), (pp. 101–124). New York: Pergamon Press.

King, T. W. (1999). *Assistive technology: Essential human factors.* Boston: Allyn & Bacon.

Klecker, B. M. (2006). The gender gap in NAEP fourth-, eighth-, and twelfth-grade reading scores across years. *Reading Improvement, 43,* 50–56.

Kruidenier, J. (2002). *Research-based principles for adult basic education reading instruction.* Washington, DC: National Institute for Literacy.

Learning Disabilities Roundtable (2005). *2004 Learning disabilities roundtable: Comments and recommendations on regulatory issues under the Individuals with Disabilities Education Improvement Act of 2004 Public Law 108–466.* Retrieved January 5, 2007 from www.nasponline.org/advocacy/2004LDRoundtableRecsTransmittal.pdf

Lenski, S. D., Ehlers-Zavala, F., Daniel, M. C., & Sun-Irminger, X. (2006). Assessing English-language learners in mainstream classrooms. *The Reading Teacher, 60,* 24–34.

Lerner, J. (2006). *Learning disabilities and related disorders: Characteristics and teaching strategies.* Boston: Houghton Mifflin.

Leslie, L., & Caldwell, J. (2001). *Qualitative reading inventory* (3rd ed.). New York: Longman.

Leslie, L., & Caldwell, J. (2006). *Qualitative reading inventory* (4th ed.). Boston: Pearson Education.

Leu, D. J., Kinzer, C. K., Wilson, R. M., & Hall, M. (2006). *Phonics, phonemic awareness, and word analysis for teachers: An interactive tutorial* (8th ed.). Upper Saddle River, NJ: Pearson Education.

Liberman, I. U. (1989). Phonology and beginning reading revisited. In C. von Euler (Ed.), *Wenner-Gren international symposium series: Brain and reading.* (Vol. 54). 207–220. Hampshire, England: Macmillan.

Lyon, G. R. (1995). Toward a definition of dyslexia. *Annals of Dyslexia, 45,* 3–27.

Lyon, G. R. (1996). Learning disabilities. *The Future of Children, 6*(1), 54–76.

Lyon, G. R., Fletcher, J. M., Shaywitz, S. E., Shaywitz, B. A., Torgeson, J. K, Wood, F. B., Schulte, A., & Olson, R. (2001). Rethinking learning disabilities. In C. E. Finn, Jr., A. J. Rotherham, C. R. Hokansan, Jr. (Eds.), *Rethinking special education for a new century* (pp. 259–288). Washington, DC: Thomas B. Fordham Foundation.

MacGinitie, W. H., MacGinitie, R. K., Maria, K., & Dreyer, L. (2000). *Gates-MacGinitie reading tests* (4th ed.). Itasca: IL: Riverside Publishing Company.

Mariotti, A. S., & Homan, S. P. (2005). *Linking reading assessment to instruction: An application worktext for elementary classroom teachers* (4th ed.). Mahwah, NJ: Erlbaum Associates.

Markwardt, F. C. (1989). *Peabody individual achievement test–revised.* Circle Pines, MN: American Guidance Services.

Mather, N., Hammill, D. D., Allen, E. A., & Roberts, R. (2004). *TOSWRF: Test of silent word reading fluency.* Austin, TX: PRO-ED.

Mather, N., & Jaffe, L. E. (2002). *Woodcock-Johnson III: Reports, recommendations, and strategies.* New York: John Wiley & Sons.

McAnally, P. L., Rose, S., & Quigley, S. P. (1999). *Reading practices with deaf learners.* Austin, TX: PRO-ED.

McCallum, R. S. (1991). Do training models influence school psychology training? *Council of Directors of School Psychology Programs Press, 10*(1), 1–3.

McCallum, R. S. (1998). A "bakers dozen" criteria for evaluating fairness in nonverbal testing. *School Psychologist,* 40–60.

McCallum, R. S., Bracken, B., & Wasserman, J. (2001). *Essentials of nonverbal assessment.* New York: John Wiley & Sons.

McEneaney, J. E., Lose, M. K., & Schwartz, R. M. (2006). A transactional perspective on reading difficulties and response to intervention. *Reading Research Quarterly, 41*(1), 117–128.

McGill-Franzen, A. (2006). *Kindergarten literacy: Matching assessment and instruction in kindergarten.* New York: Scholastic.

McGrew, K., & Woodcock, R. W. (2001). *Woodcock-Johnson III technical manual.* Itasca, IL: Riverside Publishing Company.

McKenna, M. C., & Kear, D. J. (1990). Measuring attitude toward reading: A new tool for teachers. *The Reading Teacher, 43,* 626–639.

McKenna, M. C., & Stahl, S. A. (2003). *Assessment for reading instruction.* New York: Guilford Press.

McLaughlin, G. (1969). SMOG Grading: A new readability formula. *Journal of Reading, 12,* 639–646.

Medina, A. L. (2006). The parallel bar: Writing assessment and instruction. In J. J. Schumm, (Ed.), *Reading assessment and instruction for all learners* (pp. 381–430). New York: Guilford Press.

Miles, E. (2000). Dyslexia across languages. *International Dyslexia Association Perspectives, 26*(4), 33–35.

Miller, W. H. (1995). *Alternative assessment techniques for reading and writing.* Normal, IL: Center for Applied Research in Education.

Miller, W. H. (2001). *The reading teacher's survival kit: Ready-to-use checklists, activities and materials to help all students to become successful readers.* Boston, MA: Houghton Mifflin.

Moats, L. C. (2004). Science, language, and imagination in the professional development of reading teachers. In P. McCardle & V. Chhabra (Eds.), *The voice of evidence in reading research* (pp. 267–287). Baltimore, MD: Paul H. Brookes.

National Assessment of Adult Literacy. Retrieved June 4, 2007, from http://nces.ed.gov/naal/

Naglieri, J. A. (2003). Naglieri nonverbal ability tests: NNAT and MAT-EF. In R. S. McCallum (Ed.), *Handbook of nonverbal assessment* (pp. 175–189). New York: Kluwer.

National Center for Education Statistics (2006). *National assessment of adult literacy.* Retrieved June 4, 2007, from http://nces.ed.gov/nationsreportcard/itmrls/

National Center for Education Statistics (2006). *The nation's report card: Reading.* Retrieved June 4, 2007, from http://nces.ed.gov/nationsreportcard/reading/

National Center for Progress Monitoring. (n.d.) Retrieved June 4, 2007 from http://www.studentprogress.org/chart/chart.asp#

National Institute of Child Health and Human Development. (2000). *Report of the national reading panel: Teaching children to read* (NIH Publication No. 00–4769). Washington, DC: U.S. Government Printing Office.

No Child Left Behind Act of 2001, PL 107–110, 115 Stat. 1425 (2002).

Overton, T. (2006). *Assessing learners with special needs: An applied approach* (5th ed.). Upper Saddle River, NJ: Pearson Prentice Hall.

Palinscar, A., & Brown, A. (1984). Reciprocal teaching of comprehension-fostering and comprehension-monitoring activities. *Cognition and Instruction, 1,* 117–175.

Papanicolaou, A. C., Pugh, K. R., Simos, P. G., & Mencl, W. E. (2004). Functional brain imaging: Introduction to concepts and applications. In P. McCardle & V. Chhabra (Eds.), *The voice of evidence in reading research* (pp. 385–416). Baltimore, MD: Paul H. Brookes.

Payne, D. A. (2003). *Applied educational assessment* (2nd ed.). Belmont, CA: Wadsworth/Thomson Learning.

Perie, M., Grigg, W. S., & Donahue, P. L. (2005). *The nation's report card: Reading 2005* (NCES 2006-451). U.S. Department of Education, Institute of Education Sciences, National Center for Education Statistics. Washington, DC: U.S. Government Printing Office.

Poncy, B. C., Skinner, C. H., & Axtell, P. K. (2005). An investigation of the reliability and standard error of measurement of words read correctly per minute using curriculum-based measurement. *Journal of Psychoeducational Assessment, 23,* 326–338.

Popham, W. J. (2002). *Classroom assessment: What teachers need to know* (3rd ed.). Boston: Allyn & Bacon.

Postlethwaite, T. N. (1985). International Association for the Evaluation of Educational Achievement. In T. Husten & T. N. Postlethwaite (Eds.), *The international encyclopedia of education* (Vol. 5, 2645–2646). Oxford: Pergamon.

Powell, W. R. (1969). Reappraising the criteria for interpreting informal inventories. In D. DeBoer (Ed.), *Reading diagnosis and evaluation* (pp. 100–109). Newark, DE: International Reading Association.

Powell, W. R., & Dunkeld, C. G. (1971). Validity of the IRI reading levels. *Elementary English, 48,* 637–642.

Pressley, M., Hilden, K. R., & Shankland, R. K. (n.d.). *An evaluation of end-grade–3 dynamic indicators of basic early literacy skills (DIBELS): Speed reading without comprehension, predicting little.* East Lansing, MI: Michigan State University, College of Education, Literacy Achievement Research Center (LARC). www.msularc.org/dibels%20submitted.pdf

Psychological Corporation. (2001). *Wechsler individual achievement test* (2nd ed.). San Antonio, TX: Author.

Rasinski, T. V., & Padak, N. (2004). *Effective reading strategies: Teaching children who find reading difficult* (3rd ed.). Columbus, OH: Pearson Merrill Prentice Hall.

Rasinski, T. V., & Padak, N. (2005a). *Three-minute reading assessments: word recognition, fluency, and comprehension, grades 1–4.* New York: Teaching Resources.

Rasinski, T. V., & Padak, N. (2005b). *Three-minute reading assessments: word recognition, fluency, and comprehension, grades 4–8.* New York: Teaching Resources.

Rathvon, N. (2004). *Early reading assessment: A practitioner's handbook.* New York: Guilford Press.

Rego, A. M. P. (2006). The alphabetic principle, phonics, and spelling. In J. J. Schumm (Ed.), *Reading assessment and instruction for all learners* (pp. 118–162). New York: Guilford Press.

Rehabilitation Act of 1973 §504, 29 U. S. C. §594 (2000 and Supp. 2003).

Reschly, D. J., & Grimes, J. P. (2002). Best practices in nondiscriminatory assessment. In A. Thomas & J. Grimes (Eds.), *Best practices in school psychology IV* (pp. 1337–1350). Bethesda, MD: National Association of School Psychologists.

Riverside Publishing Company (2001). *The Iowa tests. Interpretive guide for administrators.* Itasca, IL: Author.

Riverside Publishing Company (2002). *Basic early assessment of reading.* Itasca, IL: Author.

Riverside Publishing Company (2002). *Iowa tests of educational development.* Itasca: IL: Author.

Riverside Publishing Company (2003). *Iowa tests of basic skills.* Itasca, IL: Author.

Riverside Publishing Company (2006). *Linking testing to teaching: A classroom resource for reading assessment and instruction.* Retrieved June 4, 2007, from http://riverpub.com/products/gmrt/index.html

Roid, G. H. (2003). *Stanford-Binet intelligence scales: Technical manual* (5th ed.). Itasca, IL: Riverside Publishing Company.

Rosenblatt, L. M. (1982). The literary transaction: Evocation and response. *Theory into Practice, 24,* 268–277.

Rosenblatt, L. M. (1993). The transactional theory: Against dualism. *College English, 55*(4), 377–386.

Rosner, & Simon, D. P. (1971). The auditory analysis test: An initial report. *Journal of Learning Disabilities, 4,* 40–48.

Ruddell, R. B. (2002). *Teaching children to read and write. Becoming an effective literacy teacher* (3rd ed.). Boston: Allyn & Bacon.

Salvia, J., & Yesseldyke, J. E. (1998). *Assessment* (7th ed.). Boston: Houghton Mifflin.

Sanders, W. L. (1998, December). Value-added assessment. *School Administrator, 55,* 101–113.

Sattler, J. M. (2001). *Assessment of children: Cognitive applications* (4th ed.). La Mesa, CA: Jerome M. Sattler, Publisher.

Sawyer, D. J., Kim, J. K., & Lipa-Wade, S. (2000). Application of Frith's developmental phase model to the process of identifying at-risk beginning readers. In N. A. Badian (Ed.), *Prediction and prevention of reading failure.* Baltimore, MD: York Press.

Scholastic Aptitude Test (SAT). Retrieved June 4, 2007, from College Board www.collegeboard.com/splash

Scott Foresman (2007). Comprehension test. In Sidewalks–Intensive reading intervention, selection tests—teacher's manual, reading street grade 1 (p. 24). Glenview, IL: Pearson Education.

Scott Foresman (2007). High-frequency words test. In Sidewalks–Intensive reading intervention, selection tests—teacher's manual, reading street grade 1 (p. 57). Glenview, IL: Pearson Education.

Scott Foresman (2007). Phonics worksheet. In Sidewalks–Intensive reading intervention, practice book—teacher's manual, level A grade 1 (p. 70). Glenview, IL: Pearson Education.

Scott Foresman (2007). Record chart for unit tests. In Sidewalks–Intensive reading intervention, assessment book, level A grade 1 (p. 11). Glenview, IL: Pearson Education.

Scott Foresman (2007). Unit test 41–44. In Sidewalks–Intensive reading intervention assessment book, level A grade 1 (pp. 41–44). Glenview, IL: Pearson Education.

Schumm, J. J. (2006) (Ed.). *Reading assessment and instruction for all learners.* New York: Guilford Press.

Schumm, J. J., & Argulles, M. E. (2006). No two learners learn alike. In J. J. Schumm (Ed.), *Reading assessment and instruction for all learners.* New York: Guilford Press.

Scruggs, T. E., & Mastropieri, M. (2002). On babies and bathwater: Addressing the problems of identification of learning disabilities. *Learning Disability Quarterly, 25,* 155–168.

Shanahan, T. (2003). Research-based reading instruction: Myths about the national reading panel report. *The Reading Teacher, (57)*7, 646–655.

Shanahan, T. (2004). Critiques of the national reading panel report. Their implications for research, policy, and practice. In P. McCardle & V. Chhabra (Eds.), *The voice of evidence in reading research* (pp. 235–265). Baltimore, MD: Paul H. Brookes.

Shaywitz, S. E. (2003). *Overcoming dyslexia. A new and complete science-based program for reading problems at any level.* New York: Alfred A. Knopf.

Shaywitz, S. E., & Shaywitz, B. A. (2004). Neurobiologic basis for reading and reading disability. In P. McCardle & V. Chhabra (Eds.), *The voice of evidence in reading research* (pp. 417–442). Baltimore, MD: Paul H. Brookes.

Shinn, M. R. (1989). *Curriculum-based measurement: Assessing special children.* New York: Guilford Press.

Shinn, M. R. (Ed.). (1998). *Advanced applications of curriculum-based measurement.* New York: Guilford Press.

Shinn, M. R., & Bamonto, S. (1998). Advanced applications of curriculum-based measurement: "Big ideas" and avoiding confusion. In M.R. Shinn (Ed.), *Advanced applications of curriculum-based measurement* (pp. 1–31). New York: Guilford Press.

Skinner, B. F. (1953). *Science and human behavior.* New York: Macmillan.

Smith, F. (1988). *Understanding reading: A psycholinguistic analysis of reading and learning to read* (4th ed.). Hillsdale, NJ: Erlbaum.

Snow, C. E., Burns, M. S., & Griffin, P. (Eds.). (1998). *Preventing reading difficulties in young children.* Washington, DC: National Academics Press.

Spear-Swerling, L., & Sternberg, R. J. (1996). *Off track: When poor readers become "learning disabled."* Boulder, CO: Westview Press.

Stahl, S. A. (2004). What do we know about fluency? Findings of the National Reading Panel. In P. McCardle & V. Chhabra (Eds.), *The voice of evidence in reading research* (pp. 187–211). Baltimore, MD: Paul H. Brookes.

Stanovich, K. E. (1986). Matthew effects in reading: Some consequences in individual differences in the acquisition of literacy. *Reading Research Quarterly, 21,* 360–406.

Stanovich, P. J., & Stanovich, K. E. (2003). *Using research and reason in education. How teachers can use scientifically based research to make curricular and instructional decisions.* Portsmouth, NH: RMC Research Corporation.

STAR Reading (2006). Renaissance Learning. Retrieved June 4, 2007, from www.renlearn.com/starreading/software/

Stenner, A. J. (1996). *Measuring reading comprehension with the Lexile framework.* Durham, NC: Metametrics.

Strucker, J. & Davidson, R. (2003). *NCSALL research brief: Adult reading components study (ARCS).* Boston, MA: National Center for the Study of Adult Learning and Literacy.

Sweet, R. W., Jr. (2004). The big picture: Where we are nationally on the reading front and how we got there. In P. McCardle & V. Chhabra (Eds.), *The voice of evidence in reading research* (pp. 13–46). Baltimore, MD: Paul H. Brookes.

Teachers of English to Speakers of Other Languages. (1997). ESL standards for Pre–K students. Alexandria, VA: Author.

Temple, C., Ogle, D., Crawford, A., & Freppon, P. (2005). All children read. *Teaching for literacy in today's diverse classrooms.* Boston: Pearson.

Tennessee Comprehensive Assessment Program. Retrieved June 4, 2007, from www.state.tn.us/education/assessment/tsachhome.shtml

Total Reader by Edgate. (2006). Retrieved June 4, 2007, from www.totalreader.com/index.php?fuseaction=home.faq

Travers, J. F., Elliot, S. N., & Kratochwill, T. R. (1993). *Educational psychology: Effective teaching, effective learning.* Madison, WI: Brown & Benchmark.

Turnbull, R., Turnbull, A., Shank, M., & Smith, S. J. (2004). *Exceptional lives: Special education in today's schools* (4th ed.). Upper Saddle River, NJ: Pearson Prentice Hall.

Turnbull, A., Turnbull, R., & Wehmeyer, M. L. (2007). *Exceptional lives: Special education in today's schools* (5th ed.). Upper Saddle River, NJ: Pearson.

Two inquiries underway on Reading First questions. (December 2005/January 2006). *Reading Today, 23*(3), 3.

University of Tennessee, College of Education, Health, and Human Sciences. (2006, June). *Analysis of teaching for professional development.* Knoxville, TN: University of Tennessee.

Valencia, S. (1999). A portfolio approach to classroom reading assessment: The whys, whats and hows. In Barrentine, S. J. (Ed.), *Reading assessment. Principles and practices for elementary teachers* (pp. 113–117). Newark, DE: International Reading Association.

Venesky, R. L., Bristow, P. S., & Sabatini, J. P. (1994). Measuring change in adult literacy programs: Enduring issues and a few answers. *Educational Assessment, 2,* 101–131.

Voyager Universal Literacy System®. (n.d.) Retrieved June 4, 2007, from www.voyager learning.com/literacy/overview.jsp

Vygotsky, L. S. (1978). *Mind and society: The development of higher mental processes.* Cambridge, MA: Harvard University Press.

Wagner, R. K., & Barker, T. A. (1994).The development of orthographic processing ability. In V. W. Berninger (Ed.), *In the varieties of orthographic knowledge* (Vol. 1). Dordrecht, Netherlands: Kluwer.

Wagner, R. K., Torgeson, J. K., & Rashotte, C. A. (1999). *Comprehensive test of phonological processing.* Austin, TX: PRO-ED.

Walpole, S., & McKenna, M. C. (2006). The role of informal reading inventories in assessing word recognition. *The Reading Teacher,* 592–594.

Wechsler, D. (2003). *Wechsler intelligence scale for children* (4th ed.). San Antonio, TX: The Psychological Corporation.

Wiederholt, J. L,, & Blalock, G. (2000). *Gray silent reading tests.* Austin: TX: PRO-ED.

Wigfield, A., & Guthrie, J. T. (1997). Relations of children's motivation for reading to the amount and breadth of their reading. *Journal of Educational Psychology, 89,* 420–432.

Wilkinson, G. S. (1993). *Wide range achievement test* (3rd ed.). Wilmington, DE: Jastak Associates.

Wilkinson, G. S. (2006). *Wide range achievement test* (4th ed.). Lutz, FL: Psychological Assessment Resources.

Will, G. F. (2006, January 16). Ed schools vs. education. *Newsweek, CXLVII, 3,* 98.

Windingstad, S., Choate, S., Bell, S. M., & McCallum, R. S. (March, 2007). *Reliability and validity of the test of silent word reading fluency and the test of silent contextual reading fluency.* Poster presented to the 2007 annual convention of the National Association of School Psychologists, New York.

Woodcock, R. W. (1987/1998). *Woodcock reading mastery test–revised/normative update.* Circle Pines, MN: American Guidance Service.

Woodcock, R. W., & Johnson, M. B. (1989). *Woodcock-Johnson III pscyhoeducational battery–revised.* Allen, TX: DLM Teaching Resources.

Woodcock, R. W., Mather, N., & Schrank, F. (2004). *Woodcock-Johnson III diagnostic reading battery.* Itasca, IL: Riverside Publishing Company.

Woodcock, R. W., McGrew, K. S., & Mather, N. (2001). *Woodcock-Johnson III.* Itasca, IL: Riverside Publishing Company.

Woodcock, R. W., McGrew, K. S., & Werder. J. K. (1994). *Woodcock-McGrew-Werder mini-battery of achievement.* Itasca, IL: Riverside Publishing Company.

Wooten, D. A. (2000). *Valued voices: An interdisciplinary approach to teaching and learning.* Newark, DE: International Reading Association.

Yoon, J. (2002). Three decades of sustained silent reading: A meta-analytic review of the effects of SSR on attitude toward reading. *Reading Improvement, 39*(4), 186–195.

Yopp, H. K. (1995). A test for assessing phonemic awareness in young children. *The Reading Teacher, 49,* 20–29.

Zambo, D. (2006). Using thought-bubble pictures to assess students' feelings about reading. *The Reading Teacher, 59,* 798–807.

Ziegler, M., Bell, S. M., & McCallum, R. S. (in press). *Assessment of reading instructional knowledge–adult.* Washington, DC: National Institute for Literacy.

Zutell, J., & Rasinski, T. V. (1991). Training teachers to attend to their students' oral reading fluency. *Theory into Practice, 30,* 211–217.

Credits

Figure 2.1   Jeanne Chall's Model of Reading Development. McKenna, M.C. & Stahl, S. A. (2003). *Assessment for reading instruction*, Table 1.1, page 4. New York: Guilford Press.

Figure 2.2   Stage Model of Reading. Spear-Swealing, L. & Sternberg, R. J. (1996). *Off track: When poor readers become "learning disabled."* Copyright 1996. Reprinted by permission of Westview Press, a member of Perseus Books Group.

Figure 2.4   Figure 8.1 from Adams, M. J. (1990). *Beginning to read: Thinking about learning and print*, page 158. Copyright 1990. Reprinted by permission, MIT Press.

Figure 3.1   Modified Test of Print Concepts Answer Sheet adapted by Klesius & Searls (1985) in Mariotti, A. S. & Homan, S. P. (2005). *Linking reading assessment to instruction: An application worktext for elementary classroom teachers (4th edition)*, pages 17–18. Mahwah, NJ: Lawrence Erlbaum.

Figure 3.2   Unit Test, pages 41–44; Scott Foresman, Intensive Reading–Assess Book. Copyright held and reprinted by permission of Pearson Education, Inc.

Figure 3.3   Record Chart for Unit Test, page 11. Scott Foresman, Intensive Reading–Assess Book. Copyright held and reprinted by permission of Pearson Education, Inc.

Figure 3.4   Phonics Worksheet, page 70. Scott Foresman, Intensive Reading–Practice Book. Copyright held and reprinted by permission of Pearson Education, Inc.

Figure 3.5   High Frequency Words Test, page 57. Scott Foresman, Intensive Reading—Selection Tests—Teacher's Manual. Copyright held and reprinted by permission of Pearson Education, Inc.

Figure 3.6   Comprehension Test, page 24. Scott Foresman, Intensive Reading—Selection Tests—Teacher's Manual. Copyright held and reprinted by permission of Pearson Education, Inc.

Figure 3.7   Yopp, H. K. (1999). A test for assessing phonemic awareness in young children. In S. Barrantine (Ed.), *Reading assessment: Principles and practices for elementary teachers* (page 168). Originally published 1995 in *The Reading Teacher*, 49 (1), 20–29.

Figure 3.8   Examiner word lists: Preprimer through second grade. From Lauren Leslie, Joanne Caldwell Qualitative Reading Inventory–4. Published by Allyn and Bacon, Boston, MA. Copyright © 2006 by Pearson Education. Reprinted by permission of the publisher.

Figure 3.9   "Lost and Found" passage and questions. From Lauren Leslie, Joanne Caldwell Qualitative Reading Inventory–4. Published by Allyn and Bacon, Boston, MA. Copyright © 2006 by Pearson Education. Reprinted by permission of the publisher.

Figure 3.10   "The Pig Who Learned to Read" passage and questions. From Lauren Leslie, Joanne Caldwell Qualitative Reading Inventory–4. Published by Allyn and Bacon, Boston, MA. Copyright © 2006 by Pearson Education. Reprinted by permission of the publisher.

Figure 3.11   "The Bear and the Rabbit" passage and questions. From Lauren Leslie, Joanne Caldwell Qualitative Reading Inventory–4. Published by Allyn and Bacon, Boston, MA. Copyright © 2006 by Pearson Education. Reprinted by permission of the publisher.

Figure 3.14   Figure 10.2 Miscue Analysis Worksheet. From Lauren Leslie, Joanne Caldwell Qualitative Reading Inventory–4. Published by Allyn and Bacon, Boston, MA. Copyright © 2006 by Pearson Education. Reprinted by permission of the publisher.

Figure 3.19   "The Pig who learned to Read" retell. From Lauren Leslie, Joanne Caldwell Qualitative Reading Inventory–4. Published by Allyn and Bacon, Boston, MA. Copyright © 2006 by Pearson Education. Reprinted by permission of the publisher.

be reproduced or transmitted in any form or by any means, electronic or mechanical, including photocopying and recording or by any information storage or retrieval system without the proper written permission of The Riverside Publishing Company unless such copying is expressly permitted by federal copyright law. Address inquiries to Contracts and Permissions Department, The Riverside Publishing Company, 425 Spring Lake Drive, Itasca, Illinois 60143-2079.

Figure 6.4   Excerpt from TOSWRF protocol Form B (#12238). From Mather, N., Hammill, D. D., Allen, E. A., & Roberts, R. (2004). Used with permission of PRO ED.

Figure 6.5   Copyright © 2001 by The University of Iowa. Excerpt from the Word Analysis Practice subtest from the *Iowa Tests of Basic Skills (ITBS)*, page 6, reproduced with permission of The Riverside Publishing Company. All rights reserved. No part of this work may be reproduced or transmitted in any form or by any means, electronic or mechanical, including photocopying and recording or by any information storage or retrieval system without the proper written permission of The Riverside Publishing Company unless such copying is expressly permitted by federal copyright law. Address inquiries to Contracts and Permissions Department, The Riverside Publishing Company, 425 Spring Lake Drive, Itasca, Illinois 60143-2079.

Figure 6.6   Copyright © 1993 by The Riverside Publishing Company. "Directions from Nelson-Denny Reading Test, Part II Comprehension (Form G)" from the *Nelson-Denny Reading Test*, page 7, reproduced with permission of the publisher. All rights reserved. No part of this work may be reproduced or transmitted in any form or by any means, electronic or mechanical, including photocopying and recording or by any information storage or retrieval system without the proper written permission of The Riverside Publishing Company unless such copying is expressly permitted by federal copyright law. Address inquiries to Contracts and Permissions Department, The Riverside Publishing Company, 425 Spring Lake Drive, Itasca, Illinois 60143-2079.

Figure 6.7   Copyright © 2000 by The Riverside Publishing Company. "Sample questions from Reading Vocabulary Subtest" from the *Gates-MacGinitie Reading Tests (GMRT), Fourth Edition* reproduced with permission of the publisher. All rights reserved. No part of this work may be reproduced or transmitted in any form or by any means, electronic or mechanical, including photocopying and recording or by any information storage or retrieval system without the proper written permission of The Riverside Publishing Company unless such copying is expressly permitted by federal copyright law. Address inquiries to Contracts and Permissions Department, The Riverside Publishing Company, 425 Spring Lake Drive, Itasca, Illinois 60143-2079.

Figure 6.8   Copyright © 2000 by The Riverside Publishing Company. "Sample questions from the Reading Comprehension Subtest" from the *Gates-MacGinitie Reading Tests (GMRT), Fourth Edition* reproduced with permission of the publisher. All rights reserved. No part of this work may be reproduced or transmitted in any form or by any means, electronic or mechanical, including photocopying and recording or by any information storage or retrieval system without the proper written permission of The Riverside Publishing Company unless such copying is expressly permitted by federal copyright law. Address inquiries to Contracts and Permissions Department, The Riverside Publishing Company, 425 Spring Lake Drive, Itasca, Illinois 60143-2079.

Table 6.1   Standard Condition and Description, pages 53–54. From *Applied Educational Assessment w/CD 2nd edition* by Payne, 2003. Reprinted with permission of Wadsworth, a division of Thomson Learning: www.thomsonrights.com Fax 800-730-2215.

Table 6.2   Page 57, Table 2–2, External Testing Programs: Criticisms and Solutions. From *Applied Educational Assessment w/CD 2nd edition* by Payne, 2003. Reprinted with permission of Wadsworth, a division of Thomson Learning: www.thomsonrights. com Fax 800-730-2215.

Table 6.3   Table 2.3 NAEP Performance Level Definitions and Descriptions. Adapted from McKenna, M.C. & Stahl, S. A. (2003). *Assessment for effective reading instruction.* New York: Guilford Press, page 34.

Table 6.4   Copyright 2001 by The University of Iowa. "Scope and Sequence Chart" from the *Iowa Tests of Basic Skills (ITBS)* reproduced with permission of The Riverside Publishing Company. All rights reserved. No part of this work may be reproduced or

Figure 7.4   Zambo, Debby. (2006, May). Teaching Tips: Using thought-bubble pictures to assess students' feelings about reading. *The Reading Teacher*, 59 (8), 798–803.

Figure 7.5   Zambo, Debby. (2006, May). Teaching Tips: Using thought-bubble pictures to assess students' feelings about reading. *The Reading Teacher*, 59 (8), 798–803.

Figure 7.6   Tell Me What You Like! (Interest inventory). McKenna, M. & Stahl, S. (2003). Taken from *Assessment for reading instruction*. New York: Guilford Press, page 213.

Figure 7.7   Copyright © 2001 by The University of Iowa. "Class Primary Reading Profile" from the *Iowa Tests of Basic Skills (ITBS)*, page 120, reproduced with permission of The Riverside Publishing Company. All rights reserved. No part of this work may be reproduced or transmitted in any form or by any means, electronic or mechanical, including photocopying and recording or by any information storage or retrieval system without the proper written permission of The Riverside Publishing Company unless such copying is expressly permitted by federal copyright law. Address inquiries to Contracts and Permissions Department, The Riverside Publishing Company, 425 Spring Lake Drive, Itasca, Illinois 60143-2079.

Appendix A   *Standards for Reading Professionals–Revised 2003*. Professional Standards and Ethics Committee of the International Reading Association. Copyright 2004 by IRA. Reprinted with permission.

Index

A

AAT (Auditory Analysis Test), 127
Abrams, L. M., 32
Abuses, high-stakes testing, 210
Academic progress data, 11
Accommodation, 274, 299
Accommodations, high-stakes testing, 215–216
Accountability
  assessment selection/evaluation, 202, 239
  assessment's role in, 8, 10–11
  formal, group assessment, 216–221
  high-stakes testing in, 200, 209, 210
  learning disability/ELL testing, 215
  of teachers, 2, 10–11
Achievement-level policy definitions, NAEP, 217
Achievement tests, 181, 299
Acquired alexia, 40, 299
ACT (American College Test), 5, 171
Action research, 32, 299
Adams, Marilyn, 14, 15–16, 17, 18, 34, 44–47, 66
Adam's cognitive model of reading, 44–47, 66
Adaptive behavior, 61, 299
Adaptive testing, 178, 299
Adequate yearly progress (AYP)
  defined, 299
  monitoring, 153
  NCLB requirements, 10, 215
ADHD (attention deficit hyperactivity disorder), 12, 299
Administrators
  assessment selection/evaluation, 239
  IRA standard, 7
  proficiency levels, 280–281
Adult basic education
  assessment of, 63–64, 70
  assessment selection/evaluation, 239
  average rates, 110
  defined, 299
  formal, group assessment, 228
  formal individual assessment of, 189–190
  informal assessment of, 123
  progress monitoring, 160
  reading comprehension assessment, 208–209
  resources, 294
Adult Basic Learning Examination, 231, 235
Adult literacy assessment, 63, 219–221
Adult Reading Components Study, 63–64

Affective information, 256–257
Age-equivalent scores, 169–170, 191, 299
Aimline, 111, 112, 299
AIMSweb, 136, 145–148, 244, 270
Allington, R. L., 10, 17, 22, 108, 219, 243–244
Alphabetic principle
  defined, 14, 299
  developmental models of, 42, 43, 45
  transactional view of, 53
Alphabetics, 14, 299
Alternate forms
  defined, 299
  in progress monitoring, 223
Alternate forms reliability, 134
Alternative Assessment Techniques for Reading and Writing, 80
American College Test (ACT), 5, 171
Analytical Reading Inventory, 7th Ed., 129
Anderson, R. C., 21
Anecdotal, 248, 299
Armbruster, B. B., 14, 16, 20
The Art of Teaching Reading (Calkins), 33
Arter, J. A., 113
Artifacts in portfolio assessment, 114
Assessment
  cognitive variable, 257–259
  computer-based (*See* Computer-based assessment)
  consistency issues in, 134
  data, gathering/evaluation, 259–261
  defined, 4, 299
  formal, group (*See* Formal, group assessment)
  formal, individual (*See* Formal, individual assessment)
  hybrid (*See* Hybrid assessment methods)
  informal (*See* Informal assessment)
  IRA standard, 7
  learning disabilities (*See* Learning disabilities)
  multitier model of instruction (*See* Multitiered model of instruction)
  purposes of, 8–12, 70
  reading wars, 33–35
  resources, 261, 287–288
  role of, 4–6, 65–66
  selection/evaluation, 238–240
  teacher professional standards, 6–8, 280–281
  types of, 35–36
  value-added, 10–11
  writing, 240, 243–245

Assessment of Reading Instructional Knowledge-Adult form (ARIK-A), 221
Assessment-to-instruction
  entire class, 261–263
  individuals, 264–266
  overview, 276–278, 280–281
  struggling students, 265–266
Associational Fluency and Naming Facility subtest, 185
Attention deficit hyperactivity disorder (ADHD), 12, 299
Attitude inventories, 255, 278
Auditory Analysis Test (AAT), 127
Auditory memory
  defined, 49, 50, 299
  transaction view of, 55
Auditory processing, 52, 299
Authentic Text assessment, STAR Reading, 153, 155
Authentic writing in assessment, 243–244
Authority syndrome, 26
Autism, 243, 299
Automatic word, 299
Automatic word recognition. *See also* Orthography; Word recognition
  defined, 18, 58
  teaching strategies, 18–19
Automaticity, 19, 185, 299
Awareness, 48, 299
Axtell, P. K., 147
AYP. *See* Adequate yearly progress (AYP)

B

B-AAT (Berninger Modification of the Auditory Analysis Test), 127
Balanced literacy, 299
Balanced literacy theory, 34
Bandura, A., 246
Basal, 178, 179, 300
Basal series
  applications of, 2, 260
  defined, 299
  overview, 73–78, 107
Baseline, 267, 300
Basic Early Assessment of Reading (BEAR), 127, 223–225, 231
Basic interpersonal communicative skills (BICS), ELL students, 62, 63
Basic Reading Inventory, 129
Basic reading skills
  defined, 50, 58, 300
  formal individual assessment of, 194–196
  informal assessment of, 128–130
  tests, task variation, 182

Basic writing, 50, 300
BBELS (Book Buddies Early Literacy Screening), 127
BEAR (Basic Early Assessment of Reading), 127, 223–225, 231
Beck, I. L., 20
Beck, M. D., 21
Benchmarks
  defined, 24, 300
  NAEP, 216, 217
Berlin, Rudolf, 40
Berninger Modification of the Auditory Analysis Test (B-AAT), 127
Betts, E. A., 19, 21, 88, 89
Betts criteria, reading level determination, 88–89, 93
BICS (basic interpersonal communicative skills), ELL students, 62, 63
Blends, 42, 300
Blind students, 48
Bond, G. L., 17
Book Buddies Early Literacy Screening (BBELS), 127
Bos, C. S., 18, 20
Bracken, B., 63
Braille, 48
BRIGANCE® Inventories, 137–143, 147, 160, 244, 260
Brown, A., 23
Brown, C. L., 61–63
Burns, M. S., 12
Burns/Roe Informal Reading Inventory, 129
Buros Mental Measurements Yearbook, 240, 245

C

Caldwell, J., 18, 82, 91, 98, 99
California Achievement Test, 5th ed. (CAT), 231, 235
Calkins, L. M., 12, 22, 33, 97–98, 120, 226–227
Calkins, Lucy, 33, 120
CALP (cognitive academic language proficiency), ELL students, 62, 63
Cambier, Nicholas, 40
Case studies
  DBPS science education, 268–270
  DBPS special education, 266–267, 270–273
  defined, 300
  described, 26–27, 31–32
CAT (California Achievement Test), 5th ed., 231, 235
Catts Deletion Test (CDT), 127
Cause/effect determinations, 27, 30–31, 265–266
CBA (curriculum-based assessment), 105–107
CBM. See Curriculum-based measurement (CBM)
CDT (Catts Deletion Test), 127
Ceiling point, 178, 179, 300

Cerebral palsy, 243, 300
Chall, Jeanne S., 17, 33–34, 34, 41, 42, 116
Chall's stage model, 41, 42
Charles, Harley, 3, 110–111. See also Science education
Choral reading
  defined, 20, 300
  instruction tips, 296
Chronological age determination, 178–180, 202
CIBS-R inventory, 140–142
CIBS-R Standardization and Validation Manual, 142
Class Primary Reading Profile, 261, 262
Classroom observation form, 250–251
Classroom Reading Inventory, 10th ed., 130
Classroom Teacher proficiency levels, 280–281
Clay, M. M., 55, 73, 90, 102, 103–104, 104
Cloze procedure, 112
Cloze type, 300
Code-based, 300
Code-based instruction, 34
Coding miscues, 92
Cognitive academic language proficiency (CALP), ELL students, 62, 63
Cognitive complexity, 167
Cognitive models of reading
  Adam's, 44–47, 66
  inclusive, 56
  information processing, 47–51
Cognitive variable assessment, 257–259
Colleges of education, closing, 26
Comprehension
  basal reading series, 78
  CBM assessment, 112–113
  defined, 21, 42, 58, 300
  developmental models of, 42, 43, 46
  formal, group assessment, 201, 226–228, 231–234
  formal individual assessment of, 187, 192, 194–196, 272
  Gates-MacGinitie test, 208
  inclusive model of, 56, 70, 226–227
  inferential, 49, 302
  informal assessment, 79, 80, 128–130, 146, 148, 149
  information processing models of, 48–49
  instructional tips, 297
  IRI assessment of, 84–87, 89, 93–96
  ITBS/ITED assessment, 222
  listening, IRI assessment of, 100
  motivation's influence on, 247
  norm table sample, 179
  qualitative analysis, 97–100
  quasi-experiment design, 29
  resources, 291
  teaching strategies, 21–23, 34, 64
  tests, task variation, 183

think–alouds, 99
transactional view of, 53
vs. vocabulary, 21
Comprehension monitoring strategy described, 22
Comprehensive evaluation, 270, 300
Comprehensive Test of Basic Skills, 231, 235
Comprehensive Test of Phonological Processing, 184
Comprehensive Testing Program III, 231, 235
Computer-based assessment
  AIMSweb, 136, 145–148, 160
  benefits of, 157
  DORA, 154–156, 159–160
  Lexia Program, 155
  Lexile Framework, 153, 157–160
  NWEA, 155
  overview, 152–153
  Read 180, 155
  STAR Early Literacy, 154
  STAR Reading test, 153–156
  Total Reader system, 153, 155
Computers in reading instruction, 261
Concepts about Print Test, 71–73
Concurrent validity, 135, 300
Confirmation//fluency stage, Chall's model, 42
Conley, M. W., 210
Connected text
  defined, 300
  error analysis, 80–81
  miscue calculation, 92–93
Consolidated word recognition, 300
Consolidated word recognition stage, Spear-Swerling/Sternberg model, 43
Consortium on Reading Excellence (CORE) Phonics Survey, 127
Construct validity, 135, 300
Content validity, 134–136, 204, 300
Context, in literacy instruction, 53, 54, 56
Context cues, 300
Context cues analysis, 97–98
Context processor
  Adam's model, 44–46
  defined, 300
Contextual analysis, 20, 300
Controlled word recognition stage, Spear-Swerling/Sternberg model, 43
Cooperative learning, 54, 300
Cooperative learning strategy described, 23
CORE (Consortium on Reading Excellence) Phonics Survey, 127
Core programs, 2, 300
Correlation coefficients
  defined, 29–30, 51, 300
  in progress monitoring, 147
  in reliability measures, 133, 134
  in validity measures, 134–137

Correlational studies, 13, 26, 27, 29–30, 300
Council for Exceptional Children, 57
Criterion-referenced assessments
    applications of, 69, 204
    defined, 300
    described, 35, 137–138
Criterion Test of Basic Skills, 2nd Ed., 127
Crockett, Lesa. See also First grade students
    CBM assessment, 107
    described, 2
    experimental designs, 29
    informal assessment, 80–84
    observation by, 248
    reading assessment methods, 137, 264–265
Cunningham, P. M., 17, 18–19, 55, 73, 243–244
Current-form preparation, 212, 300
Curriculum-based assessment (CBA), 105–107
Curriculum-based measurement (CBM)
    applications of, 5, 107, 208–209
    defined, 301
    described, 35, 145
    fluency, 107–113
    history of, 107
    inclusive model, 70
    progress monitoring, 111–113
    teacher made/selected, 72–78, 107–113, 127
    vs. CBA, 106–107

D

Data-Based Problem-Solver Model (DBPS)
    defined, 301
    IEPs in, 274–276
    multitiered instruction in, 273
    overview, 266, 267, 278
    remediation vs. compensation, 273–274
    science education case study, 268–270
    special education case studies, 266–267, 270–273
Davidson, R., 63–64
DBPS. See Data-Based Problem-Solver Model (DBPS)
Declarative knowledge
    defined, 48, 49, 301
    in writing, 243
Decoding
    adult readers, 64
    in basal readers, 73
    Chall's model, 42–43
    in comprehension, 33–34
    DBPS case study, 270–273
    defined, 301
    in dyslexia, 59, 60
    error analysis, 105

formal, individual assessment, 166, 167, 182, 184, 185
    importance of, 13
    inclusive model of, 287
    information processing models, 49–51
    instructional tips, 295, 296
    IRI assessment, 82, 95, 100
    in learning disabilities, 58, 266-267
    phonological, 52
    in portfolio assessment, 114
    reliability testing, 133
    in think-alouds, 99
Decoding Fluency subtest, 185
Decoding stage, Chall's model, 42
Deficit model of reading, 40
Deno, Stanley, 107, 145
Dependent variable, 29, 301
Developmental models of reading
    Adam's cognitive model, 44-47
    Chall, 41, 42
    Frith's phases, 44, 45
    overview, 41
    Spear-Swerling/Sternberg, 41–44
Developmental Reading Assessment, 127, 130
Developmental Reading Assessment (DRA), 119
Developmental version, 168, 301
Diagnostic Assessments of Reading, 128
Diagnostic Online Reading Assessment system (DORA), 154–156, 159–160
Diagnostic tests, 181, 301
DIBELS. See Dynamic Indicators of Basic Early Literacy Skills (DIBELS)
Difficulty level, determination of, 120
Direct (explicit) instruction, 22, 23, 301
Disaggregate, 10
Disaggregate data, 301
Discrepancy model, 58–59, 61
Distracters
    defined, 301
    developing, 112–113
Document literacy, 220, 301
DORA (Diagnostic Online Reading Assessment system), 154–156, 159–160
DRA (Developmental Reading Assessment), 119
Dunkeld, C. G., 89
Durrell Analyses of Reading Difficulty (3rd ed.), 194, 197
Dykstra, R., 17
Dynamic Indicators of Basic Early Literacy Skills (DIBELS)
    correlation coefficients in, 135
    described, 148–152, 264
    progress monitoring via, 137, 145
Dyslexia
    decoding in, 59, 60
    defined, 17, 59–60, 301
    history, 40
    informal assessment, 155

IRI assessment, 95
    phonemic awareness, 17
    resources, 294
    student needs, 258

E

Early literacy, assessment of, 146, 154. See also Dynamic Indicators of Basic Early Literacy Skills (DIBELS)
Early Reading Diagnostic Assessment-Revised (ERDA-R), 128, 194, 197
Echo reading, 20, 301
Edformation norms, 109
Educational defensibility guideline, 211
Educational standard, 6
Edyburn, D. L., 261
Effect size, 219, 301
Efferent, 54
Ehri, Linnea, 41, 44
Eighth grade performance descriptions, NAEP, 217–218
Ekwall/Shanker Reading Inventory, 4th ed., 130
Elementary and Secondary Education Act of 1965 (ESEA), 9–10
Elementary Reading Attitude Survey (ERAS), 255–256
Elkonin blocks
    applications of, 15
    defined, 272, 301
ELL. See English language learners (ELL)
Elliott, J., 151
Elliott, S. N., 210
Emergent literacy
    Chall's model, 41, 42
    defined, 301
Emotional disturbance, 58, 301
Empirical data, 301
Empirically, 26
Engagement, 247, 301
English language learners (ELL)
    assessment, 11, 61–63, 258
    DBPS case study, 268–270
    defined, 301
    formal, group assessment, 229
    formal individual assessment of, 189, 191, 192
    high-stakes testing, 214–216
    informal assessment of, 124–125
    NCLB assessment requirements, 10
    progress monitoring, 160
    resources, 293–294
    UNIT testing, 257
Entire class, assessment-to-instruction, 261–263
Environmental influences on reading, 53, 55
ERAS (Elementary Reading Attitude Survey), 255–256
ERDA-R (Early Reading Diagnostic Assessment-Revised), 128, 194, 197
Error, 133

Error analysis technique
    defined, 301
    inclusive model, 70
    informal assessment, 80–81
    miscue analysis, 90–93, 125, 127
    norm-referenced tests, 176
Error reduction, 178
Errors per minute, 84, 301
ESEA (Elementary and Secondary Education Act of 1965), 9–10
Ethnic/racial proficiency trends, 219–221
Etiology, 40, 301
EWRT (Exception Word Reading Test), 128
Exception Word Reading Test (EWRT), 128
Explicit content, 227
Explicit instruction, 301
Explicit instruction strategy, 22, 23
Expository, 23
Expository nonfiction text
    applications of, 227
    defined, 301
    readability, 116
    student response, IRI assessment, 99–101

F

Field testing, 168, 301
First grade students
    assessment of, 137–138
    assessment-to-instruction, individuals, 264–266
    formal, individual assessment, 168–170, 172
    IRI administration, 82–87
    observation of, 248
    percentile scores, 170–171
    progress monitoring in, 142–144
    reading assessment methods, 264–266
    retelling analysis, 98–99
"Five finger" rule, 120
Flanagan, D., 181, 183
Flesch-Kincaid readability grade, 118
Fletcher, J. M., 28, 52
Floor effects, 151, 301
Fluency
    assessment of, 5
    average rates by grade level, 108–110
    CBM assessment, 107–113, 208–209
    defined, 19, 58, 302
    formal, group assessment, 224–225, 231–234
    formal individual assessment of, 172, 185–186, 192, 194–196, 272
    inclusive model of, 56
    informal assessment, 80, 128–130, 146–149
    instructional tips, 267, 296
    quasi-experiment design, 28–29
    resources, 292–293

teaching strategies, 19–20, 64
tests, task variation, 182
transactional view of, 53
true experiment design, 27–28
Fluid reasoning, 47, 50, 302
Formal, group assessment. See also High-stakes testing
    accountability, 216–221
    administration/scoring, 201–205
    adult basic education, 228
    applications of, 199–200
    assessment selection/evaluation, 229, 239
    assessment-to-instruction, entire class, 261–263
    benefits, 200–201
    characteristics, 201–205
    comprehension, 201, 226–228, 231–234
    criterion-referenced information, 204
    data, gathering/evaluation, 259–261
    data application strategies, 221–223
    described, 35, 229, 276
    English language learners, 229
    fluency, 224–225, 231–234
    high-stakes testing (See High-stakes testing)
    inclusive model of reading, 200–201
    instruction planning/progress monitoring, 206–209
    limitations, 200, 201
    orthography, 223–224
    phonemic awareness, 223–224, 231–234
    phonics, 223–224, 231–234
    psychometric data, 235–236
    scaled scores, 203–204, 210, 216–217
    standard scores, 202
    vocabulary, 201, 225–227, 231–234
    vs. individual, 180–187
    word recognition, 231–234
    writing, 244–245
Formal, individual assessment. See also Norm-referenced tests
    administration/scoring, 176–178, 191–192
    adult basic education, 190
    age/grade-equivalent scores, 169–170, 191
    assessment-to-instruction, individuals, 264–266
    basic reading skills, 194–196
    comprehension, 187, 192, 194–196, 272
    context, 200–201
    decoding, 166, 167, 182, 184, 185
    described, 35, 165–167, 191–193, 276
    development of, 167–168
    English language learners, 189, 191, 192
    error reduction, 178
    first grade students, 168–170, 172

fluency, 172, 185–186, 192, 194–196, 272
Literacy Instruction Pie, 192–193
normal curve equivalents (NCEs), 175–176
percentile scores, 170–171, 191
phonemic awareness, 184, 194–196, 272
phonics, 184, 194–196, 272
psychometric data, 197–198
reliability in, 192
score types, 168–176
standard score (See Standard scores)
test bias, 166, 188–190, 307
test selection, 189–191
validity in, 192
vocabulary, 167, 169, 186–187, 194–196
vs. group, 180–187
word recognition, 184–185, 194–196
writing, 244
Fountas, I. C., 73, 119
Four Blocks approach, 73, 260
Fourth grade performance descriptions, NAEP, 217
Fox in a Box: An Adventure in Literacy (FOX), 128
Francis, D. J., 28
Frequency count, 249, 302
Frith, U., 41, 44
Frith's developmental phases model, 44, 45
Frustration reading levels, assessment of, 83, 84, 86–89, 95
Fry, Edward, 116, 117
Fry readability graph, 116, 117
Fuchs, D., 111, 112
Fuchs, L. S., 107, 111, 112, 145
Full alphabetic coding, 43, 302
Functional literacy, 220, 302

G

Gagne, E. D., 48
Gagne, Robert, 48, 49
Garfield, 255
Gates-MacGinitie Reading Test
    adult literacy assessment, 221
    applications of, 206–208, 225–228
    described, 201, 232
    fluency assessment, 147
    psychometric data, 235
Gender proficiency trends, 219
Generalized test-taking preparation, 212
Generalized test-taking preparation, 302
Genres areas of literature, 263, 302
Gerston, R., 25
Goodman, K. S, 55, 71
Goodman, Y., 151
GOR-4 (Gray Oral Reading Tests, 4th Ed.), 194, 197

Grade-equivalent scores, 116, 169–170, 191, 302
Graphemes, 46
Graphic organizers, 22, 302
Gray Oral Reading Tests, 4th Ed. (GOR-4), 194, 197
Gray Silent Reading Tests
    applications of, 194, 197, 239
    described, 201, 232
    psychometric data, 235
Griffin, P., 12
Group Primary Reading Profile, 261, 262
Guided reading, 2, 73, 302
Gunning, T. G., 18–19
Guthrie, J. T., 212, 247, 248–249

H

Hall, D. P., 19, 55, 73
Hammill, D.D., 203
Hargis, C. H., 5, 116, 117–118
Harris, A. J., 109
Harris-Sipay norms, 110
Hasbrouck, J. E., 108, 109
Haywood, Greg. *See also* Special education
    BRIGANCE® assessment, 142
    CBM applications, 111–113
    described, 2–3
    motivation of students by, 249
    professional development, 10
    reading level assessment, 93, 95
Helper-supplied word
    defined, 302
    miscues, 90, 92
Henk, W. A., 256
Hesitation, 302
Hesitation miscues, 90, 92
High-stakes testing. *See also* Formal, group assessment
    applications of, 199–200
    controversy, 210
    defined, 10, 181, 209, 302
    ELL students, 214–216
    guidelines, 210–212
    history, 209–210
    learning disabilities, 214–216
    problems/solutions, 212–214
Homan, S.P., 71, 72, 104, 106
Humenick, N. M., 247, 248–249
Hunt, J., 157
Hybrid assessment methods
    AIMSweb, 136, 145–148
    described, 6
    DIBELS (*See* Dynamic Indicators of Basic Early Literacy Skills (DIBELS))

I

IDEA 2004. *See* Individuals with Disabilities Education Improvement Act of 2004 (IDEA, 2004)

IEP. *See* individual education program (IEP)
Implicit, 302
Inclusive model of reading
    comprehension, 226–227
    contextual variables, 259
    formal, group assessment, 200–201
    motivation, 245
    overview, 55–57, 70, 166, 287
    progress monitoring, 131–132
Independent reading levels, assessment of, 83, 88–89, 95
Independent variable, 29, 302
Individual education program (IEP)
    assessment selection/evaluation by, 215
    defined, 274–276, 302
    formal, group assessment by, 202–203
    special education, 12, 137, 141, 274
Individuals, assessment-to-instruction, 264–266
Individuals with Disabilities Education Improvement Act of 2004 (IDEA, 2004)
    benefits, 142
    CBM assessments in, 113
    disability categories, 11–12, 58
    requirements, 9–10, 57, 174, 214–215
Inferential comprehension, 49, 302
Informal assessment
    adult basic education, 123
    basal reading series, 73–78
    basic reading skills, 128–130
    benefits/limitations, 132, 276
    comprehension, 79, 80, 128–130, 146, 148, 149
    dyslexia, 155
    English language learners, 124–125
    error analysis, 80–81
    fluency, 80, 128–130, 146–149
    kindergarten students, 120–123, 125
    Literacy Instruction Pie, 160
    in miscue analysis, 90–91
    observation/interview, 71–72
    overview, 35, 69–70
    phonemic awareness, 128–130, 148, 149
    phonics, 79, 128–130
    range, 132, 133
    reliability, 132–134
    specific skill, 78–80
    validity, 134–137
    vocabulary, 128–130, 148, 149, 153–154
    word recognition, 79, 80, 128–130
    writing, 243–244
Informal reading inventories (IRIs)
    abbreviated assessment, 100
    applications of, 5, 9, 82, 125
    decoding, 82, 95, 100
    defined, 302
    described, 35, 81–82
    inclusive model, 70

limitations of, 100–102
listening comprehension, 100
miscue analysis, 90–93
qualitative analysis, 96
quantitative analysis, 87–88
teacher-made, 100
technique, 82–87, 101
text type differences, student response to, 99–100
Information processing model
    brain research support of, 49
    cognitive correlates, 49–51
    of comprehension, 48–49
    defined, 302
    memory in, 47–50
    overview, 47–48
    of phonemic awareness, 49, 50
Informed content, 227
Insertion, 302
Insertion miscues, 90, 92, 97
Instruction, planning
    assessment-to-instruction (*See* Assessment-to-instruction)
    assessment's role in, 4–6, 8–9, 239, 281
    cognitive variables in, 51
    concerns, 2, 3
    entire class, 261–263
    individuals, 264–266
    informal assessment, 200
    Literacy Instruction Pie, 64–65
    miscue patterns in, 97
    norm-referenced group data, 200
    progress monitoring in, 144, 206–209
    tips, 295–298
Instructional reading levels, assessment of, 83, 86–89, 206
Integration, information processing models of, 49
Intellectually gifted, 51, 302
Intelligence
    cognitive aspects of, 50, 51
    defined, 303
Intelligence quotient (IQ)
    defined, 171, 303
    in learning disability determinations, 58–59, 61
    reading *vs.,* 51–53
Inter-individual comparisons, 202, 303
Inter-rater reliability, 134, 303
Interest inventories, 254–255
Internal consistency reliability, 134, 303
International Reading Association (IRA), 6–7
Intra-individual, 13
Intra-individual comparison, 65, 303
Intra-rater reliability, 134, 303
Iowa Test of Educational Development (ITED), 221, 222
Iowa Tests Interpretive Guide for Teachers and Counseling, 263

Iowa Tests of Basic Skills (ITBS)
  accountability, establishment of, 202, 239
  applications of, 221, 222
  comprehension assessment, 227
  described, 232
  grades 3–8 skills assessment, 245
  group reading profile, 261, 262
  oral/reading vocabulary assessment, 225
  psychometric data, 235
  scaled scores, 203–205
  word analysis, 222–224
IQ-achievement discrepancy procedure, 174–175. *See also* Intelligence quotient (IQ)
IRA (International Reading Association), 6–7
IRIs. *See* Informal reading inventories (IRIs)
ITBS. *See* Iowa Tests of Basic Skills (ITBS)
ITED (Iowa Test of Educational Development), 221, 222

J

Journal of Psychoeducational Assessment, 240

K

Kamil, M. L., 21
Kaufman Tests of Educational Achievement II (KTEA-II), 182–185, 194, 197
Kear, D. J., 255–256
Kidwatching, 71–72, 125
Kim, J. K., 41, 44, 45
Kindergarten students
  assessment overview, 70
  informal assessment, 120–123, 125
Klesius-Searls Test, 71–73
Kruidenier, John, 123
KTEA-II (Kaufman Tests of Educational Achievement II), 182–185, 194, 197
Kucan, L., 20

L

Lack of prosody miscues, 90, 92, 303
Learning disabilities
  age/grade-equivalent scores, 169–170
  assessment of, 57–61, 155
  DBPS case studies, 266–267, 270–274
  decoding in, 58, 266–267
  defined, 303
  high-stakes testing, 214–216
  identification of, 10, 57–61, 174–175
  IQ-achievement discrepancy procedure, 174–175
  NRP on, 58
  percentile scores, 170–171
  resources, 294

Lee, S. W., 151
Lenski, S. D., 124
Lerner, J., 73
Leslie, L., 18, 82, 91, 98, 99
Letter Naming Fluency measure, 151
Leu, D. J., 16
Leveled, 303
Leveled readers books
  applications of, 2, 73, 125
  defined, 65, 303
  overview, 119–120
Lexia Program, 155
Lexile Analyzer, 158
Lexile Calculator, 158
Lexile Framework, 120, 153, 157–160, 204, 210
Lexile score, 303
Linking Testing to Teaching: A Classroom Resource for Reading Assessment and Instruction, 208
Lipa-Wade, Sally, 41, 44, 45
Listening comprehension, IRI assessment of, 100
Listening vocabulary, 20, 303
Literacy Instruction Pie
  assessment-instruction link, 261
  DBPS, 272, 273
  described, 64–65, 289
  formal, individual assessment, 192–193
  informal assessment, 160
  motivation, 246
  teacher self-assessment, 259
Logographic, 303
Logographic phase, 44, 45
Long-term memory, 47, 48, 50, 303
Lose, M. K., 54
Lyon, G. R., 52

M

MacGinitie, W. H., 227, 228
Mariotti, A. S., 71, 72, 104, 106
Math computation, assessment of, 146
Mather, N., 208
Maze, 303
Maze procedure, 112
McCallum, R. S., 63, 268
McEneaney, J. E., 54
McGill-Franzen, A., 65, 121, 122
McKenna, M. C., 19, 21–22, 41–42, 90, 97, 103–104, 107, 108, 218, 248, 254, 255–256
McKeown, M. G., 20
McLaughlin, G., 116
Meaning-based, 303
Meaning-based instruction, 34
Meaning processor
  Adam's model, 44–46
  defined, 303
Measures of Academic Progress, 155, 265
Medial letters, 42, 303
Mediated, 48, 303

Mediated process, 303
Medical model of reading, 40
Melnick, S. A., 256
Memory in information processing, 47–50
Mental retardation, 57, 174, 303
Meritocracy, 214
Metacognition
  defined, 22, 303
  in information processing models, 49
  think-alouds, 99
Microsoft Word readability scores, obtaining, 118
Miscue analysis
  coding, 92
  connected text, 92–93
  defined, 303
  described, 90–93, 125, 127
  error analysis, 90–93, 125, 127
  first grade level, 264–265
  helper-supplied words, 90, 92, 302
  hesitation, 90, 92, 302
  inclusive model, 70
  informal assessment in, 90–91
  insertion, 90, 92, 97, 302
  IRIs, 90–93
  lack of prosody, 90, 92, 303
  mispronunciation, 90, 92, 304
  omission, 90, 92, 97, 304
  qualitative analysis, 96–97
  repetition, 90, 92, 305
  reversal, 90, 92, 305
  running records, 104, 106
  self-correction, 90, 92, 97, 306
  substitution, 90, 92, 96–97, 306
  syntax, 97, 307
Miscues, 303
Mispronunciation, 304
Mispronunciation miscues, 90, 92
Moats, L. C., 18
Models of reading
  applications of, 44
  developmental, 41–46
  history, 39–41
  inclusive (*See* Inclusive model of reading)
  information processing, 47–51
  overview, 66
  transactional view, 53–55
Modification, 274, 304
Modified Concepts about Print Test, 71–73
Mohn, R. S., 32
Morgan, W. Pringle, 40
Morpheme, 304
Morphemic analysis, 20, 304
Motivation issues
  affective information, 256–257
  attitude inventories, 255
  classroom observation form, 250–251
  classroom observations, 248–249
  Elementary Reading Attitude Survey (ERAS), 255–256
  instructional tips, 297–298

interest inventories, 254–255
overview, 245–246, 278
portfolio assessment, 113, 114
Reader Self-Perception Scale (RSPS), 256
reading journals, 249
relative influence of, 246–248
resources, 293
sentence completion forms, 249, 252
solving, 9
student behaviors, 3
student interviews, 256
Thought–Bubble Technique, 252-253
Multilevel Academic Survey, 232, 235
Multiple strategy application described, 23
Multiple viewpoint stage, Chall's model, 42
Multitiered model of instruction
adequacy of, 152
assessment in, 137
in DBPS, 273
defined, 304
described, 10, 23–25
oral reading, 23–24
progress monitoring, 24–25, 142–143, 145
special education, 24

N

NAAL (National Assessment of Adult Literacy), 63, 219–221
NAEP (National Assessment of Educational Progress), 4, 212, 216–219
Narrative text fiction
applications of, 227
defined, 304
graphic organizers in, 22
readability, 116
student response, IRI assessment, 99–100
National Achievement test, 2nd ed., 232
National Assessment of Adult Literacy (NAAL), 63, 219–221
National Assessment of Educational Progress (NAEP), 4, 212, 216–219
National Center on Student Progress Monitoring, 144
National Reading Panel (NRP)
on comprehension instruction, 21–23
on the five areas of reading, 13
on learning disabilities, 58
on phonemic awareness, 16, 17
on vocabulary, 20
NCEs (normal curve equivalents), 175–176
NCLB (No Child Left Behind of 2001), 9–10, 113, 214–215, 259
Nelson-Denny test, 208, 225–228, 232, 235, 260
No Child Left Behind of 2001 (NCLB), 9–10, 113, 214–215, 259
Nondiscriminatory, 304

Nondiscriminatory comprehensive educational evaluation, 57, 304
Norm, 304
Norm group, 5, 304
Norm-referenced tests. *See also* Formal, group assessment; Formal, individual assessment
assessment method, 5–6
BRIGANCE® Inventories, 140
data application strategies, 221–223
defined, 165, 304
error analysis, 176
Normal curve equivalents (NCEs), 175–176
Northwest Evaluation Association (NWEA), 155, 265
NRP. *See* National Reading Panel (NRP)
Numeracy, assessment of, 146
NWEA (Northwest Evaluation Association), 155, 265

O

Observation-based assessment
classroom observation form, 250-251
oral reading, 71, 80
overview, 71–72, 125
special education, 248–249
Observation Survey of Early Literacy Skills, 128
Omission, 304
Omission miscues, 90, 92, 97
Onset-rime, 15, 16
Operationalization, 107, 304
Oral reading. *See also* Miscue analysis
AIMSWeb assessment, 147, 270
assessment selection/evaluation, 239
BEAR assessment, 127, 224–225, 231
CBM assessment, 107–109, 111
in comprehension assessment, 100, 105
DIBELS assessment, 148, 149, 264
expectancy rates by grade, 112
GOR-4, 194
GO2T-4, 197
inflection in, 19
instruction tips, 296
multitiered assessment, 23–24
observation assessment, 71, 80
progress monitoring, 8, 65, 111–112, 132
QRI assessment, 260
running record assessment, 102
scoring, 115
standard score assessment, 172
validity measures, 135–137
in vocabulary assessment, 105
word recognition lists, 82
Oral vocabulary, 20, 225, 304
Orthographic processing
defined, 18
developmental models of, 45, 46
inclusive model of, 56
transactional view of, 53

Orthographic processor
Adam's model, 44–46
defined, 304
Orthography
defined, 13, 14, 304
described, 18–19
formal, group assessment, 223–224
Osborn, J., 14, 16, 20
Overton, T., 4, 81, 106, 112, 114, 181, 209

P

Padak, N., 19, 55, 80
PAL-RW (Process Assessment of the Learner: Test Battery for Reading and Writing), 194, 197
Palinscar, A., 23
PALS (Phonological Awareness Literacy Screening), 128
Paraprofessional candidates, 280–281
Partner reading, 54, 267, 304
Passage Comprehension subtest, 187
PAST (Phonological Awareness Screening Test), 128
Payne, D. A., 114, 189, 211, 212, 213
Peabody Individual Achievement Test-Revised, 142, 194, 197
Pearson Product Moment correlation coefficient, 134–137
Peer-reviewed journals, 25–26, 304
Percentage mastery, 170
Percentile ranks, 168, 170–171, 191, 304
Phoneme blending, 15
Phoneme deletion, 15
Phoneme segmentation, 15
Phonemic awareness
acquisition difficulties, 40
defined, 304
described, 13–17
developmental models of, 42, 43
formal, group assessment, 223–224, 231–234
formal individual assessment of, 184, 194–196, 272
inclusive model of, 56
informal assessment of, 128–130, 148, 149
information processing models of, 49, 50
transactional view of, 53
Phonemic categorization, 15
Phonemic identity, 15
Phonemic isolation, 15
Phonics
applications of, 2
assessment of, 149
basal reading series, 76
defined, 16, 304
formal, group assessment, 223–224, 231–234
formal, individual assessment, 184, 194–196, 272
importance of, 16–17

Phonics (*cont.*)
  inclusive model of, 56
  informal assessment, 79, 128–130
  instruction strategies, 16, 17
  skills, 13, 14
  transactional view of, 53
Phonological awareness, 15–16, 128, 304
Phonological Awareness Literacy Screening (PALS), 128
Phonological Awareness Screening Test (PAST), 128
Phonological processor
  Adam's model, 44–46
  defined, 304
Pilot testing, 168, 304
Pinnell, G. S., 73, 119
Planning memory, 243
Poncy, B. C., 147
Popham, W. J., 210
Portfolio, 304
Portfolio assessment
  benefits/limitations, 113, 114
  CBM graphs, 112
  data, gathering/evaluation, 260
  decoding in, 114
  defined, 304
  described, 113–115, 127
  grading, 115
  inclusive model, 70
  kindergarten students, 122
Powell, W. R., 89
Powell criteria, reading level determination, 89, 93
Practice effect, 223, 304
Predictability logs, 124
Predictable text, 41, 304
Prediction, of reading achievement, 44, 158
Predictive Reading Profile (PRP), 232, 235
Predictive validity, 135, 136, 305
Previous-form preparation, 212, 305
Primary-SMOG Grading, 118
Primer, 82, 305
Problem of the match, 9, 305
Procedural knowledge
  defined, 48, 305
  in writing, 243
Process Assessment of the Learner: Test Battery for Reading and Writing (PAL-RW), 194, 197
Processing speed, 50, 305
Professional development, 10, 25
Professional ethics guideline, 211
Progress monitoring. *See also* Assessment
  adequacy of, 152
  adult learners, 160
  AIMSweb, 136, 145–148
  assessment's role in, 8–10, 125–126, 142–145, 239
  data, gathering/evaluation, 259–260
  defined, 305

ELL learners, 160
  first grade students, 2
  graded material for, 107
  inclusive model of reading, 131–132
  in instruction, planning, 144, 206–209
  multitiered model, 24–25, 142–143, 145
  oral reading, 8, 65, 111–112, 132
  practice effect issues, 223
  via CBM, 111–113
Proofing skills assessment, 245
Proportion of Accurate Responses calculation, 102, 104
Prose literacy, 220, 305
Prosody
  defined, 19, 305
  error analysis, 81
  miscue analysis, 90, 92, 299
PRP (Predictive Reading Profile), 232, 235
Pseudoword Decoding subtest, 184, 185
Psychometric, 305
Psychometric data
  AIMSweb, 147
  BRIGANCE® Inventories, 141–142
  DIBELS, 150–151
  DORA, 159–160
  formal group assessments, 235–236
  formal individual assessments, 197–198
  Lexile, 159
  STAR Reading, 159

Q

QRI-4. *See Qualitative Reading Inventory-4 (QRI-4)*
Qualitative Reading Inventory-4 (QRI-4)
  applications of, 227, 260, 280, 281
  described, 82, 85–87, 91, 98, 130
  wcpm calculations, 84
Qualitative studies, 13, 305
Quantitative literacy, 220, 305
Quasi-experimental study, 26-29, 305
Question answering strategy described, 22
Question generation strategy described, 22

R

Racial/ethnic proficiency trends, 219–221
Rapid automatic naming, 50, 305
Rasinski, T. V, 19, 55, 80
Rathvon, N., 149, 150, 151
Raw score representation, 168, 305
Read 180, 155
Readability, 116–119
Reader Self-Perception Scale (RSPS), 256
Reading, 12–23
  areas of, 13–14

cognitive correlates of, 257
  defined, 12–13
  factors influencing, 13
  fluency (*See* Fluency)
  importance of, 2–4
  instructional tips, 297
  orthography, 13, 14, 18–19
  phonemic awareness (*See* Phonemic awareness)
  phonics (*See* Phonics)
  teaching challenges, 2
  transactional view of, 53–55
  vs. IQ, 51–53
Reading & Reader Passages & Reading & Language Inventory Pkg., 5th Ed., 130
Reading attack strategies, assessment of, 71–72
Reading a-z, 119
Reading First, 10
Reading Fluency Subtest, 186
Reading framework, NAEP, 218
Reading Inventory for the Classroom & Tutorial Audiotape Package, 5th Ed., 130
Reading journals, 249
Reading Recovery leveled books, 119
Reading Specialist/Literacy Coach, 7, 280–281
Reading vocabulary, 20, 225, 305
Reading Vocabulary subtest, 186–187
Reading wars, 33–35, 305
Reading/writing connection, 64, 240, 243
Reason-based practices, 33, 305
Receptive vocabulary, 154, 305
Reciprocal teaching, 23, 305
Recoding
  defined, 305
  phonological process, 49, 149
Recognition. *See* Word recognition
Rego, A. M. P., 18
Reliability
  alternate forms, 134
  correlation coefficients in, 133, 134
  defined, 132–133, 176, 303, 305
  in formal, individual assessment, 192
  informal assessment, 132–134
  inter-rater, 134, 303
  internal consistency, 134, 303
  intra-rater, 134, 303
  test-retest, 134, 307
  testing, decoding in, 133
  types of, 133–134
Renaissance Learning, 153
Repetition, 305
Repetition miscues, 90, 92
Research, quantitative *vs.* qualitative, 31–32
Resources, assessment, 261, 291–294
Response to intervention (RTI) model
  adequacy of, 152
  defined, 305
  implementation, 3, 239

learning disabilities, identification of, 10, 61

oral reading assessment, 61, 143–144, 239

progress monitoring, 142–143

Retelling, 305

Retelling analysis, 97–99

Retrospective Miscue Analysis: Revaluing Readers and Reading, 128

Reversal, 305

Reversal miscues, 90, 92

Richmond Test of Basic Skills #2, 233, 235

Rimes, 305

Rosenblatt, Louise, 53–54

Rousseau, Henri, 247

RSPS (Reader Self-Perception Scale), 256

RTI. *See* Response to intervention (RTI) model

Rubric scoring, 305

Ruddell, R. B., 100, 101, 114

"Rule of thumb" criterion, 120

Running records

applications of, 104–105

defined, 305

described, 35, 102, 104, 127

inclusive model, 70

miscue analysis, 104, 106

quantifying, 104

scoring, 102–105

S

Salvia, J., 133

Same-format preparation, 212, 305

San Diego Quick Assessment, 79, 128

Sanchez, Maria, 3–4, 27–29. *See also* Adult basic education

SAT (Scholastic Aptitude Test), 5, 171

Sawyer, D. J., 41, 44, 45

Scaffold, 13, 306

Scaled scores, 203–204, 210, 216–217

Schedule for Kindergarten Literacy Assessment, 121

Schmidt, Johann, 39–40

Scholastic Aptitude Test (SAT), 5, 171

Schwartz, R. M., 54

Science education

assessment overview, 157

attention issues, 3

CBM assessment in, 110–111

DBPS case study, 268–270

reading comprehension assessment, 208

Scientifically-based instruction, 10, 25–33

action research, 32

applications of, 26–27

benefits of, 32–33

correlational studies, 13, 26, 27, 29–30

described, 25–26

quasi-experimental study, 26–29

true experimental study, 26–28

Scientifically based reading, 306

Scientifically based research, 306

Scott Foresman Reading Series, 73–78

Screening tests, 181, 306

Second Language Acquisition-Associated Phenomena (SLAAP), 62–63, 258

Section 504 of the Rehabilitation Act of 1975, 12, 215, 306

Self-correction, 306

Self-correction miscues, 90, 92, 97

Self-Correction Ratio calculation, 104

Self-efficacy, 245–247, 306

Semantic organizers, 22

Sentence completion forms, 249, 252

Sentence complexity, determination of, 116

SES. *See* Socioeconomic status (SES)

Shanahan, T., 28

Shaywitz, S. E., 12, 59

Shinn, M. R., 107, 108

Short-term memory, 47, 48, 50, 306

Sight vocabulary, 18, 82, 306

Sight word recognition, 18, 306

Sigmon, C. M., 55, 73

Single-subject studies, 26–27, 30–31, 306

Single viewpoint stage, Chall's model, 42

Sipay, E., 109

Skinner, C. H., 147

SLAAP (Second Language Acquisition-Associated Phenomena), 62–63, 258

Slope, 144, 306

Smith, F., 247

SMOG readability, 116–118

Snow, C. E., 12

Socioeconomic status (SES)

defined, 306

NCLB assessment requirements, 10, 215

variability in, 2

Spadafore Diagnostic Reading Test, 128

Spandel, V., 113

Speaking vocabulary, 20, 306

Spear-Swerling, Louise, 41, 43

Spear-Swerling/Sternberg model, 41–44

Special accommodations, high-stakes testing, 215–216

Special education

age/grade-equivalent scores, 169–170

BRIGANCE® Inventories, 137–143, 147, 160, 244

CBM assessment, 107

chronological age determination, 178–180

DBPS case studies, 266–267, 270–273

eligibility, assessment's role in, 8, 10–12, 133, 166 (*See also* Criterion-referenced assessments)

eligibility, screener tests, 181

ELL student assessment, 63

high-stakes testing, 215

IRI assessment, 85, 88, 93–96

learning disability assessment, 57–61

motivation of students, 249

multitier model of instruction, 24

NCLB assessment requirements, 10

oral reading rate gain assessment, 111–112

percentile scores, 170–171

resources, 293

staff, communication needs of, 3

standard scores in, 173–174

students, observation of, 248–249

Speech-language impairment, 57, 302

Spelling assessment, 244–245

SRA Achievement Series, 233, 236

SRI-2 (Standardized Reading Inventory), 2nd ed., 195, 197

SSR (sustained silent reading), 263, 303

Stahl, S. A., 19, 21–22, 41–42, 90, 97, 103–104, 107, 108, 218, 248, 254, 255

Standard deviation, 171–172, 306

Standard error, 176, 306

Standard nine, 175, 306

Standard scores

benefits of, 173–174, 192

defined, 171, 191, 306

formal, group assessment, 202

in learning disability determinations, 174–175

limitations of, 175

points, 58

properties, determination of, 171–173

scaled scores, 203–204, 210

in special education eligibility determinations, 173–174

Standardization, 306

Standardization sampling, 168

Standardization version, 168

Standardized, 306

Standardized assessment, 35–36, 306

Standardized Reading Inventory (2nd ed.) (SRI-2), 195, 197

Standards for Educational and Psychological Testing, 210–212

Standards for Educational and Psychological Testing, 240

Standards for Reading Professionals Revised, 6–7

Stanford Achievement Test, 202, 223, 233, 236, 239

Stanford Early School Achievement Test, 3rd ed., 233, 236

Stanines, 175, 306

Stanovich, K. E., 26

Stanovich, P. J., 26

STAR Early Literacy, 154

STAR Reading Diagnostic Report, 156, 157

STAR Reading test, 153–156

Sternberg, R. J., 41–44
Sternberg, Robert, 41, 43
Stieglitz Reading Inventory, 3rd Ed., 130
Story maps, 22, 306
Story structure, 22, 306
Strucker, J., 63–64
Student interviews, 256
Student Profile Sheet, 122
Substitution, 306
Substitution miscues, 90, 92, 96–97
Subvocalize, 46, 307
Summarization
   defined, 307
   information processing models of, 49
   strategy described, 22–23
Sustained silent reading (SSR), 263, 307
Symbolic reasoning, 258
Syntax, 307
Syntax miscue assessment, 97
Systematic instruction, 307

T

T-RAN (Test of Rapid Automatized Naming), 129
TAAS (Test of Auditory Analysis Skills), 129
TABE. See Test of Adult Basic Education (TABE)
Table of specifications, 167, 307
Task analysis, 81
Task analyze, 13, 307
TCAP (Tennessee Comprehensive Assessment Program), 202, 204
Teacher/educator
   IRA standard, 7
   proficiency levels, 280–281
Teacher self-assessment, 259
Teachers of English to Speakers of English and Other Languages (TESOL 1997), 62
Teaching to the test, 210, 223, 307
Tennessee Comprehensive Assessment Program (TCAP), 202, 204
Tennessee Comprehensive Assessment System, 244
TERA-3 (Test of Early Reading Ability), 3rd ed., 195, 197
TESOL (Teachers of English to Speakers of English and Other Languages, 1997), 62
Test bias, 166, 188–190, 214, 307
Test blueprint, 167, 307
Test of Academic Performance, 233, 236
Test of Achievement & Proficiency, 234, 236
Test of Adult Basic Education (TABE)
   applications of, 208, 223–227, 239, 260
   described, 204, 234
   literacy assessment, 221
   psychometric data, 236

Test of Auditory Analysis Skills (TAAS), 129
Test of Early Reading Ability (3rd ed.) (TERA-3), 195, 197
Test of Rapid Automatized Naming (T-RAN), 129
Test of Reading Comprehension (3rd ed.) (TORC-3), 195, 197, 234, 236
Test of Silent Contextual Reading Fluency (TOSCRF)
   applications of, 202, 203, 206–207, 221, 225
   described, 234
   psychometric data, 236
Test of Silent Word Reading Fluency (TSWRF)
   applications of, 202, 206–208, 221, 225, 239, 260
   described, 185, 234
   psychometric data, 236
Test of Word Reading Efficiency (TOWRE), 195, 197
Test of Written Language, 3rd ed. (TOWL-3), 244
Test protocols, 178, 307
Test-retest reliability, 134, 307
Test Review Criteria form, 240–242
Testing, 4, 307. See also Assessment
Texas Primary Reading Inventory (TPRI), 129, 195, 197
The Reading Teacher's Survival Kit, 80
Think-alouds, 99, 307
Thought-Bubble Technique, 252–253
Three-tier model of instruction, 10, 307
3-Minute Reading Assessments, 129
Tindal, G., 108, 109
Tollefson, N., 151
TORC-3 (Test of Reading Comprehension), 3rd ed., 195, 197, 234, 236
TOSCRF. See Test of Silent Contextual Reading Fluency (TOSCRF)
Total Reader system, 153, 155
TOWL-3 (Test of Written Language), 3rd ed., 244
TOWRE (Test of Word Reading Efficiency), 195, 197
TPRI (Texas Primary Reading Inventory), 129, 195, 197
Tracking, 76
Transactional view of reading, 53–55, 307
Travers, J. F., 106
Treatment validity, 135, 137, 307
True experimental study, 26–28, 307
TSWRF. See Test of Silent Word Reading Fluency (TSWRF)
Twelfth grade performance descriptions, NAEP, 218

U

UNIT (Universal Nonverbal Intelligence Test), 257

Universal Nonverbal Intelligence Test (UNIT), 257
U.S. Department of Education Web site, 274

V

Valencia, S., 113
Validity
   construct, 135, 300
   content, 134–136, 204, 300
   correlation coefficients in, 134–137
   defined, 134, 296, 306, 307
   in formal, individual assessment, 192
   oral reading, 135–137
   predictive, 135, 136, 305
   treatment, 135, 137, 307
   types of, 134–137
Value-added assessment, 10–11
Variability issues in reading level, 5, 8–9
Variable relationship determinations, 27
Varied-format preparation, 212, 307
Vaughn, S., 18, 20
VIP (Vital Indicators of Progress), 151
Visual memory, 307
Vital Indicators of Progress (VIP), 151
Vocabulary
   age/grade-equivalent scores, 169
   assessment, oral reading in, 105
   assessment of, 52
   basal and ceiling rules, 179
   basal reading series, 77
   vs. comprehension, 21
   defined, 20, 58, 307
   formal, group assessment, 201, 225–227, 231–234
   formal, individual assessment, 167, 169, 186–187, 194–196
   Gates-MacGinitie test, 208
   informal assessment of, 128–130, 148, 149, 153–154
   instructional tips, 296–297
   ITBS/ITED assessment, 222
   National Reading Panel on, 20
   oral, 20, 225, 304
   quasi-experiment design, 29
   reading, 20, 305
   in reading skill prediction, 55
   receptive, 154, 305
   resources, 293
   sight, 18, 306
   speaking, 20, 306
   special education, 12
   teaching strategies, 20–21, 64
   transactional view of, 53
Voyager Universal Literacy System, 151
Vygotsky, L., 157

W

W-J III DRB (Woodcock-Johnson Diagnostic Reading Battery), 181–187, 196, 198, 244, 260

Wait to fail, 307
Wait to fail method, 58–59, 61
Wasserman, J., 63
Wcpm. *See* Words correct per minute (wcpm)
WDRB (Woodcock Diagnostic Reading Battery), 196, 198
Wechsler Individual Achievement Test-II (WIAT-II), 181, 182, 184–187, 196, 197
Wechsler Intelligence for Children-IV, 257
Whole language approach, 34, 307
WIAT-II (Wechsler Individual Achievement Test-II), 181, 182, 184–187, 196, 197
Wide Range Achievement Test-3, 142
Wide Range Achievement Test-4, 181, 182, 196, 198
Wigfield, A., 247
Will, G. F., 26
Woodcock, R. W., 184, 186
Woodcock Diagnostic Reading Battery (WDRB), 196, 198
Woodcock-Johnson Diagnostic Reading Battery (W-J III DRB), 181–187, 196, 198, 244, 260
Woodcock-Johnson III Tests of Cognitive Abilities, 257
Woodcock-McGrew-Werder Mini-Battery of Achievement, 181

Woodcock Reading Mastery Test, 147, 196, 198
Word analysis
    CBM assessment, 208–209
    instructional tips, 295–296
    ITBS/ITED assessment, 222–224
    resources, 292
    teaching strategies, 64
Word blindness, 40
Word chain technique, 207, 225
Word difficulty, determination of, 116
Word families, 307
Word Identification subtest, 185
Word processing program readability scores, obtaining, 118
Word recognition
    automatic, 18–19, 58
    basal and ceiling rules, 179
    CBM assessment, 110
    formal, group assessment, 231–234
    formal individual assessment of, 184–185, 194–196
    informal assessment, 79, 80, 128–130
    IRI assessment of, 82–87, 89, 94–95
    oral reading assessment via, 82
    sight, 18, 306
    Spear-Swerling/Sternberg model of, 43, 300
Word Recognition Fluency subtest, 185

Words correct in passage, calculation, 93
Words correct per minute (wcpm)
    calculation of, 84–85, 87
    defined, 307
Working memory, 47, 48, 243, 307
World view stage, Chall's model, 42
Writing
    assessment, 240, 243–245
    instructional tips, 297
    reading journals, 249
    transaction view of, 55
WRMT-R test, 186–187

Y

Yekovich, C. W., 48
Yekovich, Frank B., 48, 49
Yesseldyke, J. E., 133
Yop, H. K., 79
Yopp-Singer Test of Phoneme Segmentation, 79, 129

Z

Z score, 172–173, 307
Zambo, Debby, 252–253
Zone of Proximal Development (ZPD), 157
ZPD (Zone of Proximal Development), 157
Zutell, J., 19